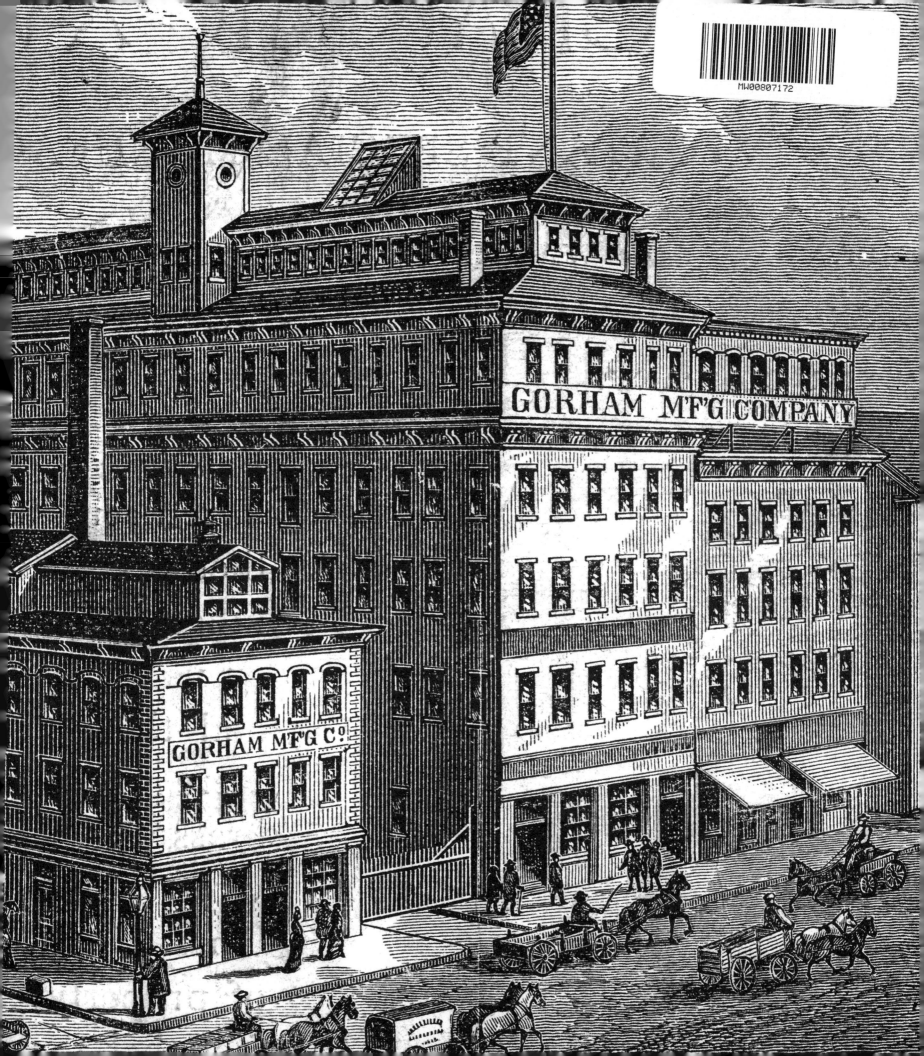

GORHAM M'F'G COMPANY

GORHAM M'F'G Cº.

GORHAM
SILVER

...ng Buildings Under Supervision OF THE DIFFERENT Watchmen.
...A. has Supervision OF Buildings in Blue,
" Red.
" Yellow.

GORH

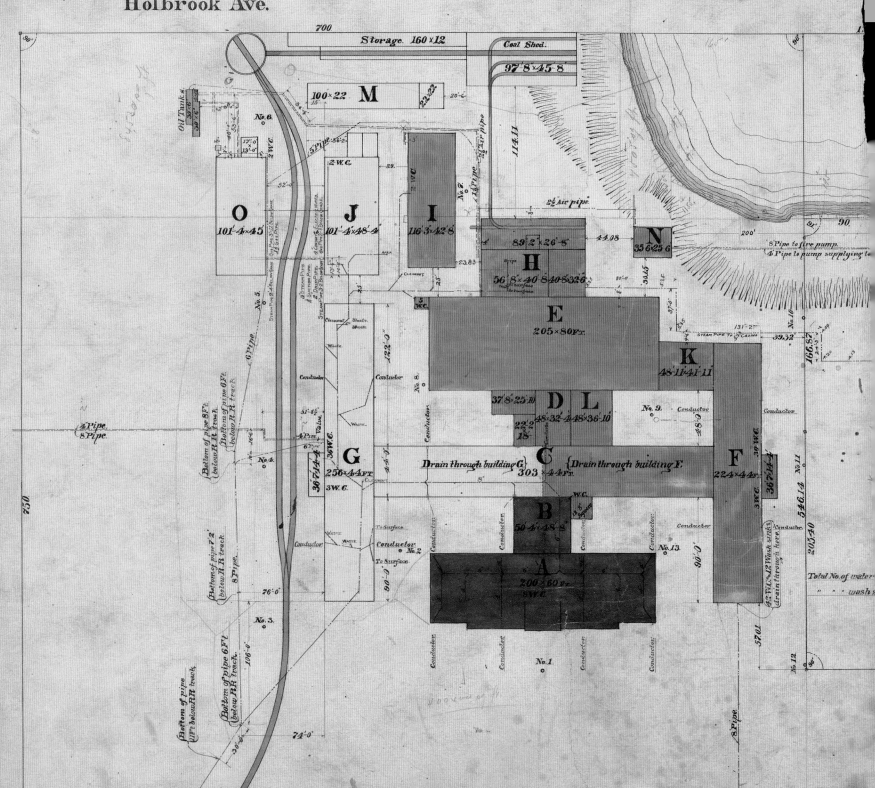

Holbrook Ave.

Adelaide Ave.

PLAN

of land belonging to the

AM MANUFACTURING CO.

Providence, R.I.

MASHAPAUG

POND.

Valve

Shed

Barn

Barn

37 × 35

Ice Houses.

Top Of Pipe
Below 300

About 261 by deed

GORHAM SILVER

DESIGNING BRILLIANCE
1850–1970

Edited by
Elizabeth A. Williams

With contributions by
Emily Banas, David L. Barquist,
Gerald M. Carbone,
Amy Miller Dehan, Jeannine Falino,
Catherine L. Futter,
Erik Gould, Ingrid A. Neuman,
John W. Smith,
Holly Snyder, Elizabeth A. Williams

CONTENTS

John W. Smith

FOREWORD

In 1831, silversmiths Jabez Gorham and Henry Webster opened a small firm on Steeple Street in Providence, Rhode Island, just a block away from where the RISD Museum now stands. At that time, Providence was growing rapidly, shifting from its earlier history that was based upon a maritime economy to creating new centers of manufacture in metals and textiles. Jabez Gorham certainly had no idea that in nearly two hundred years, thousands of works stamped with his surname would be an important part of a museum collection, much less one centered around educating the next generation of artists and designers. It's very clear to us, however, why we are so fortunate to care for this important history at the RISD Museum, located in the hometown of Gorham and generations of its workers, and long a community of makers and innovators.

Despite Gorham's Providence roots, its story is not simply local, but global. The works Gorham produced embody an epic tale of invention and reinvention: the nineteenth- and early twentieth-century ascension, powered by determination, ambition, and the relentless embrace of new technologies, followed by a post–World War II reckoning with the cumulative effects of societal change, economic downturn, and environmental issues. In every scene, the labor of the largely invisible craftsperson gleams from the table of the industry magnate and the New York shop window, from the sideboard of the middle-class newlyweds and the museum display case, still testifying to both the remarkable sensitivity of the designer's eye and maker's hand and the brutal power of the drop press.

In 1991, the RISD Museum was the grateful recipient of more than two thousand objects from Gorham's parent company, Textron Corporation, who several years earlier had given a portion of the company's business records to Brown University. In 2005, subsequent owners Brown-Forman gave the remaining records to Brown University, and, through their subsidiary, Lenox, Inc., gifted Gorham's design library to RISD Fleet Library's Special Collections and more than 2,600 design drawings to the RISD Museum. Together, these materials provide a remarkably vivid and detailed account of how these objects evolved from concept to production and how a multitude of Gorham workers played a role in the process. Today, as Providence and similar cities across the United States work to reinvent their economies for the twenty-first century, Gorham's history, and its extraordinary combination of design and technological innovation, remain both relevant and instructive.

This volume and the related exhibition were preceded by years of tireless work and creative vision, with contributions from nearly all of the RISD Museum staff. Enormous gratitude is owed to members of the RISD Museum staff who made this project a possibility, particularly Elizabeth A. Williams, the David and Peggy Rockefeller Curator of Decorative Arts and Design. Through her passion and scholarly rigor, Elizabeth has given shape and new meaning to this vast collection. Her commitment to this undertaking and her admiration and respect for the countless men and women associated with Gorham throughout its history are evident in this volume and the exhibition. Additionally, without the dedicated efforts of Emily Banas, Assistant Curator of Decorative Arts and Design; Erik Gould, Photographer; Ingrid A. Neuman, Conservator; and Amy Pickworth, Editor of Publications, this book could not have come to fruition.

Generous support for this publication and exhibition has been orchestrated by Amee Spondike, Deputy Director of Development and External Affairs; Tammie Worthington-Witczak; and Lauren Faria. Thanks also to Pam Kimel, Julia D'Amico, Matt Berry, and Colleen Mullaly. A broad range of logistics has been ably managed by Christopher Alviar, Nicole Amaral, Denise Bastien, Linda Catano, Tara Emsley, Sionan Guenther, Marny Kindness, Joseph Leduc, Jacqueline Parker, Kajette Solomon, Glenn Stinson, and Stephen Wing, Laura Ostrander, Michael Owen, Kristin Samuelson, and Thomas Morin. My appreciation also goes to the work of Sarah Ganz Blythe, Deputy Director of Exhibition, Education, and Programs, and her staff, including Christina Alderman, Brendan Campbell, Deborah Clemons, Carson Evans, Mariani Lefas-Tetenes, Alexandra Poterack, Jeremy Radtke, and Derek Schusterbauer.

In addition to my colleagues at the RISD Museum, I am grateful to the efforts of Exhibition Designer Stephen Saitas; Associate Publisher Margaret Chace and Editor Andrea Danese of Rizzoli Electa; Book Designers James Goggin and Shan James; and this volume's contributors: Emily Banas, David L. Barquist, Gerald M. Carbone, Amy Miller Dehan, Jeannine Falino, Catherine L. Futter, Erik Gould, Ingrid A. Neuman, and Holly Snyder. Enormous thanks also for the care and dedication of the many volunteers who helped clean our Gorham silver collection, and to the many other greater Providence community members who have contributed their personal insights. Many thanks also to the Fleet Library at RISD.

The involvement of other institutions has been important to this undertaking. My colleagues Cameron Kitchen and Amy Miller Dehan at the Cincinnati Art Museum and Todd A. Herman and Brian Gallagher at the Mint Museum have led the work of bringing this exhibition to both of those museums. We extend enormous thanks to the staff of the John Hay Library at Brown University for supporting research initiatives in the Gorham Manufacturing Company Archive. A generous in-kind gift from Spencer Marks, Ltd., provided authors enhanced access to those archival materials. Significant grants made this exhibition and its programming possible. We are grateful to Terry Carbone at the Luce Foundation; Elizabeth Francis and the Rhode Island Council on the Humanities; and the National Endowment for the Arts. We extend gracious thanks to the Zennovation Fund, to Karen Warfield at Textron, and, for their continued support, to Randall Rosenbaum and the Rhode Island State Council on the Arts.

Finally, I wish to extend my heartfelt gratitude to RISD President Rosanne Somerson, to RISD's Board of Trustees, and to the RISD Museum Associates and the Board of Governors. My very special thanks also goes to Dr. Joseph A. Chazan, Vicki Veh, Mary Lovejoy, Alan Nathan, Glenn Creamer, and Scott Burns.

John W. Smith
Director
RISD Museum

Elizabeth A. Williams

INTRODUCTION

Measuring a little over five inches long, with a handle fashioned as a rope-entwined harpoon and a bowl formed of a whale swimming in waves, a sterling-silver spoon (fig. 1) acquired in 1909 by the Rhode Island School of Design Museum established what is now the world's foremost collection of works made by the Gorham Manufacturing Company, today comprising nearly five thousand objects and design drawings. Drawn mainly from the RISD Museum's collection, as well as significant loans from collegial institutions and private collections, *Gorham Silver: Designing Brilliance 1850–1970* presents 120 years of the company's creations, from the beginning of Gorham's production of hollowware through its considerable successes in industrial, social, design, manufacturing, and marketing contexts. This publication endeavors to continue the invaluable research and scholarship of Gorham and American silver established and upheld by Charles H. Carpenter, Samuel J. Hough, Larry J. Pristo, Jewel Stern, Charles Venable, and numerous others.

The Gorham Manufacturing Company was an inimitable force in the city of Providence and across the globe for more than a century and a half, boldly growing from a small workshop established by one man to the largest silver company in the world. The company's approach was to design and create some of the most exceptional works ever made in silver, and then develop the most effective and inventive technologies and techniques to produce them. This outcome-oriented approach to innovation has been shared by the Rhode Island School of Design since it was founded in 1877 for the express purpose of educating students and the public about the vital role of art and design in society. Like RISD, Gorham employed an ethos and commitment to the belief that the arts and design are essential to humanity, its progress, and its wellbeing, embracing the act of conceptual and critical thinking and "connecting the hand, the mind and the heart" with highly developed skills and craftsmanship. The brilliance of the silver produced by Gorham reflected their brilliance in translating ideas into well-designed, artistically executed work.

While researching this book, I came across an 1871 article describing Gorham as "the most perfect system," noting that only such a highly functional creative, manufacturing, organizational, and marketing structure could achieve the company's accomplishments. The truly remarkable staff of the RISD Museum, the generous community of former Gorham employees and silversmiths, the vital support of colleagues in the fields of decorative arts and design and history—particularly this volume's contributors—and the project's munificent funders came together to form the extraordinary "system" that has made this exhibition and publication possible. I express my sincerest thanks and gratitude to all, as well as to the many who have brought me to the point of being entrusted with the privilege and honor of curating this project, most especially my parents, John Paul and Carol Ann Williams.

Elizabeth A. Williams
David and Peggy Rockefeller
Curator of Decorative Arts and Design
RISD Museum

1
New Bedford, Whaling City
Souvenir Teaspoon, 1891. Silver.
RISD Museum

Gerald M. Carbone and Holly Snyder

GORHAM SILVER AND AMERICAN INDUSTRIALISM

TO HANDLE SILVER AS THOUGH IT WERE PUTTY

On his first morning at sea aboard the paddle-wheel steamer *Arctic*, John Gorham (fig. 2) felt an urge to enter the engine room, though he knew it was off-limits, in order to view the gears, valves, and pistons in action. "Let's go into the engine room and see the leviathan which keeps this world in motion," he wrote in his diary on May 2, 1852.[1]

Gorham held an insatiable interest in steam power, and he intended to harness it in a new way that could give his nascent Gorham Company an edge on its competitors in manufacturing silver wares. This transatlantic voyage aboard the *Arctic* was the first leg of his quest for an audience with the world's most famous toolmaker, James Nasmyth, in the hopes of convincing him to invent a steam-powered drop press for use in making flatware—silver spoons, knives, forks, and serving utensils. Gorham, thirty-one years old, did not know Nasmyth, he carried no introduction to him, and he had no reason to believe that Nasmyth would even see him except for his own optimistic blend of self-confidence and naïveté.

Gorham's father, Jabez (fig. 4), was not thrilled with his son's ideas about employing steam power to make silverware. Father and son had been business partners until John insisted on replacing their horse, old Dick, with a fifty-horsepower steam engine to provide motive power to their little Providence, Rhode Island, shop. That was

2
John Gorham, ca. 1865. Gorham Archive, John Hay Library, Brown University

too much risk and expense for Jabez, who agreed with neighbors that installing a steam engine in the growing city's downtown created an unacceptable hazard of explosion.[2] Jabez sold his interest in J. Gorham & Son to John in 1848, four years before John set sail to meet Nasmyth with dreams of marrying a steam engine to a machine that existed only in his head.

The schism between father and son was strictly business, the result of a nineteenth-century generation gap. John held a keen interest in applying mechanical processes to the age-old craft of making silverware. He toured Springfield Armory in Massachusetts for a firsthand look at machinists making interchangeable parts for guns, and he added a spinning lathe to his shop so that his workers could make hollowware—vessels with significant depth and volume

3
Jabez Gorham's certificate of indenture, 1806. Gorham Archive, John Hay Library

This INDENTURE witnesseth,

That *Jabez Gorham Son of Jabez Gorham late of Providence in the County of Providence, deceased,*

hath put *himself* and by these Presents doth voluntarily, and of *his* own free Will and Accord, and with the Consent of *his Mother Katy Gorham of said Providence Widow*

put and bind *himself* Apprentice to *Nehemiah Dodge of said Providence Gold, Silver Smith and Jeweller*

to learn *his* Art, Trade or Mystery, and, after the Manner of an Apprentice, to serve from *the fourteenth Day of February last* for and during the Term of *Seven Years* next ensuing, to be complete and ended. During all which said Term, the said Apprentice *his* said *Master* faithfully shall serve, *his* Secrets keep, *his* lawful Commands gladly obey: he shall do no Damage to *his* said *Master* nor see it done by others, without letting or giving Notice thereof to *his* said *Master* he shall not waste *his* said *Master's* Goods, nor lend them unlawfully to any: he shall not commit Fornication, or contract Matrimony, within the said Term. At Cards, Dice, or any other unlawful Game, he shall not play, whereby *his* said *Master* may have Damage. With *his* own Goods, or the Goods of others, without License from *his* said *he* shall neither buy nor sell: *he* shall not absent *himself* by Day or by Night, from *his* said *Master's* Service, without Leave; or haunt Ale-Houses, Taverns, or Play-Houses; but in all Things behave *himself* as a good and faithful Apprentice ought to do towards *his* said *Master* and all *his* during the said Term. And the said *Nehemiah Dodge* doth hereby promise to teach and instruct, or cause the said Apprentice to be taught and instructed, in the Art, Trade or Calling, of *a Gold, Silver Smith and Jeweller* by the best Ways and Means *he* can. *And to find and allow unto his said Apprentice good and sufficient Meat Drink Washing and Lodging and also to provide him Ten Dollars worth of Clothing for each and every Year during said Term and shall put him to School the Evenings of three Winters to be instructed in reading Writing and Arithmetick*

In TESTIMONY whereof, the Parties to these Presents have hereunto interchangeably set their Hands and Seals, the *Seven* Day of *April* Anno Domini *1806* and in the *30* Year of American Independence.

Signed, Sealed and Delivered, in the Presence of

Alexr Rogers

Benjamin Gorham

Nehemiah Dodge

Jabez Gorham

Caty Gorham

such as pots, vases, urns, and the like—by bending sheets of silver over a wood form rotating on the lathe. The firm of Babbitt & Crossman in nearby Taunton, Massachusetts, had patented a technique of metal spinning whole vessels in 1834, shaving hours off the time it took to form hollowware using only hand-raising methods.[3]

Jabez, born in 1792, had learned silversmithing long before the spinning lathe and the maturation of the American system of manufacturing interchangeable parts and then of assembling the parts by mechanization.[4] He had learned his trade the old-fashioned way, as an apprentice bound out by his mother to a seven-year term with a master. His mother, Catherine, signed the indenture agreement in April 1806 (fig. 3), less than a year before she died, leaving Jabez as a fourteen-year-old orphan in the Providence household of Nehemiah Dodge, a second-generation jeweler and smith of silver and gold. In signing the indenture, the adolescent Jabez agreed not "to commit Fornication or contract Matrimony," nor to "haunt ale-houses, taverns, or playhouses," and to refrain from playing cards or dice until he turned twenty-one. For his part, Dodge agreed to "instruct" Jabez in the "art, trade, or calling of a gold, silversmith and jeweler," in the same fashion that Dodge's father, Syril, had taught him. The agreement was dated "in the 30th Year of *American* independence," 1806.[5]

Jabez found Dodge "to be a good master, kind and indulgent to the boys."[6] At twenty-one, Jabez formed a partnership with four other men to make jewelry in a second-story shop in Downcity, Providence. The partnership dissolved after five years, but Jabez kept the shop, doing business as Jabez Gorham, jeweler. He grew this company to about a half-dozen workers, which allowed him to buy a gambrel-roof wood house around the corner on Steeple Street (fig. 5) where he rented the first floor to a druggist while using the second story and attic for his own shop. Here, he created a

gold chain design that became known as the Gorham chain. He and his workers also handcrafted gold beads, earrings, finger rings, breast pins, and the like—jewelry that Gorham sold by making occasional forays to Boston and into northern New England where he peddled his wares to small-town jewelry stores. His sales trips were sometimes long and lonely affairs, as evidenced by the letters he wrote to his wife, Amey, advising her to provide tender care for their children ("wipe Amanda's nose with a soft handkerchief so as not to make it sore") and asking that she "take good care of my pig."[7]

In 1831, Jabez Gorham had taken on a partner, Henry Webster, to add spoons made of coin silver to the product line now produced by Gorham & Webster. Webster fashioned silver spoons, while Jabez oversaw the jewelry production, an arrangement that was in place for seven years until Jabez brought his youngest son, John, into the family business. The decision proved to be problematic: John clashed with the shop foreman. Through much of the early nineteenth century, foremen acted as subcontractors in manufacturing shops, setting the rules and working conditions to ensure efficient production. When push came to shove—as in John's case—it was the owner's son and not a valuable foreman who got shoved out the door.

A decade after forming Gorham & Webster, Jabez sold his interest in the firm to some Providence jewelers, leaving Webster working alone with the silver-spoon side of the business. Less than a year after the sale, Webster was offered a partnership in a spoon-making firm in Boston; he was a Boston native and wanted to return. Would Jabez be interested in buying his silver business, he asked? Jabez

had worked for thirty-five years, including his apprenticeship; he was comfortably retired with a Benefit Street house on the western slope of Providence's College Hill, a few streets up from his old shop. He said that he would buy out Webster and return to work, on one condition: that his son, John, would join him in the firm.

After getting fired from Gorham & Webster in 1838, John Gorham had tried to make it on his own, first as a farmer, then as a clerk at various businesses in Providence, New York, and Boston. Clerks belonged to a new professional class in the antebellum era. Garbed in respectability—they wore coats and ties and projected an air of gentility—they actually wielded little power and worked long hours for meager pay. Absent family connections, they had little chance of upward mobility.[8] Thus, when his father offered John a second chance in the silver business, the twenty-one-year-old found "the opportunity was particularly attractive," as he later wrote in a retrospective.[9] "It was not only a mechanical operation but one which seemed to me to possess unusual opportunities for development."

J. Gorham & Son opened in 1841, a fortuitous time for entering the silversmith's trade. The Tariff of 1842 added new fees of 20 to 30 percent to imported silver, essentially freezing foreign silversmiths out of the American market.[10] New duties on a host of other products required companies exporting into the United States to pay the American Treasury in silver or gold coins, boosting supplies of coin—silver melted from coins and fashioned into products such as silver spoons, Gorham & Son's main product. The company also made silver forks, knives, thimbles, ladies' belt buckles, combs, and Jabez Gorham's signature gold chain. All this was done in the little gambrel-roof house on Steeple Street, measuring 40 by 40 feet. A dozen men churned out the products on the first floor, whereas ten others worked in the attic burnishing the silver and gold with old Dick furnishing rudimentary horsepower by traveling around the basement in a circle.[11]

With tariff protections in place and a steady stream of coin silver flowing into the country, Gorham's gross sales increased 350 percent to $35,000 (approximately $1,160,000 today) in just four years, stretching the tiny shop's capacities. John wanted to expand. He cajoled his father into borrowing $17,000 from a local financier in order to lease a lot next door, erect a brick building four stories high, and install a fifty-horsepower motor, replacing the horse. All "seemed to be going smoothly until the mid-summer" of 1847, John recalled.

By then, Jabez "began to fully realize the magnitude of the undertaking and became exceedingly nervous over the scheme."[12] So John bought his father out of the company for $8,000 and assumed all the partnership's debts.

"I struggled along till the later part of 1849 when, needing capital to carry the business to advantage, I arranged for a partnership with Gorham Thurber," John later recalled (fig. 6).[13] Though only twenty-five, Thurber—John's cousin—brought with him a wealth of experience as the bookkeeper for the Franklin Foundry and Machine Company in Providence, Rhode Island. Bookkeepers were foot soldiers in the Industrial Revolution, employing an old technology, double-entry bookkeeping, in new ways to enhance the emerging culture of business enterprises. Industrialization created exponentially more transactions than merchants had conducted in agrarian British North America, and by midcentury

6
Gorham & Thurber advertisement in the *Rhode Island Almanac for the Year 1852*

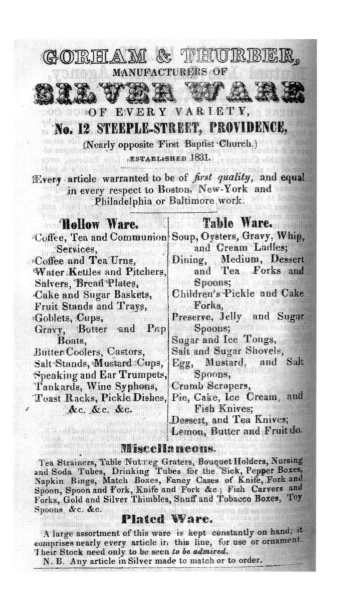

information moved at the speed of railroads and Morse code. Bookkeepers set and measured value, providing the market baseline data that made it possible to calculate profit and loss.[14]

The two young partners quickly brought on a third cousin, Lewis Dexter Jr., to join them as partner in the firm. Dexter provided more capital and another set of eyes in managing the day-to-day operations, freeing John Gorham to research manufacturing processes. Gorham's research took him to Springfield Armory, to the U.S. Mint in Philadelphia, and possibly to the large Reed & Barton silverware plant in Taunton. Reed & Barton was the successor in interest to Babbitt & Crossman, whose pioneering use of the rotating lathe for spinning hollow forms had already given a huge boost to the manufacture of silver hollowware. Before he

7
Kettle on Stand, 1850.
Gorham and Thurber.
Silver with ivory.
RISD Museum

embarked for his European tour on the *Arctic,* John Gorham had already taken advantage of this innovation and hooked turning lathes to his new steam engine to begin making hollowware in the Gorham shop. This meant that Gorham could now offer large tea and coffee services (fig. 7), first displayed at the Rhode Island State Fair in 1850, where the contemporary reviewer from the *Providence Journal* found them "perfect in design and execution" (fig. 110).[15]

In early 1852, Gorham informed his partners of his plan to go overseas in search of skilled workmen and new technologies that could give the Gorham Company an edge over its many competitors, especially Reed & Barton; Ball, Black & Co.; and Tiffany & Co. He told them, in his recollection, "That much was to be done which had never to my knowledge been undertaken by any silversmiths in this country. That although we had made considerable progress in changing our small tools to improved ones, we were still working with a class of machines only suitable to jewelers. Heavy rolls and stamps must be introduced in their places, of sufficient size and power for us to handle silver as though it were putty."[16]

The *Arctic* left the wharves of lower Manhattan on May 1, 1852, bound for Liverpool, England. "Well how sound we sleep in these steamers," Gorham wrote the next morning. "Nothing like not having the stomach too crowded to rest well," he added, a joking reference to his postdinner bout of seasickness the day before.[17] By 10:00 a.m. he was ready to sneak into the engine room, three decks below the main deck of the 2,800-ton paddle-wheel steamer. One of the firemen stoking a boiler with coal informed Gorham, "We usually expect a fine or a treat from the passengers what come down here . . . then they can come down here as often as they like and won't be asked again." Gorham gave the fireman a fifty-cent piece (equivalent to about sixteen dollars today), only to be told by an officer of the crew that the fireman "had no right to tell you so, sir, he is only one of the hands. Only the officers can give permission." Gorham retreated up one flight to the enginemen's lounge, where he sat for more than two hours observing the engine room below and making detailed notes: *4 boilers, each independent. 8 fires. 24 firemen in 3 watches. 18 coal bearers.* "What a monster. A regular Goliath," he wrote of the steam engine. "And mine a Tom Thumb. . . . Now for the deck and be sick."

As his seasickness subsided, shipboard life began to appeal to him. He spied the northern lights, icebergs, a pod of whales "sporting in the distance," two wide paths

of phosphorescence trailing in a glow behind the boat's paddle wheels. "The living is everything that can be desired. All the delicacies of a first class hotel," he noted. Then turning back to the silver business, he observed: "These steamers have a very large set of dining and [dessert] forks. Table [dessert] and tea spoons. Olive pattern, besides Tongs, Ladles, Fish knives &c and &c, furnished by Bell, Tomkins, and Black [Ball, Tompkins and Black]. Her plates and cutlery are Sheffield, all handsomely marked."

The *Arctic* steamed into Liverpool on a foggy morning, its arrival after eleven days at sea announced with the thud of a gun. Before he disembarked, Gorham talked with Michael Gibney, whom he described as "the New York silversmith" with whom the Gorham Company did some business, sending partially finished blanks to New York so Gibney could run them through his steel die rollers to press patterns such as Gorham's *Prince Albert* into the blanks. The results were uneven and the costs high. Gibney "is on a tour principally of pleasure I guess," Gorham wrote, while he himself was there seeking new processes that he intended to use to cut Gibney and his rollers from the Gorham Company's expense sheet.

Gorham toured England for nearly a month, visiting places that employed electroplating—applying thin coats of silver to objects by electrifying solutions of dissolved silver—and paying a master craftsman to teach him how to

cast molds in sand before he dropped into Nasmyth's works at Patricroft, in greater Manchester. Nasmyth was already a legendary figure, known for the steam hammer, a machine he invented to forge the large crankshafts that turned paddle wheels on steamships.[18] His hammer harnessed steam to lift an iron block weighing hundreds of pounds then, with a stroke of a cylinder, driving it down to hammer steel into shape. He modified the steam hammer to invent the pile driver.

Gorham arrived at Patricroft on Saturday, June 5, and found that "the hum of the driving belts, the whirl of the machinery, the sound of the hammer upon the anvil, gave the place an air of busy activity." Nasmyth received him and heard John Gorham's proposal: Gorham wanted Nasmyth to make a steam press that could inculcate patterns into flatware. Essentially, Gorham wanted a smaller version of the giant steam hammer; instead of hoisting a huge block of iron, it would lift the obverse half of a die containing a raised pattern above a blank of flatware resting on the sunken, or reverse, half of the die. With a stroke of the piston, the die would strike the flatware blank, inculcate the pattern, and recoil, ready to strike again.

Using drop presses to stamp patterns into flatware was nothing new. Silversmiths had long been using a couple of methods to raise the heavily weighted die before dropping it on to a blank, but they were both laborious: either hoisting it hand over hand by pulley or cranking a screw that would raise the die to height, then cranking it up again after each blow. Gorham laid out his idea to Nasmyth. "He looked at me for a moment with some astonishment," Gorham recalled, "and then asked me if I had crossed the Atlantic to get such a machine. I replied that I knew of no place to procure such a tool except from its inventor. He said he had never built one, [but] . . . would be very glad to build it for me."[19]

Nasmyth set a price of £165 to £170 (about $21,800 to $22,500 today) per machine, delivered from England to the United States. By Monday he had made drawings of the machine; when Gorham dropped in to see them, Nasmyth said to his partner: "I have been trying for years to get our manufacturers to adopt the steam press without success, and here comes a Yankee across the water expressly to have one built, and our people still use the hand drop press with several men to each machine."

Americans were not tethered to centuries-old traditions of artisanal skills, the way the British were. As Nasmyth observed, "Yankees" were mad for machinery. Gorham's curiosity about process was partly a product of the time and place where he lived: mid-nineteenth century Providence was an American center for "technological convergence," a term coined by economic historian Nathan Rosenberg to explain the synergy between inventors and manufacturers who "by doing some things successfully [create] a capacity for doing other things."[20] The city was home to a network of inventors and manufacturers who knew one another socially; they sometimes met at meetings of the Franklin Society, the Association of Mechanics, or the Rhode Island Society for the Encouragement of Domestic Industry, where speakers frequently lectured to packed houses on the latest scientific developments in batteries, illumination, chemistry, and natural science.

At home, John Gorham socialized with Lewis Dexter's young brother-in-law, Lucian Sharpe, an eponymous partner in the nascent machine tools giant Brown & Sharpe.[21] Sharpe was perhaps the first to take the American system of manufacturing interchangeable parts out of the armories and apply it to a nonweapons product: the Willcox & Gibbs Sewing Machine. In the mid-1850s, Brown & Sharpe employed William Nicholson to graduate the lines on its small tools such as rulers and protractors, skills that he later employed to cut the intricate faces of files and rasps in his own business, the Nicholson File Company.

Providence was also the place where George Corliss had arrived in hopes of finding funding for his sewing-

9
Coin-Silver Cup, 1854.
Silver. RISD Museum

machine patent, the third such patent issued in the United States. Failing to find capital, Corliss went to work for a Providence firm as a draftsman, and while there he turned his attention to improving the stationary steam engine, a hundred-year-old technology widely viewed as a backup for waterpower until 1848, when Corliss developed a system of valves to efficiently harness the steam engine's power.

Even Jabez Gorham tapped into the technological convergence pulsing through Providence. Though he was schooled in the traditional ways of an eighteenth-century jeweler's apprentice, Jabez was no Luddite. He invested in the local Eagle Screw Company, which obtained a patent for making the pointed gimlet screw.[22] Jabez's investment made him a rich retiree. In fin de siècle Providence, civic leaders boasted with little hyperbole that the city was home to the "Five Industrial Wonders of the World": Corliss Steam Engine Company, American Screw Company, Nicholson File Company, Brown & Sharpe, and Gorham Silver, each business among the largest of its type in the world.

By 1854, John Gorham's new steam press was chuffing away, stamping decorated flatware in the company's four-story building on Steeple Street. With the clank of a die, a knife, spoon, or fork was decorated, a new blank inserted, and clank, another fine piece of silver flatware was on its way to completion (fig. 8). Before the steam press, a silversmith could make a dozen spoons in a ten-hour day; silver is brittle at room temperature, so each spoon had to be briefly annealed, or softened with heat, every five or six minutes—nine times per spoon. The steam press sped up the work, eventually reducing the need for annealing to four times per spoon.

The factory's fifty-horsepower steam engine also turned wheels that the lowest-paid workers—often women, in many silver manufactories—used to polish flatware. With his steam engine powering his presses and polishing wheels, John Gorham could complete more flatware pieces within minutes than his father could have made in a day. The pieces cost less to produce and were of better quality—more consistent in thickness and weight. In addition, the engine powered the lathes for spinning up hollowware, so that by the mid-1850s Gorham was making quality tea sets, pitchers, goblets, and small items such as salts and cups for babies (fig. 9). The firm's gross sales multiplied exponentially: in 1850, John Gorham's first full year with his cousin as bookkeeper, the company sold $29,000 worth of silverwares. By the end of that decade, the Gorham Company did $397,000 (more than $12 million today) in annual sales.[23]

By employing steam to stamp and polish flatware and to spin hollowware, Gorham created

10
The Gorham plant on Steeple Street in Providence, ca. 1885. Gorham Archive, John Hay Library

11
Gorham workers,
ca. 1870s.
Gorham Archive,
John Hay Library

of gold or silver. There are pipes for the gas which lights the building ... "whispering" pipes for speaking messages from room to room, steam pipes, pipes blowing air to fan blast furnaces, pipes everywhere in the 40 rooms of this hive of humming industry.

"technological discontinuities," defined by business theorists Philip Anderson and Michael L. Tushman as "fundamentally different ways of making a product that are reflected in order-of-magnitude improvements in the cost or quality of a product."[24] Technological discontinuities can be "competence-destroying," by rendering a trade's skills obsolete, or they can be "competence-enhancing," by increasing demand for the skills embodied in the trades they are altering. The technological discontinuities created by applying steam to the manufacture of silverware were clearly competence-enhancing. Silversmiths no longer had to spend hours hand-raising hollowware to shape over a form, or hammering a steel punch to cram silver-spoon blanks into tin dies. Machinery spun up the hollowware and pounded the flatware into patterned shapes, freeing designers, diemakers, and silversmiths to worry about the finer points of the craft, particularly with hollowware: molding, casting, finishing, and chasing.

In 1868, a writer from *Harper's New Monthly Magazine* toured the "famous Gorham Silver Works" along Steeple Street, pronouncing the plant "by far the most extensive and complete in the world." The company had grown to fill forty rooms in the four-story structure (figs. 10, 11). Behind the walls ran miles of pipes that the writer, James Parton, found particularly impressive:

> There are pipes for the pure rainwater needed in many processes. There are pipes for hard water used for all the common purposes. There are pipes for carrying to the basement the water containing particles

The demands of a wartime economy had depressed Gorham sales during 1861 and 1862, the first two years of the Civil War, forcing Lewis Dexter to move his capital investment out of Gorham and into textiles. To make it easier to raise capital, the remaining partners applied to the Rhode Island General Assembly for a charter in 1863, incorporating the firm in 1865 as the Gorham Manufacturing Company, a joint stock corporation with Gorham and Thurber, each holding a third of the outstanding stock.

John Gorham took advantage of these slack years by trying out new products: casting small bronzes and making silver plate. On his trip to England he had taken notes on a technique of electrifying a silver solution to apply thin coats of silver to products; now eleven years later, Gorham set up his own experimental plate works in 1863. Two years later he paid the passage for an English expert, Thomas Shaw, to emigrate and help Gorham perfect the process before releasing a line of silver plate that allowed consumers to buy the look of true silverware at a fraction of the cost.

In 1865, Gorham's gross sales crossed the million-dollar threshold for the first time. By boosting the amount of silver wares made at the factory, John Gorham had also increased the demand for various skilled craftsmen who worked in silver: designers, molders, diesinkers, engravers, and chasers. Good silversmiths were hard to find in the United States; a master might graduate seven apprentices in seven years, not nearly enough to feed the growing appetite for trained silversmiths. Gorham began in 1850 with fourteen workers, and by 1866 they employed more than three hundred.[25]

Though Jabez Gorham likely employed a couple of African American men as silversmiths,[26] apprentices in all the metal trades were almost exclusively white men. One of the largest metalworking guilds, the International Association of Machinists, did not admit black workers until the 1940s, and even then it was largely through the intervention of the NAACP and other groups advocating for civil rights. Women had an even harder climb to make it into the ranks of metalworkers, but white women began to make initial inroads during the early twentieth century, as they were called into the manufacturing plants to take the places of men sent off to World War I.[27]

Carbone and Snyder

12
Tea and Coffee Service,
ca. 1859. Silver with gilding.
RISD Museum

13
Tea and Coffee Service, in
Gorham *Photo Catalogue*, 1869.
Gorham Archive, John Hay Library

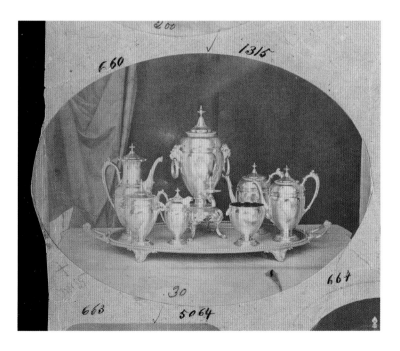

With hundreds of workers and $1 million worth of product, John Gorham had yet another new problem to contend with: inventory control. Once again he turned to an emerging technology for a partial solution. Gorham was apparently captivated with the concept of photography at its very inception. Even before he boarded the *Arctic* in 1852, he had first paused along the wharves of New York City to have his daguerreotype taken. He and his father both had distinct and revealing styles of posing for portraits: clean-shaven Jabez wore his jeweler's glasses and stared straight at the camera, his eyes scrunched in a myopic squint; bearded John looked away from the camera, gazing askance at something distant.

The advent of albumen print paper in the 1850s revolutionized the emerging business of commercial photography by allowing for the creation of multiple reproductions quickly and cheaply from a single photographic negative. It was now possible for professional photographers to expand their customer base from the affluent to less well-heeled consumers. Between 1855 and 1860, the business exploded in American cities and towns; Westminster Street, then the main commercial thoroughfare in Providence, was chockablock with

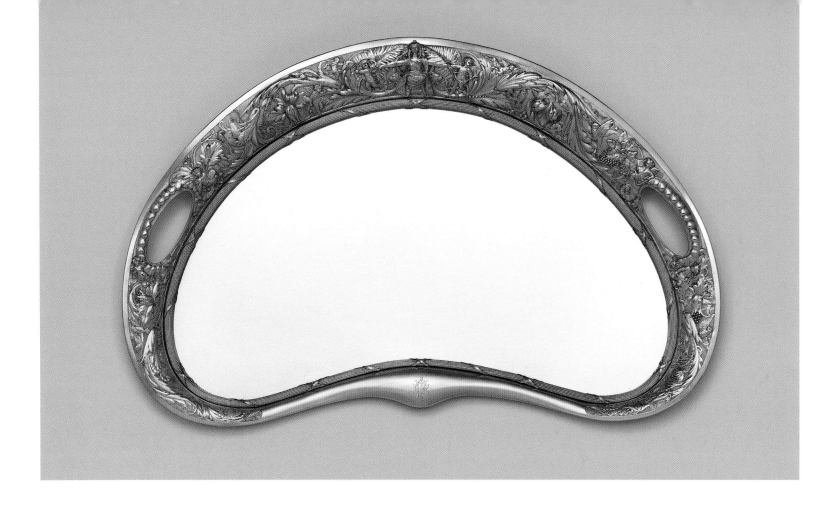

photographers' studios where a customer could not only have a photo
taken but also acquire a copy of
a well-known photograph of a celebrated person, such as Abraham
Lincoln or General Ulysses S. Grant.[28]

John Gorham did not allow his company to fall behind
in making use of this important asset. He began taking
images of silver products in 1855–56 and installed a photography studio on the top floor of the shop where he employed
two men as staff photographers, a boy as an assistant, and
a woman to mount the prints.[29] Besides being useful in track-
ing the multiple patterns and products that Gorham made,
the photographs (precisely organized for easy retrieval)
proved to be great marketing aids for its new force of traveling salesmen who could gauge a wholesaler's interest in
new products without being bogged down by carrying cases
full of silver (figs. 12, 13).

By the time Parton, the writer from *Harper's*, visited
the Gorham works in 1868, John Gorham had fully realized
his goal of harnessing machinery "to handle silver as though
it were putty." Parton observed that "the visitor is surprised
most of all to see the ponderous engines . . . used in subduing
common materials here employed in conquering the precious
metals. There is a room in which salvers [silver trays] (fig. 14)
and other large objects are stamped into form by the fall of
huge masses of iron weighing a ton and a half, the thump of
which would shake the building from its propriety if there
were not many feet of granite masonry under them, and piles
under the masonry."[30] Gorham's achievement, however, came
with a cost: one of Gorham's hands came between the dies,
and the steam press bit a
chunk out of it.

Parton's visit took
place at the forefront of
Gorham's post–Civil War
boom. An important key in
rebuilding the artisanry
that Parton saw on view in
the plant in 1868 was John
Gorham's effort to recruit

Carbone and Snyder

talent from the established centers of European—and particularly British—silver production. In 1868, George Wilkinson (fig. 15), born in the metalworking center of Birmingham, England, and trained at the Birmingham School of Design, numbered among Gorham's three-hundred-odd employees. Wilkinson had come to America to work for the Ames Co. of Chicopee (Massachusetts), manufacturers of swords, cutlery, and tools, but he did not last long there: John Gorham enticed Wilkinson to join his company in 1857 as chief designer by paying him almost three times what his other designers earned. This largesse paid dividends. Like most American silverware companies, Gorham had been producing Rococo Revival pieces, which were elaborately ornamental. Wilkinson changed that. His Neoclassical designs, emphasizing bold shapes and large areas of unornamented surface, "proved both popular and influential," giving Gorham an edge on its North American competitors.

Encouraged by his success with Wilkinson, John Gorham again cast his eyes across the Atlantic to France, Germany, and England, this time not for technology but for people steeped in the culture of metalworking. Gorham hired ninety-five experienced European immigrant craftsmen by the late 1860s—almost one-third of his workforce. He gave his workers freedom to design. Drawing on a long legacy of European craftsmanship but freed from old-world constraints, Gorham designers such as Thomas J. Pairpoint and Florentin Antoine Heller set design trends through the 1880s. In addition, the company's adoption of the British sterling standard (.925 fine) for its solid silver wares in 1868 and its introduction in 1865 of a new line of electroplated hollowware, using the process that Gorham had developed on its own during the Civil War years, set the Gorham Manufacturing Company above its competitors, which were selling cheaper wares made with only coin silver (.900 fine) and lower plating standards. By 1868, Gorham's wares were notable not just for their artistry but also for their durability and quality of manufacture.[31]

16

Presentation Water Pitcher, 1867. Silver. RISD Museum

17

Presentation Water Pitcher (detail), 1867. Silver. RISD Museum

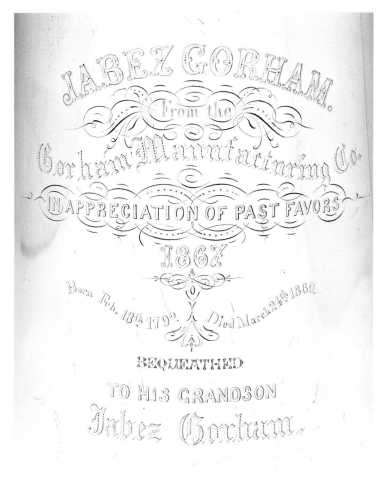

The 1870s were a dark time of trial, both for John Gorham personally and for the company that bore the family name. Jabez Gorham (figs. 16–17), once an orphaned apprentice, had died in 1869 a wealthy man. His estate included 270 shares of American Screw Company; stocks in a half-dozen banks, the Union Pacific Railroad, and the Slater Cotton Company; a couple of houses on Benefit Street; and bonds of the Black Hawk Mining Company, for a total value of $389,868—the current equivalent of $7.2 million.[32] John Gorham, too, had tried diversifying his portfolio. He invested with Isaac Thurber, his brother-in-law, in the Thurber Mining Co., chartered in 1865 "for mining gold, silver, and other metals."[33] Gorham also encouraged friends and associates to invest, including his sister, Marcy, but with unhappy results. In 1868 the local agent for R.G. Dun & Co. reported: "[John Gorham's] 'Thurber' Mine speculation is believed by some to be a swindle & that he made money by it." There is no evidence that the company was a swindle, and Gorham made no money in the volatile mining industry—on the contrary, he lost a fortune. In an overheated economy, John Gorham continued to be haunted by bad luck in his outside investments. The Panic of 1873 did nothing to help his financial woes, which appear to have escalated in the years that followed. He eventually pledged all of his shares in the Gorham Manufacturing Company to secure his debts. His disgrace was complete in 1878, when the board relieved him of executive duties and ousted him from the company he had built into an economic powerhouse.[34]

The board's actions were not without foundation, as inherent instability in both the European and American economies had already resulted in the longest economic depression of the century, which would continue at least into 1879 (the following year) and by some accounts into the 1890s.[35] Business activity across the nation declined by one-third. Gorham itself saw a precipitous drop in sales, from more than $1 million in 1873 to barely half that six years later.[36] In 1877, company officers agreed to cut their salaries in half, to $5,000. To meet his obligations in the Thurber Company, John Gorham had borrowed from Gorham Manufacturing, using his stock as collateral. When in 1875 he declared bankruptcy, Gorham Manufacturing took his stock to fulfill his pledge. Three years later he pleaded for a chance to retain his seat on the board of directors: "I have hesitated at no personal sacrifice whereby I felt the prosperity of the business could be advanced," he wrote. The board expressed its "most heartfelt sympathy for his present financial condition" but, mindful of the difficult conditions the company was still facing, turned down his request. After thirty-six years in business, the Gorham Manufacturing Company joined the relatively new trend of replacing an entrepreneurial family firm with a corporate hierarchy of salaried executives unaffiliated with the company's original founders.[37]

To replace John Gorham, the board hired a new president, William Crins, a sixty-year-old career businessman with glasses and a white beard. He became Gorham's titular president, but the real power behind the throne was Edward Holbrook (fig. 18), the company's young New York sales agent. Holbrook had married Frances Swift, the daughter of a railroad president and a Boston Brahmin, and he used his new money to buy significant shares of Gorham stock, for which purpose he also accrued a substantial debt that it took him four years to repay. By 1878 he was one of only four officers in the company, along with Crins, Gorham Thurber (John's cousin), and longtime designer George Wilkinson.

The Crins-Holbrook tandem came to power at the right moment. The effects of the Panic of 1873 began to depress the company's stock, but, owing to some sound decisions instituted by Edward Holbrook in his new role as chief agent, sales boomed in the 1880s, reaching nearly $3 million by the end of that decade. Holbrook's decision to institute a series of catalogues (fig. 230) helped to create public awareness of Gorham's product lines, and topical brochures—such as the one specially created for the monumental *Century Vase* (fig. 118) shown at the 1876 Centennial International Exhibition in Philadelphia—imbued Gorham's artistry with compelling backstories that appealed to the sensibilities of a rising affluent middle class. In addition, Gorham added new production lines for religious wares—the Ecclesiastical Division was organized in about 1885—and began a separate division for bronze casting at about the same time.[38] The four-story plant on Steeple Street was not large enough to keep pace with the many new orders these changes brought in, and there was no more room for expansion in the existing Downcity complex. So in May 1888, with Holbrook newly elected as company treasurer, the board

18
Portrait of Edward Holbrook, ca. 1910. Gorham Archive, John Hay Library

GORHAM M'F'G CO.
WORKS AT
(ELMWOOD)
PROVIDENCE, R.I.

authorized Crins to sign contracts to build a new plant, "which," Crins dryly noted in his diary, "means much hard work for me."[39]

To design the new factory in Providence, Crins hired Frank Perry Sheldon, an architect known for designing manufacturing plants; his career projects eventually included the Pacific Mills in Lawrence, Massachusetts, the Hanes cotton underwear plant in North Carolina, and more than a dozen textile factories throughout the South. Gorham's new plant rose at 333 Adelaide Avenue (fig. 19), fronting on Mashapaug Pond near the Elmwood Station streetcar stop, about three miles south of the Downcity factory. The company diverted a rail spur into the Gorham lot so that train cars could carry coal, lumber, and bullion all the way to the rear of the plant, where the silver bars began their transformative journey to shipping rooms located near the front.

The bones of Sheldon's design were the geometric H plan (pages 2–3, fig. 187), a common layout for nineteenth-century mills, which allowed for the maximum number of windows letting in natural light. Behind the cross section of

19
Drawing of Gorham's Elmwood plant, in *Views, Exterior and Interior, of the Works of the Gorham Manufacturing Company, Silversmiths*, 1892. Gorham Archive, John Hay Library

the H, he added a power plant large enough for a 450-horse-power Corliss engine—nearly ten times more powerful than the engine John Gorham had marveled over on the *Arctic*—with a five-foot stroke and a revolving band wheel twenty feet in diameter (fig. 20). By the end of 1888, the new plant was already making a significant contribution to the local economy, as building suppliers for housing noted the uptick in sales of brick and increased demand for masons. A report in the *Providence Journal* claimed "the sale of bricks for the new Gorham Manufacturing Company has been the largest transaction for the year, as the several buildings now in process of erection will employ more bricks than more than half of all the other [new] buildings combined."[40]

The roughly triangular lot of thirty-six acres was bordered by Adelaide Avenue, the rail spur, and Mashapaug Pond, which provided fresh water for washing, electroplating, and silver finishing. With its own power plant, water supply, and

20
Engine Room, in *Views, Exterior and Interior, of the Works of the Gorham Manufacturing Company, Silversmiths*, 1892. Gorham Archive, John Hay Library

The new factory complex included a handsome building of corbelled brick and granite, which stood in front of the H-shaped wings where production took place, and a four-sided clock tower, the tallest building on the site, loomed above everything (fig. 22). Visitors entered the front office building by mounting granite steps that ascended through a great archway flanked by two heavy doors, the overall effect being that this was a solid, industrious place. The new plant had taken, in all, a little more than a year to complete. By January 1890, the company was already at work testing the new boilers. Apparently the plant opened as scheduled, without fanfare, that same year in June.[42]

Holbrook's broad managerial vision, combined with the opening of the new plant, positioned Gorham to take full advantage of structural changes in the American economy that were encouraging massive growth in corporate enterprise. The Adelaide Avenue plant, with its own dedicated rail spur, allowed the company not only to enhance its production chain and better control the supply of raw materials into the works but also to prepare it for new modes of mass distribution of its finished products. As leader of the company, Holbrook's prior experience as Gorham's principal sales agent made it possible for him to oversee and coordinate mass distribution of Gorham's products to the company's benefit.[43]

Nevertheless, there were ongoing structural problems in the late nineteenth-century economy that created distinct challenges for the manufacturing

21
Silver Finishing or Coloring Room, in *Views, Exterior and Interior, of the Works of the Gorham Manufacturing Company, Silversmiths*, 1892. Gorham Archive, John Hay Library

fire station, the new Gorham plant was completely self-sustaining, with no outside utility costs. Providence was home to some of the world's best machine designers, but Gorham engineered most of its own cutting mills, grinding machines, and presses in its in-house experimental machine shop. The company did reach out locally to buy Frederick Grinnell's new automatic fire sprinkler system, built in Providence. And the Rhode Island Time Registrar Company created an elaborate timekeeping system in which workers deposited metal time checks into cylinders that vacuum tubes whisked off to the registrar's office to log each worker's presence in the complex. For heating and ventilation, Gorham looked outside of Rhode Island to the Sturtevant Company of Boston, which installed a state-of-the-art system that kept workers comfortable by means of massive fans and hidden hot-water pipes (fig. 21). At the time, Gorham's executives felt that "the health and welfare of the employee is quite as important as the convenient and economical arrangement of machinery."[41] Gorham was one of the few New England manufactories to practice progressive employee welfare, which eventually included pensions, group health care, reduced work hours, and a company savings bank—company-offered benefits that, perhaps not coincidentally, made it tougher for unions to gain traction.

Carbone and Snyder

22
Office Building, in *Views, Exterior and Interior, of the Works of the Gorham Manufacturing Company, Silversmiths*, 1892. Gorham Archive, John Hay Library

and marketing of silver wares. In December 1892, several silver manufacturers came together in a consortium they incorporated under the name the Silversmiths Company, for the purpose of addressing industry-wide problems such as the price of silver, which had begun to plunge owing to overproduction by mines in the Western states. When the Panic of 1893, driven by the oversupply of domestic silver, pressured silver manufacturing companies to the breaking point, a number of the firms in the consortium, feeling the pinch of their devalued products and focusing on their own survival, abandoned the idea of working together and sold their stock in the Silversmiths Company. Holbrook, instinctively sensing an opportunity for expansion, bought up the proffered shares until he held a controlling stake. He went on to use the Silversmiths Company as an umbrella or shell corporation to hold silver-manufacturing firms that he then bought at bargain-basement prices in the recession of the mid-1890s.

By decade's end, Holbrook controlled both Gorham and, under the aegis of the Silversmiths Company, six of its competitors; he ran the two entities independently of one another, forming the foundation for an expanding, and expansive, silver-manufacturing empire. While Gorham continued to drive the evolution of silverware design, Holbrook continued to grow his own, now privately held,

Silversmiths Company empire. By 1913, he had acquired seven more silver manufacturers from New Hampshire to New York. On the eve of World War I, Holbrook controlled as much as 40 percent of U.S. sterling silver production. This was, perhaps, not as lucrative as it sounds. Holbrook was able to buy up silver manufacturers because so few investors wanted them— the price of silver was still flat, and intense competition among silversmiths led to price-cutting and small profit margins. But it was nevertheless a shrewd choice, as it meant that Holbrook had a firm grasp on the business operations of Gorham's lower-tier competitors.[44]

Holbrook's experience as sales agent also gave him a keen appreciation for the importance of good design in driving sales. With both Holbrook and George Wilkinson on the executive board, the company placed a premium on recruiting good designers, notably Thomas J. Pairpoint in 1868 and Florentin Antoine Heller (fig. 119) in 1873 and again in 1881. Holbrook outbid Tiffany & Co. twice to gain the talents of Heller, an acclaimed French silversmith and die cutter who kept Gorham on the cutting edge by transitioning Gorham designs from Pairpont's high Victorian style to the Beaux Arts. Holbrook's next hire would prove to play an even more significant role in Gorham's fortunes: on his annual trip to Europe in 1887, Holbrook recruited eighteen-year-old William Codman to emigrate from England to supervise the company's line of ecclesiastical wares. Codman turned out to be a good hire, chiefly because his father, William Christmas Codman (fig. 134), agreed to follow him to Gorham in 1891. This marked the beginning of an incredibly prolific career for the elder Codman as the designer who helped establish Gorham's reputation as the world's top maker of consumer silverwares.

Holbrook ran a profitable and progressive, if discriminatory, company. In 1893 the Gorham works employed 1,377 workers, about half of them American born, 40 percent born in England, and the remaining 10 percent of workers generally coming from Germany, France, or Switzerland.[45] Gorham now generated a prolific array of products, both in range and output, and by the mid-1890s, workers in the photo studio were printing and filing tens of thousands of photographs a year. The Gorham works also consisted of an in-house printing department that published miniature books (such as *Cocktails—How to Make Them*) and pamphlets. One of the latter, entitled *Woman's Work at the Gorham Manufacturing Company* (fig. 192), reported:

> Employment adapted to the women in the silverware establishment of the Gorham Manufacturing Co. at Providence, RI is confined to a comparatively few of the

numerous departments of the works; such as the Case Room, wherein their work consists of lining the cases with satin or other suitable material, or blocking, or other incidental operations; in the Etching department, and also in the Photographic rooms.

It is in the Case Department that women's work is utilized to any large extent, the work being particularly adapted to the nimble deftness of touch so natural to the average woman, and foreign to the average man.[46]

In the Case Department, carpenters built exquisite wood boxes (fig. 76) to hold every silver order; women lined the insides with satin or silk and covered them with leather or chamois. Silverware shipped from the plant inside these custom-made boxes was protected by flannel bags that women stitched in the factory, at the rate of about seventy thousand bags per year.[47]

In 1899, Holbrook introduced a company pension program and built a "casino" for workers, a brick colonial-style building with a slate roof, featuring a dining room where workers could eat hot lunches at cost, bedrooms for visiting executives, a large reading room, and basement parking for four hundred bicycles, later converted into a duckpin bowling alley with six lanes (fig. 23).

When the Guns of August boomed and World War I broke out over Europe in 1914, Edward Holbrook quickly agreed to tool up for making bullet casings of brass and cupronickel to supply Serbian forces with ammunition. Within a year, Gorham had built an extension on to its main factory to make 75-millimeter cartridge casings for French and Russian

field guns. When the United States finally entered the war in 1917, Gorham built a new plant in the Phillipsdale section of East Providence to build loaded hand grenades. The plant employed two thousand people, mostly white women, who packed one hundred thousand grenades per day. Several organizations filed complaints with Rhode Island's governor alleging that Gorham (like a number of companies during this time) refused to hire women of color. According to the newspaper *New York Age,* the company "stated that it didn't hire colored women because white women refused to work with them."[48] Gorham added yet another war-related plant a block from the Providence waterfront to make shell casings for the U.S. Navy. During the war, Gorham signed at least twenty-four contracts with the U.S. military. At the same time, Holbrook was cognizant that the company would not and could not survive only on its war contracts. Toward the end of the war, in order to spur consumer purchases, Gorham issued a leaflet—without once mentioning its own silver wares—suggesting that buying American-made consumer goods was an important means of expressing patriotism.[49]

When Armistice was declared, the war work came to a sudden end just a few months before Holbrook died in May 1919, further complicating Gorham's readjustment to the post–World War I economy. The company was left rudderless in the face of chaos: Holbrook had no worthy successor lined up, William Christmas Codman had already retired as chief designer in 1914, the company had not yet developed a new set of styles for its products in the intervening years, and it was now saddled with two munitions plants, specially constructed to fulfill its war contracts, which were now of no use. After several years of poor sales, the company was forced to retrench and reorganize. In 1924, the board voted to buy the assets of the Silversmiths Company from Holbrook's heirs and hired a professional manager, Edmund Mayo. Mayo, age thirty-nine, projected a professorial mien but had no prior experience in the silver industry. He held a mechanical engineering degree from the University of Maryland and had worked for a shipbuilding company. During the war he had worked on, and perfected, tooling for drawing manganese steel into the U.S. Army helmets worn by American soldiers. He came to Gorham after having served as CEO of a metal-stamping company.

Mayo was aware of Gorham's legacy, but as a manager he was not sympathetic to the continued preeminence of Gorham's in-house design team. Instead, he subordinated design to production and marketing.[50] To introduce new design concepts and push the company forward,

23
Casino built by Edward Holbrook as a gift to employees, 1899. Gorham Archive, John Hay Library

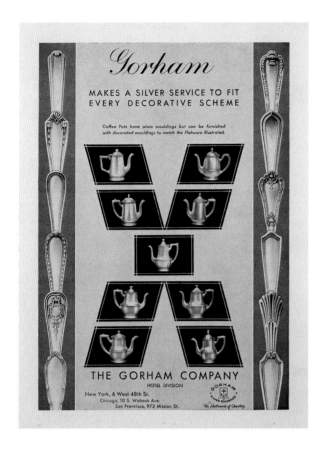

strategic additions: the Alvin Company was purchased in 1928, with its product identity and sales force retained as separate from Gorham's, and in 1929 Gorham's New York retail storefront merged with Black, Starr & Frost.

The stock market crash of October 1929 put an abrupt halt to Mayo's planning. Between 1929 and 1933, the value of silver wares produced in the United States fell by 60 percent, from $86 million to $34 million.[51] Once again, Gorham was forced to retrench. With barely two-thirds of the work that it used to have, the company turned from setting new standards to trying to survive. Much of Gorham's value resided in its vast collection of dies. Good diesinkers were as valued as the best chasers; when the company retired a flatware pattern, it locked the dies in a massive vault stocked with tier after tier of valuable dies as protection against falling into the hands of competitors. In the 1930s, Gorham revived its older, most popular patterns—*Chantilly* (fig. 65), *Strasbourg*, and *Buttercup*—as it limped through the Great Depression. With the country at an economic crossroads, Mayo perceived that the company's survival depended on obtaining more large-scale institutional contracts to supplement the declining purchase power of the formerly affluent consumers who sought out its high-end designs. A line of sturdy, if somewhat pedestrian, hotel ware was added to Gorham's offerings, and the sales staff did their best to persuade hotel chains that Gorham silver would add to hotel ambience (fig. 24).

he imported a well-known contemporary designer from Denmark, Erik Magnussen (fig. 145). Magnussen joined Gorham in 1925 as a "special designer" with his own studio, set apart from the firm's large designing room. His early work at Gorham built on traditional designs, but by 1927 he had branched out into incorporating motifs expressed by abstract artists into his new designs. Magnussen's work appealed to consumers with Modernist sensibilities for whom Gorham's dominant Colonial Revival and Academic styles seemed cliché. Just as William Christmas Codman's 1903 Art Nouveau lady's writing desk captured the movement of its generation, Magnussen's 1927 *Cubic* service (figs. 202–4, 217), entitled "the Lights and Shadows of Manhattan" (fig. 253) by the company, captured the spirit of Art Deco.

Magnussen's tenure at Gorham proved to be short; he left the company in 1929, moving to Chicago to set up on his own studio. Mayo, in the meantime, got on with the work of reorganizing Holbrook's legacy. The Silversmiths Company was dissolved, and its subsidiaries—which had previously been run independently of Gorham—were now merged into Gorham's operations. Mayo then made two

When the United States declared war on Japan and Germany in December 1941, American factories once again began ramping up

26
Assembly and fitting
of torpedo parts, 1943.
Gorham Archive,
John Hay Library

for wartime production. The federal government's immediate interdiction of the use of copper in consumer wares had forced Gorham to end manufacture of goods made in bronze and brass, as well as all of its plating work, that same month. By the middle of 1942, strict consumer rationing had evaporated the markets for toilet goods and church wares, and those product lines were discontinued. Between 1943 and 1945, the War Production Board limited the use of silver to 12.5 percent of what it had been prior to the declaration of war. In peacetime, Gorham had employed about 1,200 silver workers; by 1945, only 160 of the firm's workers were making silverware, and sterling flatware production was limited to just a dozen or so tried-and-true patterns. Gorham's facilities were thus primed to devote nearly every ounce of their effort to war work (fig. 25).

Mayo proved himself every bit as favorable to Gorham's efforts during World War II as Holbrook had been during World War I. Moreover, his experience on the engineering side of metalworking gave him the foresight to pursue various military contracts successfully. In all, Gorham made thirty-six products for use in the war effort: 40-millimeter steel cartridge casings; gun mounts; gas mask parts; parachute hardware; 75-millimeter smoke shells; castings for submarines; parts for torpedoes; tank bearings; and 20-pound fragmentation bombs (fig. 26). In May 1944, the company received the Army-Navy "E" Award for excellence in production, which was presented to representatives of the then largely female Gorham workforce with much fanfare at a public ceremony presided over by Henry Wriston, president of Brown University.[52]

In the 1950s, with the war over and postwar recovery beginning to boom, there were thoughts of expansion in the air (fig. 27). Gorham now embarked on a binge of acquisitions. At the end of the decade, it added three silverware companies and a California bronze foundry, then began to diversify into fine paper and electronics. First Gorham bought the Eaton Paper Co. of Pittsfield, Massachusetts, which held a significant share of the market in quality typing paper. In 1960, they added Pickard & Burns, Inc., a Massachusetts electronics company that conducted classified research and development for the defense industry, including the installation of guidance systems for the new Polaris missile.

Silverware still constituted 60 percent of Gorham's business, and in the early 1960s the company hired a number of young designers, including a few women, in an attempt to invigorate the company's designs. The decade also brought a wave of corporate conglomerations to the business world, as companies sought to avoid antitrust problems by amassing different businesses that were not in competition with one another while simultaneously spreading investment risk across a range of industries. They also hoped to defer taxes by acquiring new assets through tax-free stock swaps. Gorham's stock price was lower than the combined value of its assets, and this combination of the goodwill of its name, its valuable collection of flatware dies, its profitable subsidiaries, and its inventory of silver in an era of rising silver prices made it a desirable target for a hostile takeover. The company fended off several takeover attempts before approaching Textron, a global conglomerate with headquarters just miles away in Downcity Providence, to discuss a merger. In the summer of 1967, Textron agreed to fold Gorham into its assets.

In 1968, under Textron's purview, Gorham officially embarked on a diversification program into giftware and total tabletop industries, including the manufacture of china, crystal, and fine writing papers used for invitations and other correspondence related to social events. As Gorham had no expertise in any of these product lines, they relied on acquisitions to make the plan work. In 1970, for example, they acquired the Flintridge China Company in Pasadena, California, a maker of fine porcelain. The expansion continued into giftware, and Gorham began manufacturing novelty items, such as silver Christmas tree ornaments. But these efforts to keep up with the times proved to be no match for the markets; with the price of silver fluctuating, a crisis loomed perpetually in the wings. Silver became extremely volatile in the late 1970s, when a few wealthy investors attempted to corner the silver market, sending prices soaring from $6.08 an ounce in January 1979 to nearly $50 an ounce in early 1980. Extreme price fluctuations made it difficult for Gorham and other silverware makers to set value on their raw stock and finished goods. With volatile pricing, the availability of affordable stainless-steel flatware, and a shift in the United States away from formal dining habits, sales of consumer silver products slumped. Through its diversification program, Gorham now imported more than it made.

In 1986, the company downsized and moved production to the former Speidel watchband plant in Smithfield, Rhode Island. As Gorham employees worked to clear out the Adelaide Avenue building, a great number of art books, drawings, historical records, and objects were saved by individuals working with Gorham, Textron, the John Hay Library at Brown University, and the RISD Museum. A large portion of these materials were given to the John Hay Library by Textron in 1987, founding the Gorham Manufacturing Company Archive. Textron sold Gorham to Dansk International Designs in 1989, which was then purchased by Brown-Forman Corporation in 1991, and both Dansk and Gorham were incorporated into Lenox, Incorporated, which Brown-Forman had purchased in 1983. When Brown-Forman sold the Lenox division in 2005, a gift of archival materials equal to the 1987 bequest came to the John Hay Library. Today, approximately 6,200 linear feet of company records dating from the founding of the company by Jabez Gorham in 1831 to its final disposition in 2005 comprise the Gorham Manufacturing Company Archive at the John Hay Library.

27
Aerial view, Elmwood plant, ca. 1940. Gorham Archive, John Hay Library

The collection features many thousands of drawings and photographs of Gorham products; corporate, personnel, costing, sales, and advertising records; and blueprints, plaster casts, and copper printing plates. Incorporated into the collection are the records of fourteen companies acquired by Gorham over the course of its corporate life span prior to its acquisition by Textron. In 2005, Lenox also gifted nearly 1,800 volumes from the Gorham Design Library to the RISD Fleet Library and more than 2,500 design drawings were given to the RISD Museum.

Local investors bought the empty Adelaide Avenue factory but were unable to settle on a redevelopment plan, and the City of Providence acquired the complex at a tax foreclosure sale. The city and groups such as the Rhode Island Historical Preservation and Heritage Commission and the Providence Preservation Society tried to find alternative uses for the site, which had been cleaned up in 1994 by the Textron Corporation and the Department of Environmental Management. Even with a bond issue for redevelopment approved by the City Council in 1997, no viable offers emerged, and the Gorham complex was demolished in 1998.[53] Although the manufacturing facility that operated continuously from 1890 to 1986 no longer remains, the Gorham Manufacturing Company's stellar collection of nearly 1,800 silver wares endures. In 1991, Textron donated the company collection to the RISD Museum, where it continues to convey the innovations and accomplishments of the world's largest silver company.

1　John Gorham, diary of a trip to England & France in 1852, Gorham Manufacturing Company Archive, John Hay Library, Brown University, Providence, Rhode Island (hereafter GMCA).

2　John Gorham, an account of my beginning, July 1893, GMCA.

3　George Sweet Gibb, *The Whitesmiths of Taunton: A History of Reed and Barton 1824–1943* (New York: Harper and Row, 1943), 73–75. Cited in Charles L. Venable, *Silver in America, 1840–1940: A Century of Splendor* (Dallas and New York: Dallas Museum of Art / Harry N. Abrams, 1994), 13–14.

4　The American system of manufacturing was a nineteenth-century process that relied on the use of interchangeable parts and mechanization for production. The ability to separate manufacture from assembly allowed for the division of labor. See David A. Hounshell, *From the American System to Mass Production, 1800–1932: The Development of Manufacturing Technology in the United States* (Baltimore: Johns Hopkins University Press, 1984).

5　Original indenture of apprenticeship for Jabez Gorham with Nehemiah Dodge, April 2, 1806, GMCA.

6　John Gorham, draft notes on the history of the Gorham Company, January 13, 1894, GMCA, quoted in Charles H. Carpenter Jr., *Gorham Silver, 1831–1981* (New York: Dodd, Mead & Company, 1982), 23.

7　Jabez Gorham, correspondence with Amey Thurber Gorham, October–November 1819, GMCA. For quoted sections of letters, see Carpenter, *Gorham Silver, 1831–1981*, 25–26.

8　Brian P. Luskey, *On the Make: Clerks and the Quest for Capital in Nineteenth-Century America* (New York: New York University Press, 2010), 1–20.

9　John Gorham's history, 1893, notebook with 32 pages of J.G.'s draft, GMCA.

10　For further information, see Venable, *Silver in America, 1840–1940*, 19–33.

11　See *The Sales Manual and the History of the Gorham Company* (Providence: Gorham Manufacturing Company, 1932), 2. Information given by Henry C. Bushnell, who made the first dies for Gorham in 1843 and authored an unpublished manuscript, "Recollections of the Early History of the Gorham Company," cited in Carpenter, *Gorham Silver, 1831–1981*, 30.

12　John Gorham, handwritten history of Gorham, January 13, 1894, GMCA.

13　John Gorham, an account, July 1893, GMCA.

14　Michael Zakim, "Bookkeeping as Ideology: Capitalist Knowledge in Nineteenth-Century America," *Common-place* 6, no. 3 (April 2006). See also Michael Zakim, "Producing Capitalism: The Clerk at Work," in *Capitalism Takes Command: The Social Transformation of Nineteenth-Century America*, ed. Michael Zakim and Gary Kornblith (Chicago: University of Chicago Press, 2012), 223–48.

15　*Providence Journal*, September 29, 1850, 2.

16　John Gorham, an account, July 1893, GMCA.

17　John Gorham, diary, 1852, GMCA.

18　James Nasmyth, *James Nasmyth, Engineer: An Autobiography*, ed. Samuel Smiles (London: John Murray, 1883), 39–42; see also "Nasmyth, Alexander" in *Encyclopaedia Britannica: A Dictionary of Arts, Sciences, Literature and General Information* (11th ed.), vol. 19 (Cambridge: Cambridge University Press, 1911), 248–49; Joseph Wickham Roe, *English and American Tool Builders* (New York: McGraw-Hill Book Company, 1916), 81–97.

19　John Gorham, an account, July 1893, GMCA.

20　Nathan Rosenberg, *Perspectives on Technology* (Cambridge: Cambridge University Press: 1976), 230.

21　Lucian Sharpe, "Journals of Lucian Sharpe," unpublished manuscript, 1848–50. Brown and Sharpe Collection, New Box 29, Rhode Island Historical Society Library.

22　Welcome Arnold Greene, *The Providence Plantations for 250 Years* (Providence: J. A. and R. A. Reid, 1886), 264–65.

23　Carpenter, *Gorham Silver, 1831–1981*, 51.

24　Philip Anderson and Michael L. Tushman, "Technological Discontinuities and Dominant Designs: A Cyclical Model of Technological Change," *Administrative Science Quarterly* 35 (1990): 604–33.

25　Venable, *Silver in America, 1840–1940*, 74. See also "Manufacturing and Mechanical Industry of Rhode Island. Silver Ware—Gorham Manufacturing Company," *Providence Journal*, May 19, 1871.

26　A detailed Roster of Gorham Craftsmen, compiled over the course of many years by Samuel J. Hough, includes Owen Salisbury of "Snow Town," a predominately African American neighborhood in what was then the north-western corner of Providence. He was listed as a thirty-year-old laborer in 1830. Eleven years later, he was elevated to silversmith, an unusually long apprenticeship period. James Salisbury, also of Olney Street in Snow Town, appears on the roster as a silversmith in 1850, twenty years after Owen's first appearance. In his will, Jabez Gorham left $1,000 to the Providence Association for the Benefit of Colored Children.

27　See, for example, Paul Frymer, *Black and Blue: African Americans, the Labor Movement, and the Decline of the Democratic Party* (Princeton: Princeton University Press, 2008), 52–70; National Industrial Conference Board, *Wartime Employment of Women in the Metal Trades* (Boston: National Industrial Conference Board, 1918).

28　James Reilly, "The History, Technique and Structure of Albumen Prints," *AIC Pre-Prints* (May 1980), 93–98.

29　Alden vs. Gorham, 1867. John Gorham's history, 1893, Sydney S. Rider Collection, John Hay Library.

30　James Parton, "Silver and Silver Plate," *Harper's New Monthly Magazine* 37, no. 220 (September 1868): 443.

31　*The Sales Manual and the History of the Gorham Company* (Providence: Gorham Manufacturing Company, 1932), 5.

32　The will of Jabez Gorham, 1869, GMCA.

33　*Acts and Resolves Passed by the General Assembly* (Providence: Oxford Press, 1865), 134.

34　Like the Panics of 1837 and 1857, the Panic of 1873 was the result of multiple causes, chief among them overly optimistic projections of investor appetite for bonds to finance the Northern Pacific Railroad's planned trans-continental line. The Philadelphia bank of Jay Cooke & Co. could not sell enough of the bonds it held to meet other obligations; when word got out that Cooke & Co. was running short on cash, a run on the bank ensued, precipitating a panic that hit Rhode Island particularly hard. The state's largest concern, A. & W. Sprague, closed—putting 12,000 people, mostly textile workers, out of work. Scott Reynolds Nelson, *Nation of Deadbeats* (New York: Alfred A Knopf, 2012), and William G. McLoughlin, *Rhode Island: A History* (New York: W. W. Norton and Co., 1970), 166–68.

35　Nicolas Barreyre, "The Politics of Economic Crises: The Panic of 1873, the End of Reconstruction, and the Realignment of American Politics," *Journal of the Gilded Age and Progressive Era* 10, no. 4 (2011): 403–23. http://www.jstor.org/stable/23045120.

36　Carpenter, *Gorham Silver, 1831–1981*, 90.

37　Alfred D. Chandler, *The Visible Hand* (Cambridge, MA: Belknap Press of the Harvard University Press, 1977), 1–4.

38　For more information on production of bronzes and ecclesiastical ware, see Carpenter, *Gorham Silver, 1831–1981*, 141–59.

39　The authors wish to thank Mr. Charles Chapin, who retains William Crins's diary and allowed its research, For quoted sections of the diary, see Carpenter, *Gorham Silver, 1831–1981*, 136–40.

40　"Masons' Building Materials," *Providence Journal*, January 1, 1889, 7.

41　*The Sales Manual and History of the Gorham Company* (Providence: Gorham Manufacturing Company, 1932), 6.

42　*Providence Journal*, January 11, 1890, 3.

43   Chandler, *The Visible Hand*, 285–86, 484.

44   Venable, *Silver in America, 1840–1940*, 223–27.

45   Gorham Manufacturing Company, *Woman's Work at the Gorham Manufacturing Company, Silversmiths* (Providence and New York: Gorham Manufacturing, 1892).

46   Ibid.

47   Ibid.

48   *New York Age*, November 9, 1918.

49   "Are You Practicing False Patriotism?" (New York: Gorham Manufacturing Company, 1918). Copyrighted that same year by E. Le Roy Pelletier, likely the author of the text, the leaflet may have reprinted a text originally published elsewhere, though attempts to identify a prior printing have so far proved fruitless.

50   On page 254 of *Gorham Silver*, Carpenter points to William Codman's reliance on old designs and Mayo's hiring of Erik Magnussen to make the point that Mayo was not persuaded by the efficacy of having an in-house design team.

51   Venable, *Silver in America, 1840–1940*, 229–30.

52   "Pictorial Review of the Official Presentation of The Army-Navy 'E' Award for Excellence in Production to the Men and Women of the Gorham Manufacturing Company, Providence, Rhode Island. Friday, May 29, 1944, 3:10 P.M." (Providence: Gorham Manufacturing Company, 1944). The brochure includes photographs of Gorham's wartime workforce. For further details on Gorham's war production work, please see Gorham Manufacturing Company, *Report to the War Department, Boston Ordnance District . . . of the methods used to manufacture the 40 mm Steel Cartridge Case* (Providence: Gorham Manufacturing Company, 1944). This report includes a photo array showing and describing each step of the process, and details the equipment used for manufacturing the shells.

53   For more information see: the Gorham Documentation Project for the City of Providence Department of Planning and Development and the Rhode Island Historical Preservation & Heritage Commission, prepared by Erik Gould, Erik Carlson, and Joshua Safdie, 1998.

GORHAM WORKS
1860s–1870s

28
Medallion Pitcher, 1864.
Silver. RISD Museum

29
Wine Decanter Set (detail),
ca. 1865.
RISD Museum

30
Wine Decanter Set, ca. 1865.
Shreve & Co., retailer.
Silver and glass. RISD Museum

31 *(overleaf)*
Tea and Coffee Service, 1871.
Silver with gilding and ivory.
RISD Museum

32
Creamer and Sugar Bowl, ca. 1865.
George Wilkinson, designer, and
Shreve, Stanwood & Company, retailer.
Silver. RISD Museum

33
Creamer (detail), ca. 1865.
RISD Museum

34
Ice Bowl, 1866, and Ice Tongs, 1869.
Both silver with gilding. RISD Museum

35
Ice Bowl (detail), 1866. RISD Museum

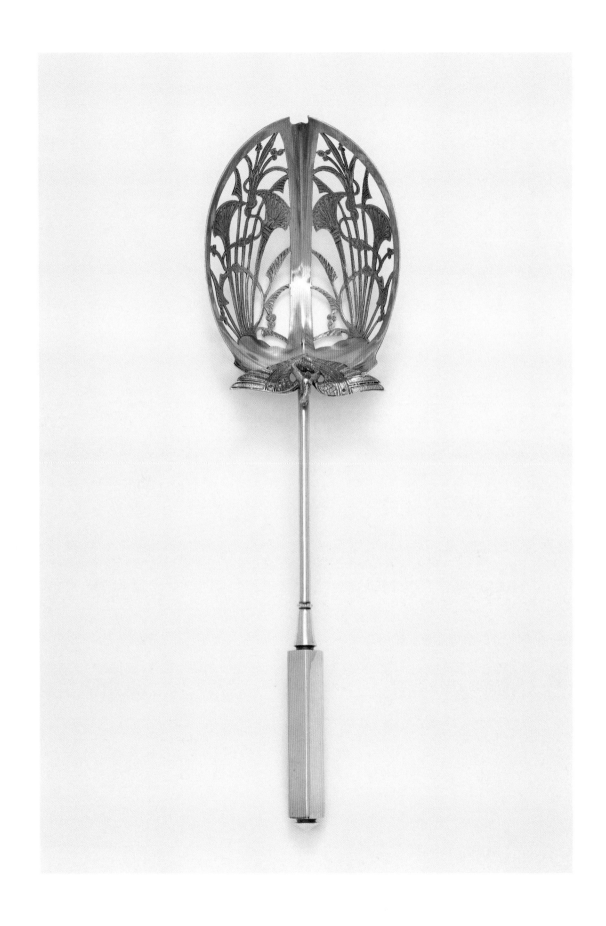

36
Isis Ice Serving Spoon, ca. 1871.
George Wilkinson, designer.
Silver with gilding. RISD Museum

37
Isis Ice Serving Spoon (detail),
ca. 1871.
RISD Museum

38
Pattern 500 Tea and Coffee Service, 1871.
Silver with ivory. RISD Museum

39
Pattern 500 Urn with Stand (detail),
1871. RISD Museum

40
Hot-Water Kettle and Stand, 1874.
Silver with gilding and ivory. RISD Museum

41
Fruit Stand (detail of fig. 69), 1871.
Silver with gilding. RISD Museum

Jeannine Falino

GORHAM SILVER AND SOCIAL ASPIRATIONS

EXCEEDINGLY SPLENDID

The appearance of a dinner table set with silver for a large party is so exceedingly splendid that we can hardly wonder that fashion has adopted this metal for her own. . . . Show me the way a people dine, and I will tell you their rank among civilized beings.

Harper's New Monthly Magazine, 1868[1]

The importance of good manners has been a subject of discussion for centuries.[2] One of the most famous American examples is the "Rules of Civility & Decent Behavior in Company and Conversation" copied out by George Washington in 1747, when he was about fifteen years old. Washington's rules were derived from existing publications, most of which trace their lineage to *de Civilitatae morum puerilium (On Civility in Children)*, written by Erasmus about 1530, and which equated good manners with virtuous behavior.[3] Washington's 110 rules governed manner and deportment, of which no less than fourteen addressed the subject of table manners.[4] These include admonitions to "feed not with Greediness" and noting, "It's unbecoming to Stoop much to ones Meat Keep your Fingers clean & when foul wipe them on a Corner of your Table Napkin." Washington's father died when the future president was only eleven years of age, and family finances prevented him from traveling abroad for a formal education. Yet ambition drove him to acquire the knowledge, bearing, refinement, and the well-appointed home for which he became renowned. His copybook testifies to an early awareness of etiquette and its role in society.

In Washington's world, the British colonial elite was a landed gentry whose ancestors were among North America's earliest European settlers. Upward mobility occurred infrequently, except through marriage, as was the case for Washington. In this homogeneously Caucasian and exclusionary society, everyone knew one another or knew of one another through relations and friends.

The hereditary order of Washington's world began to shift with the increased influx of European immigrants and the rise of commercial and industrial activity beginning in the 1830s, which opened new pathways to wealth and influence. It led to a fluidity in a rising middle class whose status was marked by personal achievements and personal wealth rather than circumstances of birth. These individuals solidified their new status with purchases of domestic and personal products, endowing them with meaning in their desire to become accepted members of polite society.

By the 1850s, Gorham was an established silversmithing firm that actively sought to embrace the desires and

42
Water Pitcher,
Gorham & Thurber, 1851.
George Babcock, engraver.
Silver. RISD Museum

aspirations of its consumers even as it helped to shape the evolving nature of silver consumption itself. By this time, etiquette books, silver manufacturer brochures, and domestic magazines had grown in number to serve those seeking advice on the proper selection of such items and their uses. In this way, American silver became the most desirable medium for expressing gentility, sophistication, and wealth, and Gorham was more than ready to meet this rising demand for refined wares. An 1853 Gorham advertisement (fig. 225) emphasized "the stock of silver . . . at their ware room, comprising nearly every article desired for ornament or utility"; an 1852 example (fig. 110) noted the "rich stock of the finest quality of silver" and the "great variety of silver articles manufactured at this establishment" (fig. 42).

The ability to purchase fine goods was one thing; the genteel knowledge to use them correctly and within the bounds of good manners was another. The potential for moving up the social ladder through proper dress, comportment, home decoration, and dining drove a market for prescriptive literature. Etiquette books served as a helpful guide to safely navigating polite society, and more than two hundred such books were printed between 1870 and 1917. Some published earlier in the nineteenth century continued in popularity for decades, as in the case of Eliza Farrar, spouse of a Harvard professor, who wrote *The Young Lady's Friend* in 1836, which

was reprinted as late as 1880.[5] The role of authors was to impose structure on the growing middle class, perceived as an ever-changing and increasingly disorderly society. "Etiquette writers and other apostles of civility saw themselves battling for far bigger stakes than how best to eat asparagus. Their enterprise must be viewed with the larger concern of how to establish order and authority

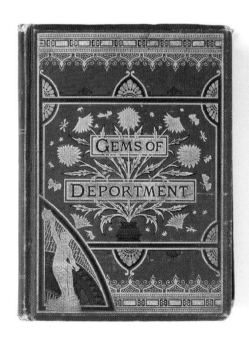

in a restless, highly mobile, rapidly urbanizing and industrializing democracy."[6]

It was clear that help was needed. Foreign observers had taken note of American manners—or lack thereof—at the table, remarking upon their haste and lack of refinement. Knives and spoons were the standard implements of the table through a major portion of the nineteenth century, as they had been for centuries; the spoon for liquids, and the knife (or knives) for cutting, piercing, securing, and eating directly from the edge of the blade. The fork was another matter, evolving from the two-tine carving fork, which was originally used to secure meat while being cut with the knife. It did not become a standard personal utensil at the American table until the third quarter of the nineteenth century, when it finally supplanted the knife as the primary tool for conveying food to the mouth.

The shift to forks began in Italy in the early seventeenth century. One writer in 1608 provided the following description:

> The Italian[s] . . . use a little fork when they cut their meat. For while with their knife which they hold in one hand they cut the meat out of the dish, they fasten the fork, which they hold in their other hand, upon the same dish, so that whatsoever he be that sitting in the company of others at the meal, should unadvisedly touch the dish of meat with his fingers from which all at the table do cut, he will give occasion of offense . . . having transgressed the laws of good manners. . . . [T]he Italian cannot by any means indure [sic] to have his dish touched with fingers, seeing all men's fingers are not alike clean.[7]

It was the improper use of forks in the service of personal hygiene at the table that led one astonished foreigner to recount a visit to New York in 1833. While eating breakfast at a hotel, the writer was "surprised to hear calls from all sides for forks, the use of which I could not divine; as I had already seen that the American has no need of them for eating, but uses his knife alone, with wonderful dexterity. A waiter brought several plates full of forks, and set them in the middle of the table. The gentlemen . . . immediately fell upon the forks; each secured one, rose, and repaired to some part of the room . . . [and] began at their ease to pick their teeth and pare their nails."[8] By 1881, etiquette books, such as *Gems of Deportment and Hints of Etiquette* (fig. 44), made it quite clear that to "pick the teeth with a fork . . . may be safely set down as vulgar."[9]

45
Tea and Coffee Service, 1873–75. Silver with gilding and ivory. RISD Museum

tea and coffee service (fig. 45) complete with such specialized forms as a waste bowl with a gilded interior, designed to receive the dregs from a teacup before the cup was refilled. Together with the set's ornamentation and shining surface, it proclaimed the refined manners and good taste of its owner.[11]

By the mid- and late nineteenth century, as women assumed a greater role in selecting objects for the home, they applied the knowledge absorbed from social acquaintances, genteel parents, and etiquette publications to create identity and shape their domestic world. Their purchases coincided with a rapidly exploding world of manufactured goods in the form of furniture, glass, ceramics, silver, and textiles for home use and decoration. Gorham increased the market for silver by offering an assortment of forms and designs to suit every desire, which, by 1874, meant that they were producing about 125 different object types and nearly 1,000 individual objects from which consumers could choose, ranging from bonbon bowls to spectacle cases and sugar dusters to cake baskets (fig. 46).[12] The output increased to such a degree that by 1880, Gorham conceded

47
Oyster Forks, 1879.
Silver with gilding.
RISD Museum

46
Cake Basket, 1874. Silver with gilding. RISD Museum

The concept of personal cleanliness in public was relatively new to a world that lacked indoor plumbing until the late nineteenth century. With advancements in hygiene came the fear of giving offense and the heightened awareness of social environments, especially the fear of transgression at the dinner table.[10] These concerns eventually brought the fork into full use as a means of distancing individuals from their food as well as their dining companions, and illuminated the social tension between the convivial and the individual that etiquette books sought to balance.

The advance of the middle class meant the construction of new homes that included dining rooms, a significant space that was separate from the rest of the house and appeared in building plans of the period. It was an improvement over the kitchen where many had previously taken their meals. Historian Clifford E. Clark Jr. has identified the dining room as the "sacred center of middle-class family life" within which the family could shape its image with furnishings and the practice of correct behavior at the table and, in the process, could establish an idealized community insulated from the unruly world beyond (fig. 43). Following the lead of the upper class, the middle class filled their dining rooms with significant cultural and behavioral content such as a Gorham

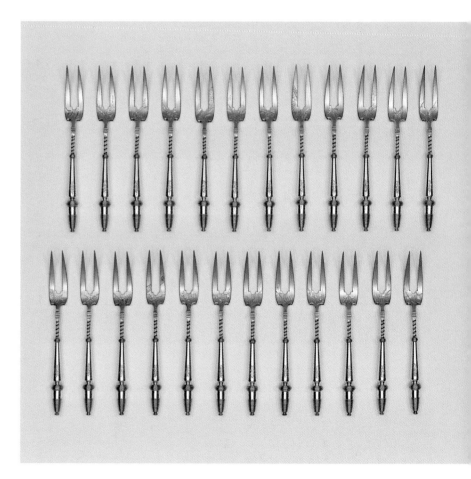

Falino

American Woman's Home (1869) by Catharine R. Beecher and Harriet Beecher Stowe, and its dedication page, which honored "The women of America in whose hands rest the real destinies of the republic, as moulded by the early training and preserved amid the maturer [sic] influences of home."[15]

As the nineteenth century progressed, women began to incorporate a wider array of food into their household menus. Oysters were plentiful on the Eastern Seaboard, long feasted upon by Native Americans, and they were a common meal for the working class in the nineteenth century. Their status improved by the 1840s as canning made them into delicacies transported to inland cities, and ceramic oyster plates and delicate oyster forks (fig. 47) transformed them into attractive additions to the dining table. By contrast, celery was considered an elite vegetable; it was first cultivated in Kalamazoo, Michigan, where celery farms flourished beginning in

that it could not publish them all in their entirety: "The innumerable variety and the rapid succession of new forms and style of decoration has [sic] prevented our issuing a complete catalog."[13] Women sought to assemble these refined goods, each to their taste and means, in small ways and large, in pieces and in large sets, to make the dining room a focus of family gatherings and a training ground for the practice of good manners and hospitality.

Women were generally considered central to the running of American households and to domestic life since the eighteenth century. During the nineteenth century, however, they assumed increasing responsibility for the purchase of food and other goods, while their husbands worked outside the home to generate family wealth. Running the household was one of the few active roles open to middle-class women during this period, which contributed to the fusion of their identity with their domestic environment in what has been called a "cult of domesticity."[14] They became avid students of etiquette and interior-design publications and, thus armed, the guardians of a protected interior world and a moral refuge from the changing world around them, where genteel behavior in all its outward manifestations served as a sign to others of the quality of life within. The crucial role of women in this endeavor is evident in the title of *The*

the 1850s. This quickly led to the creation of celery vases in silver or glass for holding the stalks and their leafy tips vertically in the manner of a bouquet (fig. 48).[16] Sardines became an exotic food for Americans owing to their European origins, and with the advent of canning and the success of sardine factories in Maine during the 1870s, a fashion arose for sardine containers and serving forks and

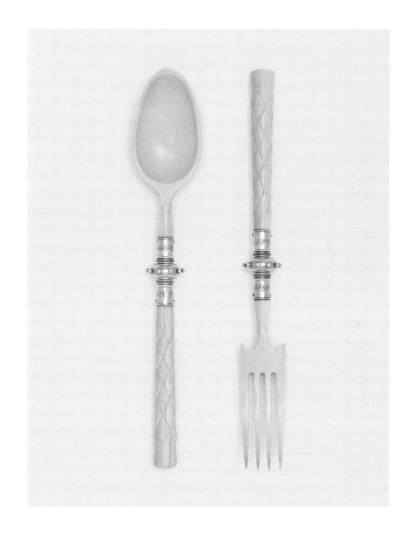

tongs (fig. 103).[17] Often served as a first course, turtle soup was held in great esteem in nineteenth-century America and became a symbol of refined Victorian dining. Illustrating an important theory of design, the vessels' forms indicate their contents (fig. 49).

Transportation and refrigeration brought dramatic changes in diets and dining patterns to Americans around the country. To prevent spoilage, refrigerated railcars packed with harvested blocks of ice were designed to ship frozen meat from Chicago; fish from the Great Lakes and the Atlantic and Pacific coasts; and eggs, dairy, fruits, and vegetables to far-flung destinations across the country. Meanwhile, late nineteenth-century hotels, restaurants, and middle- to upper-class homes began to acquire their own iceboxes, as they were called, so that perishable goods could be kept cold longer, allowing for better planning and execution of meals.[18] Beyond its functional purpose, the pleasures of iced food and drink led to inventive hollowware

and flatware designs by Gorham that evoked a frigid and faraway Arctic world such as ice cream slices (fig. 50), ice cream spoons (fig. 52), and ice cream plates (fig. 83). Ice bowls with tongs and spoons (figs. 34–37, 121) were shaped in the forms of rugged icebergs with polar bears that prepared guests for chilled and frozen delights.

The new foods gave rise to a proliferation of custom-designed serving utensils by Gorham and other silver manufacturers.[19] They included macaroni servers and pastry servers (fig. 266), butter knives, nutcrackers (fig. 86), and butter plates (figs. 123, 175). Asparagus servers were devised to grasp a group of stalks for transfer to the plate, thus forever banning the use of fingers, a practice that had been prevalent a few decades earlier. Thus as middle- and upper-class consumers planned their menus, they also contended with an awareness of these specialized implements and hollowware to handle each delicacy, and the need to acquire them, as promoted by manufacturers.

In the same manner, fresh salad greens called for salad dishes, salad forks, and salad servers (fig. 51). Lettuce and other greens were available seasonally, and by 1900 they were cultivated in hothouses. Lettuce first appeared in the American home in the 1830s, when it was included as an ingredient for lobster and chicken salads. By the 1840s, greens were served alone with an oil and vinegar dressing.[20] Gorham met this growing interest in salad dishes as early as the late 1860s; by 1905 *The Gorham Salad Book, With Rules for Dressings and Sauce* detailed the varied sorts of dishes that could be assembled with meat, fish, shellfish, eggs, nuts, fruit, and even cheese, with one essential rule that the food must be served cold.[21]

When the first shipments of oranges arrived on the East Coast in the 1870s, diners were at last able to indulge their appetites the proper way, with orange cups designed to hold half of the fruit in place, and by using orange knives, also called peelers, and spoons with pointed tips to better extract sections.[22] Gorham's Furber service included fruit forks and knives (figs. 72, 84), along with a set of fruit plates (fig. 76), each depicting a different variety, celebrating the bounty of American agriculture. Meanwhile, according to Elizabeth F. Ellet's *New Cyclopedia of Domestic Economy, and Practical Housekeeper* (1873), large fruit stands (page 8, figs. 69, 114, 168) emerged to contain imported novelties including bananas, sugarcane, prickly pears, and oranges, among other fruit, which provided beauty to the sideboard or dining table and, according to at least one writer, a conversational focus for gentlemen at the table, when the ladies had departed, to discuss "freetrade, colonial policy, etc."[23]

The bowls of spoons, wide and rounded since the sixteenth century, were gradually narrowing in order to more neatly enter the mouth, in keeping with early admonishments to keep the mouth closed while eating.[24] With regard to desserts, spoon bowls (fig. 52) were often gilded to prevent the acid in fruits from discoloring silver. Large sugar tongs, used in the colonial era for cone sugar (sugarloaves), gave way to smaller and more delicate versions for grasping sugar cubes, and pierced spoons were designed to sift granulated sugar.[25] In all, the rage for new patterns and specialized serving pieces was a peculiarly American phenomenon, fueled by competing silver manufacturers like Gorham, who manufactured more than fifty different patterns in the mid-1870s—a number that doubled to one hundred within ten years. Such a profusion of manufacturing designs that supported a multitude of serving pieces contrasted with the British, in their "supine conservativism" according to one writer, of producing a handful of traditional designs such as "fiddle or *Old English,*" with little

52
Ice Cream Spoon, 1879. Silver with gilding. RISD Museum

desire to expand into new patterns or specialized forms.[26]

Notwithstanding the profusion of these goods and the desires they kindled in nineteenth-century consumers, a heavy emphasis on proper utensils and usage, aided and abetted by etiquette guides, could also prevent the true expression of good manners. For instance, as peas entered the mainstream of American gastromony, so, too, did the discussion of how best to eat them—with a knife or a fork? The struggle between desire and comportment led to a story in 1873 entitled "Hyper-Gentility" in *Scribner's Monthly* that mocked the way in which manners prevented the enjoyment of good food.[27] The story recounts three "high-toned ladies . . . so extremely proper in their manners" who were served peas at the home of a country friend. The two-tined fork at each place setting was useless for eating the tiny peas. The family used their knives as was still common in the 1870s, but the ladies denied themselves the pleasure of peas that were

54
Dining room, Leland
Stanford residence. ca. 1878.
Stanford Libraries

53
Table setting for dinner
à la française, ca. 1870

of honor later surprised her with a gift of two dozen oyster forks.[28] The anecdote illustrates how fully Gorham, among other silver manufacturers, had achieved market penetration among both men and women with specialized forms that were considered essential components of a dinner service.

Before a single piece of silver was purchased, however, there were a few important decisions to consider: Service à la française or à la russe? How many guests must one plan for? And how extensive a service, in terms of place settings, serving implements, and hollowware, is needed? What style should be chosen for the service? Must it be in harmony with the room furnishings? These questions and many more were addressed in detail by etiquette manuals.

Originating in France and based upon banquet-style meals of the sixteenth century, service à la française, or French-style service, is considered the most elaborate and demanding of all serving styles. It was practiced in Europe before its adoption in the British colonies during the eighteenth century. Those who aspired to serving dinners à la française followed a strict symmetry on the dining table in which all the dishes, laden with food and set with fine dinnerware, were arranged to greet the guests (fig. 53). Primacy was given to main dishes that were placed around the center of the table, while side dishes were interspersed among them. Guests were expected to serve themselves and pass dishes from one to another, with waiters nearby to assist.[29]

The magnificent and heavily laden spread of ceramics, glass, and silverware used in service à la française impressed visitors even as it exhausted them. The table was reset for each course, adding to what was a long and, for some, a tiresome meal. As stated by Eliza Farrar in *The Young Lady's Friend* (1837), "[A] dinner, well performed by all the actors in it, is very fatiguing, and as it generally occupies three hours or more,

"fresh, green, plump, and luscious, and so delightfully hot and tempting," because it violated the rules of etiquette. The author pointed out the foolishness of such fixations while ignoring the central tenet of proper behavior—to adapt yourself to others. Nevertheless, difficulties such as these led to the introduction of three, and eventually four, tines in forks.

Missing oyster forks apparently did not diminish Mrs. Charles Frederick Manderson's view of her Washington dinner party one evening in 1891. She decided to let her guests, who were all male, use "ordinary forks," and she considered the dinner was a success despite this omission, since her guests were unlikely to be concerned with such niceties. This gendered perspective backfired, however, when her guest

55
Diagram of a table set for
a multi-course dinner, *Demorest's
Family Magazine*, 1891

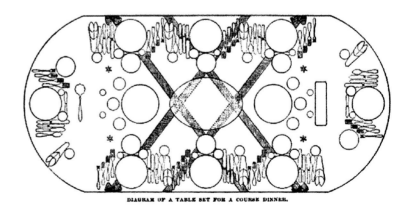

DIAGRAM OF A TABLE SET FOR A COURSE DINNER.

56
Dining room with table set,
Potter Palmer mansion,
Chicago, ca. 1895–1902.
Art Institute of Chicago

most persons are glad to go away when it is fairly done."[30] Not all homes adhered to such a high standard as the one visited by Farrar.

The setting and rules of behavior for service à la française as described were an ideal intended for an expanding middle class, few of whom could execute a dinner on such an exacting scale. The guidelines provided by etiquette books of the era were intended for readers to make their own choices according to their own means and depending upon the occasion.

The same was true for the shift to service à la russe, which took hold gradually during the nineteenth century. Introduced into France by the Russian ambassador to Napoleon, Prince Aleksandr Borisovich Kurakin, in 1811, popularized in Europe by the 1860s. and adopted in America in the 1870s, dining à la russe enabled Victorians to further distance themselves from direct contact with the food. Each course, of which there may have been as many as fifteen, was served by waiters to guests one at a time; any preparation, such as carving meat, was completed by servants in the kitchen and the meal was often served from the sideboard (fig. 54). It was not uncommon for decorations on the numerous dining implements and serving vessels to be related to the type of food contained within.[31]

This arrangement reduced the number of serving dishes on the table at any one time, but multiplied the number of servants necessary, as well as the quantity and shape of individual dishes and flatware required for diners throughout the course of the meal (fig. 55). It drove the marketplace

to produce multiple sets of elegant dinner services and new forms such as oyster plates. Without a large display of food on the table, the center became a stage for the lavish display of flowers and large ornamental objects made of silver, glass, or ceramic (fig. 56). As the nineteenth century progressed and more complex dinners evolved, so, too, did the number of specialized eating and serving implements designed for their use.[32] Implicit in these developments were the assumptions that the host could supply all the required costly equipage and that guests were expert in the manner of manipulating their food. Elite settings such as these were unrealistic models for Americans living on middle-class incomes, since few households possessed the requisite servants, funds, or knowledge gained from books or experiences to entertain on such an aristocratic level. In the last analysis, each family compromised to achieve their ideal as promoted by prescriptive literature and manufacturers alike to the extent they desired or were able to afford.[33]

At the end of the meal, men often retired to a separate room to share in smoking and drinking, two activities that were also well supported by Gorham's industrious design and manufacturing enterprise. All manner of smoking devices, such as humidors (fig. 206), cigar lamps (fig. 177), ash receptacles, and match

57
Match Safes, 1881–ca. 1900.
Silver with gold and copper.
RISD Museum

safes (fig. 57) in a multitude of designs, as well as decanters (fig. 60), wine coasters, and drinking flasks (fig. 233), were made for purchase individually and also in sets. Although antismoking efforts in the late 1800s condemned women smokers for rejecting their role as the standard-bearers of proper behavior in the family—smoking being considered a sign of loose morals—the truth is that many did smoke, just as in earlier decades they had taken snuff, although much of this activity took place within the home rather than in public. Women no doubt purchased these goods with themselves as well as their husbands in mind.[34]

The plethora of silver vessels and services made by Gorham for the consumption of tea and coffee responded to and influenced the formal ceremony of the late afternoon event, known as tea, and the country's predilection for coffee. The *Ladies' Home Journal* eloquently described the accoutrements of the tea table in 1884: "The tea-table is as a flower of this growth that we call home. . . . [I]t is the shore where the drift from the waves that surged through the day, is deposited. Foolish things and useless things, and true and precious things are stranded there."[35] Among the precious things made by Gorham to be "stranded" on the tea table were sets of tea flatware, tea bells, tea balls, and strainers, in addition to the elaborate services. Suggesting that the strict etiquette rules demanded during the evening meal could be slightly relaxed at afternoon tea, the *Cosmopolitan Cook and Recipe Book* suggested in 1888 that tea time was "charming when contrasted with the anxieties, formality and etiquette of the dinner table."[36] Nonetheless, successful hostesses followed protocol by sending invitations for tea, as it was one of the most important female social activities in the nineteenth century, described in *Gems of Deportment and Hints of Etiquette* as lasting two hours during "which time is usually spent in chatting, eating, and exchanging social ideas" (fig. 58).[37]

The services that invariably led the order of images in Gorham's internal albums of product photographs typically included a teapot and a coffeepot, often accompanied by a sugar and cream set, and a waste bowl. More elaborate services added a hot-water kettle on a stand, and a hot-milk pitcher and tray. Coffee was served at breakfast, and following European customs, black coffee was served after dinner. These coffeepots for black coffee are elegantly tall and slender with extenuated spouts and were usually sold with a small tray and sugar bowl (figs. 59, 91). Etiquette books suggested serving the robust beverage "after a hearty dinner, especially if the food is rich in animal oil, a small cup of strong, black coffee, drank without milk, but with a liberal allowance of sugar is found to promote digestion and a lively flow of spirits. . . . [N]o dinner is complete without this *café noir*."[38]

With rising incomes and with homes to decorate, silver began to enter American life in greater quantities. Thanks to an 1842 tariff of 30 percent on imported gold and silver, whether plate or solid, middle- and upper-class

58
Stereographic photogragh,
1899. "Gossip—at
every sip a reputation dies"

consumers were able to purchase competitively priced American silver, some for the first time in their lives. Benefits from the tariff were compounded by the discovery of the massive Comstock Lode in Nevada, the greatest silver strike in modern history, which yielded vast quantities of the ore, consequently lowering its price while retaining its luxury status. The protective tariff was raised to an impressive 65 percent by 1930, which allowed consumers to enjoy American-made silver at low prices for almost nine decades. The competition it unleashed among silver manufacturers led to a dazzling era of silver production in the United States with an ever-changing buffet of choices for consumers.

Elite expenditures may have spurred the appetite of average Americans for silver. One conspicuous consumer was Chicago insurance magnate Henry Jewett Furber (fig. 71). From 1866 to 1880, he engaged Gorham to produce a silver-gilt service for twenty-four, in what would ultimately become the company's largest commission, eventually totaling 816 pieces in all, of which 687 were flatware and 129 hollowware. As a measure of their significance, Gorham placed several items, including the service's epergne (figs. 73–74), on view in the Gorham display at the Centennial International Exhibition of 1876 in Philadelphia.

The initials of the financier's wife, Elvira Irwin Furber (fig. 70), were engraved on each of the 816 pieces (figs. 85, 87). When engraved with a woman's initials or coat of arms, silver's

ancient reputation as a valued commodity gained additional strength as a form of investment against an uncertain future, as well as one that could be passed along as a sentimental possession to succeeding generations,[39] demonstrating women's involvement in purchasing silver and the expanding role of females in determining household taste. Silver manufacturers strove to offer female consumers a plethora of silver designs that appealed to their interests, from all manner of flowers to historical patterns like Gorham's *Mythologique* (figs. 154, 189, 191), and curving designs such as the Rococo or Art Nouveau, as well as the Japanesque, as opposed to Gorham's early *Medallion* designs (fig. 28) that were more masculine in their appeal.

Not all could afford silver on such a magnificent scale, but the extraordinary growth and allure of silver-plated goods meant that the "middling classes" could also possess flatware, tea services, or other table wares that looked like silver without paying the cost of sterling. Patented in 1840 by George and Henry Elkington in Birmingham, England, the electrolytic method of depositing a fine layer of silver on a base metal was quickly adopted in the United States where it found a wide audience. Gorham began experimenting with electroplating in 1863 and began production in 1865, with the objective of producing "plated ware which shall have all the splendor and durability of the best plate, at about one-fourth the cost. Thus a silver tea service, which in solid silver would be worth five or six hundred dollars, costs in this superior kind of plated ware from one to two hundred dollars."[40]

The popularity of silver plate led to inventive and sometimes short-lived forms, like card receivers, tilting ice pitchers, pickle jars, spoon racks, moustache cups, and revolving butter dishes, each in a dozen or more styles to suit the taste of the buyer.[41] The Victorian taste for visually complex surfaces was easily met by silver plate manufacturers, who used quantities of both cast and applied elements to create surface interest. In the end, the consumer's purse determined the choice of sterling versus silver plate. Those who could pay for solid silver appreciated the differences in material and craftsmanship between it and silver plate. Nonetheless, those who chose silver plate got exactly what they wanted, elegance on a budget.

Silver for the dining room as described thus far omits flatware made for the tiniest members of the nuclear family—children. Beginning in the 1850s, changing cultural attitudes toward child development included a discussion of their socialization through the use of dining implements (fig. 61). By the 1890s, if not earlier, silver manufacturers addressed this market by selling instructive items like the loop handle

61
"For Tiny Hands"
Gorham
advertisement, 1924

spoon with its curved grip; the food pusher, which aids in moving food onto the fork; as well as small sets that included flatware, cups, and plates that mimicked adult versions of the same, all of which were produced by the firm. Decoration sometimes included popular subjects drawn from children's literature, such as Little Bo-Peep, as produced by Gorham. While made in both sterling and plated silver, the choice of solid silver as the proper medium for these utensils, beyond economic concerns, related to the ceremonial aspects of such gifts and their perceived value as heirloom items, especially in the case of porringers, forms that had long fallen out of general use.

Many gifts were meant to demonstrate emotional bonds of love and friendship. As such, prospective buyers were targeted by an industry that learned to capitalize on events marked by celebration.[42] The transformation of

62
Dressing Set,
ca. 1890. Silver.
RISD Museum

gift giving from a personal, homemade object to one that was manufactured led to dismay among observers like Ralph Waldo Emerson, who in 1844 wrote that "the only gift is a portion of thyself. Thou must bleed for me. . . . But it is a cold, lifeless business when you go into the shops to buy me something which does not represent your life and talent, but a goldsmith's."[43]

Nevertheless, by the 1870s, the fashion for gift giving in general was in full swing, served by the silver industry with the production of countless novelties. Aside from souvenir spoons, which became a national passion, Gorham enticed buyers with a seemingly infinite variety of personal items such as dresser sets (fig. 62), scent bottles, picture frames, and table ornaments such as bonbon baskets, as well as leather items having silver decoration or accessories, such as handbags, cigarette lighters, and fitted luggage that included "every traveling convenience," at a range of prices to satisfy all budgets.[44] The text of Gorham advertisements was designed to convey confidence in the quality and taste of their goods, as stated in a 1909 advertisement: "Gorham Silverware possesses every desirable attribute for household use or gift; it is pre-eminently artistic and refined, and its permanency of character enhances its acceptability."[45] With each Christmas season, the firm advertised their wares

in a similar fashion, and in 1918, during wartime, they demonstrated sensitivity, even as they pressed the value of silver purchases: "In these times when economy is a badge of patriotism, Gorham sterling silverware is one of the most sensible Christmas offerings imaginable. For it is a gift that lives long after the giving, enriching the recipient. Yet costing no more than the giver can reasonably afford to spend."[46]

Emerson and others notwithstanding, the sacred bond of matrimony became a secular business opportunity that the silver and jewelry industry strove to dominate, along with florists, caterers, and photographers, among others. Welcoming window displays, targeted advertisements, and trained salespeople enticed buyers, while at the wedding celebration itself gifts were handsomely arrayed for inspection, the displays looking much like the showcases of the stores from which they came. These public viewings had the potential to create competition and anxiety among well-meaning guests, who, knowing their gift would be displayed, often strove beyond their means to give something of value. James Wells Champney's oil painting *Wedding Presents* (fig. 63) (ca. 1880) features guests, including one sharp-eyed elderly lady, jostling one another to survey wedding gifts that include one colonial-style caster, and suggests the intensity of interest in the type and likely value of such gifts.

Silver's popularity on these occasions was attested to by etiquette expert Mrs. John Sherwood (Mary Elizabeth Wilson Sherwood), who wrote upon viewing one such display, "The first thing which strikes the eye . . . is the predominance of silver-ware. Not only the coffee and tea sets, but the dinner sets and the whole furniture of the writing table, and even brooms and brushes, are made with repoussé silver handles."[47] Such was the prevalence of silver at weddings that *Harper's Magazine* opined that "there are few families among us so poor as not to have a few ounces of silver plate, and forlorn indeed must be the bride who does not receive upon her wedding-day some articles made out of this beautiful metal."[48] Gorham capitalized upon its long history as a purveyor of fine silver in a *Vogue* advertisement of 1910, which stated: "going back nearly one hundred years, Gorham silverware has been the 'Wedding Silver' of three successive generations. Today, 'Gorham' and 'Wedding Silver' are almost synonymous terms" (fig. 64).

Newspaper announcements of elite weddings in the late nineteenth century are replete with mentions of multiple silver services for the table or tea, along with specialized items such as sets of tea or dessert spoons given by prominent relatives and friends of the family. By contrast, young couples of the mid- to late nineteenth century received an assortment of objects, including silver, in various forms and styles that were dependent upon the sentiments and purses of their guests, as is evident from the arrangement

63
James Wells Champney,
Wedding Presents, ca. 1880.
Oil on canvas. Museum
of the City of New York

of gifts seen in the Champney painting. This latter impromptu method of gift giving predates the twentieth-century fashion for wedding registries at small-town jewelry shops or department stores, where well-wishers could purchase selections from a pattern pre-selected by the bride and groom.

64
"Wedding Silver"
Gorham advertisement,
1910

The growing fashion for accumulating large sets of a single pattern was promoted by manufacturers. Beginning in the 1890s, they encouraged a unified approach to style and pattern by producing handsome advertising brochures devoted to a single flatware design, a tactic that also was intended to improve sales of complete patterns. Gorham's *Versailles* booklet was typical of such brochures—a small, fine-quality publication with illustrations, it was accented by text that drew upon historical and architectural elements of French history as inspiration for flatware that "finds a

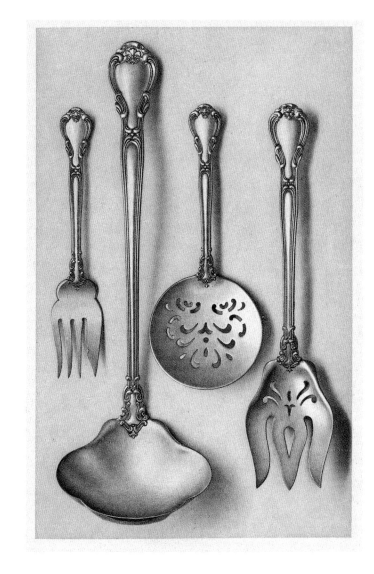

"A Dining Room—Louis XV
Period" and "The Chantilly Pattern—
Cold Meat Fork, Soup, Ladle,
Tomato Server and Salad Fork," from
*Silver for the Dining Room: Selected
Periods* by John S. Holbrook, 1912

welcome and well deserved
place in the American home."[49]

For those seeking a
distinguished pattern for their
home, John S. Holbrook's
*Silver for the Dining Room,
Selected Periods* (1912) offered
an excellent guide. Holbrook, a vice president of Gorham,
described the thicket of confusing styles that bewildered
prospective buyers, distilling them into "their purest and
best forms." Each chapter begins with an elegant engraving
of a historical interior (fig. 65), followed by photographs of
Gorham silverware inspired by that period style. Chapter
headings listed stylistic eras such as the Florentine, Jacobean,
Louis XIV, Louis XV, and Louis XVI, and three distinct
Georgian periods, among others. The silver patterns featured

in each chapter bore an identical or loosely related name,
such as *Chantilly* (fig. 65), to match the Louis XV interior, or *Baronial*, for the Jacobean interior. In a brilliant
stroke of advertising, the grand historical interiors were
sprinkled with objects resembling Gorham silver, allowing the reader to linger within these architectural spaces
and imagine owning silver with such rich associations.
The book concluded with a final section on Gorham's Art
Nouveau–inspired *Martelé*—by then already seventeen
years old—stating that "the time was ripe for a new sort of
silverware."[50] Printed on heavy, deckle-edged paper, with
illustrations in sepia and photographs of the company
silver, the volume was intended to convey confidence and
quality to consumers.

Despite the consumption of silver being at its peak
for a service for twelve at the turn of the twentieth century,

societal changes came with the arrival of World War I. Even before this, the elaborate rituals of the dining room began to suffer from the lack of servants in middle- and upper-class homes. Finding and retaining capable servants, who knew their way around a dining room, became a critical concern.[51] As early as 1897, etiquette authority Mrs. Sherwood noted the difficulty of ordering the household so that two servants could do the work for an entire middle- to upper-class household. As she wrote: "When life was simpler, this was done without murmuring; but now it is difficult to find good and trained servants, particularly in New York, who will fill such places."[52] The so-called "servant problem" regarding the loss of largely Irish or African-American domestic staff increased as many fled the poor pay and societal disdain of domestic service for blue- and white-collar jobs in the early decades of the twentieth century.

Chafing dishes may have become popular at the turn of the twentieth century as a way to create simpler meals with little or no staff. Descended from an ancient lidded, tripodal form, sometimes called a brazier, and heated from below, the chafing dish was revived during the 1890s and its merits celebrated in dozens of books devoted to the subject. The renewed popularity of the chafing dish was attributed to New York City's most luxurious hotel, the Waldorf-Astoria, which used it to serve such post-theater guests as financier J. P. Morgan and actress and singer Lillian Russell.[53]

The performance-related nature of the chafing dish may have been part of its appeal, as many recipes call for making the meal within the dish itself, rather than simply using it for serving and retaining the food's heat, as is still common today. Gorham produced several books to promote the chafing dish, each of which were filled with recipes that typically relied on a sauce with a main dish, whether eggs, fish, meat, game, vegetables, dessert, and even nuts.[54]

H. M. Kinsley, restauranteur at Holland House in New York and at his eponymously named site in Chicago, in his introduction for a Gorham publication, described several reasons for the form's sudden popularity, all of which addressed subtle shifts in society: a trend toward informality at the table; the ongoing desire for elegance; and the changing nature of the household, its management, and the involvement of both men and women in the kitchen. He described the convivial atmosphere encouraged by use of the chafing dish, as follows: "The Chafing Dish not only makes possible the sincerest expression of the most perfect hospitality, but it seems the true symbol of good fellowship. It develops a spirit of royal camaraderie."[55] That spirit may be inferred from one of its more popular dishes, called Welsh rarebit,

which consists of butter, egg, cream cheese, mustard, and beer, warmed and served on toast.

For those who were challenged by the high standards of entertaining, and who wished to eat informally, whether communally or singly, but with style, Kinsley offered his opinion on the chafing dish: "Like all beneficent things it is not for the rich alone. It ministers in more or less elegant form to all sorts and conditions of men. It is of infinite convenience to those who nurse the sick and must prepare food at irregular hours. It is a boon to the journalist who, after his nightly toil, enjoys a repast in his own home. The busy housewife whose burdens are lightened by one maid calls the Chafing Dish 'the woman's friend.'" The book included twenty illustrations of Gorham chafing dishes in sterling, silver plate, and one made of bronze and copper, which appealed to all incomes. Among the many designs was one unique example designed to sway with the movement of a yacht, along with special long-handled chafing spoons.

And as one of the few pieces to address gender at the table, Kinsley noted that it offered "one of the undisputed arts where a man and woman may share equal privileges and triumphs. A man may prove his skill in cooking with it without detracting from his dignity and a woman can scarcely manipulate it without adding to her charm." The chafing dish enjoyed popularity from the 1890s through the 1920s, before it was revived again in the 1940s, when readers were assured that the chafing dish was "not too complicated for a resourceful cook—excellent for either the man or woman at the helm of a chafing-dish—they will add imagination to the most informal of after-theatre parties and do wonders for your reputation as a cook."[56]

The popularity of the chafing dish, and the informal meals it was designed to conjure up, may have served as a bellwether for changing approaches to dining and domestic life around the turn of the twentieth century. Other labor-saving devices began to appear as household servants dwindled in number and more and more women took part in activities outside of the home. The advent of electric-powered vacuum cleaners and washing machines at the beginning of the twentieth century helped with the household, while frozen and canned foods continued to aid meal preparation, but these inventions did little to revive the centrality and sanctity of the dining room.[57] Instead, the pace of daily life (and fewer, if any, servants) left less time to care for silver and other time-consuming preparations for formal dinners. When they did occur, meals were less frequent and reduced in scale.

Silver manufacturers nevertheless strove to keep their product in the public eye using paid advertisements, brochures, and via product placement in articles for a growing number of midmarket and upscale women's and shelter magazines like *House Beautiful, Arts & Decoration,* and *Vogue* that appealed to the consumer's desire for objects of beauty, symbolic meaning, heirloom value, and artistry. Antiquarian and writer Edward Wenham expanded his articles on historical silver in *Art & Decoration* to include contemporary topics, such as "Table Silver, the Traditional Gift." He advised that if "we select carefully, the probability is that the object will be preserved through many generations, and in later years be esteemed to the same extent as the works of Paul Revere,"[58] suggesting the potential for increased value and enhanced status with such purchases.

Brides held fast to their desire for silver flatware and serving pieces even as many realized their inexperience in making such a momentous

66
Modern American Coffee Service, 1928. Erik Magnussen, designer. Silver with ebony and ivory. Philadelphia Museum of Art

selection. Prescriptive literature emphasized "correctness" as a way of assuaging such concerns and, in this manner, continued to be a valuable guide for those who wished to follow in the steps of their mothers and grandmothers. By 1931, however, even etiquette doyenne Emily Post had to admit that times had changed, acknowledging that "twenty-five years ago, the dining room of a well-appointed house looked like a silver shop." She offered suggestions to reduce the amount of silverware needed in the modern household, at one point stating candidly that "a certain few of these implements" could be "made to do double service by being washed in the pantry" during the meal, although her preference was for a complete service. Post's simplified service, consisting of 116 pieces, had more to do with reducing the number of specialized forms that had been at their height thirty years earlier; Post also suggested silver plate as an economical substitute for sterling silver in serving dishes, candlesticks, and other larger forms. Post's advice must

have come as a relief to many young brides who wed during the Great Depression and strove for elegance on a budget.

Table-setting guides published in the 1920s and 1930s acknowledged the dramatic shifts taking place in American society. Most, like Post, took a practical approach and recommended less silver for the dining table, while emphasizing the importance of making correct and therefore socially acceptable choices, which revisits early writing on proper behavior and its unspoken potential for public shame. This subject is evident from the titles of other booklets published by silver manufacturers, including Gorham's *The Art of Table Setting* (1929).[59] All were designed to put prospective consumers at ease regarding the intricacies of table settings and their uses while stressing the importance of choosing the proper pattern, one that was harmonious with the dining room itself.[60] Some featured reassuring text by luminaries from the world of women's magazines, and many if not most were intended as advertising literature, presented to prospective brides and others at department or jewelry stores.

Hoping to find a younger, more sophisticated market for silver, Gorham boldly updated its portfolio of historical designs in 1927 with modern hollowware by Danish artist Erik Magnussen (fig. 145). Using simple cylindrical forms and black synthetic handles, with a hint of Neoclassicism, Magnussen's *Modern American* line was a streamlined design offering a limited number of forms, such as a tea service with tray (figs. 66, 147), a pitcher, salt and pepper shakers, and a cocktail service, the latter of which met the emerging trend for mixed drinks. Similarly, console sets, some mounted with ivory for a touch of luxury, consisting of a compote centerpiece and two candlesticks, were intended to provide a focal point on the dining table or fireplace mantel without dominating a room with quantities of silver. These simple but effective centerpieces were approved by a writer for the *New York Times*, who wrote in 1928, "Console settings of sterling silver has [*sic*] become so popular that the usual three pieces—a pair of candlesticks and a bowl for flowers—have been developed by silverware designers so that almost any type of interior may have its appropriate ware."[61] But as with the standard-bearer for this new initiative, the *Cubic* service (figs. 202–4, 217), also designed by Magnussen, few were ready to bring the avant-garde into their homes.

Advertising could not, however, prevent the inevitable changes in a society with less time for the formalities of entertaining and a growing impatience for the care that silver demanded. Articles in the 1940s and 1950s urged owners to get more "joy" out of their silver through the pleasures of polishing, suggested the purchase of "casual" silver, and offered ideas to "keep your silver busy" by getting it out of storage and on view in the home.[62] The cajoling nature of these articles suggests that their target audience was losing touch with silver.

Yet, by the 1950s, young veterans returning from World War II were bent upon marrying and buying a home, two life-changing events that are frequently accompanied by gifts of silver and dinner parties set with the family's best dinnerware (fig. 255). Silver may have entered households as gifts or purchases, but it was typically relegated to the china cabinet or lined storage cases and used only for special occasions. A growing preference for informality throughout the home made the mass-produced, easy-care products like ceramics, glass, stainless steel, plastic, and aluminum an attractive and inexpensive alternative for daily living (fig. 67).

The zeitgeist of the modern domestic age was best captured by Russel and Mary Wright, whose *Guide to Easier Living* (1950) promoted multifunctional forms for casual dinners, thus reducing the total number of items needed for entertaining.[63] Acknowledging that America's servant population was long gone, they upturned the gender balance by creating a fresh model: the "new-style host" and "hostess," who share responsibilities for purchasing, cooking, preparing drinks, and looking after visitors. Moreover, they made guests a key part of the activities, from food preparation to serving and clearing dishes. Their relaxed attitude extended to the table, where the "new-style guest" "knows that using the right fork is less important than helping with the party,"[64] and implying that hosts couldn't care less about proper handling of flatware. To reduce labor, they suggested cutting the amount of flatware from thirty-eight "conventional settings" to twenty-one "family cafeteria" pieces, or a knife, a spoon, and a fork per setting, and encouraged the use of stove-to-table and refrigerator-to-table utensils, dishes, and cookery.[65]

The *Guide to Easier Living* offered solutions to a post–World War II culture in flux, with a fast-paced lifestyle that valued simplicity and practicality over the quaint mannerisms of yesteryear. Gorham responded to these cultural shifts with simplified designs that were informal in appearance, often biomorphic in shape, and adaptable to varied use. The company introduced *Trend* coffee service and candlesticks (1952), *Directional* creamer and sugar bowl (1955),

Tri-round casual dishes (1963), and *Starburst* candelabra (1967), using terms that evoked a modern tempo. Jewel-toned enamels and colorful glass elements sometimes adorned these new forms, adding to their decorative appeal in the home.[66]

Post–World War II Americans enjoyed their leisure time by indulging in smoking and drinking, and Gorham met this resurgent cocktail culture with new smoking and drinking accessories, including novel designs like their martini spike (1967–70), which dispensed vermouth through a syringe set within a silver mount. Martini pitchers, which doubled as beverage servers (fig. 68) and were accompanied by long spoons for stirring, were offered as part of Gorham's *Modern* line, designed by Donald H. Colflesh. Also by Colflesh, the *Circa '70* line (figs. 201, 218–19) emphasized bold biomorphic lines.

By 1970 silver had begun to yield its cherished place in the home, but its influence continues to the present as a reliable indicator of taste, refinement, and character, owing to the values placed on its forms and to the behavior associated with its use. Today's aspiring young men and women look to online websites for guidance on properly setting a table and the correct way to hold a fork, just as their predecessors in the nineteenth century consulted etiquette guides.[67] As with the rules copied painstakingly in the 1700s by George Washington, their motives for self-improvement are the same—upward mobility, the respect of peers, and the fellowship of a civilized and well-mannered society.

68
Modern Beverage Server
and Stirrer, 1959.
Donald H. Colflesh, designer.
Silver and plastic.
RISD Museum

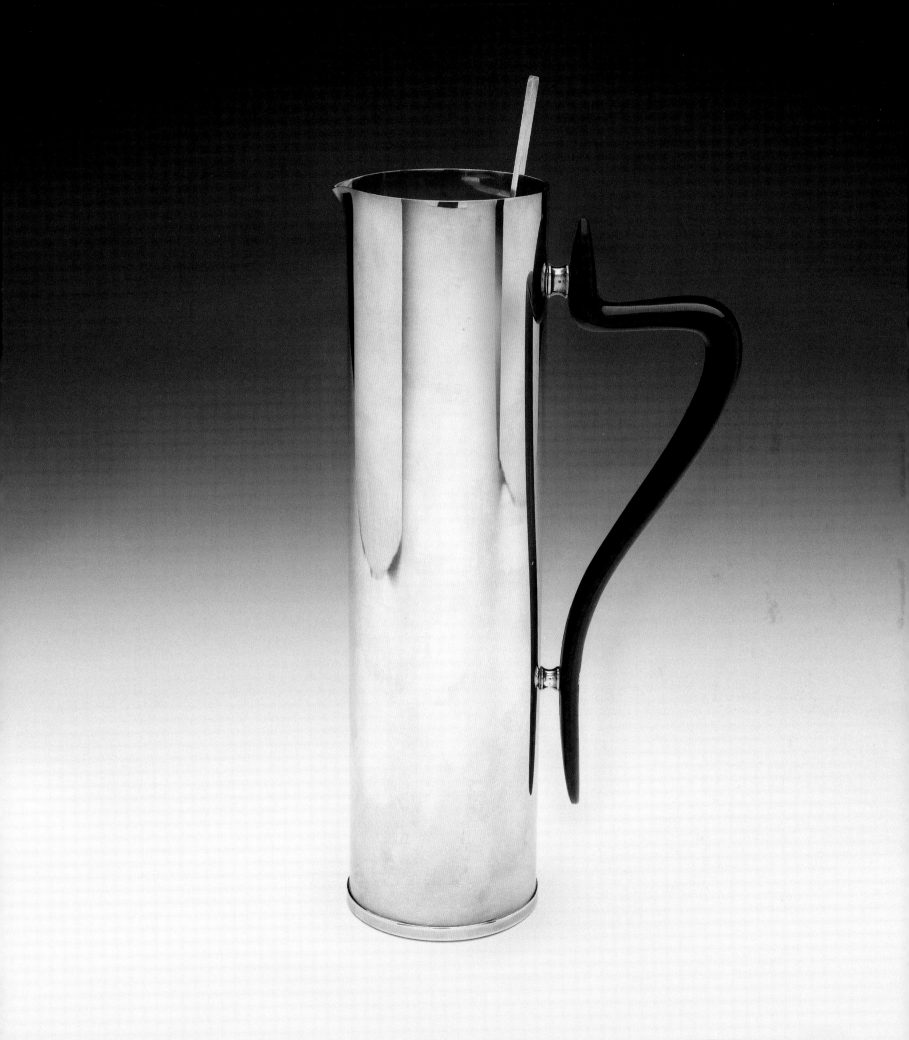

1   James Parton, "Silver and Silver Plate," *Harper's New Monthly Magazine* 37, no. 220 (September 1868): 434.

2   Norbert Elias, "The Development of the Concept of Civilité," in *The History of Manners*, vol. 1 in the series *The Civilizing Process*, trans. Edmund Jephcott (New York: Pantheon Books, 1982). See also Arthur M. Schlesinger, *Learning How to Behave: A Historical Study of American Etiquette Books* (New York: Cooper Square Publishers, 1968).

3   See Erika Rummel, ed., *The Erasmus Reader* (Toronto: University of Toronto Press, 1990), 101, for the influence of the Erasmus text on Western society.

4   Washington's handwritten rules are in the Library of Congress. For an analysis of Washington's text and its source, see *George Washington's Rules of Civility and Decent Behaviour in Company and Conversation*, ed. Charles Moore (Boston and New York: Houghton Mifflin Company, 1926), xi–xv.

5   "Eliza Ware Rotch Farrar," in *Notable American Women, 1607–1950, A Biographical Dictionary*, 3 vols., ed. Edward T. James (Cambridge, MA: Belknap Press of Harvard University Press, 1971), 2:601–2.

6   John F. Kasson, "Rituals of Dining: Table Manners in Victorian America," in *Dining in America: 1850–1900*, ed. Kathryn Grover (Amherst, MA, and Rochester, NY: University of Massachusetts Press / Margaret Woodbury Strong Museum, 1987), 119.

7   Thomas Coryate, *Crudities Hastily Gobbled Up in Five Months*, 1608, cited in Henry Petroski, *The Evolution of Useful Things* (New York: Alfred A. Knopf, 1992), 8–9.

8   "American Manners in 1833," translated from a German work by a Correspondent of the Atheneum, *Dublin Penny Journal* 3, no. 126 (Nov. 29, 1834), 170–71. Up to this date, the knife, with the blade facing the mouth, was commonly used at the table.

9   Martha Louise Rayne, *Gems of Deportment and Hints of Etiquette: The Ceremonials of Good Society, Including Valuable Moral, Mental and Physical Knowledge* (Detroit: Tyler & Co., 1881), 213.

10 Bathtubs and showers in the United States were not generally found in households until the late nineteenth century, and soap was not commonly used for washing the skin until about the 1860s. Richard L. Bushman and Claudia I. Bushman, "The Early History of Cleanliness in America," *Journal of American History* 74, no. 4 (March 1988): 1213–38.

11 Clifford E. Clark Jr., "The Vision of the Dining Room, Plan Book Dreams and Middle-Class Realities," in *Dining in America 1850–1900*, ed. Kathryn Grover (Amherst, MA, and Rochester, NY: University of Massachusetts Press / The Margaret Woodbury Strong Museum, 1987), 146–50.

12 These figures based upon Gorham's 1874 photo book, Gorham Manufacturing Company Archive, John Hay Library, Brown University, Providence, Rhode Island (hereafter GMCA).

13 Gorham Manufacturing Company, *Catalogue*, Autumn 1880.

14 Beverly Gordon, "Woman's Domestic Body, The Conceptual Conflation of Women and Interiors in the Industrial Age," *Winterthur Portfolio* 31, no. 4 (Winter 1996): 281–301.

15 Catharine E. Beecher and Harriet Beecher Stowe, *The American Woman's Home: or Principles of Domestic Science, being a Guide to the formation and Maintenance of Economical Healthful, Beautiful, and Christian Homes* (New York: J. B. Ford and Company, 1869), n.p.

16 "Oysters," *The Oxford Encyclopedia of Food and Drink in America*, 1: 487. Celery farms were concentrated in "Celery City," as Kalamazoo, Michigan, was known, beginning in the 1850s. http://www.kpl.gov/local-history/business/celery.aspx, accessed March 31, 2018. The move from celery stands to low plates had begun about 1900, according to chef and cookbook author Jessup Whitehead in *The Steward's Handbook and Guide to Party Catering* (Chicago: Jessup Whitehead, Publishers, 1903), 269. "The fashions change as to the method of serving; the tall celery glasses set upon the table form the handiest and handsomest medium, but having become so exceedingly common they are discarded at present at fashionable tables, and the celery is laid upon very long and narrow dishes."

17 Commercial canning came into use in the United States as early as 1821, and home canning was made safer with durable vacuum seals introduced with Mason jars in 1858. Andrew F. Smith, ed., *The Oxford Encyclopedia of Food and Drink in America*, 2 vols. (New York: Oxford University Press, 2004), 1:184–85. The United States Army was consuming canned sardines by 1857. "The latest news, received by magnetic telegraph from Washington," *New-York Daily Tribune*, July 28, 1857, 5.

18 Iceboxes were the norm until refrigerators for home use were invented in 1913. Oscar Edward Anderson, "The Growing Need for Mechanical Refrigeration, 1860–1890," in *Refrigeration in America* (Princeton: Princeton University Press, 1953), 37–70. "Forty-five per cent of the ice sold in New York in 1879–1880 went to private families. In Boston and Chicago they bought thirty-three per cent. About half that sold in Baltimore and Philadelphia was purchased for the home, and in New Orleans, where ice consumption was low, sixty-nine per cent went to domestic buyers," according to Anderson, 53. By 1907, 81 percent of New York City families possessed ad hoc containers for storing food with ice as well as purpose-built iceboxes, as cited in *Robert Coit Chapin, The Standard of Living among Workingmen's Families in New York City* (New York: Charities Publication Committee, 1909), 136.

19 For discussions of specialized forms, see Susan Williams, *Savory Suppers & Fashionable Feasts, Dining in Victorian America* (New York: Pantheon Books / Strong Museum, 1985), 108–14, and Charles L. Venable, *Silver in America, 1840–1940, A Century of Splendor* (Dallas and New York: Dallas Museum of Art / Harry N. Abrams, 1994), 128–41.

20 Miss [Eliza] Leslie, *Directions for Cookery in Its Various Branches* (Philadelphia: Carey & Hart, 1849), 203.

21 *The Gorham Salad Book, With Rules for Dressings and Sauce* (Providence: The Gorham Company, 1905).

22 Williams, *Savory Suppers*, 108.

23 Elizabeth F. Ellet, *The New Cyclopedia of Domestic Economy, and Practical Housekeeper* (Norwich, CT: Henry Bill Pub. Co., 1873), 125–29, cited in Williams, *Savory Suppers*, 108.

24 Concern for proper behavior of the mouth is mentioned in eight of the rules of civility copied by Washington, including number 97. "Put not another bit into your mouth till the former is swallowed. Let not your morsels be too big for the jowls."

25 Sugar cubes were not available in the United States until sometime after 1875. Regan Hofmann, "How the Victorian Obsession for Order Created the Humble Sugar Cube," *Saveur*, February 22, 2017, https://www.saveur.com/history-sugar-cube, accessed February 5, 2018.

26 A. St. Johnston, "American Silver-Ware," *Magazine of Art* [London] 9 (1886): 13–18.

27 "Hyper-Gentility," *Scribner's Monthly* 5, no. 5 (March 1873): 643.

28 "Fun at the White House . . . and Mrs. Manderson's Missing Silver," *Omaha World*, May 24, 1891.

29 For other descriptions of dining à la française, see Damon Lee Fowler, ed., *Dining at Monticello* (Chapel Hill: University of North Carolina Press, 2005), 14, and Stephen Schmidt, "When Service à la Française Met Service à la Russe," http://www.manuscript-cookbookssurvey.org/when-service-a-la-francaise-met-service-a-la-russe/, accessed September 13, 2018.

30 Eliza Ware Rotch Farrar, *The Young Lady's Friend, by a Lady* (Boston: American Stationers' Company, 1837), 349.

31 Leila Southard Frost, "A Course Dinner, Table Appointments and Service," *Demorest's Family Magazine* 28, no. 2 (December 1891): 110–14.

32 Smith, ed., *Oxford Encyclopedia of Food and Drink in America*, 1:397–400.

33 For an assessment based upon archeological findings in Harper's Ferry, Virginia, see Michael T. Lucas, "À la Russe, à la Pell-Mell, or à la Practical: Ideology and Compromise at the Late Nineteenth-Century Dinner Table," *Historical Archaeology* 28, no. 4, An Archaeology of Harpers Ferry's Commercial and Residential District (1994), 80–93.

34 Dolores Mitchell, "The 'New Woman' as Prometheus: Women Artists Depict Women Smoking," *Woman's Art Journal* 12, no. 1 (Spring–Summer 1991): 3–9.

35 "Around the Tea Table," *Ladies' Home Journal* 2, no. 1 (December 1884): 2; cited in Venable, *Silver in America, 1840–1940*, 130.

36 *The Cosmopolitan Cook and Recipe Book* (Buffalo: Dingens Brothers, 1888), 12; cited in Grover, *Dining in America 1850–1900*, 10–11.

37 Rayne, *Gems of Deportment*, 257.

38 Joseph B. and Laura. E. Lyman, *The Philosophy of House-keeping* (Hartford, CT.: Goodwin & Betts, 1867), 322; cited in Williams, *Savory Suppers*, 128.

39 Jennifer Goldsborough, "The Proliferation of Cutlery and Flatware Design in Nineteenth Century America," in Sarah D. Coffin, et al., *Feeding Desire, Design and the Tools of the Table, 1500–2005* (New York: Assouline / Cooper Hewitt National Design Museum, 2006), 186–89.

40 Parton, "Silver and Silver Plate," *Harper's New Monthly Magazine*, 445.

41 For a useful history on the history of silver plate and a selection of range of makers and forms, see Dorothy T. and H. Ivan Rainwater, *American Silverplate* (West Chester, PA: Schiffer Publishing, 1988). Charles Venable, "The Silverplated Ice Water Pitcher: An Image of a Changing America, 1850–1900," *Material Culture* 9, no. 1 (Spring 1987): 39–48.

42 Barbara Penner, "'A Vision of Love and Luxury': The Commercialization of Nineteenth-Century American Weddings," *Winterthur Portfolio* 39, no. 1 (Spring 2004): 1–20.

43 Ralph Waldo Emerson, "Gifts," in *The Collected Works of Ralph Waldo Emerson*, vol. 3 (Cambridge, MA: Belknap Press of Harvard University Press, 1971), 94, cited in Penner, "A Vision of Love and Luxury."

44 Two-page Gorham advertisement for travel cases, handbags, travel suitcases in *Vogue*, September 24, 1903.

45 Gorham text advertisement, *Vogue*, October 9, 1909.

46 Gorham Christmas advertisement, *Vogue*, December 1, 1918.

47 Mrs. John Sherwood [Mary Elizabeth Wilson Sherwood], *Manners and Social Usages* (1884; repr., New York: Harper and Brothers, 1897), 117.

48 Parton, "Silver and Silver Plate," *Harper's New Monthly Magazine*, 434.

49 *Versailles* (Gorham Manufacturing Co., ca. 1890–1910), GMCA.

50 John S. Holbrook, *Silver for the Dining Room, Selected Periods* (Cambridge, MA: University Press, 1912), xiii. This trend continued through the 1930s, according to one article that cautioned brides to "take all things into consideration in choosing the table ware that will grace the dining room and make or mar meals. . . . Get for yourself . . . china and glass and silver that go with Early American maple, or . . . Eighteenth Century reproductions, with their sense of dignity and charm." Edna Deu Pree, "Period Silver and China for Brides," *American Home* 20 (June 1938): 37.

51 For an analysis of the servant problem in the United States, see Faye E. Dudden, "Experts and Servants: The National Council on Household Employment and the Decline of Domestic Service in the Twentieth Century," *Journal of Social History* 20, no. 2 (Winter 1986), 269–89. Dudden notes that "in 1870 over one half of all women workers were domestic servants and in 1900 servants still numbered about one-third of all employed women, by 1950 the ranks of domestic servants had shrunk to insignificance."

52 Sherwood, *Manners and Social Usages*, 357. Two servants, as noted by Mrs. Sherwood, were probably for middle- or upper middle-class homes. The number of servants in a household depended upon the size of the home and the presence of a servants' wing. The fashionable residences on Euclid Avenue in Cleveland, home to John D. Rockefeller, among others, and also known as Millionaires' Row, were staffed by eight to twelve servants. Dan Ruminski and Alan Dutka, *Cleveland in the Gilded Age: A Stroll Down Millionaires' Row* (Mount Pleasant, SC: Arcadia Publishing, 2012).

53 Sylvia Lovegren, *Fashionable Food: Seven Decades of Food Fads* (New York: Macmillan, 1995), 206.

54 Thomas J. Murrey and Gorham Manufacturing Company, *Good Things from a Chafing Dish* (Providence: Livermore & Knight), 1890; H. M. Kinsley and Gorham Manufacturing Company, *One Hundred Recipes for the Chafing Dish* (New York: Gorham Manufacturing Co., 1894); *The Chafing Dish Book* (Providence: Livermore & Knight, 1899), reprinted 1905; *The Tiny Book of the Chafing Dish* (Providence: Livermore & Knight, 1905).

55 Kinsley, *The Chafing Dish Book*, 21–22. Additional quotations from the book are taken from these pages.

56 "Chafing-dish comeback," *Vogue* 95, no. 5 (March 1, 1940): 76–77; 120–21.

57 Smith, "Frozen Food," 523.

58 Edward Wenham, "Table Silver, the Traditional Gift," *Art & Decoration* 32 (December 1929): 74–75.

59 Claudia Quigley Murphy, *The Art of Table Setting* (New York: Claudia Quigley Murphy, 1921). The book appears to be self-published, but a Gorham decorative border on the title page, bearing the company's marks, signals their involvement.

60 For an exhaustive review of such booklets, which also included the care of silver, see Dorothea Burstyn, "Evolution of Dining Habits, Modes of Entertaining and Marketing Methods as Revealed by American Silver Makers' 'Etiquette' Books," *Silver Studies, The Journal of the Silver Society* 25 (2009): 19–28.

61 Walter Render Story, *New York Times,* March 1928, as cited in Patricia Kane, "Master of Modern Silver: Erik Magnussen Masterpieces revealed," *Antiques & Fine Arts*, Summer 1914. https://www.incollect.com/articles/master-of-modern-silver-erik-magnussen, accessed April 11, 2018.

62 Mathia Doris and Dorothy Horrigan, "More Joy from Your Silver," *Better Homes and Gardens* 18 (May 1940): 49; "It's a Trend! Silver for Casual Use," *Better Homes and Gardens* 31 (October 1953): 120–22, 139; F. Huttenlocher, "Keep Your Silver Busy," *Better Homes and Gardens* 31 (September 1953): 126. "Hideaway's a Poor Place for Silver," *Chicago Daily Tribune,* July 2, 1961; ProQuest Historical Newspapers: *Chicago Tribune* pg. S A4.

63 Mary Wright and Russel Wright, *Mary and Russel Wright's Guide to Easier Living* (New York: Simon and Schuster, 1950; repr., Salt Lake City: Gibbs Smith, Publisher, 2003).

64 Ibid., 35.

65 Ibid.

66 For the definitive discussion of the new forms and colors of midcentury American silver, see Jewel Stern, *Modernism in American Silver: 20th-Century Design* (New Haven: Yale University Press, and Dallas: Dallas Museum of Art, 2005).

67 Aspirational behavior, particularly among those moving from the lower to upper class and especially in the case of nonwhites in white society as "class-passing." Arwa Mahdawi, "'Class-Passing': How Do You Learn the Rules of Being Rich?" *Guardian*, February 1, 2018, https://www.theguardian.com/us-news/2018/feb/01/poor-americans-poverty-rich-class, accessed May 16, 2018.

Elizabeth A. Williams

THE GORHAM FURBER SERVICE

> The beauty of the ordinary American table, with its snowy damask and china, sparkling cut-glass and lustrous utensils of silver . . . is a power, and one that goes too near the springs of moral as well as aesthetic culture to be lightly esteemed by the most serious observer.

William C. Conant for *Scribner's Monthly*, 1874[1]

Inspired by Greek, Roman, Italian, Egyptian, English, French, American, Russian, and Japanese design, the silver service on the table of Henry Jewett and Elvira Irwin Furber reflected nineteenth-century America's interest in and absorption of international cultures. Fashioned to serve twenty-four guests and stored in twenty custom-fit oak cases, the 816 pieces constituting one of the largest American silver services of its time were made by the Gorham Manufacturing Company between 1866 and 1880, a pivotal moment in the stylistic development of American silver and in the exacting refinement of upper-class dining practices. The rising importance of elaborate dining customs and extravagant accompanying dining services was observed by famed French chef and author Urbain Dubois, who wrote, "[T]he Americans, those robust gourmets who, newly arrived in the arena, have nevertheless made remarkable progress, in cooking as well as

69
Pair of Fruit Stands, 1871.
Silver with gilding.
RISD Museum

70
Elvira Irwin Furber,
ca. 1869. Neville Public
Museum of Brown County

71
Henry Jewett Furber,
1869. Neville Public
Museum of Brown County

gastronomy. But the luxuries of the table in that country of voracious appetites have assumed such extraordinary proportions as to make one involuntarily think of the famous excess of the feast of Ancient Rome."[2]

Henry Furber (fig. 71) grew up in the small village of Rochester, New Hampshire, a member of a New England family of modest means whose earliest immigrant to the British colonies arrived in 1635. Furber began life with little indication that he would become a successful entrepreneur.[3] During his junior year at Bowdoin College in Maine in 1860, Furber decided to take a job as the superintendent of the public school system in Green Bay, Wisconsin, to earn extra money for tuition.[4] Family tradition claims that Furber arrived in Green Bay with fifty cents in his pocket and no

living arrangements, prompting his decision to knock on the door of postmaster and lawyer Alexander J. Irwin in search of a place to stay. Irwin welcomed Furber into his own home, which he shared with his wife and five daughters. In 1862, Furber passed the Wisconsin state bar exams, joined one of the city's leading attorneys to form a partnership, and married Irwin's daughter Elvira (fig. 70), whose monogram, EIF (fig. 87), would soon grace each piece of the Furber service.

Furber developed an interest in the insurance business, the catalyst by which the young lawyer would make his fortune. He joined the Metropolitan Fire Insurance Company of Green Bay in 1865 as a special agent, quickly moving up the ladder to serve as general manager at the company's headquarters in Chicago and then as vice president in New York. He next took the position of vice president of the Universal Life Insurance Company in 1867 and North American Life Insurance in 1874.[5] By the end of that year, the Furbers had purchased more than $15,000 (or about $330,000 in today's currency) of silver from Gorham.[6]

The Furbers traveled extensively in Europe, and Henry was known to be especially partial to design inspired by the Italian Renaissance, as evidenced by the purchase of a seventeen-pound, thirty-two-inch silver and gilt kidney-shaped tray with a mirrored center (fig. 14). Furber bought the tray, made by Gorham in 1874, at the 1876 Philadelphia Centennial International Exhibition. In J. S. Ingram's *The Centennial Exhibition Described and Illustrated*, it is described as a "massive silver salver with elegant fretwork . . . one of the finest specimens of *repoussé* chasing ever executed in this country and valued at $3,000, at which price it was purchased by a New York gentleman."[7] Known as the *Cellini Salver*, named after the renowned sixteenth-century Mannerist sculptor and goldsmith Benvenuto Cellini of Florence, the work is rimmed by bound fasces, an ancient Roman symbol of magisterial power and strength in unity, and decorated with classical putti representing the arts. The salver is the epitome of the Renaissance Revival style advanced at Gorham by Thomas J. Pairpoint, who had joined Gorham in 1868 and who designed the salver as well as several other significant works in the service.

An intricately wrought pair of fruit stands (figs. 69, 168) made in 1871 also joined the Furber service. They measure a foot and a half in length and are decorated with the Roman goddess of the harvest, Ceres, as well as foxes and grapes (fig. 41) that reference Aesop's fables. The Furber stands resemble ancient Russian drinking vessels known as *kovsh*, typically fashioned in the form of a floating duck and produced in pairs, one silver and one gold. During feasts and weddings, dark mead was drunk from the golden vessel and light mead from the silver vessel. Gorham's costing ledgers indicate that these fruit stands were the only two produced, each requiring three hundred hours of labor.[8]

One reason for the Furbers' orders for elaborate and decorative wares for the table was a change in dining customs in the United States. Prior to and shortly after the Civil War, refined meals were served à la française (fig. 53), by which serving dishes full of food were placed directly on the table all at once by servants, and diners would serve themselves from the dishes. Dining à la russe (figs. 54–56) was introduced to France in 1811 by the Russian ambassador to Napoleon, Prince Aleksandr Borisovich Kurakin. This style, popular in Europe by the 1860s and adopted in the United States in the 1870s, called for the creation of new types of vessels to fill the Victorian dining room with splendor. In this scenario, diners would seat themselves at a table where flowers and fruits, often displayed in ornate centerpieces or epergnes, had replaced the food, which servants presented in a series of courses, each of which was brought out separately when the previous course was finished. Often the decorations found on the numerous serving vessels related to the type of food for which they were intended. An 1874 *Scribner's Monthly* article discusses the "symbolical works of art that hint the special purpose of every vessel and utensil they adorn."[9]

Exemplifying in majestic form the showy centerpieces that arrived with à la russe dining, the 1872 epergne (figs. 73–74) is the grandest and most complex piece of the Furber service. Dressed in a silver gown embedded with gilded stars, Columbia stands on a globe and holds a gilded garland aloft with the assistance of two putti.[10] Adorned with golden hummingbirds, the shell-shaped bowls were for flowers. The oblong bowls, mounted with sterling repoussé plaques featuring allegorical representations of Love and Contentment, were to be filled with fruit. In addition to its classical motifs, the form of this epergne derives from an eighteenth-century British model, providing evidence that American silversmithing is founded upon British traditions.

By 1876, the Furbers had purchased more than fifty significant pieces of sterling silver hollowware, including a twelve-piece tea and coffee service (figs. 45, 85), pickle dish (fig. 78), wine decanter (figs. 128, 129), celery vase (fig. 48), compotes (fig. 78), table bell, butter dish (fig. 78), cake plate, bread plate (fig. 87), pitchers, plateaus, cruet sets (fig. 79), tureens (fig. 78), fruit stands, sauceboats (figs. 78, 173), salts (fig. 122), platters, trays, a basket (fig. 46), wine coolers, vases, goblets, and an ice bowl with tongs (figs. 34–35). The service would ultimately comprise 129 pieces of hollowware.

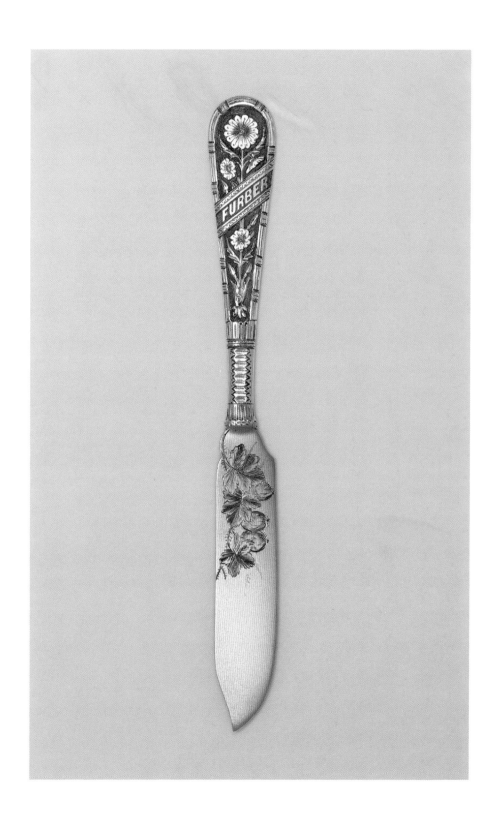

72
Fruit Knife, 1879. Silver with gilding.
RISD Museum

73
Epergne, 1872. Silver with gilding.
Plateau, 1876. Silver with gilding
and mirror. Both Thomas Pairpoint,
designer. RISD Museum

74
Epergne (detail), 1872.
RISD Museum

Williams

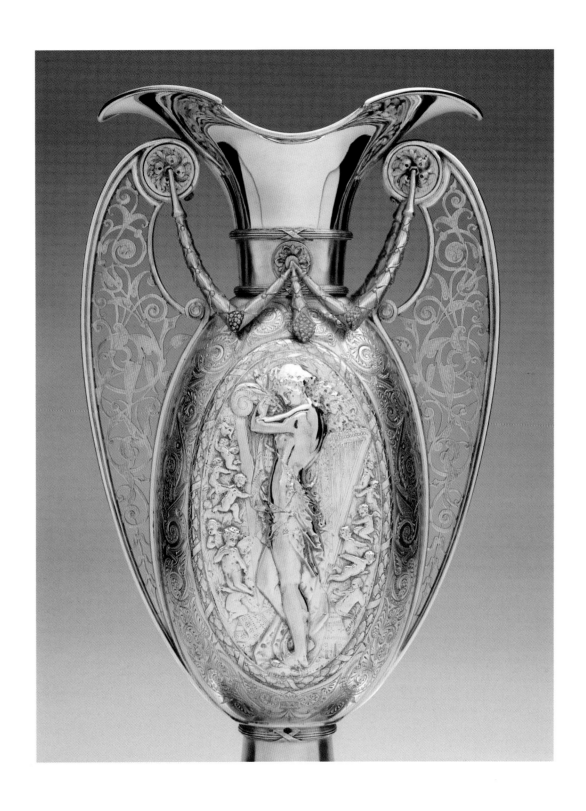

75
Cellini Vase, 1875. Thomas Pairpoint, designer.
Silver with gilding. RISD Museum

Gorham selected at least four significant pieces from the Furber service to be displayed in its pavilion at the 1876 Centennial International Exhibition in Philadelphia (fig. 223). The epergne, commanding a prominent position in the window flanking the entrance (fig. 220), is joined by the *Cellini Vase* (figs. 75, 116), an elaborate oval vessel adorned with gilded flanged sides, designed by Pairpoint. The epergne is illustrated in *Gems of the Centennial Exhibition* on what is described as a "looking-glass plateau."[11] Although the Furber service does not include the same plateaus pictured, it does feature three massive mirrored examples (figs. 73, 81) decorated with a reduced replica of the Parthenon frieze depicting horsemen participating in a Panathenaic procession. Along with the *Cellini Salver*, a Furber service pitcher with repoussé plaques of Venus was also exhibited in Philadelphia (figs. 89, 90).

"The Silver Age," an article published in the December 1874 issue of *Scribner's Monthly*, relates a seemingly fictitious account of an excessively sumptuous dinner given by a wealthy New York couple, who bear an extraordinary similarity with the Furbers and their service. Although the Furbers are not mentioned in particular, the silver wares depicted are credited to Gorham, and two pieces from the Furber service, the *Cellini Salver* and the pitcher with Venus, are illustrated in the essay.[12] The number to be served on a generously proportioned table, which is "twelve yards long and two yards wide" and "filled closely enough for good effect with 'jewelry in silver' from Gorham's," happens to be twenty-four, and the table's center is commanded by "a magnificent silver *epergne* . . . heaped and overhung with a great cone of the richest flowers . . . which rests on four massive feet, as if floated on a silver sea, or more literally a burnished 'plateau' . . . that mirrors back the beauty." The essay contains a particularly detailed description of what could certainly be the fantastical pair of Furber fruit stands with ladle-shaped bowls that seemingly glide on lithe tendrils of vines with small clusters of grapes. At the fictitious table, guests partake of fruits and nuts presented from "a sort of fairy barge . . . where grapes are piled within and dangle over the sides, . . . where a baffled fox clings falling from his leap at the high clusters."

Continuing the visualization of the opulent scene, the essay describes the "millionaires, ambassadors, generals, admirals, authors, and the President of the United States" being "marshalled to their places . . . to admire the display . . . the indescribable beauty of the new style of tureens" (fig. 78). As if the author were partaking in a dinner serviced by these Gorham wares, he gives special attention to the form: "But what soup or nectar of Jove, is worthy to rest in that elysium of art which we profane with the name of tureen! The white glory of its interplay sheen and shade, lit up again with dewy sparkle of cut foliage festooned to either side, then surprised by a delicate molding of gold, and reflected back on itself from the mirror-like plateau or tray beneath . . . if thou couldst have seen this silver picture wreathed in golden haze."

Drawing attention to the popularity of ice bowls, the essay describes "bowls of crushed ice rimmed with pendent icicles of frost-silver, and their bases piled with rugged arctic scenery, in blocks and bergs and polar bears—all these are so at home in the expressive metal that they seem to cool with air." An ice bowl of this exact description, accompanied by a pair of ice tongs in the form of harpoons with ropes twisted around the handles, was purchased by the Furbers (figs. 34, 35).

Sitting down to the Furbers' table, one would have been confronted with a bevy of Gorham flatware—687 pieces in all. The majority of serving and dining utensils are the *Angelo* pattern, which debuted in about 1870. In addition to the *Angelo* pattern (figs. 80, 266), also known as No. 10, the Furber service comprises nine other distinctive patterns, including *Eglantine* berry spoons, similarly decorated ice cream spoons, No. 290 egg spoons with unicorn finials, No. 5 Japanesque fruit knives and forks (figs. 84, 228), *Japanese* pattern forks (fig. 101), No. 45 oyster forks (fig. 47), and silver-handled salad forks overlaid with an elegant gilded lattice. A special pattern was used for the twenty-four individual asparagus tongs, sardine tongs (fig. 103), and sugar tongs, decorated with an *F* entwined in foliage on one side and a unicorn on the other. Another pattern was customized for twenty-four fruit knives with a diagonal border reading FURBER (fig. 72). Elaborate engraving on the tines, bowls, and blades further customizes the flatware.

The apparent gap in Furber service invoices between 1877 and 1878 may be attributed to a number of factors, but a vigorous renewal of orders in 1879 signaled a seismic stylistic shift in the aesthetics of both the service and the Gorham Manufacturing Company. Japan's display at the 1876 Philadelphia Centennial International Exhibition had swept in a trend, igniting the American Aesthetic movement and transforming preferences in silver design. The Furbers embraced this new style, as evidenced in Gorham's 1878 Japanesque water set (fig. 102). Consisting of a pair of cups and pitcher with an oval tray, the set combined the simplicity, exoticism, and naturalism of Japanese design, which was considered particularly avant-garde and innovative in nineteenth-century America. Reflecting the intended contents, the Japanesque hand-engraved decorations cleverly depict a watery lower half swimming with fish and turtles, while the sky above is populated with butterflies and dragonflies in the manner of Katsushika Hokusai's *Manga* imagery. Although the ornamentation on the water set is radically different from the pieces in the service made before this time, it can be imagined that the sustained use of sterling silver with gold in a combination of smooth and matte textures with engraved ornament ensured a harmonious appearance on the table and celebrated the nineteenth-century ardor for mixing together various styles, creating an eclectic yet concordant whole.

Noting the growing interest in Japanese design, the 1874 *Scribner's Monthly* article uncannily describes twenty-four salts (fig. 122) and pepper shakers (fig. 174) of the Furber service yet to be ordered, marveling at "the iridescent oxides and golds on the dainty little butterflies just flitting over the edges of the silver salt-cellars, and the fanciful form of the chased pepper-bottles . . . within reach of every hand." The individual salts with gold-washed bowls and pepper shakers—twelve with gilt tops and twelve with silver tops—are all engraved with the unique motifs. In the same vein, measuring a mere three inches square, the Furber-service butter dishes are a microcosm of Japanese surface textures, mixed metals, and ornament. Each of the twenty-four dishes depicts a different design of engraved Hokusai-style birds, butterflies, flowers, bamboo shoots, and textile patterns, rendered in matte silver and gold against textural backgrounds.

There are 260 pieces of Gorham Japanesque silver in the service, including twenty-four each of ice cream plates (fig. 83), fruit plates, salt and pepper shakers, butter dishes (figs. 123, 175), berry spoons, ice cream spoons, fruit knives, fruit forks, fish forks, butter knives, and a pair of tazzas. These wares were often sold in sets packaged in custom-made wood cases, such as the dessert set shown in the company's photo album of the 1870s, featuring plates and knives similar to those in the Furber service (fig. 76).

The pair of tazzas and twenty-four fruit and twenty-four ice cream plates are all rendered in silver with a matte gilt ground, and each is finely engraved with a differing realistic design of fruits, flowers, and foliage that incorporates shading achieved with various tones of gold on the silver. The mixed metals are examples in Gorham's repertoire of adapting the Japanese sensibility of freely employing metal alloys and patinas to be used as various colors in the creation of a broad palette of the medium. The twenty-four ice cream spoons with pointed matte gold bowls (fig. 52) are cast on each side with a profusion of gilded and variously patinated leaves, fruits, and flowers reminiscent of the tightly placed,

allover designs found on Japanese metalwork. Similarly, the twenty-four berry spoons in the *Eglantine* pattern feature mixed-metal naturalistic ornament; the bowls are described in the inventory as being "in the shape of an Oriental fan."

The Japanesque design of the Furber fruit knives and forks (fig. 84) derives from handles of *kogatana* (small knives carried in the sword scabbard) known as *kozuka*, an important part of Japanese sword fittings.[13] Possessing cast, sometimes of bronze (fig. 228), handles with silver and gilded decorations of mythological figures, birds, marine life, horses, military furnishings, masks, deer, bulls, and flora, the forks and knives feature tines and blades decorated with engraved Aesthetic floral and textiles patterns. Introduced by an unknown designer, the pattern, referred to as No. 5 by 1881, was limited to dessert knives and forks, later expanding to fish forks.

The completion of the Furber service culminated in 1880 with the purchase of ten sterling silver oval meat and fish platters with Renaissance Revival borders. An 1880s newspaper clipping chronicles a lavish dinner given by the Furbers featuring more than a dozen courses, with a menu of "clams, and consommé, five wines and liqueurs, scalloped lobster, filet mignon, mushrooms, roasted chicken, veal sherbets, strawberry omelet, cheese, fruit, petits fours and the usual variety of vegetables and salads."[14] The article noted that the "sideboard epergnes were

76
Case for Dessert Set.
Gorham *Photo Catalogue*, 1873–79.
Gorham Manufacturing Company
Archive, John Hay Library

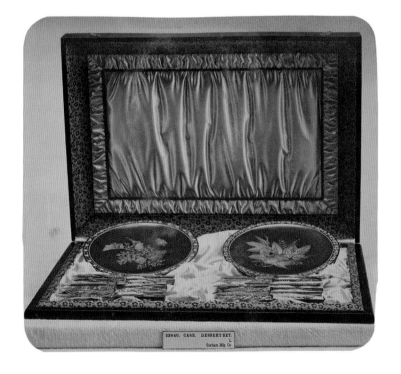

filled . . . and carnations and roses overflowed from silver vases," and claimed "no kindred occasion in America has ever inspired its equal."[15]

Elvira died in Florence in 1912 and Henry died in Chicago in 1916. His estate, valued at more than $6 million (or $138 million today), was given to his oldest son, William Elbert Furber, and his youngest son, Frank Irwin Furber; his middle son, Henry Jewett Furber Jr. (1865–1956), was bequeathed nothing.[16] It is theorized that Henry Jr. was seen by his father as "too strong a man in his own right— too keen competition for his father—to be willed anything of his father's millions," but Elvira, who owned the Furber service at the time of her death, thought otherwise and willed it to Henry Jr.

Said to be a less extravagant and flamboyant man than his father, Henry Jr. achieved a number of distinctions in his life, including a PhD in economics from the University of Halle-Wittenberg in Germany, admission to the Illinois bar, election to president of the International Olympic Games Association of 1904, and the award of the French Legion of Honor for an invention of his that was capable of locating submarines and aircraft via sound-wave technology.[17] With his primary residence at the Chicago Athletic Association, Henry Jr. had chosen a simpler life than his parents and decided to sell the Furber service back to Gorham through the Swann Auction Galleries of New York in the 1940s.[18] H. T. Brenner, Gorham merchandise manager, wrote to Benjamin Swann on August 23, 1949, relating that after seeing pieces from the Furber service the previous week in New York, "We believe that we should like to have pieces from the collection as examples of early Gorham work for our present-day craftsmen and we would be interested in seeing the entire collection with this in mind."[19] Contemplating whether Gorham wished to purchase part of or the entire collection, Brenner wrote directly to Henry Jr. on September 14, 1949, indicating, "It may be that we could handle the entire collection for you or it may be more advantageous mutually for us to select some of the more important things."[20]

It took only a few months for the decision to be made: on November 8, 1949, a van picked up the Furber service crates in New York and returned them to Providence, where the service became part of the company's corporate collection and was used for numerous promotional purposes until it was given to the RISD Museum.[21] On November 18, 1949, Brenner sent a letter to Furber enclosing a $25,000 check for the purchase of the complete Furber service, saying that the arrival of "your grand silver service" at the Gorham Manufacturing Company "has created a lot of enthusiasm among my associates and everyone is tremendously pleased that we have had the good fortune to bring these pieces back to Providence."[22]

1   William C. Conant, "The Silver Age," *Scribner's Monthly* 9, no. 2 (December 1874): 198.

2   Urbain Dubois, *Cuisine artistique*, 1886; cited in Harvey A. Levenstein, *Revolution at the Table: The Transformation of the American Diet* (New York and Oxford: Oxford University Press, 1988), 17.

3   Phyllis Meras, "The 17 Trunks of Silver Came Back to R.I.," *Rhode Islander* (July 19, 1959), 12.

4   For information on Henry Jewett Furber and Elvira Irwin Furber, see Terry Heller, "A Sketch of the Lives of Henry Jewett Furber, Sr. and Jr." from the *Sarah Orne Jewett Text Project*, Coe College online resource, 2013. Furber received his degree from Bowdoin College in 1861.

5   "North American Life Troubles," *New York Times*, February 28, 1977. "Sued for Four Millions. The Universal Life Insurance Company's Troubles," *New York Times*, July 18, 1877.

6   Statement of account from Dec. 30, 1874. Gorham Manufacturing Company Archive, John Hay Library, Brown University, Providence, Rhode Island (hereafter GMCA). The sum of $15,000 in 1874 is the equivalent of about $333,000 in 2018.

7   J. S. Ingram, *The Centennial Exposition, Described and Illustrated, Being a Concise and Graphic Description of This Grand Enterprise*, 1876 (repr., New York: Arno Press, 1976), 309. Also mentioned and illustrated is an 1874–75 pitcher decorated with an allegorical relief of Venus lighting the torches of the Loves from the Furber service, 307, 311.

8   Gorham Manufacturing Company, Costing Ledger, Silver Hollowware, No. 2, 1866–1873, fruit bowl 775, GMCA.

9   Conant, "The Silver Age," 207.

10 For a contemporary description of the epergne, see George Titus Ferris, *Gems of the Centennial Exhibition* (New York: D. Appleton & Company, 1877), 12.

11 Ferris, *Gems of the Centennial Exhibition*, 13.

12 Conant, "The Silver Age," 197–209.

13 Joe Earle, *Lethal Elegance: The Art of Samurai Sword Fittings* (Boston: Museum of Fine Arts, Boston, 2004), 30, 234, 235. Kanzan Satō, *The Japanese Sword: A Comprehensive Guide*, trans. Joe Earle (New York: Kodansha International, 1983), 162, 198.

14 "Biography of Henry Jewett Furber," File II, Furber Collection, Historical-Museum, GMCA.

15 Ibid.

16 Meras, "The 17 Trunks of Silver," 11–12. The $6 million Furber estate was worth about $138 million in today's purchasing power.

17 Heller, "A Sketch," 5.

18 Letter to Benjamin Swann of Swann Auction Galleries from H. T. Brenner, Gorham Merchandise Manager, dated August 23, 1949. File II, Furber Collection, Historical-Museum, GMCA.

19 Ibid.

20 Letter to Henry Jewett Furber Jr. from H. T. Brenner, dated September 14, 1949, File II, Furber Collection, GMCA.

21 Letter to Henry Jewett Furber Jr. from H. T. Brenner, dated November 2, 1949. File II, Furber Collection, GMCA.

22 Letter to Henry Jewett Furber Jr. from H. T. Brenner, dated November 18, 1949. File II, Furber Collection, GMCA.

77
Soup Tureen, 1873.
Silver. RISD Museum

Williams

78
Tureens, Sauceboats,
Salts, Compotes, Fruit Stand,
Pickle Dish, and Butter Dish,
1873. Silver with gilding.
RISD Museum

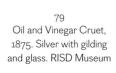

79
Oil and Vinegar Cruet,
1875. Silver with gilding
and glass. RISD Museum

80
Angelo Flatware Set,
ca. 1870. Silver with gilding.
RISD Museum

81
Candelabra, 1879.
Silver with gilding.
Plateaus, 1876. Silver with
gilding and mirror.
All Thomas Pairpoint, designer.
RISD Museum

82
Candelabrum (detail),
1879. RISD Museum

83
Ice Cream Plate, 1879.
Silver with gilding.
RISD Museum

84
Melon Forks, 1879.
Silver with gilding.
RISD Museum

85
Waiter, 1873.
Thomas Pairpoint, designer.
Silver with gilding.
RISD Museum

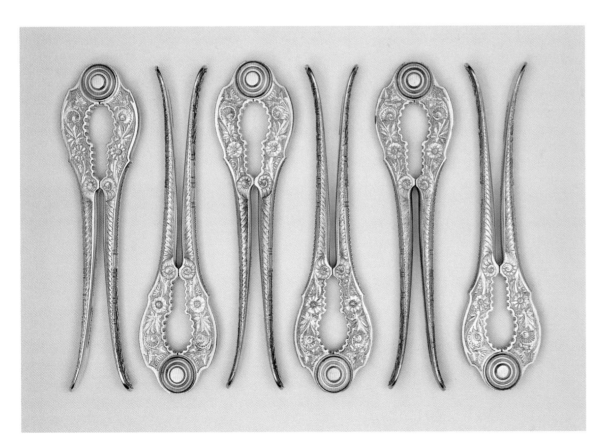

86
Nutcrackers, 1879.
Silver with gilding.
RISD Museum

87
Bread Plate, 1871.
Silver with gilding.
RISD Museum

88
Grape Shears, 1879.
Silver with gilding.
RISD Museum

89
Pitcher, 1874.
Silver with gilding.
RISD Museum

90
Pitcher (detail), 1874.
RISD Museum

GORHAM WORKS
1870s–1890s

91
Coffeepot, ca. 1890.
Copper and silver with ivory.
RISD Museum

雞

鶯

張志和

玉子章

93
Vase, 1880.
Silver with copper and brass.
RISD Museum

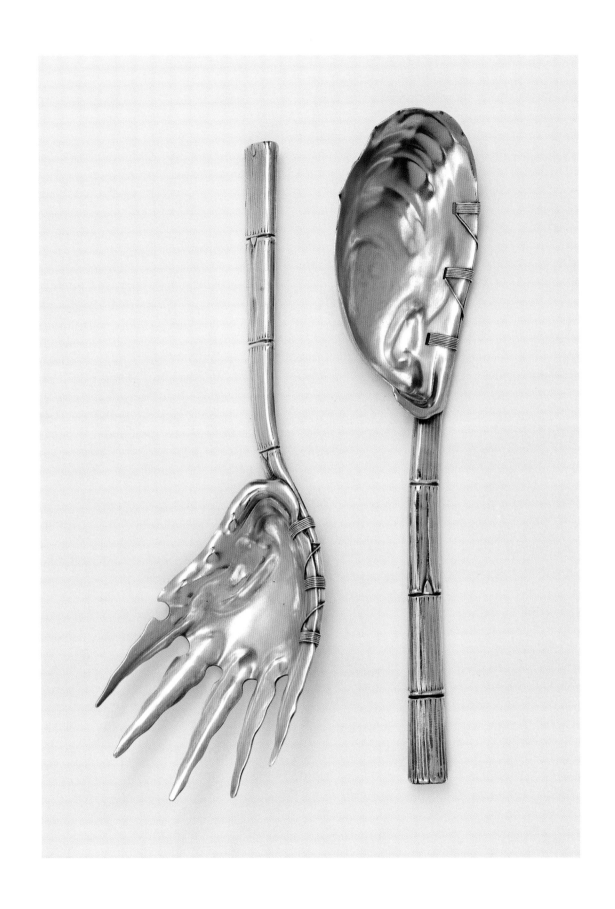

94
Salad Servers, ca. 1880.
Silver with gilding.
RISD Museum

95
Tureen on Stand, 1881.
Silver with copper.
Collection of Kathy Field Malavasic

96
Tureen, 1884.
Silver.
RISD Museum

97
Teapot and Stand (detail), 1871.
RISD Museum

98
Teapot and Stand, 1871.
Silver.
RISD Museum

99
Coffee and Tea Service, 1886.
Silver with gilding and wood.
RISD Museum

100
Cream Jug (detail), 1886.
RISD Museum

101
Fish Forks, 1879.
Silver with gilding.
RISD Museum

102
Water Set, 1878.
Silver with gilding.
RISD Museum

103
Sardine Tongs (detail), ca. 1879.
Silver with gilding.
RISD Museum

104
Vase, 1879.
Silver with copper and brass.
The Nelson-Atkins Museum of Art

105
Gorham casting patterns
from the 1800s
in original drawer, 2018.

106
Trophy Cup, 1883.
Ivory, silver, and glass.
RISD Museum

107
Trophy Cup (detail), 1883.
RISD Museum

112

108
Tea Caddy, 1880.
Silver with gilding.
RISD Museum

David L. Barquist

DESIGNING GORHAM SILVER

ʎ

THE RESTLESS LABORATORY

From the time that the Gorham Manufacturing Company commenced hollowware manufacture in the early 1850s, the designers employed by the company were a key factor in its success. John Gorham initially obtained designs from silversmiths in New York City, but beginning in 1857 with George Wilkinson, the company hired a succession of European-trained men as design directors. Wilkinson, together with his compatriot Thomas J. Pairpoint and Florentin Antoine Heller, situated the company's production within the traditions of European stylistic developments. This was seen as beneficial to both the company and the country at large. One reporter observed in 1868, "They have brought from foreign lands artisans and artists to exercise and (what is of much more importance) to communicate their skill and knowledge in the United States."[1]

During the post–Civil War era, an expanding marketplace of silver wares created by industrialized technology and a nearly limitless supply of metal from the mines in the American West allowed Gorham's designers to create more innovative work. They took inspiration from a wide range of cultures and historical traditions, frequently combining disparate motifs and techniques in individual objects. Under William Christmas Codman, who succeeded Wilkinson as design

109
Urn with Stand,
1871. Silver.
RISD Museum

director in 1891, the firm simultaneously embraced historical revivals and created *Martelé*, the most innovative American silver in the Art Nouveau style. In the decades after Codman's directorship, historical revival styles accounted for the largest share of the company's production, despite a brilliant experiment with Modernism with the Danish silversmith Erik Magnussen. It was not until the decades after World War II that a significant portion of Gorham's production again reflected innovative designs.

Early Hollowware in the
Rococo Revival Style

The company, known as Gorham & Thurber from 1850 to 1852, initially produced hollowware in designs typical of the Rococo Revival style fashionable in American and European urban centers. For drawings and wax models for their first tea and coffee service, the company turned in 1850 to an unidentified New York City silversmith, perhaps an associate of the silversmith Michael Gibney (born ca. 1815), who had been supplying Gorham with flatware in his version of the English *Prince Albert* pattern since the mid-1840s.[2] The design for the tea and coffee service, described in 1868 as in "the old Chinese pattern," featured the pear-shaped bodies, naturalistic cast elements, and lavish repoussé-chased decoration common to tea services made

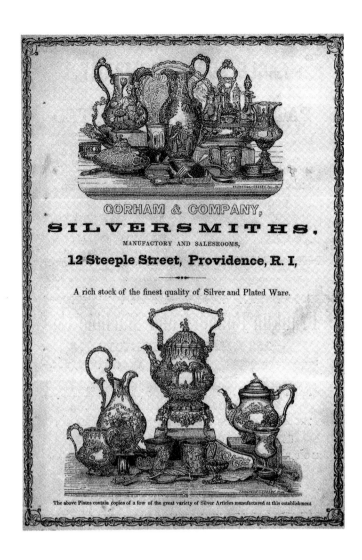

110
Gorham & Company
advertisement, 1852. Gorham
Archive, John Hay Library

contemporaneously in Boston, New York, and Philadelphia from the mid-1840s onward.[3] John Gorham later recounted that the drawings were made "under my instruction . . . where the individual pieces were appropriately decorated with something pertaining to its own character—for instance the Coffee pot had mountings of the Coffee Plants, leaves & buds[,] the body being chased with scenes from his Coffee Plantations."[4] The designer apparently did not consider his work Gorham's exclusive property: "Not holding in awe these unknown men of Providence, [he] dishonorably sold the same design to a New York silversmith; so that when next a member of the [Gorham] Company was on Broadway he was horrified to see a facsimile of their tea set in a shop window."[5]

Within two years, Gorham & Company was producing a full range of hollowware in the Rococo Revival style, as seen in an advertisement that depicted "a few of the great variety of Silver Articles manufactured at this establishment" (fig. 110). As with the tea and coffee service, the majority of these pieces were typical examples of hollowware with pear-shaped bodies (fig. 111) overlaid with naturalistic ornament, copying designs made for a decade or more by silversmiths in other American urban centers. The salt composed as a scallop shell supported by a piece of coral mounted on a rocaille base was identical to salts made by R. & W. Wilson of Philadelphia between 1825 and 1846.[6] More

111
Tea Service, Gorham & Thurber,
1850. Silver. Art Institute of Chicago

Barquist

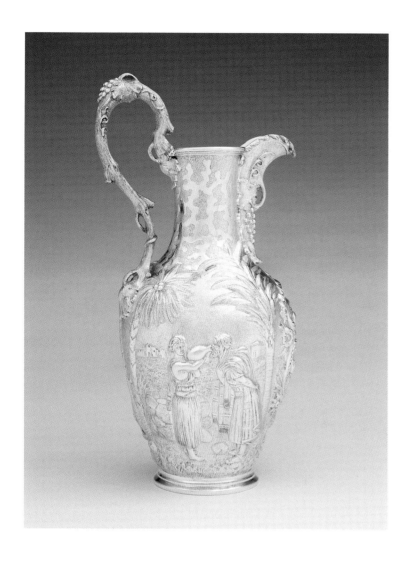

112
Rebekah at the Well Pitcher,
Gorham & Company, 1852. Silver.
Cincinnati Art Museum

paralleling a stylistic change that
was taking place in American
decorative arts at large. Born in
England, Wilkinson had studied
at the Birmingham Society of Artists in the early 1830s, after
which he was apprenticed to a local silversmith. He subsequently worked for the Birmingham firm of William Gough
and registered a design for a flatware pattern "in the style of
the Alhambra," which Gough exhibited at the Birmingham
Exhibition of Manufactures and Art in 1849.[9] Brought to the
United States in 1854 by the Ames Manufacturing Company
in Chicopee, Massachusetts, Wilkinson joined Gorham in
1857 and after a brief departure in 1860 rejoined the company
in December of that year as chief designer, the position he
would hold until his death.[10]

Wilkinson's English training was evident in the *Union
Vase* (fig. 113), a monumental punch bowl on a stand that
Gorham produced in 1864. Donated by the silversmiths and
jewelers Bailey & Company of Philadelphia to the Great
Central Fair of 1864, held to raise funds for sick and wounded
Northern soldiers in the Civil War, the *Union Vase* measured
40 inches in height, exclusive of its verd-antique marble
base, and it contained six hundred troy ounces of silver.[11]
The hemispherical punch
bowl, based on ancient Roman
prototypes, stood on a tripod
base, also inspired by Roman
bronze examples, adorned

113
Union Vase, 1864. George Wilkinson,
designer, in Gorham *Photo
Catalogue,* 1872. Gorham Archive,
John Hay Library

unusual was the *Rebekah at the Well Pitcher* (fig. 112) represented (in reverse) at the top center of the advertisement. It
featured a ubiquitous grape-stock handle and spout, but the
chased decoration was copied from a print after the 1833
painting *Rebecca at the Fountain* by Horace Vernet, an early
indication of the company's interest in directly emulating
European sources.[7] In the same year that this advertisement
appeared, John Gorham made his first trip to Europe.

George Wilkinson and
the Néo-Grec Style

Gorham continued to make objects in the Rococo Revival style
into the late 1860s, including tea services in the "old Chinese"
design with the same castings but different chased ornament.[8]
However, the arrival in 1857 of George Wilkinson (1819–1894)
(fig. 15) accelerated the company's transition from stock Rococo
Revival designs to classical- and Renaissance-inspired forms,

with implements of ancient, medieval, and modern warfare. Winged personifications of History, Fame, and Peace, as well as a helmeted figure of the goddess of Liberty holding a staff with a Phrygian cap, further carried out the classical theme. For models, Wilkinson turned to English exhibition and presentation pieces of a decade earlier, such as those exhibited at the Crystal Palace in 1851, or the Pompeian dessert service designed by Auguste-Adolphe Willms for Elkington & Co., Britain's largest and most important nineteenth-century manufacturer of silver and electroplated wares, and exhibited at the 1862 International Exhibition.[12] A critic for one American journal hailed Gorham's punch bowl as "the finest and most elaborate specimen of fine art in silver that has ever been made in an American workshop."[13] Hyperbole aside, a decade earlier, John Chandler Moore of New York had produced the *Four Elements* centerpiece with large three-dimensional figures in 1851–53, and Tiffany & Co. had made the even larger Woodlawn Cup by 1860.[14]

114
Fruit Dish from Cyrus W. Field Dinner Service, 1866. Silver with gilding. Museum of the City of New York

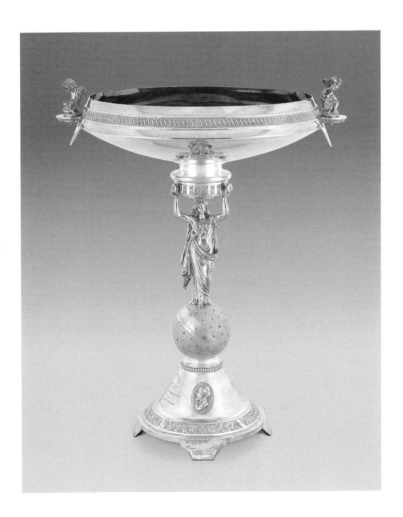

Wilkinson's impact on more routine productions of the Gorham factory is illustrated by the dinner service made in 1866 for presentation to New York merchant and entrepreneur Cyrus W. Field (fig. 114) and the *Pattern 500* tea and coffee service of 1871 (figs. 38–39, 109), both produced in the first decade of his directorship.[15] The objects' geometric shapes were derived from ancient Greek and Roman vessels, modified by exaggerated outlines, flared rims, and angular handles and bases. Undecorated, highly polished surfaces contrasted with cast, die-stamped, etched, and engraved ornament; the extensive repoussé work seen in the 1850s was used sparingly. The ornament comprised a virtual inventory of classical and Renaissance motifs: bands of ivy, grapevines, and laurel leaves; three-dimensional figures of draped maidens, winged putti, and lions; low-relief roundels of putti; male, female, and grotesque masks on handles and spouts; and openwork anthemia and animal's-paw feet on bases. Profile medallions inspired by ancient cameos were particularly popular, and *Harper's New Monthly Magazine* noted that Wilkinson's *Medallion* pattern (fig. 28), produced in both hollowware and flatware that was patented in 1864, "has had a great run among persons fond of the original and peculiar."[16] In other instances ancient Egyptian rather than Greco-Roman details were chosen, such as the sphinxes on the bases of a creamer and sugar bowl from about 1865 (figs. 32–33) or the company's *Isis* pattern (figs. 36–37).

Such designs were a striking departure from the Rococo Revival of mid-century, and the press was eager to underscore their innovative character. An 1868 article in *Harper's New Monthly Magazine* illustrated similar objects made by Gorham and noted: "Ten years ago the Providence makers dared not produce their best—dared not abandon the old forms endeared to the public by habit and protected by fashion. Many a time they were obliged to modify or lay aside a fine design only because the taste of the public was not 'up to it'—it was too simple, too violent a departure from established patterns, or else it was 'chased beyond the market.' At present they find the public taste responsive to their own."[17] Gorham's designs were simplified interpretations of recent European work, French as well as English. The exaggerated, geometric shapes, flared rims, and angular handles of Gorham's productions shared similarities with metalwork made in England by Elkington and in Paris by Ferdinand Barbedienne, Christofle, and others. Christofle exhibited a silver tea and coffee service in the 1862 London International Exhibition with bodies based on Greek vase shapes and similar angular handles, reliefs of classical figures, and three-dimensional putti; copies of the exhibition's illustrated catalogue as well as *Modèles de l'Orfévrerie Christofle* were recorded in the design library in 1871.[18] In 1863 an English

115
Designing and Modeling
Room, in *Views, Exterior
and Interior, of the Works of
the Gorham Manufacturing
Company, Silversmiths,*
1892. Gorham Archive,
John Hay Library

critic described such works as "that peculiar development of the Greek style which has distinguished the ornamental designs of France for the last few years, called 'Néo-Grec.'"[19] Other American silver manufacturers were producing objects contemporaneously in the same style, including Tiffany & Co. and John R. Wendt of New York, suggesting common sources of inspiration.[20]

The wealth of historical and contemporary references made by these objects reveals the importance of Gorham's design library, even at this relatively early date. John Gorham recorded buying design books and prints in London and Paris on his second trip to Europe in 1860, when he visited what he referred to as the Kensington Design School (presumably the Normal Training School of Art, a forerunner of the Royal College of Art) and the South Kensington Museum in London and the Louvre and the Musée du Luxembourg in Paris. The copy of Owen Jones's 1856 *Grammar of Ornament* in the design library was almost certainly among the unspecified books he purchased from its publisher, Day & Son, in September 1860.[21] By 1862, one visitor to the Gorham factory reported, "The

designer's room is a large neat office, and contains a library of the most costly works on ornamental art."[22] Five years later, another visitor observed, "[T]he artists' room—is a kind of magazine or storehouse of beautiful forms, which have been gathered in the course of years by Mr. George Wilkinson.... Here is a large and most costly library of illustrated works in every department of art and science."[23] In addition to illustrated books, by 1871 the design library included albums of drawings, prints, and photographs; plaster casts of medallions, ancient gems, and classical and Renaissance sculptures; parian and majolica ceramics; a Wedgwood vase; bronze sculptures and objects; and electrotypes (fig. 115).[24] *Harper's* reported in 1868:

> Upon being shown into the Designing Room of the
> establishment, the visitor is surprised to find himself
> in an apartment which has the appearance of a library.
> It is indeed well stored with books, and with illustrated
> works of the costliest description. All beauty is akin.
> A designer may get from an arch of the Cologne
> Cathedral an idea for the handle of a mustard-spoon,
> and infuse the spirit of a gorgeous mosque into the

design of a caster. He may borrow from the gnarled branch of a brave old oak a crook for a pitcher-handle, and imitate the droop of a vine in the bend of its spout. Antique vases, the Elgin marbles, books of animals, birds, fishes, flowers, trees, portraits, pictures, statuary, architecture, and all other accumulations of grace and beauty, may be useful to those whose business it is to cover with grace and beauty the tables of mankind.[25]

116
Cellini Vase, 1875, with stand, 1874. Both silver with gilding. Both Thomas Pairpoint, designer. RISD Museum

Thomas J. Pairpoint and Florentin Antoine Heller

In 1867, both John Gorham and George Wilkinson made trips to Europe to see the Exposition Universelle (International Exposition) in Paris and possibly to recruit Thomas J. Pairpoint (1838–1902) as a designer and modeler for the company. Pairpoint began working in Providence in the autumn of 1869.[26] Born in London, he was the son and brother of silversmiths in

the firm of William Pairpoint & Sons.[27] Several sources state that Thomas Pairpoint served an apprenticeship in Paris; he is known to have worked with the French silversmith Léonard Morel-Ladeuil (1820–1888), who from 1859 to 1885 worked in England as a designer of exhibition pieces for Elkington & Co.[28] Pairpoint subsequently worked as a designer and chaser for several London silversmiths, including Lambert & Rawlings and Harry Emanuel. British critics recognized Pairpoint as a rising talent; the *Art Journal* described him in 1862 as "a young English artist, who gives promise of holding rank beside the most famous of his contemporaries."[29] At the Exposition Universelle of 1867 in Paris the *Art Journal* singled out a bloodstone cup with silver mounts "modelled and wrought in repoussé by the excellent artist, Thomas Pairpoint."[30] By 1879, after he had worked at Gorham for a decade, an article in the *Jewelers' Circular and Horological Review* hailed Pairpoint as "one of the most skillful and artistic designers of the present day, having a reputation that is world wide."[31]

117
Plate 12 in Martin Riester, *Ornements du 19me siecle: inventès et dessinès par divers artistes industriels et gravès,* ca. 1851. Special Collections, Fleet Library at Rhode Island School of Design

Pairpoint's background in the sculptural tradition of Morel-Ladeuil was reflected in many of the objects produced at Gorham after his arrival. Classical figural elements as well as relief ornament increased dramatically in both quantity and their overall scale on objects, as seen in what one article called the *Feast of Flowers* centerpiece (fig. 73), and pitcher from the Furber service (figs. 89–90), whose decorative elements were published as Pairpoint's work.[32] The centerpiece's plateau, as well as the candelabra and a pair of smaller plateaus from the Furber service, also featured the horsemen from the Panathenaic procession frieze from the Parthenon, copied from plaster reproductions of the Elgin marbles in the design library (figs. 81, 170–72). A characteristic Pairpoint design was the *Cellini Vase* (figs. 75, 116) of 1874–75, also acquired by the Furbers.[33] The tall, ovoid body with flaring rim and base and high, scrolling handles was a characteristic French Néo-Grec form; a similar design (fig. 117) was published in Martin Riester's *Ornements du 19me siècle* of about 1851, a copy of which was in the Gorham design library.[34] On the Gorham vase this composition was dominated by the repoussé plaque by Pairpoint of a partially draped female figure standing in front of a harp, surrounded by winged putti. Pairpoint's vase appears to have been inspired by works such as Mathurin Moreau and Michel Auguste Madroux's *Education of Achilles Vase*, designed for Christofle and exhibited at the 1867 Paris Exposition Universelle that featured the same ovoid body, flaring rim and base, and large-scale central plaque with figures in high relief.[35]

The French character of Pairpoint's designs is particularly evident in the objects that he created as competition or exhibition pieces, most notably his entry for the 1875 design competition to create a vase to honor the poet and editor William Cullen Bryant and the *Century Vase,* designed jointly with Wilkinson for the Philadelphia Centennial International Exhibition of 1876 (fig. 118). The basic form of his proposal was a Greek amphora with volute handles, which Pairpoint dramatically attenuated in the Néo-Grec manner; a contemporary review called it "of a purely Grecian character, gracefully elongated to monumental proportions."[36] Pairpoint's vase had far more sculptural ornament than those of his competitors; another critic described the base as "the most original feature of this design," with its three-dimensional groups of classical figures illustrating Bryant's poems.[37]

Although the jury did not choose Pairpoint's design, it served as preparation for creating the *Century Vase*. On the latter work, the boat-shape vase all but disappeared

E 1393
E 1394 end view showing back
E 1395 top section showing vase

beneath the high relief and figural ornament that embellished it. Pairpoint presumably had the principal role in the *Century Vase*'s design, particularly given its close relationship to the design of Morel-Ladeuil's *Helicon Vase*, designed in 1871 for Elkington & Co.'s display at the 1872 International Exposition in London.[38] The *Century Vase*'s elaborate iconographic program was divided into three sections: base, plinth, and vase. Featuring the figures of a Native American and a buckskin-clad pioneer, the base was ornamented with native plants, conveying the idea that the "fertility of nature has constituted the first element, the very foundation, of national growth and prosperity."[39] Supporting a slab of granite framed by a border of thirty-eight stars, which symbolized "the unity and solidity of the government on which rest the thirty-eight States," the base included figural representations of War and Peace from which the United States came into existence. The plinth was ornamented with festoons of laurel leaves supported by bison heads, framing medallions of Fame with a portrait

118
Century Vase, 1876. Thomas Pairpoint and George Wilkinson, designers. In *Gorham Photobook Silver No. 1,* 1872–79. Gorham Archive, John Hay Library

119
Florentin Antoine Heller
in his studio, 1892

of George Washington on the front
and Philosophy and Diplomacy with
a portrait of Benjamin Franklin on
the back, two founding fathers whose
achievements literally and figuratively underpinned the
country. On the front of the vase itself was a relief of Genius
recording American achievements in art, science, and literature, whereas on the back was a relief of Invention honoring
American innovations in transportation, manufacturing,
mining, and agriculture. The vase's cover represented the
figure of the United States towering over Europe, Asia,
and Africa, "all generously contributing their wealth, taste,
skill, and industry to adorn the natal festivities of their
sister, the youngest in the family of nations."

Another French-trained designer at Gorham during
these years was Florentin Antoine Heller (1839–1904) (fig. 119),
who had studied briefly at the École des Beaux-Arts in Paris.
In 1872 Heller came to the United States to work at Tiffany
& Co., and the following year he joined Gorham as a designer
and die-cutter. [40] For the Centennial International Exhibition
Heller created the *American Shield* (fig. 120), as indebted to
French and English models as Pairpoint and Wilkinson's
works. The elongated proportions, dramatic poses, and flut-
tering draperies of the female figures in the border personify-
ing Equality and Liberty are similar to classical figures
modeled by Albert-Ernest Carrier-Belleuse, Frédéric-Auguste
Bartholdi, and others, whose work in turn was inspired
by French Renaissance artists such as Jean Goujon and

Francesco Primaticcio, an Italian painter, architect, and
sculptor who spent most of his life in France. Moreover,
dishes and shields with the same format of a central element
surrounded by a border of allegorical figures were designed
by the French designer Auguste-Adolphe Willms for
Elkington & Co.: the *Four Elements* dish exhibited in London
in 1862 and the *Medusa Shield* shown in Philadelphia in 1876. [41]

The 1870s was a decade of significant stylistic innovation at Gorham, and the figural ornament and classical
motifs of these grandiose exhibition pieces were to a large
extent unrepresentative of the directions taken by the company's designers. Although the *Century Vase* had been
hailed by some in the American press as "a masterpiece which
is unsurpassed in purity of material, in felicity of design
and in excellence of finish," its derivative character did not
escape notice, and Charles L. Venable, author of *Silver in
America, 1840–1940*, has pointed out that by the mid-1870s
these large-scale exhibition pieces with allegorical figures
had fallen out of favor with many art critics. [42] Pairpoint's
departure from Gorham in 1878 might be interpreted
as owing to Gorham's shift away from the Néo-Grec style
that he espoused. The company's designers increasingly
were drawn to exotic, non-European sources of inspiration,
as evidenced by the ice bowls (figs.
34–35, 121) that featured polar
bears, icebergs, and other Arctic
imagery, reflecting the contemporary interest in Arctic exploration
as well as the purchase of Alaska
by the United States in 1867. [43]

120
The *American Shield* and
Furber service candelabrum,
shown in *Choice Examples of
Sterling Silver Ware: The Products
of the Gorham Mfg Co:
Silversmiths*, 1893. Gorham Archive,
John Hay Library

121
Ice Bowl, 1871;
Ice Spoon, 1874. Both silver.
Dallas Museum of Art

Inspiration from Japan

By the early 1870s, there was also a growing enthusiasm in the United States and Europe for Japanese art. Reviewing the Centennial International Exhibition in Philadelphia, one critic hailed the Japanese exhibit:

It . . . is filled in every part with a rich and valuable display, the variety and beauty of which are one of the great surprises of the Exhibition. . . . A number of bronze vases are included in this collection, which are the wonder and admiration of all visitors. They are of beautiful shapes, and are ornamented with such a profusion of engraving and chasing—the conceptions of which are droll and intricate—that a photograph would be necessary to give an accurate idea of them. The work is unique and cannot be reproduced by the most skillful artificer in either Europe or America.[44]

122
Salt, 1879.
Silver with gilding.
RISD Museum

Turning away from the classical figurative decoration of the Néo-Grec style, designers at Gorham began devising ornamentation with plants, birds, insects, and other subjects taken from nature. The designers had many points of contact with the arts of Japan, through imported Japanese objects as well as several seminal books on Japanese art and culture in the company's design library, including at least seven of the fifteen volumes of Katsushika Hokusai's (1760–1849) *Manga* (figs. 92, 179).[45] Large displays of Japanese art were featured at the London International Exhibition of 1862 and Paris Exposition Universelle of 1867, where Pairpoint had his work exhibited and which both John Gorham and George Wilkinson also visited. No designers' names have been connected to the Japanese-style silver made at Gorham. As design director, Wilkinson presumably was sympathetic to the new style, even if he did not work in that mode. Carpenter observed that Pairpoint's series of articles "Art Work and Silver," published in 1879–80, did not mention Japanese art.[46]

The Gorham designers' earliest response to this fascination with Japanese art was engraved ornament of fans, diagonal patterned bands, roundels, and cropped images of plants, birds, and insects (figs. 122, 123), all rendered with the lack of shading and perspective found in ukiyo-e prints, although these motifs could also be found in Japanese textiles, lacquer, enamels, and ceramics, as well as metalwork. Identical engraved or flat-chased decoration, sometimes highlighted with bright cutting or parcel gilding, was made by Elkington & Co. and other British silver manufacturers, and this ornament is often termed "Anglo-Japanese."[47] A set of shallow bowls engraved with these motifs, made at Gorham in 1869, are some of the earliest—if not the earliest—known pieces of American silver in this Anglo-Japanese style.[48] Gorham designers applied this type of decoration, usually engraved but sometimes chased, on a wide range of traditional forms in the 1870s and early 1880s, such as a water pitcher and cups

Henry and Elvira Furber acquired in 1878 (fig. 102), as well as the salts, pepper shakers (fig. 174), and butter plates (figs. 123, 175) they purchased in 1879,

126
Fruit Plate, 1881. Silver
with gilding and copper.
Dallas Museum of Art

which featured a different design
on each individual piece. Motifs such
as swallows swooping to chase
butterflies were ubiquitous Anglo-
Japanese images that Gorham designers repeatedly
employed. They could be found in a large number of
Japanese and European print sources, including Hokusai's
Manga and John Ward's *Motifs for Panel and Other
Decoration*, both in Gorham's design library.[49] Gorham's
copy of George Audsley's 1875 *The Keramic Art of Japan*,
one of the first and most important books on Japanese
art to be produced in the English language, provided an
image of a trio of Japanese ceramic plates in blue and white,
the largest depicting a tiger emerging from a densely foliated background. In 1881, Gorham produced a
hand-hammered and elaborately chased version of the
square plate (fig. 124) copied directly from the Japanese
ceramic model.[50]

Gorham designers also created pieces in the Japanese
style that departed from standard forms and traditional
decorative techniques, more as art objects than utilitarian
wares. Although not always based directly on Japanese
models, the shapes were simplified and more geometric, in
keeping with Japanese aesthetics. Objects of this type
are recorded in photographs as early as 1873, when a series

127
Oyster Tureen, 1885,
and Stand, 1884. Silver.
Dallas Museum of Art

of tea caddies were made with simple,
rounded shapes inspired by ceramic and
lacquer vessels; their only decoration was
die-rolled borders and figural finials.[51] A
group of similarly austere tablewares made in 1874 had rectilinear or spherical bodies with handles made to resemble bamboo.[52]

Slightly later Japanese-style art objects with simplified forms were ornamented with two- and three-dimensional
appliqués instead of the engraving or repoussé decoration
used on Anglo-Japanese pieces. Frequently these appliqués
were highlighted against textured, patinated, or colored backgrounds (fig. 95). These treatments were inspired in part by
the Japanese metalwork exported to and exhibited in the West,
much of which was made of bronze, iron, and various alloys
ornamented with patinated and textured surfaces and applied,
high-relief ornament.[53] A more direct influence on such pieces
were the Japanese-style objects made by Tiffany & Co. for their
display at the Paris Exposition Universelle of 1878. Designed
by Edward C. Moore, these pieces featured organic, irregular
shapes, surfaces textured to resemble hammering, and colored
appliqués made of gold, copper, and mixed-metal laminates
like *mokume-gane*. Tiffany & Co.'s exhibit created a sensation
and had a profound impact on American silver manufacturers.[54]

Although Gorham had made Japanese-style objects
with hammered surfaces prior to 1878, the numbers increased

l'oeil, inspired by Japanese bronze and multi-metal objects like an *okimono* by Shaomi Katsuyoshi, with leaves inhabited and eaten by insects.[58] Other objects, including a pitcher (fig. 125) of 1882, two tureens (figs. 96, 127), and a punch bowl (fig. 184), featured carp swimming in water rendered as stylized S-curves, a subject found in many ukiyo-e prints, including volume 13 of Hokusai's *Manga* in the company's design library. On the pitcher and the tureens, the breaking waves were depicted with stylized, clawlike foam and spray copied directly from prints by Hokusai, such as his renowned *The Great Wave Off Kanagawa* of 1830–33.[59]

Americans were eager to claim these works as uniquely American; in part this was true because of the lack of guild or other legal restrictions in the United States on combining precious and nonprecious metals in the same object, enabling the rich combinations of color and texture that Tiffany and Gorham achieved. Gorham proclaimed the novel qualities of their "'American Curios,' exhibiting the most marked effects in form and surface decoration" in

129
Wine Decanter Stand
(detail), 1873.
RISD Museum

130
Bud Vase with Enameled
Decoration, 1877.
Silver and gilding with
enamel. Newark Museum

dramatically in the years following the Exposition Universelle. Two vases demonstrate Gorham's different approach to Japanese-inspired aesthetics and its designers' fascination with Japanese mixed-metal laminates and alloys. Gorham's 1879 *Curio* vase (figs. 104, 180) is composed of silver with speckles of brass and copper fused into it under pressure, while an 1880 vase features a hammered surface and mixed-metal appliqués, such as the circular medallions with an owl and swallow (figs. 93, 105). A review of an exhibition in 1880 at Gorham's Union Square showroom in New York observed that "an odd plate, and one of rich design, has an inlaying of various metals, producing a mottled effect."[55] Company photographs document only a handful of small pieces of hollowware made with this innovative metal, which also was employed for *Curio* flatware (fig. 181).[56] The combination of different colored metals also inspired Gorham's short-lived lines of copper objects with hammered and patinated surfaces and silver appliqués (fig. 91), introduced in 1881, and *Banko Iron Ware* objects with silver appliqués (fig. 178), introduced in 1883.[57] In the 1880s, Gorham's designers took the Japanese influence in another direction. Instead of using chased backgrounds contrasted with two-dimensional appliqués and different colored metals, they created objects ornamented

128
Wine Decanter Stand, 1873.
George Wilkinson, designer.
Silver with gilding and glass.
RISD Museum

with allover repoussé chasing and three-dimensional elements. Some of these pieces, such as a fruit plate of 1881 and pitcher of 1879 (figs. 126, 176) were conceived as a kind of trompe

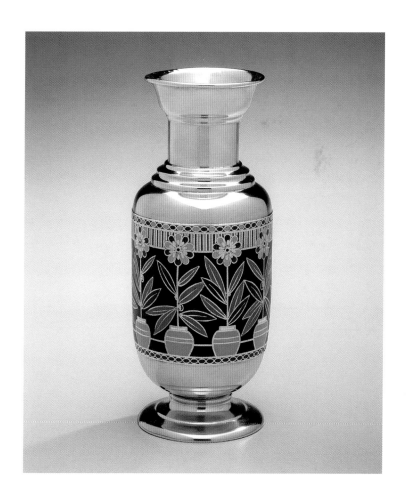

an 1879 advertisement that also stated, "The productions of our Factory the present season . . . indicate the most thoughtful consideration and study of what is new in DECORATIVE ART."[60] As Elizabeth A. Williams demonstrates in her dissertation "Designing a New Mold," American critics also hailed such wares as artistic innovations that surpassed Japanese models.[61] In 1877 one critic commented approvingly on objects made "in tones too subdued and delicate to yield a motive to the ordinary purchaser. . . . [This trait] is especially characteristic of the mature refinement of Japanese art, into the spirit of which our leading silver artists have drunk deeply of late, if one may judge by the prevalence of Japanese style in the novelties pouring forth from the restless laboratories of Gorham and Tiffany. We have seen a tea caddy from the Gorham works, close enough to the slumberous oriental antiquity of tone to seem like some Japanese heirloom."[62]

131
Elephant Fruit Stand, 1881. Silver with gilding. Manoogian Foundation, courtesy the Detroit Institute of Arts

Stylistic Diversity, 1870–90

Despite the reference in 1877 to the "prevalence of Japanese style," Japanese-style objects were only one part of Gorham's production in the 1870s and 1880s. The company's photographic records document a range of styles, including a significant percentage of Néo-Grec and Egyptian Revival modes being made in any one year, such as the wine decanter stand (figs. 128, 129) made in 1873 for the Furber service. Gorham's designers also produced a few art objects in the English Aesthetic style, inspired by design reformers such as William Morris and Christopher Dresser. As has been noted, the English design reformers were inspired by Japanese art, which to some extent overshadowed their influence in the United States.[63] A silver-gilt and cloisonné enamel vase (fig. 130) of 1877 is an exceptional example of American silver in the English Aesthetic taste, notwithstanding the use of cloisonné enamel, undoubtedly inspired by the tremendous popularity of Japanese work in this medium. The vase's simple shape reflects the influence of Dresser's

and sent to Japan for decoration as late as 1897.[69] Its popularity was superseded in part by designs that borrowed from different Middle and East Asian traditions to create an "exotic" style that made less specific references to its sources than did the Japanese-inspired objects. A fruit stand (fig. 131) of 1881, designed as a carpet supported by elephants, and a pitcher formed from two entwined snakes (fig. 185) of 1885, evoked Mughal Indian and other non-European sources but were not based on any specific prototypes, just as the repoussé decoration on a tea and coffee service (figs. 99, 100) of 1886 combined motifs taken from Asian architecture, textiles, and metalwork. As Williams has shown in her dissertation, Gorham's so-called "Turkish" coffeepots were actually based on Persian prototypes and were frequently embellished with Japanese-style appliqués (fig. 91).[70]

The repoussé chasing found on Gorham's Japanese and other exotic-style objects of the 1880s reflected a larger shift in popularity to hollowware with "allover" floral repoussé chasing. Few pieces in this style appear to have been produced during the 1860s and 1870s, although this decoration presumably could have been executed on special order.[71] In 1880, however, a repoussé tea service with ornament inspired by eighteenth-century Rococo models was included in the "heliotypic illustration" in the company's 1880 catalogue (figs. 132, 230), surrounded by hammered, Japanese-style wares; the text noted that the service was "selected as examples of Repoussé. To this department we have been giving particular attention, and having largely increased its working force, we are producing unquestionably the most desirable line of Repoussé Work in Hollow Ware and Small Wares which the trade demands."[72] By 1889, the publication that accompanied Gorham's display at the 1889 Exposition Universelle illustrated only one "Japanesque" tea service and multiple forms with lavish repoussé chasing, some described as "Rococo in style."[73]

metalwork, and the band of potted flowers embodies his advocacy for bilateral symmetry and repetition in ornament.[64] None of Dresser's publications are known to have been in the Gorham design library, although it did contain F. Edward Hulme's *A Series of Sketches from Nature of Plant Forms* of 1863, which echoed Dresser's theories.[65] The vase's ornament also could have been inspired by English designers influenced by Dresser, such as the dado wallpaper of lilies in pots designed by Walter Crane for Jeffrey & Company or the sunflower balustrade from Thomas Jeckyll's cast-iron pavilion, both exhibited at the Philadelphia Centennial International Exhibition in 1876.[66] Crane's illustration of "Little Bo Peep" from his *Baby's Opera* of 1877 was engraved on plates made at Gorham in 1878 and 1879.[67] Walter Wilkinson (1853–1894), George's son, possibly designed this vase. He began working at Gorham in 1868 and in his twenties created drawings in a similar English Aesthetic taste that appeared in company advertisements and catalogues. One of his drawings used in an 1878 advertisement featured a similar vase with the flowers in relief.[68]

The popularity of Japanese-style silver peaked in the early 1880s and slowly declined over the latter years of that decade, although silver dealers Spencer Gordon and Mark McHugh have as recently as 2016 discovered a group of about 100 pieces of "Special" hollowware that Gorham manufactured

The Gilded Age and Eclectic Historicism

Objects in historical revival styles also became more popular after 1880. A few interpretations of various historical styles were made as early as the 1860s, such as the "Fancy Goblet" apparently made as a special item in or before 1869 that closely copied late sixteenth-century cups made in Nuremberg; the company owned a later Russian example dated 1745.[74] With the arrival of designers such as Florentin Antoine Heller, who were trained in the tradition of the École des Beaux-Arts, which stressed the study of historical models, Gorham's

133
Atalanta Prize Cup,
1887. Silver. Philadelphia
Museum of Art

decoration created a much richer surface. Elements like the masks of Neptune and a sea monster were inspired by sixteenth-century Dutch silver in the so-called Auricular style, whereas the figures of Nereids resembled contemporary sculpture by Jean-Baptiste Carpeaux or illustrations by the German artist Franz Simm, whose book of figural compositions entitled *Al Fresco*, published in 1885 was in Gorham's design library.[76] The *Atalanta Cup* was prominently featured in the frontispiece to the company's autumn 1888 catalogue (fig. 135) as well as in the company's display at the World's Columbian Exposition held in Chicago in 1893 (fig. 236).[77] Many more affordable interpretations of historical European designs were put into production, such as the flatware patterns designed by Heller between 1882 and 1894, with evocative names like *Fontainebleau, Medici, Cluny, Nuremburg, Old Masters, Versailles,* and *Mythologique* (figs. 154, 189, 191).[78]

Another historical-revival style that gained popularity in the 1880s imitated eighteenth-century English Georgian-American Colonial objects. Again as early as the 1860s, Gorham made "to order for Mr. Kendrick" a dome-covered tankard that copied Colonial New England models, albeit with a hexagonal body instead of a tapered cylinder and a floral finial.[79] A cream pot and sugar bowl with fluted, urn-shaped bodies and flat handles of an early nineteenth-century style was recorded in 1878, as was a pear-shaped, three-footed cream pot copying mid-eighteenth-century examples, with the addition of allover floral chasing, and an apple-shaped teapot with a wood handle that also closely copied mid-eighteenth-century examples was made in 1880.[80] In 1884 a mid-eighteenth-century-style tea and coffee service was made as a "Special" with inverted pear-shaped bodies, although the set was embellished with historically incorrect gadrooning and wood handles on every vessel.[81] Undecorated versions of the three-footed cream pot were illustrated in the company's 1888 catalogue.[82] The inspiration for some of these objects may have come from historical silver in the corporate collection that Gorham had formed, three items of which were illustrated in John H. Buck's

134
William Christmas Codman,
ca. 1895. Gorham Archive,
John Hay Library

production during the last quarter of the nineteenth century easily responded to demand for objects that evoked past epochs of European history to which Americans felt themselves to be the heirs, often by combining the styles of several eras into a single object in nontraditional ways. A spectacular example of this kind of synthetic historicism is the prize cup of 1887, commissioned by financier Jay Gould for his steam yacht *Atalanta* (figs. 133, 232). Heller probably was the designer; his sculpture *La Vendage* in Gorham's exhibit at the 1889 Paris Exposition Universelle similarly featured female figures in artfully intertwined poses, surmounted by a stylized mask.[75] The *Atalanta Cup*'s classical imagery, baluster shape, and exaggerated handles and rim looked back to the Néo-Grec style of the 1860s, although the complex interplay of cast, repoussé, chased, and etched

Old Plate, published by Gorham in 1888; other pieces were lent to the Washington Inaugural Centennial Exhibition in New York in 1889, for which Buck organized the silver section.[83] *Old Plate* was one the earliest publications to include images of early American silver, as well as a "chronological list of American plate" with the names of some makers identified.[84]

William Christmas Codman and *Martelé*

The arrival in 1891 of William Christmas Codman (1839–1921) (fig. 134) as design director intensified Gorham's historicist bent. Born in Norwich, England, he had worked as an ecclesiastical designer for the Medieval Revival architect George Gilbert Scott and subsequently for Elkington & Co.[85] His first designs at Gorham were for the 1893 World's Columbian Exposition in Chicago, where a multiplicity of styles, historical and contemporary, was put on show. The Gorham exhibit included older objects, including the *Century Vase* and the *Atalanta Cup*, as well as many newly made objects that evoked different historical periods:

use of the shell and its jeweled strap-work mounts were inspired by late sixteenth- and early seventeenth-century northern European proto-types.[88] The *New York Times* critic wrote, "Highly representative American art in silver is found in . . . very graceful and beautiful centrepieces in a Louis XVI plateau, the centrepieces being of polished nautilus shell, mounted with silver, studded with jewels, and surmounted and supported by beautifully modeled sea nymphs and dolphins."[89] The *Art Amateur* similarly praised Gorham's exhibition as "thoroughly artistic" and described as "chief among" its display the "fine prize cup made of a nautilus shell set in the Renaissance manner with figures, shells and other ornaments in gold and precious stones."[90] The exaggerated contrapposto and sinuous draperies of the central caryatid figure also reflect Codman's awareness of contemporary European Art Nouveau, or Jugendstil, design (fig. 136), a similarity that becomes apparent when this figure is compared with the female caryatid on the Cyrus Field service of a quarter century earlier (fig. 114). Female caryatid supports were a stock element of classically inspired silver, so it is difficult to link this figure to a specific source, although it is strikingly similar to the central support of a centerpiece illustrated in a catalogue issued by the Württembergische Metallwarenfabrik in Germany.[91]

Codman's most important contribution at Gorham was the *Martelé* line, which he initiated in 1896 with the support of Gorham's president, Edward Holbrook. Steeped in the principles of the British Arts and Crafts movement, particularly the belief that design and execution should never be separated, craftsmen and designers collaborated to execute *Martelé* objects. This approach was sufficiently different from the normal process at Gorham that the craftsmen who worked on the *Martelé* line received special training under Codman and worked under "an enlightened policy of control" that allowed opportunities for individual expression.[92] After a preliminary exhibition as "wrought sterling silver" in New York in 1897, the *Martelé* line was given its formal debut in Paris at the 1900 Exposition Universelle, where *Martelé* objects accounted for more than half of Gorham's display. The focal point of the exhibit was the impressive dressing table and stool (fig. 138).[93] A tankard chased with hops plants (fig. 139) was another spectacular object featured in the exhibition.[94] Just

a claret jug (fig. 150) with jeweled mounts in the Renaissance manner; a basin in the style of Paul de Lamerie, a renowned London-based silversmith active in the first half of the eighteenth century; a wine pitcher (fig. 153) with masks and reliefs following Baroque models; and a jeweled, silver-gilt *Dancers Plaque* with inset enamels of putti and figures taken from eighteenth-century French fêtes galantes.[86] The *New York Times* enthusiastically praised the revival-style objects in Gorham's exhibit, singling out one dessert service whose "design is pure Italian Renaissance" and another that "is correct Louis XVI in design."[87]

One of the most commented-upon objects was Codman's *Venus* or *Nautilus Centerpiece* (fig. 137), whose

as the name *Martelé* referenced the idea of direct contact with the maker's hammer, the tankard's curvilinear design underscored the metal's malleability. Instead of copying elements of historical models, most of the ornament was taken directly from nature, and although a tankard is a traditional silver form, this example bore little relationship to historical examples. As Horace Townsend wrote in his essay for the book Gorham published to accompany the exhibit, "The work they produced should be of its own century. Beautiful as is the work of the 'Little Masters' of the past it yet speaks in a dead and forgotten tongue. The designer of to-day, if he is a true artist, must create and not copy."[95] Critics and exposition judges agreed; Gorham was awarded the grand prix for metalwork, Edward Holbrook was made a chevalier of the Légion d'honneur, and Codman received a gold medal.[96] The French critic Roger Marx wrote admiringly of Gorham's exhibit, "On ne se lasse point d'admirer le talent et l'imagination dépensés libéralement, en prodigue [One never tires of admiring talent and imagination expended liberally, lavishly]."[97]

Both Codman's contemporaries and subsequent scholars have acknowledged *Martelé* silver as one of the greatest expressions of the Art Nouveau style in the United States. In 1912, art critic Evelyn Marie Stuart wrote, "Here indeed is a new school, a distinctive type, a fresh beauty as novel and as characteristically our own as our Rookwood pottery or Tiffany glass."[98] Nevertheless, in creating these designs Codman synthesized a number of historical and contemporary influences. The subtle, hammered surfaces had their origin in the chased, textured backgrounds first used in the 1880s by British Arts and Crafts metalsmiths including the Guild of Handicraft and Gilbert Marks.[99] The "whiplash" lines and curves likewise appeared in England in the 1880s in designs by A. H. Mackmurdo and were taken up in the 1890s in metalwork and jewelry by C. R. Ashbee, Philippe Wolfers, Henry van de Velde, and Edward Colonna.[100] Having popularized "hammered" surfaces on its Japanese-style silver in 1878, Tiffany & Co. went on to produce a series of objects that featured high-relief repoussé decoration of large-scale flowers against textured backgrounds. Contemporary English and

139
Martelé Tankard, 1900.
William E. Jordan, chaser.
Silver. Collection of
Suzanne and Joel Sugg

140
Ewer and Dish, 1900.
Robert Bain, chaser.
Silver. Collection of
Suzanne and Joel Sugg

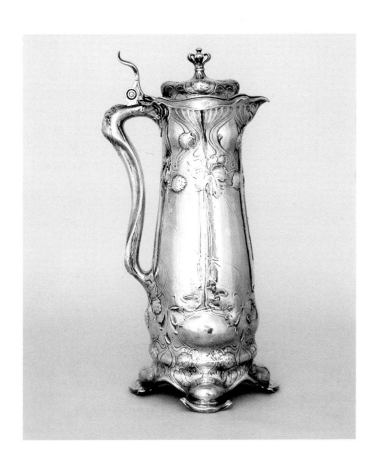

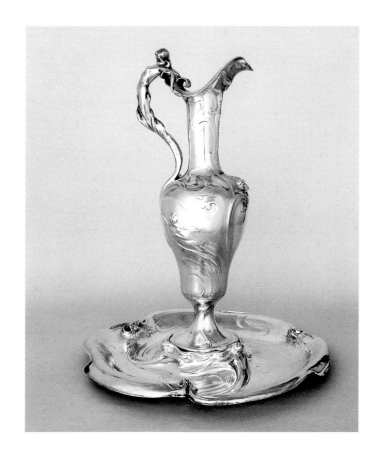

141
Centerpiece, 1903.
Edwin Everett Codman,
attributed modeler, and
Robert Bain, chaser. Silver.
Cincinnati Art Museum

Continental European metalworkers created irregularly shaped objects with naturalistic floral decoration, most notably the pewter manufacturers J. P. Kayser Sohn and Jules-Paul Brateau.[101] All these sources would have been known to Codman and other Gorham designers through publications and periodicals in the company's design library, including *L'Art* and *International Studio*. Samuel Hough has demonstrated that some of the marine creatures found on pieces of *Martelé* silver were derived from *Das Their in der decorativen Kunst* of 1896 found in Gorham's design library, and L. J. Pristo has noted the similarity of a *Martelé* mirror to one by Henri Nocq published in 1897.[102]

Other *Martelé* objects were inspired by historical models. As American silver historian W. Scott Braznell has demonstrated, sets of tall ewers and basins, such as the example made in 1900 (fig. 140), had a form and marine-theme decoration modeled on Dutch Mannerist silver of the late sixteenth and early seventeenth centuries.[103] The

spectacular *Martelé* centerpiece of 1903 (fig. 141) recalls the *Atalanta* prize cup with its classical figures of Neptune and Nereids; the figure of Neptune standing within a shell has its source in European print sources extending back to the sixteenth century.[104] The figural handles derive from Baroque prototypes like Charles Frederick Kandler's wine cistern of 1734 that Buck illustrated in *Old Plate*.[105] The silver mounts for a wine pitcher (fig. 153) and claret decanter (fig. 143) exhibited in Paris in 1900 similarly featured Baroque-inspired ornament, including a mask of Bacchus and a Daphne-like female figure emerging from grapevines on the pitcher.[106] Although *Martelé* silver was innovative as a collaboration of designers and craftsmen who produced objects largely in the latest Art Nouveau style, both the company and critics situated it squarely within long historical tradition. At a preview exhibition in New York of the objects being sent to the Exposition Universelle, the *New York Observer* commented, "This really is a revival of the ancient art practiced in the sixteenth century by Cellini, when men worked out by hand

versions, using similar organic shapes and large-scale, naturalistic floral decoration. As Braznell has demonstrated, these imitations were realized in a variety of ways.[110] Reed & Barton created a line of objects, with wavy rims and feet and superb hand-chased ornament, some of which were made in the same standard of .950 silver.[111] A few of these pieces appear to have been copied directly after Gorham examples, including a tankard that is strikingly similar, with the same dimensions as one shown in Paris in 1900 (fig. 139).[112]

Stylistic Simplification and Historical Revivals

Townsend described *Martelé* production at Gorham as an *imperium in imperio* ("empire within an empire"), but in fact some of the chasers who executed *Martelé* objects also worked on pieces in other styles.[113] Between 1897 and 1916, the years of development and peak production of *Martelé*, both Codman and the company also lavished great attention on objects they continued to make in historical-revival styles, which were less eclectic and more historically accurate than they had been in the 1880s and early 1890s. The writing table and chair (figs. 197, 207–9) that Codman designed in 1903 for the 1904 Louisiana Purchase Exposition (the Saint Louis World's Fair) was a late example of that earlier eclectic style, combining multiple forms inspired by Rococo furniture with inlaid decoration in the style of Baroque marquetry, swans' heads on the chair copied from Empire furniture, and silver mounts in the Art Nouveau style.

Within a decade, John S. Holbrook, the son of Edward Holbrook, criticized such productions: "The time has gone by for a hodge podge and potpourri of all the arts playing discord. Our tendency to-day is to isolation, selection, and purification of all historic styles."[114] Gorham shifted focus and instead of combining disparate motifs from a variety of sources, designers followed individual models. Some of these were special production pieces like the silver and ivory tankard made in 1898 (fig. 142), closely based on seventeenth-century German examples that were being collected contemporaneously by J. P. Morgan and other wealthy Americans.[115] Codman's *Chantilly* flatware (fig. 65) and hollowware, first introduced in 1895 and subsequently modified, was based on French Régence and Louis XV designs, and became the company's most popular pattern.[116]

The culmination of this phase of Codman's design work was the 129-piece dinner service made by Gorham between 1909 and 1911 for Senator William A. Clark of Montana.[117] Described by Codman's son as in the style of

with patient and loving care the beautiful ideas their minds conceived. . . . The Gorham Company are to be congratulated upon the revival of the ancient silversmith's art."[107]

Martelé objects were among the finest American statements of the Art Nouveau style and also were among the earliest in the medium of silver, along with some designs of the 1890s by John T. Curran for Tiffany & Co. and Charles Osborne for the Whiting Manufacturing Company.[108] Gorham also produced Art Nouveau–style objects that were part of the *Athenic* line, a companion to the *Martelé* line introduced in 1901, such as a cigar box (fig. 206) and a pair of candelabra (figs. 213–214, 244).[109] The critical acclaim and extensive press that greeted the *Martelé* line inspired other American silver manufacturers in the years following the Paris Exposition Universelle to produce their own

143
Martelé Claret, 1900.
George W. Sauthof, chaser,
and J. Hoare & Company,
glassmaker. Silver and glass.
Collection of
Suzanne and Joel Sugg

William Christmas Codman's son William observed in 1930, "The service designed by William C. Codman for the late Senator Clarke [*sic*] . . . is considered the best example of this period in silver executed in modern times . . . monumental, stately, may we say regal."[120]

In 1914 Codman retired and returned to England; his son William succeeded him as chief designer. The elder Codman's departure could be interpreted as the end of the Gilded Age at Gorham. In the years after World War I, nationwide trends of rising wages for labor and falling numbers of household servants resulted in a decline in demand for silver that was increasingly costly to produce. Art lines like the Japanese-inspired wares of the 1870s or *Martelé* had given Gorham great critical notoriety but were not always

the "Louis XIV period," objects like the tureen and plateau were not copied from specific examples of seventeenth-century French silver but instead employed moldings, shells, animal's-paw feet, satyr's masks, strapwork, and gadrooning taken from a variety of designs and objects of that era to create an object that evoked its magnificence, a process that could be described as "isolation, selection, and purification."[118] Residences like Alva and William K. Vanderbilt's Marble House in Newport, Rhode Island, used a similar vocabulary of motifs drawn from period sources to create an evocation of the ancien régime so popular with wealthy Americans during the later years of the Gilded Age. In 1912 John S. Holbrook described the Louis XIV style: "For large banquet halls, great entertainments, and the magnificent homes of wealth, no more suitable style can be chosen."[119]

144
Plymouth Coffee and Tea Service, in *The Gorham Mark*, 1916. Gorham Archive, John Hay Library

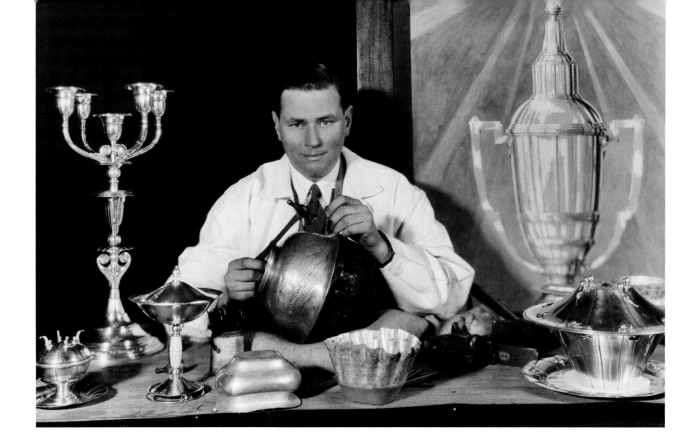

economically viable. As Venable has observed of the years following World War I, the drive in the silver industry was to maximize efficiency. An internal review of Gorham in 1923 recommended reducing the number of patterns and designs in production, as well as introducing new designs only "in the exceptional case" rather than bringing out new designs annually as had been done in the past.[121]

Simpler Neoclassical designs like the *Plymouth* pattern (fig. 144), which was introduced in the first decade of the twentieth century, not only were less expensive to produce but also appealed to consumers in the heyday of the Colonial Revival style. In an address to the New York School of Applied Design for Women in 1918, John S. Holbrook stated, "In the revival of taste to-day the demand for Colonial examples and Colonial reproductions is one of the most hopeful signs we see, in my opinion, for the development of a sincere, pure, and true style of American art. . . . The chief characteristics of the Colonial style, as evidenced by the examples, are a careful study of form, and the shapes showing strongly classic tendencies and a marked repression in the use of ornament."[122] The *Plymouth* pattern derived from late eighteenth- and early nineteenth-century objects with fluted, urn-shaped bodies, such as tea services made by Paul Revere Jr. of Boston and James Musgrave

of Philadelphia.[123] Unlike their historical antecedents, different objects in the service had identical bodies, with broad outlines and sharply tapered bases. A tea and coffee service in this as-yet unnamed pattern appeared in Gorham's 1906–7 catalogue, and a slightly simplified version, now "known by the name of 'Plymouth,'" was presented in the 1908–9 catalogue as "meet[ing] all requirements in a modern, modest home."[124] The timing of its introduction was in sync with the growing enthusiasm for all things Colonial; in 1906 the Museum of Fine Arts, Boston, mounted the first exhibition of early American silver.[125] A copy of this exhibition catalogue was in Gorham's design library, as was nearly every book on the subject of early American silver published in the years following.

Erik Magnussen and European Modernism

The younger Codman's enthusiasm for the Colonial style was shared by American critics and consumers at large but was at odds with stylistic developments abroad, and the general lack of sympathy for Modernist works prevented the United States from participating in the 1925 Exposition Internationale des Arts Décoratifs et Industriels Modernes in Paris. Organized to demonstrate the recovery of French luxury-goods industries from World War I, the dazzling display jolted Gorham and other American manufacturers into the realization that their designs were no longer "modern." In that same year, Gorham president Edmund Mayo hired Erik Magnussen (1884–1961) (fig. 145) as "Designer (special work)"; he apparently worked independently of chief designer Codman. Born in Denmark, Magnussen trained as a sculptor and worked as a chaser in Copenhagen and Berlin before establishing his own silver shop in Copenhagen in 1909. In the 1910s and early 1920s his silver and jewelry were exhibited in Denmark, France, Germany, and Brazil.[126] A 1926 candy dish (fig. 146) and pair of candlesticks (fig. 215) Magnussen designed in 1927 and executed in 1928 demonstrate his grounding in Danish silver design of the first two decades of the twentieth century. At once abstract and organic, their fluted shafts with curved sides, colored stones, subtly hammered surfaces, and curvilinear, beaded brackets reflected silver made by Georg Jensen, Mogens Ballin, and their contemporaries.[127] As the art historian and curator Jewel Stern has pointed out, Gorham may have chosen Magnussen because his Scandinavian Modern style was considered more sympathetic to American taste than avant-garde French, German, or Austrian silver.[128] Contemporary critics admired this style; art critic and art historian Helen Appleton Read wrote approvingly of a group of Modernist dishes and boxes: "Mr. Magnussen's designs, which have won for him an international reputation, not only because of their exquisite craftsmanship, but because of the variation of patterns and their imaginative detail, has [sic], therefore, been an effective means of extending an interest in modern decorative art."[129]

Magnussen was capable of more progressive designs, however, as demonstrated by a compote he designed in 1926 that resembled metalwares by Josef Hoffmann of about 1915.[130] His *Cubic* coffee service of 1927 (figs. 202–4, 217), composed of sharp angles highlighted with oxidized and gilt decoration, was inspired by American and European Cubist painting. The set was accompanied by a small group of other pieces, such as salad servers (fig. 148). Gorham originally intended Magnussen's *Cubic* designs to be put into production, but the sharply divided critical reaction to the coffee service when it was exhibited in New York (fig. 253) led the company to reconsider.[131] In 1928 Gorham introduced Magnussen's *Modern American* hollowware and flatware (figs. 66, 147), which featured simple, geometric forms ornamented only with bands of incised lines and ivory finials. A promotional brochure hailed *Modern American* as "more than just modern—a prophecy," and some critics responded enthusiastically, describing it as "quite in tune with the modern

note" and praising its "forthright honesty."[132] The line was commercially unsuccessful, however, and Magnussen left Gorham in October 1929, working in Chicago and Los Angeles before returning to Denmark in 1939.

Gorham made other ventures into Modernist-style silver. Some were in the French Art Moderne style, including the *Franconia* and *Hunt Club* patterns, as well as some late examples of *Martelé* that featured geometric forms with abstract ornament instead of organic shapes with naturalistic decoration.[133] Others showed Magnussen's influence, such as a covered box with ball feet designed by Charles F. Simms, which Read praised as a Modern object that

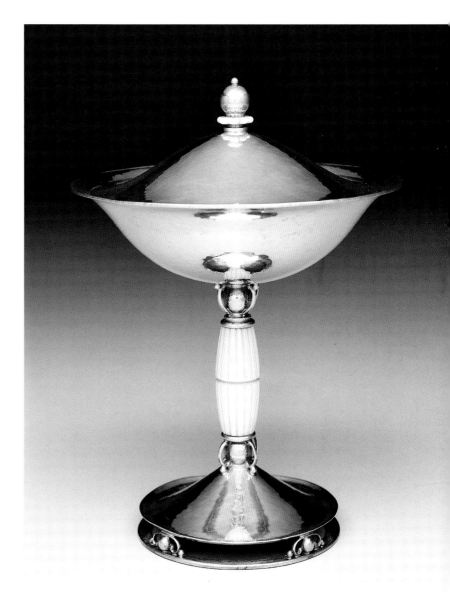

146
Candy Dish, 1926.
Erik Magnussen, designer,
and Spaulding & Co., retailer.
Silver and ivory.
Dallas Museum of Art

"does not require a readjustment of the aesthetic sense to enjoy."[134] Over the next two decades, however, with the strictures of the Great Depression and World War II, the company primarily relied on historical revival styles. *Plymouth* pattern hollowware continued to be offered in catalogues of the 1930s and 1940s; in 1948 *Vogue* featured the pattern with the comment, "Not one piece insists upon a period décor; each has the sociability of excellence."[135] William Codman's 1930 history of silver design omitted any reference to Magnussen's work and dismissed Modernism by stating, "Recently a style so called 'Modern' has been introduced to the public, but it does not appear to have made much headway; and it only remains to be said that the fashion worthy of a place in succession to the best of the

Georgian and Colonial periods has yet to be devised."[136] Perhaps because of Codman's influence, Gorham created nothing of the caliber of the spectacular Art

147
Design for *Modern American* Coffeepot, 1928. Erik Magnussen, designer. Graphite on paper.
RISD Museum

Moderne objects made in the 1930s and 1940s by Tiffany & Co. from the designs by Arthur Leroy Barney, Charles B. Blake, and Oscar Riedener.[137] Codman's retirement in 1938 presumably allowed for the Modernist cocktail service and tea service that Gorham exhibited in the "House of Jewels" at the 1939–40 New York World's Fair; their design has been attributed by Braznell to the German-born and trained Albert Feinauer (1886–1955), who began work at Gorham in 1934.[138]

Organic Designs in the Post–World War II Era

The generation of Gorham designers after World War II, including design director Richard L. Huggins (b. 1929) and staff designers Phillip B. Johnson (1899–1992) and Alexandra Solowij Watkins (b. 1933), embraced the biomorphic, "organic design" style that had been gestating since the early 1940s. These designers also were influenced by the enduring popularity of silver by Georg Jensen; Gorham had made some hollowware

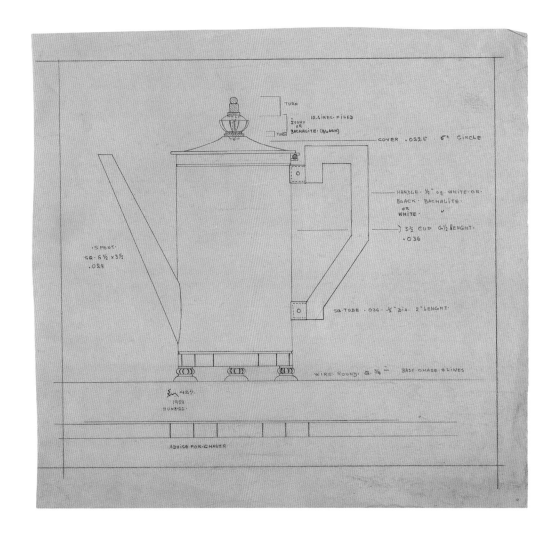

in the 1940s that closely copied earlier Jensen models.[139] As Jewel Stern has observed, the fluid, undecorated shapes of Gorham's *Trend* line of 1952 and *Directional* of 1955, both in sterling, as well as *Modern* of 1959 in electroplate (fig. 68), took inspiration from a variety of media including Eva Zeisel's ceramics and Tommi Parzinger's brass and silver pitchers of 1933 to 1941.[140] The most inspired interpretation of biomorphism at Gorham was the *Circa '70* hollowware (figs. 201, 218, 219) designed in 1958 by Donald H. Colflesh (b. 1932). Colflesh had been hired in 1956 when he graduated from the Pratt Institute in New York; he had also studied in the early 1950s with Frederick A. Miller at the Cleveland Institute of Art.[141] The influence of Miller's concept of "stretching" metal is apparent in the *Circa '70* tea and coffee service, as are the iconic hollowware designs by Henning Koppel for Georg Jensen, most notably his jugs of 1948 and 1952.[142] According to a company brochure, the *Circa '70* line of hollowware was intended to evoke "a feeling of flowing vertical motion [and] the upward look to space," and an internal Gorham newsletter described it as "the forward looking *Circa '70*, a collection whose advanced design illustrated the spirit of the future in sterling."[143] Gorham clearly intended this service as a higher-quality alternative to manufactured silver of the period, using ebony for the handles and finials, lids that were uniquely sized to each vessel, and, most significantly, a design with complex contours that required special, time-consuming fabrication. Unintentionally but fittingly, *Circa '70* was to be the last contemporary hollowware line made by the company.

In more than a century of manufacturing hollowware beginning in 1850, the Gorham Manufacturing Company fostered the careers of a succession of important designers. Charged with creating wares that would give the company a leading share of the market for silver goods, these designers frequently created exceptional examples of American art in silver. In some instances these designs proved too costly to be sustainable in the marketplace, but Gorham's legacy was its perseverance in offering innovative styles that embodied and even transformed American taste. As stated by the company's hollowware catalogue in 1889: "It has been the theory of the Gorham Company that all articles within its sphere of manufacture, however commonplace or humble, could be made beautiful as well as useful; and it has aimed to advance American civilization by observing, in all its work or product, that perfect harmony between purpose, proportion, and ornamentation, which satisfies at once the mind and the eye, and which, by combining the spirit of truth with the spirit of beauty, at once educates and refines."[144]

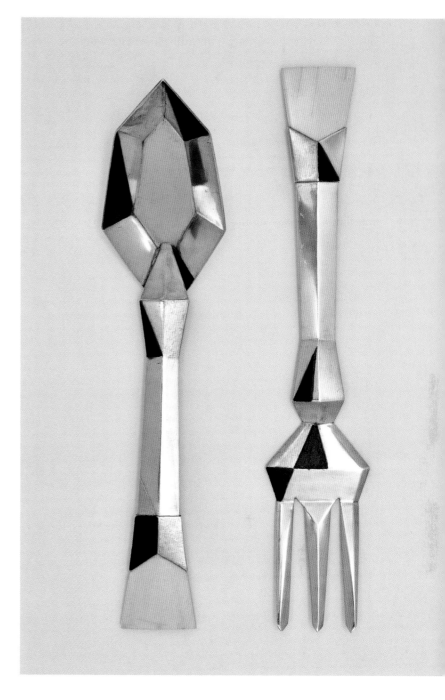

148
Cubic Salad Set, 1927.
Erik Magnussen, designer.
Silver with patinated and
gilt decoration and ivory.
RISD Museum

1 James Parton, "Silver and Silver Plate," *Harper's New Monthly Magazine* 37, no. 220 (September 1868): 447.

2 Charles H. Carpenter Jr., *Gorham Silver, 1831–1981* (New York: Dodd, Mead, 1982), 32.

3 Parton, "Silver and Silver Plate," *Harper's New Monthly Magazine*, 438.

4 John Gorham, autobiography, 1893, Gorham Manufacturing Company Archive, John Hay Library, Brown University, Providence, Rhode Island (hereafter GMCA). See also Samuel Hough, "An Incunabulum of Gorham Silver," *Silver* 26 (May–June 1994): 8–9.

5 Parton, "Silver and Silver Plate," *Harper's New Monthly Magazine*, 438.

6 Barbara McLean Ward and Gerald W. R. Ward, *Silver in American Life: Selections from the Mabel Brady Garvan and other Collections at Yale University* (Boston: David R. Godine, 1979), cat. 79. A salt of this design marked by Gorham & Thurber is illustrated in George Thompkins and Carolyn Thompkins, "A Century of Gorham Salts," *Silver* 19, no. 2 (March–April 1986): 19.

7 Amy Miller Dehan, "An Apt and Noble Gift: Gorham's Rebekah Pitcher," *Gastronomica: The Journal of Food and Culture* 9 (Winter 2010): 14–18. The present location of Vernet's painting, exhibited at the Salon of 1835, is unknown; multiple prints after it were issued beginning in 1834 with an aquatint published in Paris by Goupil et Vibert, *Les Juifs dans l'orientalisme* (Paris: Musée d'Art et d'Histoire de Judaïsme, 2012), 112.

8 A hot-water kettle in this pattern, No. 10, with a flower finial and chased decoration of cartouches enclosing a diaper pattern, was recorded as Model No. 1909, photograph no. 713, in an 1869 photograph book, GMCA.

9 Elaine Draper, "'The Silver King,'" *Silver* 23, no. 2 (March–April 1990): 16–17.

10 Elaine Draper, "George Wilkinson: The Gorham Years," *Silver* 24, no. 2 (March–April 1991): 22–23; see also Charles L. Venable, *Silver in America, 1840–1940: A Century of Splendor* (Dallas and New York: Dallas Museum of Art / Harry N. Abrams, 1994), 49.

11 Charles J. Stillé, *Memorial of the Great Central Fair for the U.S. Sanitary Commission* (Philadelphia: U.S. Sanitary Commission, 1864), 119–20. E. C. Chick, "American Art in Solid Silver," *The Aldine Press: A Typographic Art Journal* 3 (March 1870): 3.

12 See the Lumley, Montefiore, and Hartlepool Testimonials made by Hunt and Roskell of London, illustrated in *The Art-Journal Illustrated Catalogue: The Industry of All Nations, 1851* (London: The Art-Journal, 1851), 57–59; John Culme, *Nineteenth-Century Silver* (London: The Hamlyn Group, 1977), 158–59; *The Art Journal Illustrated Catalogue of the International Exhibition, 1862* (London: J. S. Virtue, 1863), 240.

13 Chick, "American Art in Solid Silver," 3.

14 Deborah Dependahl Waters, "'Silver Ware in Great Perfection': The Precious-Metals Trades in New York City," in Catherine Hoover Voorsanger and John K. Howat, eds., *Art and the Empire City: New York, 1825–1861* (New York: Metropolitan Museum of Art, 2000), 364; John Loring, *Magnificent Tiffany Silver* (New York: Harry N. Abrams, 2001), 6–7, 76–77.

15 Deborah Dependahl Waters, Kristen H. McKinsey, and Gerald W. R. Ward, *Elegant Plate: Three Centuries of Precious Metals in New York City* (New York: Museum of the City of New York, 2000), 2: cat. 322.

16 D. Albert Soeffing, *American Medallion Flatware* (New York: New Books, 1988), 100–101; Parton, "Silver and Silver Plate," *Harper's New Monthly Magazine*, 443.

17 Parton, "Silver and Silver Plate," *Harper's New Monthly Magazine*, 448.

18 *Cassell's Illustrated Exhibitor* (London and New York: Cassell, Petter & Galpin, 1862), 95; Gorham Inventory, List of Assets, 1871, GMCA.

19 J. B. Waring, *Masterpieces of Industrial Art and Sculpture at the International Exhibition* (London: Day & Son, 1863), 1: pl. 10. For examples of French metalwork, see *The Second Empire, 1852–1870: Art in France under Napoleon III* (Philadelphia: Philadelphia Museum of Art, 1978), cat. III–1; Elizabeth Aslin, *French Exhibition Pieces 1844–78* (London: Victoria and Albert Museum, 1973), cat. 12; *Decorative Arts, 1848–1889* (Paris: Réunion des musées nationaux, 1991), 15; Simon Jervis, *Art and Design in Europe and America, 1800–1900* (New York: E. P. Dutton, 1987), 80–81.

20 Waters et al., *Elegant Plate*, 2: cats. 377–78; David Revere McFadden and Mark A. Clark, *Treasures for the Table: Silver from the Chrysler Museum* (New York: Hudson Hills, 1989), cats. 4, 11.

21 Gorham visited Day & Son on September 1, 3, and 7 (John Gorham, diary, April 23–September 23, 1860, GMCA). Among other book purchases he recorded were "6 vols of HC." Books – Florentine Galery [*sic*] & c." on May 30 and books acquired at a store at 400 Oxford Street on June 27 and 30. He recorded buying "some prints from Shop & Childrens Books" in Paris on August 19. Gorham visited the Kensington Design School on May 21, the South Kensington Museum on May 16, 22, 23, and 25, the Louvre and the Musée du Luxembourg on August 19, and an otherwise unspecified "School of Art" in London on September 3. Jones's *Grammar of Ornament*

was recorded in the 1871 inventory of the design library (Gorham Inventory, List of Assets, 1871).

22 "A Great Silver Ware Manufactory," *Scientific American* 6 (June 28, 1862): 408.

23 James Parton, "Among the Workers in Silver," *Atlantic Monthly* 20 (December 1867): 733.

24 Gorham Inventory, List of Assets, 1871.

25 Parton, "Silver and Silver Plate," *Harper's New Monthly Magazine*, 443.

26 Although Carpenter, *Gorham Silver, 1831–1981*, p. 68, states that Pairpoint began working at Gorham in 1868, Samuel Hough records the company's first payment to Pairpoint in November 1869 (Samuel Hough, "Roster of Gorham Craftsmen). The latter date is corroborated by Providence city directories, which list a "Pairepont" living on Jewett Street in 1870; the entry was corrected to Thomas J. Pairpoint, "designer, Gorham M'fg. Co.," at 13 Jewett Street the following year (*The Providence Directory for the Year 1870* [Providence: Sampson, Davenport & Co., 1870], 188; *The Providence Directory for the Year 1871* [Providence: Sampson, Davenport & Co., 1871], 196).

27 Leonard E. Padgett, *Pairpoint Glass* (Des Moines, IA: Wallace-Homestead, 1979), 79.

28 Dorothy T. Rainwater and Judy Redfield, *Encyclopedia of American Silver Manufacturers*, 4th ed. (Atglen, PA: Schiffer, 1998), 240–41. For Morel-Ladeuil, see *Birmingham Gold and Silver, 1773–1973* (Birmingham, UK: City Museum and Art Gallery, 1973), cat. D15 spp.

29 *The Art Journal Illustrated Catalogue of the International Exhibition, 1862* (London: J. S. Virtue, 1863), 151.

30 *The Illustrated Catalogue of the Universal Exhibition: Published with the Art Journal* (London: Virtue and Company, 1868), 203. See also Shirley Bury, "The Source and Influence of Virtuoso Silverwork at International Exhibitions," *The Decorative Arts in the Victorian Period*, Occasional Paper XII (1989), The Society of Antiquaries of London, 38.

31 "Jottings," *Jewelers' Circular and Horological Review* 10 (September 1879): 161.

32 "American Art-Work in Silver," *Art Journal* (New Series) 1 (1875): 373–74; William C. Conant, "The Silver Age," *Scribner's Monthly* 9, no. 2 (December 1874): 200. A full description and history of the Furber service is provided in Elizabeth A. Williams, "Designing a New Mold: The American Silver Industry and Japanese Meiji Metalwork 1876–1893," PhD diss., University of Kansas, 2015, 94–114. Other examples of Pairpoint's style include vase model 1089, which featured large-scale dolphin handles and a figure of a Nereid in high relief, with her head and one of her arms in three dimensions, and oval plaques of Bacchus and a bacchante

33 that adorned a variety of forms, including a pair of model 1331 goblets (photographs nos. 1398, 647, Photograph Book "No. 1," GMCA).

33 The plaque from the *Cellini Vase* was illustrated in Conant, "The Silver Age," 197.

34 Martin Riester, *Ornements du 19me siècle: inventés et dessiné par divers artistes industriels et gravés part Martin Riester* (Paris: Turgis, 1851), n.p.

35 *Illustrated Catalogue of the Universal Exhibition 1868*, 273; see also *The Second Empire 1978*, cat. III–6. The *Education of Achilles Vase* is now in the Musée d'Orsay, Paris; see Marc Bascou, Marie-Madeleine Massé, and Philippe Thiébaut, *Musée d'Orsay: Catalogue sommaire illustré des arts décoratifs* (Paris: Éditions de la Réunion des musées nationaux, 1988), 56.

36 "The Bryant Testimonial Vase," *Art Journal* (New Series) 1 (1875): 147.

37 "The Bryant Testimonial," *Jeweler's Circular and Horological Review* 6 (July 1875): 138.

38 Venable, *Silver in America, 1840–1940*, 158–60.

39 The interpretation of the *Century Vase*'s iconography and the quotations are taken from Alexander Farnum, *The Story of the Century Vase* (Cambridge, MA: Riverside Press, 1878), n.p.

40 Samuel J. Hough, "The Gorham American Shield and The Damascened Plate for the 1889 Paris Exposition," *Silver* 26 (September–October 1994): 12–13; the *American Shield* is now in the Driehaus Collection, Chicago. Hough amplifies and corrects the account of Heller's life and career found in Carpenter, *Gorham Silver*, 121–22. Referring to a 1935 document in the Gorham archives, Carpenter states that Heller received a gold medal from the Paris Salon in 1870, but Heller was not recorded as an artist exhibiting at the Salon in that year or as receiving a medal.

41 *Art Journal Illustrated Catalogue of the International Exhibition, 1862*, p. 229; J.T.B., "Elkington & Co.'s Contributions to the Philadelphia Exhibition," *Birmingham Daily Post*, reprinted in George A. Sala, *Descriptive Essay: Elkington & Company, Philadelphia International Exhibition of 1876* (London: Sutton, Strange and Company, 1876), 30. The *Medusa Shield* appears in a stereograph entitled "Elkington's Repoussé Work" by the Centennial Photographic Company in the collection of the Philadelphia Museum of Art, accession number 1968-20-19. For Willms, see the "Design Since 1824" section of the Elkington & Company website, https://elkingtonandco.com/shop/content/8-designers (accessed January 12, 2018).

42 "The Century Vase," *Jewelers' Circular and Horological Review* 7 (November 1876): 149; Venable, *Silver in America, 1840–1940*, 160.

43 Samuel J. Hough, "The Class of 1870 Gorham Sterling Ice Bowls," *Silver* 22, no. 5 (September–October 1989): 30–32; Robert McCracken Peck, "Icy Embellishments: Arctic Imagery and the Decorative Arts," *Antiques* 171, no. 2 (February 2007): 73–76.

44 James C. McCabe, *The Illustrated History of the Centennial Exhibition* (Philadelphia, Chicago, and St. Louis: National Publishing Company, 1876), 414–15.

45 See Williams, "Designing a New Mold," 58–69, for a discussion of European and Japanese books on Japanese art in the Gorham design library, and ibid., 50–54, for a discussion of Japanese objects used by designers at Tiffany & Co.

46 Carpenter, *Gorham Silver, 1831–1981*, 105.

47 Ellenor M. Alcorn, *English Silver in the Museum of Fine Arts, Boston, Volume II: Silver from 1697 including Irish and Scottish Silver* (Boston: MFA Publications, 2000), 289–91. Additional examples in this style by Elkington & Co. and other British manufacturers are illustrated in Elizabeth Aslin, *The Aesthetic Movement: Prelude to Art Nouveau* (New York and Washington, DC: Frederick A. Praeger, 1969), figs. 89, 90; Stuart Durant and Hannah Oorthuys, *The Aesthetic Movement and the Cult of Japan* (London: The Fine Art Society, 1972), 35–40; Culme, *Nineteenth-Century Silver*, 189.

48 Carpenter, *Gorham Silver*, 103.

49 Katsushika Hokusai, *Hokusai Manga* 4 (Nagoya, JP: Tôhekidô, 1816): 14–15; John Ward, *Motifs for Panel and Other Decoration* (Birmingham, UK: J. Ward, 1881), pls. II, V. The latter publication postdates the Furber service pieces, but this motif can be found in English sources of the 1870s.

50 George Ashwood Audsley, *The Keramic Art of Japan Vol. 1 & 2* (London: Henry Sotheran & Co., 1875), pl. VIII.

51 The tea caddies were recorded as model Nos. 90 and 105, photograph nos. 172 and 173, in Photograph Book "No. 1," GMCA.

52 Tea service, model. No. 1365, photograph no. 74; butter dish, model No. 580, photograph no. 371; dessert sugar and cream, model no. 1445, photograph no. 948; berry set, model nos. 630 and 1295, photograph no. 1893; all in photograph book "No. 4," GMCA.

53 Joe Earle, *Splendors of Meiji: Treasures of Imperial Japan, Masterpieces from the Khalili Collection* (St. Petersburg, FL: Broughton International Publications, 1999), 64–67.

54 Loring, *Magnificent Tiffany Silver*, 30–36; Williams, "Designing a New Mold," 55–56.

55 "Silver in Artistic Forms," *Jewelers' Circular and Horological Review* 11 (November 1880): 212.

56 William P. Hood Jr., John R. Olson, and Charles S. Curb, "That Curious *Cairo* Pattern," *Silver* 34, no. 5 (September–October 2002): 26–27; Williams, "Designing a New Mold," 89–93. Objects made of multimetal at Gorham include cups, model Nos. B.3 and B.8, photograph nos. 1857 and 1851; tea caddy, model No. A.100, photograph no. 1855; salts, model Nos. B.9 and A.99, photograph nos. 1859 and 1860; Photograph Book "No. 1," GMCA.

57 *Gorham Manufacturing Company, Silversmiths*, trade cat. (New York: Gorham Manufacturing Company, 1881), p. 11; *Catalogue of Sterling Silver and Silver Plated Wares of the Gorham M'f'g Company, Including Examples of Their Productions in Other Metals*, trade cat. (New York: Gorham Manufacturing Company, Autumn 1883), 8.

58 Earle, *Splendors of Meiji*, 68, cat. 35.

59 Williams, "Designing a New Mold," 75–76; Akiko Mabuchi et al., *Hokusai and Japonisme* (Tokyo: National Museum of Western Art, 2017), 242–45.

60 Advertisement, *Jewelers' Circular and Horological Review* 10 (October 1878): xi.

61 Williams, "Designing a New Mold," 55–56.

62 "Ornamental Art in America: Silverware," *Jewelers' Circular and Horological Review* 8 (September 1877), as transcribed in *Silver* 23, no. 3 (May–June 1990), 13.

63 David A. Hanks and Jennifer Toher, "Metalwork: An Eclectic Aesthetic," in *In Pursuit of Beauty: Americans and the Aesthetic Movement* (New York: Metropolitan Museum of Art, 1986), 255.

64 Ibid. See also Christopher Dresser, *The Art of Decorative Design* (London: Day and Son, 1862), 82–83, 91–94.

65 F. Edward Hulme, *A Series of Sketches from Nature of Plant Forms* (London: Day and Son, 1863); Carpenter, *Gorham Silver*, 82, notes that this title was in the design library "since the 1860s."

66 Crane's wallpaper and Jeckyll's balustrade were illustrated and described in Walter Smith, *The Masterpieces of the Centennial International Exhibition Illustrated, Volume II: Industrial Art* (Philadelphia: Gebbie & Barrie, 1876), 5, 7, 403, 407. A copy of this publication was in the Gorham design library.

67 Walter Crane, *The Baby's Opera* (London: Frederick Warne & Co., 1877), 37. The 1878 "Little Bo-Peep" plate was recorded as model No. 200 in photograph book "No. 4," GMCA; the 1879 "Little Bo-Peep" child's plate was recorded as model No. B.77, photograph no. 2028 in Photograph Book "No. 1," GMCA.

68 *Jewelers' Circular and Horological Review* 9 (October 1878): 175. The vase in the drawing was made by Gorham and recorded as model A6, photograph no. 1671, in Photograph

Book "No. 1," GMCA. For Walter Wilkinson, see Hough, "Roster of Gorham Craftsmen." In 1883 the *Jewelers' Circular* credited, apparently in error, their new masthead in the same English Aesthetic style to "William" Wilkinson "whose work has done so much to popularize their [Gorham's] goods," (*Jewelers' Circular and Horological Review* 14 [February 1883]: 2). Presumably this reference was to Walter Wilkinson; George Wilkinson did have a son named William (1855–1919), but there is no record of his working for Gorham.

69 Spencer Gordon and Mark McHugh, "Global Exchange: How the Craftsmanship of Two Cultures Met in Gorham's 'Japanese Work' Silver," *Antiques* 185, no. 1 (January–February 2018): 102–9.

70 Williams, "Designing a New Mold," 74–75.

71 A cup with repoussé floral decoration, model No. 49, was recorded in photograph no. 116 in an 1869 photograph book, GMCA; a photograph of a hot-water urn with chinoiserie repoussé chasing was recorded without a model number as a special order for C. R. Smith & Company in photograph no. 566 in another 1869 photograph book, GMCA.

72 *Gorham Mfg. Co. Silversmiths* (New York, October 1880), n.p.

73 *Choice Examples of Sterling Silver Ware: The Productions of the Gorham Mfg. Co., Silversmiths* (New York: Gorham Manufacturing Company, 1889), n.p.

74 The cup, with no model number, was recorded as photograph no. 241 in an 1869 photograph book, GMCA. For German examples, see J. F. Hayward, *Virtuoso Goldsmiths and the Triumph of Mannerism, 1540–1620* (London: Sotheby Parke Bernet, 1976), figs. 178, 413, 415, 515. The Russian cup was illustrated in John H. Buck, *Old Plate, Ecclesiastical, Decorative, and Domestic: Its Makers and Marks* (New York: The Gorham Manufacturing Company, 1888), 110.

75 *Choice Examples of Sterling Silver Ware*, 1889.

76 For Auricular-style silver, see Hayward, *Virtuoso Goldsmiths*, fig. 638; A. L. den Blaauwen, *Nederlands Zilver/Dutch Silver* (The Hague: Staatsuitgeverij, 1979), cat. 36; Jan Rudolph de Lorm, *Amsterdams Goud en Zilver* (Amsterdam: Rijksmuseum, 1999), cats. 11, 14. For Carpeaux, see *The Second Empire* 1978, 213–18. Franz Simm, *Al Fresco: Wandschmuck-mostive in 12 Tuschzeichnungen* (Munich: F.A. Ackermann, 1885).

77 *Catalogue of Sterling Silver and Silver Plated Wares of the Gorham Manufacturing Co., 1831–1981* (New York: Gorham, Autumn 1888). The frontispiece illustration shows the prize cup on its original wood base with silver mounts, now lost; a drawing of the cup also appears in

the frame of the text for the frontispiece. I am grateful to Spencer Gordon and Mark McHugh for information that the *Atalanta* prize cup was exhibited in Chicago.

78 *Choice Examples of Sterling Silver Ware*, 1889, introduction.

79 Recorded as model No. 1633, photograph no. 364 in an 1869 photograph book, GMCA.

80 The urn-shaped "Dessert Sugar & Cream," was recorded as model No. 1955, photograph no. 956 ½, and the three-footed cream pot as model No. A.40, photograph no. 411, all dated 1878, in Photograph Book "No. 4," GMCA. The apple-shaped teapot was recorded as model No. B81, photograph no. 5079, dated 1880, in Photograph Book "Large Photograph Catalogue," GMCA.

81 Recorded with no model number as photograph no. 2800 in Photograph Book "No. 3," GMCA.

82 *Catalogue of Sterling Silver and Silver Plated Wares*, 1888, 109.

83 Buck, *Old Plate*, 123, 135; Venable, *Silver in America, 1840–1940*, 268.

84 Buck, *Old Plate*, 108, 153–54.

85 Carpenter, *Gorham Silver, 1831–1981*, 203–4; L. J. Pristo, *Martelé 950-1000 Fine: Gorham's Art Nouveau Silver* (Phoenix, AZ: Heritage Antiques, 2002), 10.

86 A photograph of the Lamerie-style basin is in the album "Photographs Exhibited at Chicago Columbian Exposition 1893," GMCA; the *Dancers Plaque* is in the collection of the Newark Museum, accession number 2017.4.

87 E.H.E., "Silver at the World's Fair," *New York Times*, September 20, 1893.

88 For German, Dutch, and English examples, see Hayward, *Virtuoso Goldsmiths*, figs. 522, 661; Blaauwen, *Nederlands Zilver/Dutch Silver*, cat. 7; Timothy B. Schroder, *The Art of the European Goldsmith: Silver from the Schroder Collection* (New York: American Federation of Arts, 1983), cat. 33. See also Venable, *Silver in America, 1840–1940*, 155–56.

89 E.H.E., "Silver at the World's Fair."

90 "Gold and Silverware and Jewelry," *Art Amateur* 29 (August 1893): 72.

91 Graham Dry, intro., *Art Noveau Domestic Metalwork from Württembergische Metallwarenfabrik: The English Catalogue 1906* (Woodbridge, UK: Antique Collectors' Club, 1988), 67. This catalogue dates thirteen years after Codman's design, although the centerpiece itself could be an older design.

92 Carpenter, *Gorham Silver, 1831–1981*, 227; Pristo, *Martelé 950-1000 Fine*, 12.

93 Pristo, *Martelé 950-1000 Fine*, 54.

94 Carpenter, *Gorham Silver, 1831–1981*, 233, 237–38; Pristo, *Martelé 950-1000 Fine*, 218.

95 Horace Townsend, "An Artistic Experiment," *The Gorham Manufacturing Company Silversmiths* (New York: Gorham Manufacturing Co., 1900), 33–34.

96 Pristo, *Martelé 950-1000 Fine*, 54–57.

97 Léonce Bénédite et al., *Exposition Universelle de 1900: Les Beaux-Arts et Les Arts Décoratifs* (Paris: Georges Petit, 1900), 486.

98 Evelyn Marie Stuart, "The American Renaissance in Silversmithing" *Fine Arts Journal* 27 (September 1912), 581, as quoted in Venable, *Silver in America, 1840–1940*, 258. For subsequent assessments of *Martelé*, see Carpenter, *Gorham Silver, 1831–1981*, 232; John Webster Keefe and Samuel J. Hough, *Magnificent, Marvelous Martelé: American Art Nouveau Silver* (New Orleans: New Orleans Museum of Art, 2001), 33–49.

99 Alan Crawford, *C. R. Ashbee: Architect, Designer & Romantic Socialist* (New Haven and London: Yale University Press, 1985), 313–18; Annelies Krekel-Aalberse, *Art Nouveau and Art Deco Silver*, trans. Patricia Wardle (New York: Harry N. Abrams, 1989), fig. 4.

100 Yvonne Brunhammer, et al., *Art Nouveau Belgium France* (Houston, TX: Institute for the Arts, Rice University, 1976), 302–3, 314–16; Gabriel P. Weisberg, *Art Nouveau Bing: Paris Style 1900* (New York: Harry N. Abrams, 1986), 148–51; Dedo von Kerssenbrock-Krosigk and Claudia Kanowski, *Modern Art of Metalwork: Bröhan-Museum, State Museum of Art Nouveau, Art Deco and Functionalism (1889–1939), Berlin* (Berlin: Bröhan Museum, 2001), 22–23; Martin Eidelberg, *E. Colonna* (Dayton, OH: Dayton Art Institute, 1983), 12–13.

101 Elizabeth McGooey, ed., *American Silver in the Art Institute of Chicago* (Chicago: Art Institute, 2016), cat. 60; Alcorn, *English Silver in the Museum of Fine Arts*, cat. 201; Wendy Kaplan et al., *The Arts and Crafts Movement in Europe & America: Design for the Modern World* (Los Angeles: Los Angeles County Museum of Art, 2004), figs. 2.16, 2.20; Krekel-Aalberse, *Art Nouveau and Art Deco Silver*, pl. II, fig. 172; John Heskett, *German Design 1870–1918* (New York: Taplinger, 1986), 41–42; Kerssenbrock-Krosigk and Kanowski, *Modern Art of Metalwork*, 196–99, 383; Bascou, Massé, and Thiébaut, *Musée d'Orsay*, 42–43.

102 Keefe and Hough, *Magnificent, Marvelous Martelé*, 173, 291; Pristo, *Martelé 950-1000 Fine*, 24–25.

103 Wendy Kaplan et al., *"The Art that Is Life": The Arts & Crafts Movement in America, 1875–1920* (Boston: Museum of Fine Arts,

1987), 156. For a prototype ewer by Adam van Vianen, see Hayward, *Virtuoso Goldsmiths*, pls. 628–29. Pristo, 220.

104 For example, see Hayward, *Virtuoso Goldsmiths*, fig. 158.

105 Buck, *Old Plate*, fig. 133.

106 The most celebrated image of Daphne being transformed into a laurel tree, certainly well-known to Gorham's designers, is Gianlorenzo Bernini's *Apollo and Daphne* of 1622–25 (Galleria Borghese, Rome).

107 "A Revival of Cellini's Art," *New York Observer*, March 1, 1900. Venable, *Silver in America, 1840–1940*, 258, notes an 1899 promotional article that situated *Martelé* within a long historical tradition.

108 Loring, *Magnificent Tiffany Silver*, 182–89; Venable, *Silver in America, 1840–1940*, 152–53.

109 Carpenter, *Gorham Silver, 1831–1981*, 218; Samuel J. Hough, "Notes from the Gorham Archives," *Silver* 21, no. 4 (July–August 1988): 17.

110 W. Scott Braznell, "Floral Art Nouveau Silver and the Chaser Christopher M. Whalen," *Silver* 47, no. 1 (January–February 2015): 20–27.

111 Ibid., 20–21.

112 Illustrated in an advertisement for Louis Wine Ltd., *Silver* 31, no. 5 (September–October 1999): 8.

113 Keefe and Hough, *Magnificent, Marvelous Martelé*, 22–24; T. Wells, "Clemens Friedell: The Master of the Monogram," *Silver* 35, no. 6 (November–December 2003): 20–22.

114 John S. Holbrook, *Silver for the Dining Room: Selected Periods* (Cambridge, MA: The Gorham Company, 1912), xiii.

115 Examples owned by Morgan are illustrated in Linda Horvitz Roth, ed., *J. Pierpont Morgan, Collector: European Decorative Arts from the Wadsworth Atheneum* (Hartford, CT: Wadsworth Atheneum, 1987), cats. 28, 31, 32.

116 Carpenter, *Gorham Silver, 1831–1981*, 209; Samuel J. Hough, "Chantilly Centennial Studies," *Silver* 28, no. 1 (January–Feburary 1996), 18–21; no. 2, (March–April 1996), 16–18.

117 Samuel J. Hough, "The Gorham Silver Service of Senator Clark," *Silver* 29 (January–February 1997): 18–23.

118 For a Louis XIV tureen made by Claude II Ballin, see Alain Charles Gruber, *Silverware* (New York: Rizzoli, 1982), 139, fig. 181.

119 Holbrook, *Silver for the Dining Room*, 17–18.

120 William Codman, *An Illustrated History of Silverware Design* (Providence: The Gorham Company, 1930), 23.

121 Venable, *Silver in America. 1840–1940*, 228–30, 274–75.

122 John S. Holbrook, *The Art of the Silversmith and Its Development* (New York: The Gorham Co., n.d.), 16, 18.

123 Examples of silver hollowware with fluted, urn-shaped bodies by Paul Revere are illustrated in Beth Carver Wees with Medill Higgins Harvey, *Early American Silver in the Metropolitan Museum of Art* (New York: Metropolitan Museum of Art, 2013), cat. 84; examples by James Musgrave are illustrated in *Philadelphia: Three Centuries of American Art* (Philadelphia: Philadelphia Museum of Art, 1976), cat. 141.

124 *Catalogue of Sterling Silver Ware by the Gorham Manufacturing Co.*, 1906–7, 13-J; *Addenda Catalogue of Sterling Silver Ware by the Gorham Manufacturing Co.*, 1908-9, 136-K.

125 *American Silver in the Work of Seventeenth and Eighteenth Century Silversmiths* (Boston: Museum of Fine Arts, 1906).

126 Carpenter, *Gorham Silver, 1831–1981*, 258.

127 For silver by Jensen and Ballin, see Kerssenbrock-Krosigk and Kanowski *Modern Art of Metalwork*, 36, 63–64.

128 Jewel Stern, *Modernism in American Silver: 20th-Century Design* (New Haven: Yale University Press, and Dallas: Dallas Museum of Art, 2005), 26.

129 Helen Appleton Read, "Twentieth Century Decoration: The Modern Theme Finds a Distinctive Medium in American Silver," *Vogue* 72 (July 1, 1928): 98.

130 Kerssenbrock-Krosigk and Kanowski, *Modern Art of Metalwork*, 531.

131 Reviews are discussed in Venable, *Silver in America, 1840–1940*, 278–80; Stern, *Modernism in American Silver*, 28–30; John Stuart Gordon, *A Modern World: American Design from the Yale University Art Gallery 1920–1950* (New Haven: Yale University Art Gallery, 2011), 57.

132 "Modern American" brochure (New York: Gorham Manufacturing Company, 1928); "American Decorative Art at the Art Center," *Good Furniture* 32 (January 1929): 47, as quoted by Stern, *Modernism in American Silver*, 31–32.

133 Samuel J. Hough, "A Note on the Durgin/Gorham Hunt Club Hollowware," *Silver* 29 (May–June 1997): 24–25; Stern, *Modernism in American Silver*, 86–88; Pristo, *Martelé 950–1000 Fine*, 19–21.

134 Read, "Twentieth Century Decoration," 58. For a similar bowl designed by Simms, see Gordon, *A Modern World*, 41.

135 *Gifts of Silver*, Gorham sales catalogue, October 1939, unp.; *Gifts of Silver*, Gorham sales catalogue, October 1941, unp.; "Sterling Silver . . . to Give," *Vogue* 111 (May 1, 1948): 150–51.

136 Carpenter, *Gorham Silver, 1831–1981*, 256–57; Codman, *An Illustrated History*, 1930, 72.

137 Loring, *Magnificent Tiffany Silver*, 240–47.

138 W. Scott Braznell, "Modern Expression in American Silver: The Designs of the Weimar Émigré Albert Feinauer (1866–1955), *Winterthur Portfolio* 44, no. 4 (December 2010): 289–95.

139 Stern, *Modernism in American Silver*, 143–44.

140 Ibid., 220–27; Gordon, *A Modern World*, 225.

141 Stern, *Modernism in American Silver*, 257.

142 For Miller, see Jeannine Falino, ed., *Crafting Modernism: Midcentury American Art and Design* (New York: Abrams, 2011), 187–88; for Koppel's jugs, see David A. Taylor and Jason W. Lasky, *Georg Jensen Holloware: The Silver Fund Collection* (London: The Silver Fund, 2003), 293, 298.

143 Text is from paper tag accompanying the *Circa '70* service; "Biggest Annual Sales Conference Held; New Designs in All Lines Introduced," *Gorham Perspective* 1 (August–September 1960): 3, GMCA.

144 *Choice Examples of Sterling Silver Ware*, 1889.

GORHAM WORKS
1890s–1900s

149
Whiskey Decanter, 1892.
Silver and glass.
RISD Museum

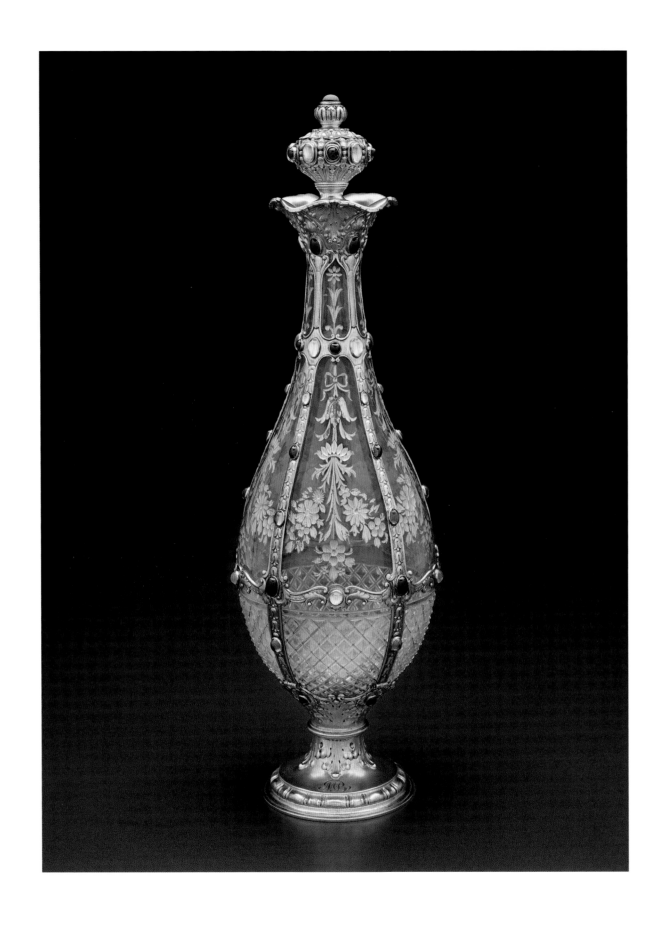

150
Claret Jug, 1893. Silver with gilding,
cut glass, amethysts, garnets, moonstones.
Museum of Fine Arts, Boston

151
Design drawing for a pitcher, ca. 1893.
Gorham Archive, John Hay Library

152
1893 World's Fair Ring, 1892.
Silver.
RISD Museum

153
Wine Pitcher, 1893.
Silver with gilding and glass.
The Nelson-Atkins Museum of Art

154
Sugar Tongs depicting Minerva,
Mythologique pattern, 1894.
Florentin Antoine Heller, designer. Silver.
RISD Museum

155
Apostle Spoons, 1894.
Silver.
RISD Museum

156

Joseph Jefferson Cup, 1895–96.
William Clark Noble, modeler. Silver.
New Orleans Museum of Art

157
Admiral Dewey Cup, 1899.
William Christmas Codman, designer.
Silver with porcelain and oak.
Chicago History Museum

158
Design for the *Admiral Dewey Cup*, 1899.
William Christmas Codman, designer.
Graphite, watercolor, and gouache on paper.
RISD Museum

157

159
Martelé Wine Pitcher, 1900.
William Christmas Codman, designer; Edward Zior,
chaser; J. Hoare & Company, glass manufacturer;
Shreve, Crump & Low, retailer. Silver and glass.
High Museum of Art

160
Design for a *Martelé* Ewer, ca. 1900.
Graphite, watercolor, and gouache on paper.
RISD Museum

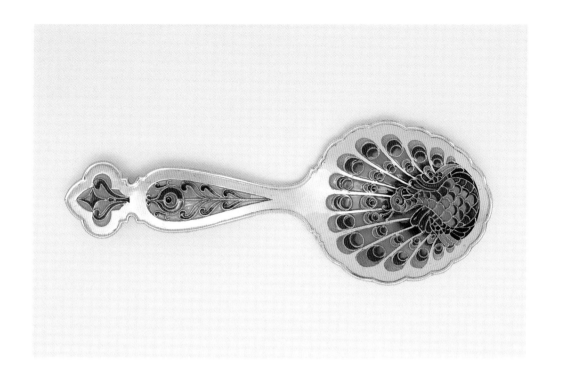

161
Bonbon Spoon, ca. 1893.
Silver with gilding
and plique-à-jour enamel.
RISD Museum

162
Pendant, 1900.
Gold, pearls, frosted green glass,
diamonds, enamel, and rubies.
RISD Museum

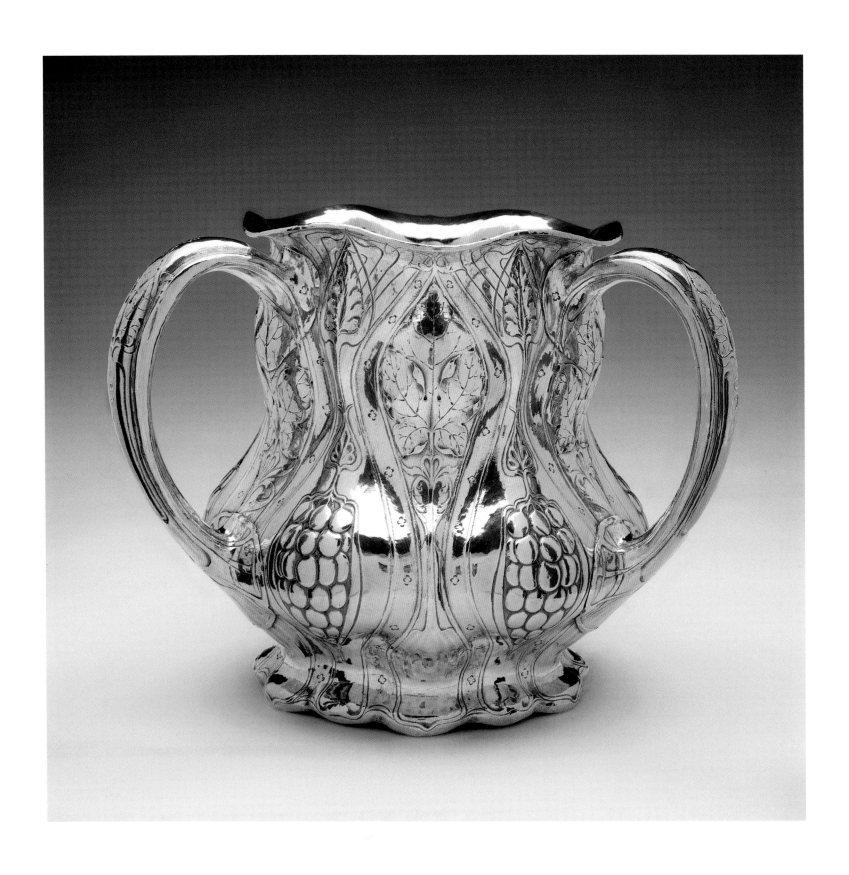

163
Martelé Billings Cup, 1899.
William Christmas Codman, designer; Herbert C. Lloyd,
chaser; Spaulding & Co., retailer. Silver.
RISD Museum

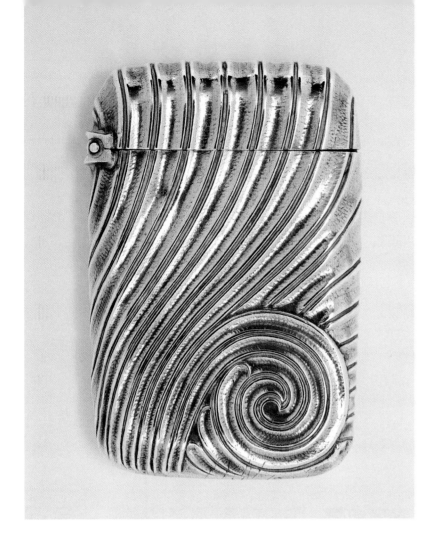

164
Match Safe, ca. 1889.
Silver.
RISD Museum

Elizabeth A. Williams

CREATING GORHAM SILVER

THE MOST PERFECT SYSTEM

Through all the mechanical complications and the various processes of manufacture the object in progress passes, as though regulated by clock work, so related, each to each, as to form a harmonious whole—a single machine, as it were, into which enters the raw material and out of which comes the perfected product.

The Providence Plantations for 250 Years:
An Historical Review of the Foundation, Rise
and Progress of the City of Providence, 1886[1]

The brilliance of a finished piece of silver arrests the eye, its form engages the brain, its weight is pleasing in the hand. Gorham customers have long appreciated the company's wares as the end products of good design, capable of existing for centuries. The successful transformation of a nascent idea in the designer's mind and the manipulation of a bar of silver into a fully realized finished work of Gorham silver was an unseen yet considerable and complex process, relying on the combination of critical thinking, technological ingenuity, aesthetic sensibilities, industrial acumen, and a strong embrace of the possibilities. It was the journey from the conceptual to the physical that realized the company's inventive approach and persevering endeavor to build what was

described in 1871 as "the most perfect system . . . all is in keeping with an artistic idea, and artistic purpose."[2]

Before the 1847 retirement of Jabez Gorham (fig. 4), who founded the company in 1831, spoons, forks, and other smallwares were produced by hand.[3] Powered by a horse plodding in a circle in the basement, the workshop at 12 Steeple Street, Providence, Rhode Island (fig. 5), consisted of a first floor for manufacturing—with an iron safe built into the brickwork—and an attic where the burnishing was done. Working from 5:00 a.m. until 8:00 p.m. with one hour each for breakfast, lunch, and dinner, the employees numbered about fourteen men, most of whom had been there since 1831, and "vacations were unheard of." The business operated in the manner of the era, which Jabez's son, John (fig. 2), described as "the day of the small things," until 1847, when "a material change in the business took place, which, as future events proved was an important factor, if not the one of greatest significance in the formation of the Gorham Manufacturing Company." John Gorham engaged his entrepreneurial aptitude and visionary intuition to initiate a seismic shift in the traditions and scale of New England silver production. As he recounted, "The difficulties of making silverware with jeweler's tools with inadequate room and power had been growing more

165
Gorham casting patterns
from the 1800s in
original drawer, 2018

and more apparent. The old horse had become overloaded; steam power was a necessity. It was evident that if progress was to be made and the business extended, there must be a revolution in the method of manufacturing. Heavy rolls and presses must be had and lathes and tools of much greater magnitude." The plans that John proposed to his father were a radical and risky undertaking: "To erect a large building for the purpose of dividing it with workshops for jewelers and similar trades, supplied with power, was, so far as we knew, an untried experiment. Wise heads predicted failure. To no extent had steam power been hitherto applied to the manufacture of Jewelry or Silverware and—worse than ale, as the first whisperings of steam boilers to be placed in the heart of the city, strong objections were raised."[4]

A 110-by-40-foot lot on Canal Street was leased for one hundred years, and plans to erect a four-story brick building were underway. John negotiated a loan through a broker with Richmond Bullock, president of the Commercial Bank, who advanced sums as the building progressed until the total reached $9,000. While the building was under construction, the broker informed John that no further funds would be furnished. Not one to be deterred, John went directly to Bullock and invited him to the building site so that he "could see for himself what I was doing with his money." Bullock found John down in the basement with the workmen, building a part of the foundation for the fifty-horsepower engine that would power the new building, run under the gangway to power the old building, and reach beyond to power other buildings. Bullock was impressed. John recalled, "I remember his pleased look." The twenty-five hands then employed at Gorham would not yet fill the new building; the idea was to build beyond their current needs, renting both space and power to other businesses—mainly jewelers—until Gorham expanded to capacity. Power was made available to jewelers across the street, such as G. & S. Owen at 9 Steeple Street, by means of underground shafting connected to Gorham's engine.[5] Although Jabez was initially in support of the expansion, he withdrew from the business as the foundations were being laid in the summer of 1847. As sole proprietor, John oversaw the completion of the building in 1848; it soon filled with "good paying clients." This revenue would repay John's debt to Bullock, who came to believe in the enterprise, loaning a total of $17,000 (about $545,000 today).[6] John Gorham's gamble and contribution to the region's manufacturing development would be recognized before the end of the century: "The marvelous development of the Gorham Manufacturing Company is a potent illustration of the great results which competition, enterprise and mechanical genius have wrought in the industries of New England."[7]

With steam power installed, the next key to Gorham's growth and success was John Gorham's procurement of steam-powered machinery specifically engineered for making silver. He traveled to England and France in 1852, seeking Scottish engineer James Hall Nasmyth, who invented the steam hammer, patented in England in 1842.[8] Nasmyth agreed to adapt his steam hammer to power a drop press capable of forming silver flatware in a single mechanized strike, thus eliminating the physical labor of repeatedly raising the drop press. The arrival of this engineering endeavor in Providence not only marked Gorham as the first American silver company with a steam-powered drop press for the purpose of making silver wares but also entrenched the enterprising nature of Gorham into the next century. The company was built and grew upon the effective and profitable combination of systematic processes—both in terms of machinery and business—and original artistic talent. Interrelated ledgers documented inventory, casting and stamping dies, costing records, and silver control; along with photo albums, design drawings, and trade catalogues, they formed a complex network of organizational, promotional, and administrative tools that enabled continual expansion of scale, diversity of product, and technological advancement. An 1892 article recognized the necessity of Gorham's by then well-established modus operandi, stating, "Only the strictest system could push on this enormous amount of labor and conserve the profits."[9]

Gorham's trajectory followed an attitude that silver manufacturers in the United States were primed to surpass those in Europe and would do so by placing the time-honored traditions of silversmithing inherited from Britain within the context of American industrialism. An 1868 article published by *Harper's New Monthly Magazine* clearly described the transformation from the 1830s norm of a shop to that of a manufactory, boldly claiming that "it may be laid down as a rule that whatever branch of manufacture can be profitably carried on in the United States on a great scale, we shall beat the world in it."[10] Continuing on to more specifically address the advancement of the manufacture of silver, the article noted the exponential advantage of the present Gorham manufactory that was "filled with ingenious machinery . . . which multiplies each man's productive power, and increased his ability to produce uniform excellence beyond computation."

By 1860, there were about 150 men employed at the company, two stories had been added to the new building, and John had purchased the estate west of 12 Steeple Street from Jabez, occupying a considerable portion of it. A 156-page 1862 inventory ledger meticulously lists the entire contents of more than thirty rooms filled with machinery, tools, dies, gas fittings and pipes, workbenches, stock materials, and fixtures.[11] By 1875, approximately 450 Gorham employees occupied sixty-nine rooms, and the manufactory had spread to the boundaries of North Main, Steeple, Canal, and Friend Streets in an area reported to be 140 by 200 feet (fig. 10).[12] In the same year, William Conant, a writer for *Scribner's Monthly*, toured the works, claiming, "After walking for half a day, and to complete exhaustion, I was congratulated on having seen a full half of the Gorham Manufacturing Company's establishment!"[13] He breathlessly described a bustling environment of myriad activities:

> In the city of Providence, I have seen under one roof an entire block of buildings filled with shafting and belting from steam-engines of the largest size, connected by steam elevators and pipes throughout, for communication, illuminating and heating gas, air blast, live steam and exhaust steam, water hot, cold, hard and soft; machines of incredible ingenuity and efficacy without number; foundries for casting in iron, brass, silver, gold, and all other metals required; machine shops for every metal, and also for woodwork; blacksmiths' shops, rolling-mills, lathes drills, milling and planing machines; shearing, punching, shaping and embossing machines; lofty shops and ponderous machines for die stamping; large rooms devoted to melting and refining furnaces; to various metallurgical processes; to electro-plating and gilding; to photography; to metal spinning; to finishing by hand and machinery, in more stages, modes and apartments than could be carried away in memory; apartments in long succession, occupied by artist and draughtsmen, some by engravers, some by chasers, some by embossers, some by die engravers, some by dies hardeners, some by tool makers, some by weighters and packers, some by fancy case makers in wood, morocco, velvet.[14]

By the time of Conant's visit, most Gorham employees specialized in different skills and processes, each working at a particular location within the facilities where the necessary equipment and resources for that task were housed. Although John Gorham hired skilled European silversmiths, the majority of his employees were Americans trained in specific silversmithing skills. An 1879 account of this division of labor notes at least twelve separate trades in which Gorham apprentices were trained.[15] One room, however, launched the processes for all that would follow.

An early history of Gorham states that the "informing soul of all this beautiful labor dwells in the Designing Room."[16] The belief in the importance of a design library was already apparent in John Gorham's thoughts as he embarked on his second trip to Europe in 1860. Multiple pages of his diary from the trip note his activities of "buying more books . . . purchasing nick nacks [*sic*] . . . selecting bronzes all day."[17] The listing in the 1862 inventory ledger notes that more than thirty books, folios, prints, plaster casts, bisques, crockery, stoneware, photographs, silver models, and electroplates found their way to "Wilkinson's Room," also known as the Design Room, a suite occupied by George Wilkinson (fig. 15), the company's head designer, who had trained in Birmingham, England.[18]

On May 16, 1860, John Gorham met Giovanni Ferdinando Franchi at the South Kensington Museum in London, where Franchi held the title of electrotypist, to purchase examples of Franchi's electrotypes of renowned

166
Design drawing,
Pattern 170 Coffeepot, ca. 1869.
Gorham Archive,
John Hay Library

metalworks from various cultures and time periods in the museum's collections.[19] Underscoring the era's belief that reproduction electrotypes and plaster casts could serve as effective teaching tools, improving the public's taste, John felt they could also be of great service at the factory, "educating our American workmen."[20] After obtaining "a mass of material which formed the nucleus of the present Museum of the Company," John Gorham continued to expand the collection, realizing "that to make a success . . . we must have the best examples of what has been accomplished in other countries where the highest talents in Silver and Metal have encouraged for long periods of time."[21]

Although the ability to simply reproduce a model was possible, Gorham was, by the 1860s, already recognized for their influence on taste and originality in design, and finding "the public taste responsive to their own . . . whatever the Designing Room at Providence approves wins prompt applause."[22] The first step in Gorham's process of transforming a new idea into a physical object was often worked out by the designer through a series of drawings that progressively achieved greater levels of refinement and specificity

of construction. An 1871 *Providence Journal* article notes that these drawings, often executed on Bristol board, were not "mere sketches," but illustrated individual objects "finished to the minutest detail, and in some cases colored."[23] A group of drawings on board, some stamped November 1, 1869, includes a coffeepot (fig. 166) with an elegantly looped handle ornamented with foliage and topped with a butterfly finial. Suggesting that the insect had momentarily alighted upon the lid, the naturalistic character of the rendering is countered by the detailed precision with which the coffeepot is drawn. A border, identified as No. 5, is applied to the vessel's body, sketched with a hint of the pattern's foliated design. Other numbers identify the base to be attached to the body, as well as the pattern number and object type: No. 170 Coffee. Comparing the drawing with a No. 170 tea service (fig. 167) substantiates the successful translation from the designer's intent to the completed product.

The physical production of silver wares of any type also relies on the material itself. Initially American silver firms, including Gorham, used coin silver, a

167
Tea Service, 1860.
Silver with gilding.
RISD Museum

standard of 90 percent silver alloyed with 10 percent copper. In 1868, Gorham adopted the British sterling standard of 92.5 percent silver, alloyed with 7.5 percent copper, as most companies had by the late 1860s. Foreign coins from South and Central America, American dollars and half dollars minted from newly discovered mines such as the Comstock Lode in Nevada, and bricks of pure silver and gold were purchased in New York from precious-metal trading firms on Wall Street, where "a long row of large, smooth kegs of Mexican or Peruvian dollars rough from the mint" were counted by a line of young gentlemen, and "little trays full of doubloons, half-doubloons, and various other kinds of gold coin" could be observed.[24]

Upon arriving at Steeple Street, the metals were weighed; coins were torn apart and tossed together in a mass to ferret out counterfeits by noting how the metal twisted and the sound it made as it fell onto the pile. In the melting room, the broken coins were mixed in crucibles with pure silver to achieve a sterling standard, which was regularly confirmed by the testing of ingots by the United States Assay Office on Wall Street. The melter carefully gauged the silver's temperature by appearance and then, at precisely the right degree, poured the molten metal into wide bars or thinner bars known as skillets. In about 1870, 200 to 400 ounces of silver by weight were melted each day, although approximately three tons of silver may have been in various states of production throughout the facility.[25]

The silver bars were then rolled flat into sheets, a process that could require several passes to achieve the desired uniform thickness. Many production processes, including rolling, required that the silver be annealed, or heated, to restore its malleability between treatments. The flattened silver was cut into various shapes: strips, sheets, or disks. These elements were shaped using a lathe or steel dies, a two-part block or roll of steel into which a pattern had been cut or "sunk." Dies were used with machinery that forced the silver into the desired shape or pattern. Production essentially split into two paths: one for flatware, individual utensils, and serving utensils, and another for hollowware vessels and decorative wares.

The No. 170 teapot is composed of a dozen parts, and its creation required approximately the same number of steps and processes.[26] First, a worker formed the top and bottom of the hollowware body by using blunt tools to press a sheet of silver against a shaped wood form, known as a chuck, as it spun on a spinning lathe. To form vessels with openings narrower than their bodies, such as the teapot, sectional chucks were devised of multiple parts fastened to a core, or

key, that fell into easily removable pieces when the key was removed. During the spinning process, the silver was annealed an additional four or five times. The spout and circular handles were cast as two halves in iron dies and soldered together; the leaves were cast separately and soldered to the handles.[27] Vessels meant to hold hot liquids required ivory insulators that were skillfully cut, inserted, and pinned into the handles. The butterfly finial on the lid was cast as a single piece and carefully attached to the lid with minute amounts of solder on each of the six legs. The two parts of the vessel's body were painstakingly fit together and the seam covered by a decorative border created by passing the metal through small patterned rollers. An engraver applied the circular garlanded medallion and the monogram, and the bands of tightly spaced geometric patterning were achieved by engine-turned engraving, also known as guilloche, a process conducted on another type of lathe.[28] The lid was hinged and attached, the foot ring was attached, and the handle and spout were soldered to the engraved body. Finally, the teapot was finished and polished in a process of successive steps.

Free of identifying numbers, a polychrome design drawing (fig. 169) depicting one of a pair of unique fruit stands (fig. 168) from the Furber service serves as a conceptual drawing, working through the composition of the parts and indicating the subtle shading of the silver from white highlights to dark contrasts, the elements that were to be gilded, and the sheen of the metals. The original drawing shows a fox functioning as a sort of foot, one paw raised to bat down a bunch of plump golden grapes that adorns one end of the vessel. The finished work features two foxes facing front and back in the middle of the bowl, entwined in a more complex arrangement of vines laden with grapes. Unburdened by the bowl's weight, they spring forth in motion, their tails aloft. The vessel's female figure now rests on a substantial volute of silver that elegantly echoes the bending branches, rather than balancing precariously on an extended back foot with toes barely making contact with the vine. The drawing's diaphanous textile is missing in the finished work, although the figure's connected thumbs and index fingers continue to suggest her intention to prevent the now-absent material from floating away. Illustrating the creative process from imagined to material, the drawing creates an elegant, animated mise-en-scène with a poised tension between elements that ultimately may not have been technically feasible when translated to precious metals, thus precipitating revisions that resolved practical issues while maintaining the overall aesthetic vision.

The depiction of metal selections and finishes also underwent revisions from the drawing to the finished works. The

168
Pair of
Fruit Stands,
1871. Silver
with gilding.
RISD Museum

169
Presentation drawing,
Furber Fruit
Stand, ca. 1871.
Gorham Archive,
John Hay Library

Williams

gilding, which in the rendering adorned only the tantalizing grapes of the fox's desire, now covers the entire undercarriage of vines, both foxes, and the plentiful clusters of grapes. The mate more closely follows the color scheme of the design drawing with two golden foxes, who must settle for silver grapes. The differentiating hints of the metals' sheen, softness, and texture in the drawing are dramatically realized in the completed works. The drawing's washes of color and tone were translated into their metallic equivalents, the drawing implements replaced by tools and treatments applicable to three-dimensional realizations. The highly polished silver undersides of the bowls reflect the sinuous entanglement of branches cast with naturalistic bark and leaves with softly stippled surfaces contrasting under a network of veins polished smooth and shiny (fig. 69). The foxes' grisaille fur bristles into finely detailed shaggy coats of gold (fig. 41), covering a perceived physicality of the animals' taut muscles and tendons. Many pieces in the Furber service incorporate gilded areas, often in a satin finish, achieved by acid etching of the silver's surface to create an overall softly textured surface. This interplay of gilding and sterling served to aesthetically harmonize the numerous forms of large services, especially those such as the Furber service, which incorporated multiple stylistic characteristics and were collected over a period of time.

The fruit stands' gilded surfaces were achieved by electro-gilding, a process by which the silver object is placed in a solution containing gold, through which an electrical current is passed, causing a layer of gold to adhere to the silver's surface.[29] The longer the object was left in the solution, the thicker the layer of gold. Although Gorham did not begin commercially producing electroplated silver until 1863, the 1862 ledger lists "gilding apparatus," including connecting wires, copper racks for holding the objects in the solution, and ten quarts of "#1 Solution containing 23 40/100 grs. gold per qt."[30] As described in James Napier's *A Manual of Electro-Metallurgy: The Application of the Art to Manufacturing Processes*, a publication in Gorham's library, instructions for electro-gilding state that the silver must be cleaned, scratched with a metal brush, and immersed in the gold solution multiple times, brushing in between each."[31] Previous to electro-gilding, mercury gilding, also known as fire gilding, was employed. In that process, a mixture of gold and mercury was applied to an article and heated, causing the mercury to dissipate. Unfortunately, mercury volatilized by the heat was inhaled and absorbed by the silversmiths, the effect of which was "most pernicious, and destructive to human life.... Paralysis is common

170
Stamped borders in
Gorham Old S Book, 1885.
Gorham Archive,
John Hay Library

among them and the average of their lives is very short."[32]

Though less toxic than mercury gilding, electro-gilding presented significant health concerns. Napier dedicated attention to this matter, stating that "every new trade, or operation gives rise to a new disease." He urges those engaged in the electroplating business to carry out the practice in "lofty well-ventilated rooms," lest the chemicals cause "a benumbing sensation in the head, with pains ... shooting along the brow."[33] Gorham had clearly already taken heed, providing what were described as light, clean, and airy workrooms. A Battery Room existed by 1862, taking the precaution of placing the battery used for electro-gilding in another room. In accordance with Napier's instructions, the connecting rods were brought from the battery to the vats, so that Gorham's workmen were spared inhaling the hydrogen gas given off by the arsenic zincs.[34]

Exemplifying Gorham's frequent incorporation of silver and gilded stamped borders, the more than 2-foot-tall

171
Miniature cast of the
Parthenon frieze, 1820.
John Henning I, artist. Plaster.
RISD Museum

epergne (figs. 73, 74) and the nearly
3-foot-tall pair of candelabra (fig. 81)
from the Furber service represent
in majestic form an interest in
Renaissance Revival design and
showy centerpieces overflowing with fruits and flowers to
adorn the table. Designed by Thomas J. Pairpoint, this
ensemble, as well as the three accompanying silver and gilded
plateaus, are a considered amalgamation of classical motifs
infused with a strong aspect of Victorian eclecticism. Of
particular interest are the 2-inch-high stamped decorative

borders of the plateaus and the candelabra, a reduced-scale
replica of the fifth-century B.C.E. Parthenon frieze, featuring
the Panathenaic procession celebrated every fourth year
on the occasion of Athena's birthday. Like the small border
applied to the No. 170 coffeepot, this border, identified as
No. 1265 in the company's photo album (fig. 170), was one
of many patterns in an ever-expanding repertoire designed
by the company. Produced in varying
widths and styles, the stamped borders
could be applied to almost any vessel
in nearly innumerable ways. Phidias, who

172
Candelabrum (detail),
1879. Silver with gilding.
RISD Museum

is believed to have been the sculptor of the original frieze, chose which aspects of the celebration to depict, as did Pairpoint, who drew selective imagery from the north and west Parthenon facades.

The source for Gorham's reduced Parthenon frieze replica was a set of plaster casts made by the Scottish sculptor John Henning I (1771–1851), who gained consent to draw the marbles from Thomas Bruce, seventh Earl of Elgin and former British ambassador.[35] Henning then carved the frieze in reverse in a 1:20 ratio in slate, from which multiple plaster casts were made and sold in sets, comprising thirty-six sections over 24 feet long in total.[36] The Parthenon frieze casts were often sold together with the sculptor's other important casts, including portrait medallions and plaques after the Raphael cartoons. Gorham's 1862 inventory lists "Elgin casts" in the rooms of George Wilkinson, along with medallion plaster casts and "Cartoons from Raphael."[37] A comparison of the plaster casts (fig. 171) to the plateau friezes clearly confirms Henning's edition as the design source, with figural spacing and breaks from one cast to the next faithfully replicated in the silver.

The Furber service plateaus, one large and two smaller, achieve a lively progression of figures that go around clockwise, handily turning the corners in continual movement, replicating the Parthenon. The largest plateau features a twice-repeated combination of six plaster-cast plaques of the north facade, with the fifth and sixth plaques illustrated in a Gorham photo album. Accurate in their sequence to the ancient model, they depict a tightly packed cavalcade of more than fifty riders and horses rhythmically organized in overlapping groups. The two smaller plateaus combine four plaster-cast plaques that are also repeated twice as they move clockwise around the perimeter. Juxtaposing passages from both the north and west facades, the figures master rearing horses and maneuver horse-drawn chariots. The bases of the candelabra are ornamented with imagery from the north and west facades, one following the cavalcade model (fig. 172) and the other utilizing less compact sections of the charioteers. Pairpoint's choice of balancing the ancient sequences with original sequences evidences an intentional design choice, offering a variety of views for diners sitting in front of these three works, which undoubtedly were often placed contiguously on the table to grand effect.

Just as a repertoire of stamped borders was applied to Gorham's myriad forms, cast elements were also designed and made for repeat use, at the ready to become one part of many that composed a piece of silver. Solid-silver components such as feet, handles, finials, and decorative elements were

designed and modeled and then made by pouring molten metal into a mold. Over many decades, Gorham workers made hundreds of thousands of bronze casting patterns (figs. 105, 165), the positive three-dimensional master models from which negative molds can be made and used to cast positive models in silver or other metals. Still extant, hundreds of large wood drawers, filled with twelve thousand pounds of solid-bronze casting patterns, reveal an important aspect of the company's ability to create new wares by combining existing elements.[38] Gorham's enormous inventory of casting patterns was managed by a series of die ledgers; there are five extant ledgers dating from 1887 to 1943.[39] Each casting pattern is stamped or tabbed with a number that was listed with its corresponding drawer number and often the model number of the object for which it was made. An example is 4886, a winged figure with a human upper body and foliate lower body (fig. 173), which was used on eighteen Furber service vessels, including soup, gravy, oyster, and sauce tureens (fig. 78). In the 1887–90 Ledger No. 1, the casting pattern is listed as "bas relief," followed by four more casting patterns of the same description, presumably of other sizes scaled to the range of vessel sizes. Beside the description is the number 190, the model number for the series of tureens. Gorham silversmiths used the ledgers to locate desired casting patterns, putting a card in the drawer noting the part that they had removed for use. These figures, listed with a location of drawer

173
Sauceboat (detail),
1873. Silver.
RISD Museum

312, tray 6, were found in the correct drawer nearly a century and a half after the works were made (fig. 165).

The arrival of the Aesthetic movement saw Gorham silversmiths shifting away from classical sources and increasingly using Asian aesthetics and techniques. The display of Japanese wares at the 1876 Centennial International Exhibition held in Philadelphia fueled the mania in the United States for Japanese design, which played a significant part in the development of the American Aesthetic movement, spanning the 1870s to the early 1890s. For the nineteenth-century Western audience, mixing precious silver and gold with base metals such as copper, iron, bronze, and steel initially reduced the value of the object. Whereas the amount of labor was not completely dismissed, often the significance and importance of the artistic merit were not sufficiently factored into the retail price of metalwork in Europe or America. The British designer Christopher Dresser, the first Western designer to visit Japan, determined, "The Japanese are the only perfect metal-workers which the world has yet produced, for they are the only people who do not think of the material, and regard the effect produced as of greater moment than the metal employed. To them, iron, zinc, bismuth, gold, silver, and copper, are only so many materials with which things of beauty may be produced, and the one is as

acceptable as the other, if perfect appropriateness is seen in the application of the material, and if the result produced be satisfactory and beautiful."[40]

To American silver companies, the alloys, coloring, and patination of metals developed over the centuries by Japanese metalworkers were almost as revelatory as Japanese imagery. Brilliantly colored metals soon made their way into American creations, which were compared to metallic paintings by 1879: "The introduction of a new metal or alloy susceptible of assuming almost any color give to the silversmith a palette only less varied than belongs to the painter and makes it possible to emulate not only the forms of nature in this class of decoration, but the many hues as well."[41] In addition to appliqués of bronze, copper, brass, silver, gold, and alloys inspired by Japanese wares, Gorham began experimenting with patinated and oxidized surfaces and textured surfaces achieved through chasing and traditionally hammered metalwork.

Several important Furber service pieces featuring a traditional interplay of silver and gilded surfaces were shown in Gorham's pavilion at the 1876 Centennial International Exhibition, but shortly thereafter a shift embracing Asian metallurgy became manifest in the service. An 1878 Furber service gilded-silver water set (fig. 102) comprising a pitcher, two cups, and a tray was decorated with butterflies, dragonflies, turtles, and fish in the manner of Katsushika Hokusai's *Manga*. A year later, three twenty-four-piece sets of individual salts (fig. 122), pepper shakers (fig. 174), and butter dishes (figs. 123, 175) brought an expanded spectrum of metals into the mix. Combinations of yellow gold, rose gold, and silver form a palette of metallic colors used for geometric borders and textures punctuated with naturalistic elements that effortlessly turn the corners of the four-sided salts and pepper shakers. A graceful pine branch takes a downward diagonal direction, eventually leveling to form a welcoming perch for a bird.

An untitled album of Gorham metallurgical formulas and processes gathered from the late nineteenth to the early twentieth century lists compositions for gold ranging from 14K to 22K, including bright gold, Roman gold, white gold, green gold, and rose gold.[42] These gold tones were achieved through immersion in multiple different gold solutions, mixed to the formulas' specifications. For the salts with yellow gold, rose gold, and silver, all areas except those to be gilded were masked with a nonconductive stopping-off varnish that prevented the formation of electrolytic deposits. Each gilding color required a different

174
Pepper Shaker, 1879.
Silver with gilding.
RISD Museum

application of the stopping-off varnish, with a separate bath for each gilding color. Here, the silver areas were kept varnished throughout the gilding process; rose-gold and yellow-gold areas were each masked off once. An ice cream plate (fig. 83) in the Furber service featuring rose-gold strawberries, green-gold foliage and cherries, and silver strawberry flowers on a yellow-satin-gold ground therefore necessitated three maskings and immersions.

Flatware was similarly gilded in multiple tones, as seen with the Furber *Eglantine* berry spoons, and ice cream spoons, both with cast handles. Tantalizing plump fruits contrast with one another in yellow gold, rose gold, and silver hues, with several of the ice cream spoons featuring ripe berries accentuated with dark oxidation for emphasis (fig. 52). As described in the formula and process book, entire objects were immersed in oxidizing solutions "until color suits" or the solution was applied with a brush to particular areas. The oxidation could be applied cold or heated for more lasting effects.

Gorham workers translated subtle two-dimensional shading into three-dimensional texturing using chasing and engraving. The twenty-four butter dishes from the Furber service are small studies of Japanese textures such as *neko-gaki*

(cat scratches), *amida yasurime* (radiating lines), *tsuchime* (hammer marks), *shigure yasuri* (vertical file marks emulating falling rain), *yasuri* (fine vertical file marks) and *ishime ji* (rough surface tooled with a punch resembling stone).[43] One of the dishes (fig. 175) centers a silver and gilded butterfly on a bed of deep, loosely overlapping horizontal gouges, framed by circular scallops and a border of imprecisely arranged triangular shapes. Whereas a similar treatment for all the various patterns is plausible, a close look at the back of the dish reveals that the triangles and horizontal gouges were individually chased into the dish and thus can be seen on the reverse, while the remainder of the decorations were engraved, a process that removes metal from the surface, but does not impress the metal so as to be shadowed on the backside.

In addition to using a variety of textures on a single piece, Gorham silversmiths also chose to use a single texture as a contrasting decorative ground on which to apply mixed-metal ornamentation. By the late 1870s, Gorham designers began to make relief and fully three-dimensional replications of specific *Manga* images in silver, copper, and bronze. Positive casting patterns in lead or the metal of the chosen motif were made by hand, then appliqués were

176
Pitcher, 1879.
Silver with gilding and
copper. Museum of
Fine Arts, Houston

cast and soldered on to the hollowware. This style is found on a four-sided footed vase (fig. 93) made in 1880; chasing marks can be seen as clearly on the exterior as the interior. The vase is decorated with cast-copper appliqués of a fork-plumed bird flying over a grassy mound, and two decorative circular medallions (fig. 105) have expertly "let in" to the vessel's surface, a process that involves cutting circles the same size as the medallions and precisely fitting and soldering the pieces in the holes. The vase is completed with a copper rooster and hen standing on a mound of silver granulations and a brass butterfly floating above. The rooster and hen bear a marked similarity to an overlapped pair surrounded with chicks depicted in volume 15 of *Manga* (fig. 92), where they are one of four framed images of birds on a two-page spread.

In the same vein, the *Four Seasons Pitcher* (fig. 176), an important example of Gorham's trompe l'oeil work, represents a pivotal time in the company's design legacy, as it continued to develop its own version of mixed-metal works in response to the Aesthetic movement. The realistic copper cherries with gold-washed silver leaves and the handle formed as a branch not only characterize the company's deft skill

in fashioning realistic creations of nature but also mark the introduction of copper as a sculptural material beyond molded appliqués. Other examples of trompe l'oeil include salad servers (fig. 94) fashioned as gilded oyster shells lashed to bamboo handles, and a tea caddy seemingly covered with a cloth tied with a bow (fig. 108).

In 1881, Gorham introduced a line of copper-bodied wares (fig. 177) that featured a range of color tones, including a red lacquer-like patina, and metal appliqués, many of which had been oxidized. The "Turkish" coffeepots (fig. 91) were often finished with a rich, deep reddish-brown glossy patina, often referred to as "red copper." A reporter for the *Jewelers' Circular and Horological Review* described the line in 1882: "Copper predominates, . . . the colors are dark warm reds of finest polish, mellowing into yellowish browns; scales and shadings . . . wine tinted. . . in warmest red tints, [with] . . . the highest polish." This finish was typically achieved by heating the copper to produce a thin film of red-brown cuprous oxide on the surface, which was then polished to a lustrous glaze and immersed in a solution to create an even color over the entire object.[44] Often referred to as the *Royal-Copper* finish since the 1870s, metallurgy manuals note that a final polish with a paste of rouge powder achieves an "excellent enamel lustre surface."[45] Determining Gorham's finish process for copper has been elusive, but included in the company's formula and processes album are two cards for "Royal Copper Finish," pasted on to the same page, each calling for birch extract and water to be used as the coloring solution into which the heated copper was to be immersed.[46] On the following page is a typewritten letter by Rupert A. Nock, a London silversmith working at Gorham from 1896 to 1905, describing a nineteenth-century process by which a vessel was heated then immersed for ten to thirty-five seconds—or until the depth of color required had been reached—in a solution of saltpeter crystals (potassium nitrate) that liquefied when heated to a dull red.[47]

In a similar departure from the expected use of silver, in 1883 Gorham experimented with a line of iron hollowware with Japanesque silver appliqués, known as *Banko Iron Ware*. The bodies were patinated with a deep red-brown texture and often accented with metal granulations of silver and copper, appearing to be randomly sprinkled on the surface or clustered to form mounds on which figures stood or palm or gnarled pine trees sprang. Much in the same way as the silver and copper vessels, silver appliqués of robed Japanese figures, fish, crabs, flowering prunus branches, insects, birds, and dragons in the manner of Hokusai explore the textured surfaces with lively animation. The line featured at least thirty-eight pieces, including vases, bonbon boxes, and card boxes, as well as a stand and four differing toddy kettles fashioned as traditional iron sake kettles with the characteristic straight tubular spout and swinging bail handle.[48] The No. 22 toddy kettle (fig. 178) heightened the globular aspect of the traditional form, inspiring Gorham designers to accentuate the circularity with a three-dimensional dragon whose body had to be painstakingly shaped to hug the curves. Underscoring the era's aesthetic association of smoking with the customs of Eastern cultures, pieces of *Banko Iron Ware* included cigar trays (some with lighters), cigarette cases, match boxes and vases, ashtrays, and tobacco bowls and jars.

Gorham designers also became intrigued by a labor-intensive Japanese metalworking process known as *mokume-gane*, which produced mixed-metal works comparable in appearance to burled wood grain. In this technique, alternating layers of different metals are fused together in a billet, or small ingot of metal, then subjected to filing, gouging, and carving to purposely create deformations and irregularity.[49] As the billet is hammered into a thin sheet, the wood grain pattern emerges. By varying the metal type and alloy formulations and manipulating the deformation and hammering processes, myriad color palettes, patterns, and sheens can be created. After first encountering *mokume-gane* at the 1876 Centennial International Exhibition in Philadelphia, Gorham experimented with adapting the process, creating hybrid versions of this

mixed-metal alloy technique. Instead of laminating sheets of metal together to be manipulated into a pattern, the company's designers randomly scattered thin fragments of metals such as copper and brass onto sheets of silver that were then heated to soften and partially fuse the metals.[50] Next, the sheets were rolled pursuant to the degree of textures desired. These sheets were shaped to form vessels, used as decorative elements on vessels, or transformed into flatware handles.

One of the most significant pieces of Gorham's *mokume-gane*, an 1879 vase (figs. 104, 180) decorated with the samurai warrior from the fifteenth volume of Hokusai's *Manga* (fig. 179), was made for Bailey, Banks & Biddle, a Philadelphia retailing firm, underscoring the degree to which the 1876 Centennial International Exhibition's display of Japanese *mokume-gane* impacted the local market.[51] The fissures between the vase's partially fused metals create a textural complexity absent in traditional *mokume-gane*. Debuting in May 1879, a flatware line known as *Curio* featured handles made from blanks of the fused material that were then subjected to the great force of the drop press.[52] *Curio* was not a full-line pattern; Gorham's costing ledger lists thirty-one pieces that were offered. Similar to Gorham's *Japanese* flatware pattern, the bowls of *Curio* spoons and ladles were often engraved with Japanesque designs, and many handles (fig. 181) feature cast-appliqué Japanesque decorations, including cranes, birds, bamboo, flowers, foliage, and geometric patterns. The costing records reveal

177
Cigar Lighter, ca. 1900.
Copper with mixed metals.
RISD Museum

chasers, who had been producing extraordinary repoussé chased work since the 1850s. Gorham's chasers were some of the most skilled silversmiths in the field, commanding the highest pay for years of training and experience. In 1862, the Chasing Room provided 70 feet of workbenches and fourteen stools at which the chasers sat "in rows, each with a piece of plate under treatment, filled with hardened pitch to facilitate its ornament."[54] By 1892, the number of chasers neared one hundred; they continued to sit in long corridors "where the full light from long windows fell upon their work" (fig. 182).[55]

Repoussé is a French word meaning to push up; the word *chasing* derives from the French word *chasser*, which means to drive out or chase around. Dating from antiquity, the technique of repoussé chasing describes two processes: one that pushes the basic decorative design from the inside outward and another that entails the refinement of that design on the vessel's exterior. The two processes are used in conjunction, each requiring great skill, patience, and expertise. For the repoussé work, workers placed vessels on a curved tool with a domed beak, called a snarling iron. The other end of the snarling iron was held in a vice as the chaser hit the shank of the

the prohibitive expense associated with producing this complicated and labor-intensive pattern. By 1880 the pattern was absent from the company's catalogues.[53]

The final phase of Gorham's adaptation of the Japanesque is found in a series of silver hollowware formed of intricate repoussé-worked patterns roiling with waves, fish, and other sea creatures. The style included one of the most famous Hokusai images—*The Great Wave Off Kanagawa (Kanagawa oki name ura)*, or more simply, *The Great Wave*, from the artist's ukiyo-e print series *Thirty-Six Views of Mount Fuji*. Enormous azure waves stacked upon one another and ending in frothy white hooks punish three small boats while the majestic Mount Fuji is diminished in the background and repeated in one of the foreground waves.

Distinctive clawlike waves are found often in *Manga*, including on at least seventeen pages in the volumes known to be owned by Gorham. Tureens, punch bowls, lamps, and pitchers made by the company in the 1880s bear waves irrefutably modeled on Hokusai's examples, but as they are compositions realized in three dimensions, credit should go to Gorham's

181
Curio Fork, 1879–80.
Silver with copper and brass.
RISD Museum

iron with a hammer. This repercussion caused the beak to push out the silver at the desired point, producing the design. As the piece was rotated, the process was repeated. Completed vessels were filled with pitch (fig. 183), a malleable substance primarily of asphaltum and coal tar, which reinforced the vessel during chasing, a process of decorating by shaping—as opposed to removing—the surface of the metal with a hammer and steel tools. The pitch was composed in varying hardnesses to accommodate the type of chasing to be conducted. The process and formula album lists the pitch formula of Nicholas Heinzelman, an eccentric Swiss silversmith brought to Gorham by Edward Holbrook in 1885. A monograph published by Gorham in 1918 described Heinzelman as developing "under the most untoward circumstances into one of the most individually distinguished chasers and modelers this country has ever known."[56]

Chasers used hundreds of tools of various shapes and sizes, which they often made themselves. Chasing was

they penetrate the sea's surface. The lidded hand-raised tureen appears to gyrate with the strong diagonals of waves that encompass its circular form, while the tureen with stand virtually spins out of control as high-relief fish leap and dive into the waves, nearly missing the crabs and lobsters also caught in the roiling waters. Finally, an 1885 punch bowl (fig. 184) takes the series to its apex with a marine scene that seemingly swells and sloshes, as its liquid contents would when served with the matching ladle with a gilded shell-shaped bowl. On one side, a golden-eyed carp splays its fins to clear the swirling whitecaps, and on the other side a dragon with gold eyes and tongue rides waves beneath an undulating rim populated with crabs, fish, and shells. Realistically hand-chased Japanesque waves on this collection of wares are accompanied by incredibly lifelike cast elements, such as the handles formed as coral branches and the finial formed as a sea urchin on the lidded tureen; the handles formed as crabs and the finial formed as a lobster on the tureen and stand; and the handles formed as shells on the punch bowl and its ladle formed of scallop shells.

One of the most unusually creative and daringly experimental designs of repoussé work by Gorham, a pitcher (fig. 185) with a pair of life-size snakes coiled to compose the body, spout, and handle of the vessel, is an outstanding example of one

184
Punch Bowl and Ladle, 1885. Silver with gilding. Museum of Fine Arts, Boston

183
Gorham employee pouring pitch into a vessel. Gorham Archive, John Hay Library

a painstaking process that could take many hours, depending on the difficulty and intricacy of the design. Tabulations calculated in Gorham's costing ledgers reveal that elaborately chased tea services from the late 1880s (figs. 99–100) could require more than seven hundred hours of chasing, representing nearly three months' effort by a chaser working a sixty-hour week. In a ten-man department, producing this single service meant committing 10 percent of its capacity for a quarter of a year.[57]

Raised by hand rather than spun on a lathe, a series of important vessels made in the mid-1880s exemplifies not only the talents of Gorham's chasers but their ability to transform these age-old skills into original and innovative creations. An 1882 silver pitcher (fig. 125) twists with pike and carp swimming in waves that crest at the vessel's neck, which is gripped by a taunting dragon. The pitcher's handle is formed by the dragon's curved body; its tongue is unfurled onto the rim and its back legs clutch the pitcher's base. A lidded tureen (fig. 96) and a tureen with stand (fig. 127) continue the dynamism of *The Great Wave*, featuring carp that literally jump from the water, as indicated by the rings created around their bodies as

182
Chasing Room in *Views, Exterior and Interior, of the Works of the Gorham Manufacturing Company, Silversmiths*, 1892. Gorham Archive, John Hay Library

salad servers (fig. 186) are encrusted with shells, crabs, sand, and strands of seaweed tangled with fish. The servers and all the wares in the pattern are fully finished on the front and back. The extant casting patterns of small shells, crabs, and other marine creatures consist of identical forms on a multi-pronged tree so that many small-scale elements could be cast at once. The concentric undulating rings of the oyster-shell-shaped serving end of the spoon appear to be awash with the receding tide that has deposited a tiny shell and grains of sand into the spoon's gilded bowl.

By the late 1880s, Gorham was operating at new heights, with a staff of 2,800. The need for larger facilities was realized, and a 30-acre plot of land was purchased in the Elmwood neighborhood of south Providence. Architectural plans were developed using the company's input regarding the features and layout of the buildings (fig. 187). The scale, modernity, scope, and self-sufficiency of the plans reflect Gorham's far-reaching goals, ambitions, and aspirations, with unalloyed recognition and respect for their employees' knowledge, capabilities, and needs. A company sales manual emphasized "the value which the Company has always placed upon the services of those who have grown up with it, for without the practical knowledge which comes only from actual experience in the more subordinate positions, the President and his advisors who arranged these buildings could never have properly appreciated the needs of the men and the business."[58] William Crins was the president of Gorham during the construction of the Elmwood plant, which began in 1889. Aptly conveying the day-to-day atmosphere of a pivotal time in the company's history, nine extant diaries written from 1888 to 1900 by Crins note the decision on May 19, 1888, by the Board to build the new plant, "empowering me [Crins] to make contracts." [59] That daunting task, Crins wrote, "means much hard work for me." By 1889 Crins was visiting the new Elmwood works daily, overseeing progress and lamenting when "things are going rather drag-gy."[60] The new Elmwood works (fig. 19) opened in 1890 with its own water supply, power plant, railway spur, and a campus of spacious, well-ventilated, and well-lit interconnected buildings that supported each phase of production.

of the company's trompe l'oeil works. Rendered with detailed scales in deep relief, the reptilian bodies appear capable of unwinding and slithering away.

An important source of Gorham's inspiration was its location in Rhode Island, also known as the Ocean State. Casts—often taken from live examples—shifted from serving as ornamentation decorating hollowware vessels to becoming the elements that formed the objects themselves. In 1884, Gorham launched a line of silver and gilded flatware and smallwares in the *Narragansett* pattern, its name originating from the Native American tribe that occupies the coast of Rhode Island and eponymous with the inlet on the north side of the Rhode Island Sound, Narragansett Bay. Looking as if they were plucked from the nearby bay, the *Narragansett*

From the time of John Gorham's first pursuit of drop presses adapted for use with silverware on his 1852 journey to England until the company moved to its new location, Gorham had debuted more than 115 flatware patterns. Located in the heart of the facility complex, the Preparatory Room (fig. 8) was described in an 1892 *Jewelers' Circular* as a space laden with heavy lines of shafting, powering a multitude of machines. Here is where "the heavy work is executed. Lumps of shining metal are rolled into sheets, and cut up and stamped into the forms of spoons, forks and other designs . . . the solid mass of unshaped metal grows into beauty of form under the quick, sharp action of huge steel machines, which do their work with almost a human impulse."[61] Much of machinery was designed and constructed by Gorham for their own specific needs. Silver came from the adjacent Bullion Room, a vaulted chamber with thick fireproof walls, protected by a great steel door, in which "stores of silver in bars, bricks, ingots, and blank forms were piled up in large pigeon-holes."[62] First, the sterling was flattened into sheets by massive rolling mills precisely calibrated to produce the correct gauge. Next the silver was run through blanking machines, which cut from

186
Narragansett Salad Set, ca. 1885. Silver with gilding. RISD Museum

the sheet basic outlines of the flatware forms, called blanks. An 1892 photo album produced by Gorham to showcase their new facility includes twenty-eight photographs of various areas of the plant populated with employees at work. An image of the Preparatory Room shows workers operating the twenty-four drop presses of "modern design," connected by massive cast-iron frames that also carried the automatic driving mechanism (fig. 188). The Preparatory Room, designed to resist the strain of the heavy machinery and its effects, was constructed with a 7-foot-thick foundation of concrete and solid granite, to which the drop presses were mounted. Around the perimeter of the drop presses were low banks of wood shelves that housed the dies: two-part steel forms that were "sunk," or cut out, with the flatware designs (fig. 190). The bottom or back part of the die was placed into the stationary part of the drop press, and the top, or front, part was raised and then dropped with great force onto the silver blank placed between the two halves, imparting both the utensil's design and its shaped form. Each form and size in each flatware pattern required an individual die. Active dies were held in the Preparatory Room and those not in use were kept, in order, in a vaulted storeroom. The 1892 photo album noted their importance to the company's production:

> Not the least interesting feature of this Preparatory Room is the collection of dies, tools, and templates. They are not by any means the least valuable of its features, in fact, they make up a large proportion of the value of the entire plant. There are thousands of them, all marked, numbered, and registered alphabetically, so that they can be put into active service on a minute's notice. They represent the labor of years, and pose an artistic value not to be calculated.[63]

A rare unfinished sample set of Gorham's *Mythologique* pattern (fig. 191) serves as exemplary model, combining elaborate detailing—the result of hours of modeling by hand—with remaining evidence of the drop press's mechanized brute force. The pattern was designed by Florentin Antoine Heller (fig. 119), a French silversmith whose precision in designing and executing the dies was noticed by critics lauding him as "an inspired artist . . . and a workman possessing a skill without a rival— a hand for which no obstacle exists."[64] A sixty-page promotional booklet (fig. 189) illustrates the twenty-four mythological designs on the seventy-two pieces offered for dining, an

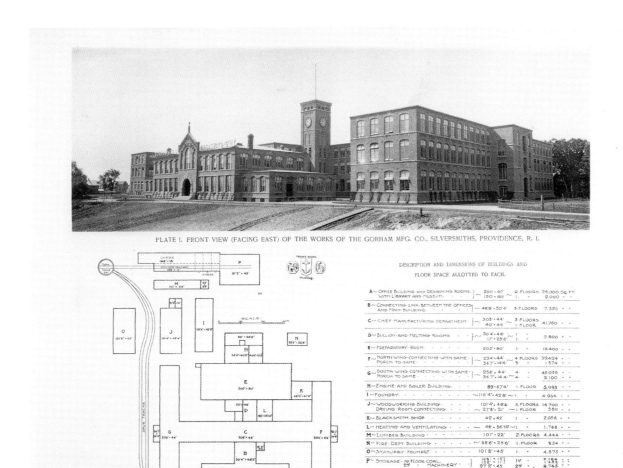

PLATE I. FRONT VIEW (FACING EAST) OF THE WORKS OF THE GORHAM MFG. CO., SILVERSMITHS, PROVIDENCE, R. I.

187

Front view (facing east), in *Views, Exterior and Interior, of the Works of the Gorham Manufacturing Company, Silversmiths*, 1892. Gorham Archive, John Hay Library

activity that could not have been undertaken with this example. The polished refinement of the handle designs starkly contrasts with the untrimmed metal between the fork tines and around the top of the sugar tongs (fig. 154), evidencing the drop press's power.

Although Gorham hired a number of experienced designers and silversmiths from Europe, training workers at home was a priority and a crucial process, providing a continual source of well-trained employees. An article lauding Gorham's showing at the 1889 Paris Exposition Universelle recognized that they had "pursued the theory that their establishment should be educational in the broadest sense, and they have constantly brought forward young *Americans* of their own training, who have become valuable assistants, and many of them artists of the highest rank in their respective departments."[65] With more than one thousand employees at the new Elmwood works, the investment in training was a significant undertaking. Apprenticing for a particular skill could take years before achieving a level of acceptable competency,

let alone the status of mastery. As acknowledged, "To have been educated in the Gorham shops is the highest recommendation that an applicant for a position as skilled artisan can give, and is acknowledged as sufficient indorsement [*sic*] whenever presented."[66]

Heller's flatware designs (fig. 155) reflected stylistic shifts away from Aesthetic movement naturalism and asymmetry in the 1890s, moving back to the order of antiquity and in new directions for materials combined with silver. A range of wares juxtaposing silver with glass, ceramics, and enamel was shown in quantity in Gorham's pavilion at the 1893 World's Columbian Exposition in Chicago (figs. 235, 236), where drawn curtains shielded busy workmen from "the curious throng."[67] Gorham's displays at the World's Fair were described as "sunbursts of splendor [that] will amply repay the public for waiting for a wealth of beauty as yet veiled to them," with "remarkable specimens of enamel work" called out in particular.[68] Filling three bays of the pavilion, the enameled wares were produced in the company's New York branch under the direction of Count Gyula de Festetics, a Hungarian artist and enamelist hired by Gorham to create

VIEWS, EXTERIOR AND INTERIOR, OF THE WORKS OF THE
GORHAM M'F'G CO., SILVERSMITHS, AT PROVIDENCE, R. I.
PLATE XVII. A.   SOUTH SECTION OF PREPARATORY ROOM.
DIMENSIONS OF ENTIRE ROOM, 205 FT. X 80 FT.

188
South Section of Preparatory Room,
in *Views, Exterior and Interior,
of the Works of the Gorham
Manufacturing Company,
Silversmiths*, 1892. Gorham Archive,
John Hay Library

enameled wares that rivaled those by European makers.[69]

An 1894 company-produced pamphlet relates that Festetics's designs were largely executed by young American women selected for their "artistic tendencies" and trained extensively in enameling.[70] This is one of several tasks deemed "employment adapted to women" and as described in another Gorham publication entitled *Woman's Work at the Gorham Manufacturing Company*, which clearly states that female employment was "confined to a comparatively few of the numerous departments of the works."[71] Photographs depict women at long workbenches, their heads bent over, assiduously toiling on typically small-scale enameled plaques that were fit into silver boxes, toilet sets, or grouped together on larger-scale wares such as vases, ewers, and salvers. An intricate silver jewelry box (fig. 193) featuring an enameled lid is typical of the Renaissance and mythological subject matter of these enamels, which required multiple layers of

the vitreous substance to be painstakingly built up, fired, and polished. Certain areas on the lid, such as the man's red pants, were enameled over foils, which provided both a metallic flash and greater sense of depth visible under the glassy stratums. The presence of the intertwined *C* and *F* in the enamel of the lid suggests that Count de Festetics may have contributed his enameling talents to this particular creation. The work of Festetics and his female assistants earned seven awards at the World's Columbian Exposition for enamel and silverwork, bringing "success to Gorham's venture into this technically challenging process."[72]

Gorham continued its forays into experimental enamels in the 1890s, showing works of plique-à-jour enamels, a process by which translucent enamels are applied one color at a time and held by surface tension within the openings created by a filigree framework of twisted wires. French for "open or against the light," plique-à-jour enamels were first developed in the twelfth century and revived in the 1890s, becoming very fashionable despite their fragile nature and high cost.[73] Gorham was one of only two American makers of this type of enamelware, and recent research reveals that the

company made about sixteen unique samples in 1893, with half being exhibited in Chicago.[74] Fashioned about the same time, a gilded silver bonbon spoon (fig. 161) features a jewel-toned peacock whose "beauty is only half appreciated until it is held up to the light, when it has the translucence of stained glass and looks like embedded jewels."[75]

Gorham's coupling of silver and glass also garnered great attention, a combination achieved by mechanically attaching silver mounts to an existing piece of glass, blowing the glass into a metal framework, or the electro-deposition of silver on the surface of the glass. Fully finished glass was supplied by well-known American glass companies such as J. Hoare and Company of Corning, New York, and T. G. Hawkes & Company, also of Corning, who provided the cut-crystal body of a wine pitcher (fig. 153), dominated by a magnificent grotesque satyr mask, shown in Chicago in 1893. A diamond-patterned cut-glass and gilded claret jug (fig. 150) with a gilded silver mount studded with amethysts, garnets, and

moonstones was also shown at the fair. An illustrated Gorham exposition publication including a rendering of the work, describes the process of "decorating portions of the glass with fired gilt," and summarizes the final result: "With the addition of the silver-gilt frame in highly ornamental repoussé the culmination is reached, a truly dazzling product of the glass worker's and metal worker's arts."[76]

Reversing the process of mounting a finished piece of glass, the "blown-in" glass technique begins with a complex framework of silver or gilded silver, into which a glass body is blown. As described in a review of Gorham's 1893 display, "[T]he effect produced by the glass bulging from the interstices of the metallic frame in rounded forms is similar to that of so many jewels, carbuncles or crystals, as the glass is colored or white."[77] Much trial and effort went into perfecting this process, a delicate balance between the force required for blowing the hot glass and the preservation of the finely wrought frame, into which many hours of labor had already been invested. The company showed a great deal of jewel-toned blown glass in its Chicago pavilion, such a pitcher whose watercolor design drawing (fig. 151) aptly simulates the shifting nuances of the brilliant blue glass suspended within an elaborate, classically inspired gilded mount.[78] This technically challenging process was looked upon as "a new

departure and is employed only by the Gorham Mfg. Co. It marks a decided step in advance of previous attempts in the line of decorative metal-working."[79]

Electro-deposition on glass was hailed as the most modern of the methods used by Gorham to join glass and silver, as it employed an "electric process, the genius of Electricity obediently doing and undoing according to the will of his new-found master, Man!"[80] However, it was women who carried out the steps to produce these fashionable wares (fig. 192). The glass was coated with a metallic-based flux such as silver nitrate, which attracted the silver in an electroplating bath and completely covered the object in a layer of silver. The design was painted on to the vessel with a heavy black resist varnish, then the object was placed in an acid bath, reversing the electrical process that had attracted the silver and dissolving areas not protected by the varnish, revealing the "sparkle of the glass through the net-work of silvery scroll" (fig. 149).[81] Similar to connections it formed with glass companies, Gorham forged a relationship with the Rookwood Pottery, decorating their earthenware vessels with silver electro-deposit overlays (fig. 194). Founded in Cincinnati by Maria Longworth Nichols Storer, Rookwood produced highly prized ceramics that were typically

192
Woman painting silver overlay on ceramic, in *Woman's Work at the Gorham Manufacturing Company*, 1892. Gorham Archive, John Hay Library

decorated by American women. However, this particular example, an 1890 ewer (fig. 238) with dragons encircling the body in tandem with swirling silver, was painted by the Japanese artist Kitaro Shirayamadani, who was hired by Storer in 1887.

As silver progressed through various stages and hands at the Elmwood works, both women and men conducted parallel tasks that met finished works at the end of manufacturing process. One of the forty-plus awards won by Gorham at the 1893 World's Fair was not for silver but for the chests (fig. 76) in which the wares were stored, described as possessing "novel and useful construction . . . thorough and elegant cabinet joining . . . [and] superior and artistic finish of exterior and interior." Although seemingly secondary to the silver wares themselves, the cases produced by the company were an important part of the business beginning in 1868.[82] An 1871 account notes the morocco leather and velvet cases filling the packing room that were destined for the "most distant cities in the Union."[83] The 1882 autumn catalogue bemoans "clumsy morocco cases," offering over seventeen varieties of wood and 280 lining materials, including more than forty shades of satin.[84] At Elmwood, wood was delivered by train to the Lumber Building, then taken as needed to the large two-story Carpenter's Shop, to which a steam-powered drying kiln for the rough lumber was attached. The first floor was filled with woodworking machinery, and the second floor housed the carpenters and case makers. Once constructed, the cases, chests, and trunks were sent to the second floor via a bridge that connected to the

south wing of the Main Building. The case department—where fabrics were sewn into the interiors and the blocks that held the wares in place were covered with fabric and glued down—employed the largest number of females. Per *Women's Work*, "to the experienced needle-woman, the handling of the silks, satins . . . comes with ready facility."

In addition to gracing innumerable American tables, Gorham silver celebrated the accomplishments, achievements, and vision of Americans in all types of endeavors, including sports, civic leadership, military service, and the performing, literary, and visual arts. In 1895 colleagues of the acclaimed nineteenth-century actor Joseph Jefferson commissioned Gorham to honor his theatrical legacy with a monumental three-handled loving cup (fig. 156) that is an outstanding example of Gorham's presentation wares, a sector of silver production in which they flourished and excelled. Designed by New England sculptor William Clark Noble, the cup was first modeled in plaster (rather than through a series of drawings) and presented to Jefferson in advance of its completion in cast solid silver.[85] Reasons for the early presentation most likely included the amount of time and the level of difficulty demanded by the work. A *Providence Journal*

193
Jewelry Box, ca. 1890. Count Gyula de Festetics, enameler. Silver and enamel. RISD Museum

Williams

article from January 1896 indicates that the plaster model "presents some unusual difficulties and will be a matter of some time."[86] A popular form of the day, the three handles took the form of Jefferson in his most celebrated roles— Rip Van Winkle, Bob Acres from *The Rivals*, and Dr. Pangloss from *The Heir at Law*—and the three panels in between depicted intricately chased scenes from the first two plays and a dedicatory panel hailing Jefferson as "The Dean of the Dramatic Profession." Underscoring the difficulty of casting such a vessel in solid silver, more than 20 inches tall and weighing more than 60 pounds, the process took 456 hours—360 for casting the figures—and 209 for the chasing.[87] Much of the work took place in Gorham's Experimental Room (pages 4–5). Located on the second floor adjacent to the Design Room and Library, it was where designers and silversmiths worked through production challenges.

Three years later, Gorham was commissioned to make the largest silver presentation work in its history. The *Admiral Dewey Cup* (fig. 157) celebrated Admiral George Dewey, a national hero after his 1898 victory in Manila Bay during the Spanish-American War. Standing 8 feet 6 inches tall, the four-part cup features intricately wrought scenes of Dewey's home in Vermont, his valor in battle, and his triumphant return to the United States. Chronicling the history of the country and its gratitude for the armed forces, the sponsorship of the Dewey cup's production was made possible by 70,000 Americans, each of whom donated a dime that was melted down to fashion the cup. Housed in the cup's oak base, a silver-covered album lists the names of all contributors. Under William Christmas Codman's direction, the cup was completed in four weeks and featured a three-cornered base composed of sea creatures with scaly bodies fashioned from overlapping dimes; this decoration was also used for the border around the lid and the base. A comparison between the finished cup and its nearly full-scale original watercolor design drawing (fig. 158) reveals changes and revisions that occurred during the transformation from creative concept to physical manifestation: the three figures standing upon the lid were reduced to a single figure of Victory who now holds aloft the enameled portrait of Dewey.

In contrast to the formal classicism of the 1890s, the Art Nouveau style of the turn of the twentieth century was shown in great quantity and with much success. Under the direction of William Christmas Codman, Gorham launched *Martelé,* one of their most popular styles. The line's name derives from the French verb *marteler* ("to hammer"), referencing the hand-hammered finish. The visual evidence of the

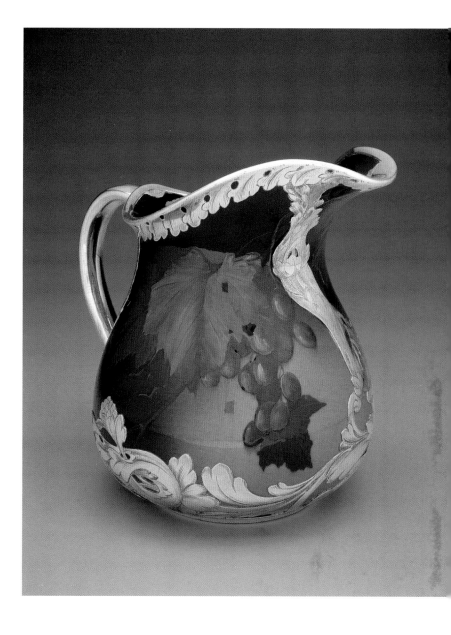

194
Pitcher, 1893.
Constance Amelia Baker, decorator, and Rookwood Pottery, ceramic manufacturer. Earthenware with glaze and silver. Museum of Fine Arts, Boston

hand of the silversmith and the curvaceous, undulating forms and decorations of the style were enhanced by the company's eventual use of .950 and .9584 fine silver, which was considerably more malleable than .925 sterling silver. Although Codman began to design in the Art Nouveau style the year after the 1893 World's Columbian Exposition in Chicago, the first official piece of *Martelé* produced was a three-handled loving cup that was entered into the company's Makers and Finished Weights ledger on November 21, 1896.[88] *Martelé* was especially challenging to produce and required designers possessing adroit abilities to adapt two-dimensional drawings into three-dimensional realizations, a feat that often demanded an insightful reading of sketchy renderings. To facilitate the demanding process of *Martelé's* production, William Christmas Codman formed a special training school at Gorham in 1896 for silversmiths who were able to produce a quantity of *Martelé* substantial enough to show at an invitational event on November 15, 1897, at the Waldorf-Astoria, the luxurious New York hotel, to which the press were given a private preview.[89]

A review by the *Jewelers' Circular* underscores the challenge of transforming the design into the physical form: "While the designs are generally from one man, W. C. Codman . . . the articles themselves were wrought under his direction by different skilled silver workers, and show to a considerable extent the individuality of the makers."[90] The recognition that a design was conceived by one person on paper and often executed by another in silver is often clearly manifested in the various forms of extant *Martelé* design drawings, which may begin as a sketchy likeness with hand-written suggestions and revisions (fig. 211), progress to precise silhouettes with technical specifications (fig. 210), and culminate in the finished product (fig. 212). A polychrome presentation drawing (fig. 195) of a three-handled loving cup features whiplash curves from which "wild columbines" of red and yellow

enamel flowers and green leaves sprout. These curves are repeated in the three strands of silver that appear to grow from the vessel's body to connect with the handles, yet they are not present on the finished loving cup (fig. 196). This may indicate that, despite the dramatic effect they lend to the drawing, their fragility was not technically feasible or functionally practical. The drawing did provide guidance for the 110 hours of chasing that achieved the shimmering, swirling surface. This work was done by George W. Sauthof, ranked one of the top chasers at Gorham by 1900.[91] Along with tankards (fig. 139), ewers, and claret jugs (figs. 143, 159), the loving cup was one of about 154 *Martelé* pieces shown at the Paris 1900 Exposition Universelle, the site of Gorham's official international launch for the line, which achieved sweeping success. [92]

The centerpiece of *Martelé's* debut was a solid-silver dressing table and stool (fig. 138) wrought from seventy-eight pounds of silver over the course of 2,300 hours of labor. William Christmas Codman (fig. 134) was awarded the silver and gold medals, Gorham president Edward Holbrook (fig. 18) was made a chevalier of the French Légion d'honneur, and the Gorham Manufacturing Company secured the grand prix for metalwork.[93] Into the early 1900s, *Martelé* continued to be

197
Martelé Writing Table, 1903.
RISD Museum

shown at world's fairs, often accompanied by pieces from the *Athenic* line, which was similar in its hand-wrought Art Nouveau style but included copper and other materials. A watercolor design drawing (fig. 200) shows a group of three elegantly attenuated silver vases embellished with sinuous copper handles and accents that encircle enameled peacock feather plaques, one of which (fig. 199) was shown at the 1901 World's Fair, the Pan-American Exposition held in Buffalo, New York. A cigar box (fig. 206) with an applied decoration of silver lashes is representative of the *Athenic* wares with hand-hammered copper bodies shown at the 1902 First International Exposition of Modern Decorative Arts, held in Turin, Italy.

A writing desk and chair (figs. 197, 207–9) were conceived and created to be showstoppers in the sea of stunning objects

at the 1904 Saint Louis World's Fair, the Louisiana Purchase Exposition. Their magnificent design and superior workmanship brought Gorham the Grand Prize in silversmithing at the fair. Although various Gorham employees and outside specialists contributed more than ten thousand hours of labor to create the desk and chair, William Christmas Codman is credited with its design, and it is his signature carved in one of the inside drawers. What Codman imagined in two dimensions was translated into three dimensions by a cadre of artists who fashioned the desk and chair from wood and silver and painstakingly inlaid them with an array of prized materials. The hours of labor accrued for various processes and the quantity and cost of each material were documented on costing slips (fig. 198) and ledgers that Gorham had used to keep track of an object's information since the late 1860s. The costing slips for this set indicate that approximately fifty pounds of silver were

C C X	Writing Desk,
	St. Louis Exposition,
	SEP 23 1903

Silver
Making
Drawing
Stamping
Spinning
Turning
Casting
„ Chas.
Piercing
Ivory
Stoning
Bobbing
G. R.
Burnishing hand
„ lathe
Finishing

C C Y	Chair,
	St. Louis Exposition,
	SEP 23 1903

Silver
Making
Drawing
Stamping
Spinning
Turning
Casting
„ Chas.
Piercing
Ivory
Stoning
Bobbing
G. R.
Burnishing hand
„ lathe
Finishing

198
Costing slips for *Martelé*
Writing Table and Chair,
1903. Gorham Archive,
John Hay Library

used. Made of ebony, the table is banded around the top with burled thuya wood and a molding of ivory. Inlays of silver, ivory, exotic woods, and mother-of-pearl constitute a dizzying array of complex arabesques, covering the top, sides, and back. Symbolism cast in silver abounds in the ornamentation. The table legs rest on small pads of ivory that echo the spoon-shaped feet and are embellished with exquisite Renaissance Revival female masks (pages 6–7, fig. 209), each representing one of the four seasons: winter is surrounded by pinecones, spring by lilies, summer by wild roses, and autumn by grapes and chrysanthemums. The silver gallery atop the writing table is formed of intertwined poppies, and the mirror is decorated with morning glories, referencing night and day.

After winning scores of awards for dazzling silver displays exhibited during the continuous stream of international expositions held since the mid-nineteenth century, Gorham did not present a single object for display at the 1925 Exposition des Arts Décoratifs et Industriels Modernes held in Paris, where only works of "new inspiration and real originality"

were accepted and "reproductions, imitations and counterfeits of ancient styles [were] prohibited."[94] The Paris exposition served as a catalyst in recasting the direction of Gorham and its design staff, which that year included its leading Modern designer, Danish émigré Erik Magnussen (fig. 145). Gorham hired Magnussen, who came to Providence from Copenhagen in 1925, giving him his own studio, which was elegantly appointed and separate from the crowded space the other designers shared under William Codman's close watch.[95] The company emphasized Magnussen's celebrity, often limiting his product lines to about twenty-four pieces. These works were assigned their own series of model numbers and stamped with the designer's distinctive maker's mark: a vertical zigzag *E* crossed with a horizontal zigzag *M*.[96] Magnussen developed

199
Athenic Vase, 1901.
Silver with copper and enamel.
Chrysler Museum of Art

Williams

his style in the same artistic circle as Georg Jensen, so it is not surprising that his early creations for Gorham were in the vein of contemporary Danish silver design, characterized by simplified shapes with hand-planished surfaces and embellished with stylized organic curvilinear and spherical ornament, such as his candlesticks (fig. 215) and candy dish (fig. 146) of sterling and ivory.

Magnussen's next creation would be his most memorable and most radical, positioning Gorham in the vanguard of Modern design among American silver firms. Resplendent with a gleaming surface of sterling, gold, and dark-patinated silver triangular facets, the designer's *Cubic* coffee service (figs. 204, 217) was a three-dimensional manifestation of the fragmented objects of everyday life that Cubist artists depicted in two-dimensional renderings, which the designer had boldly depicted with contrasting metallic tones in his own drawing

(fig. 203). Consisting of a coffeepot, creamer, sugar bowl, and tray, the service was designed, executed, and marked by Magnussen and created an immediate sensation when it was displayed in the company's Fifth Avenue showroom (fig. 253). A blueprint (fig. 202) depicting the *Cubic* sugar bowl reads like a series of angular buildings rising from the ground, suggesting the American city and its soaring skyscrapers, along with the emergence of industrial design and its modern, streamlined image. Described by Gorham as an "impressionist tea set . . . based on tall buildings seen from various perspectives and from sun shadows on set-back skyscrapers," the service was hailed as "The Lights and Shadows of Manhattan" by the company (fig. 253).[97]

Although Magnussen's inspiration may have been modern, his skills and techniques were firmly tied

200
Drawing of *Athenic* Vases, 1901. Gorham Archive, John Hay Library

NATIONAL ADVERTISEMENT PHOTOGRAPHY BY TONI FICALORA

Circa '70

Circa '70 is an enriching expression of new American design concepts, in luxurious weight sterling silver. As the artists uses lights and shadows to give life and dimension to his work, so did the designer use, with Circa '70, the black ebony finials, the soft satin grey finish, and the contrast of gentle curves and bold sculptured forms.

1461 Coffee, Cap. 3 pts, Ht. 11½" $255.00
1462 Tea, Cap. 2¾ pts. 235.00
1463 Sugar with cover 90.00
1464 Cream, Cap. ¾ pt. 70.00
FOUR-PIECE SERVICE $650.00

ANNIVERSARY SPECIAL!
With this four-piece service . . .

YOU WILL RECEIVE FREE!
The matching Trend Gallery Tray with sterling silver rim (Illustrated) Regularly $79.50 (#1081 diam. 18" Black Formica Center) or the matching YC787 Silverplated Tray (Diameter 22") Regularly $65

. . . or you can apply the $79.50 retail value of the Trend tray against the purchase of the #1468 Circa '70 Sterling Tray ($575 retail)

201
Gorham advertisement featuring *Circa '70* coffee and tea service, 1961. Gorham Archive, John Hay Library

to European goldsmithing traditions. Underscoring his dedication to his art, the gilded sections of the coffee service were achieved through use of the historical yet toxic technique of mercury gilding. Later Magnussen would claim to have spent three hours a day for a year rediscovering the "lost art" of this process, melting flakes of gold into mercury to spread upon the silver, heating it to evaporate the "deadly mercury vapors that rise under a torch."[98] As Magnussen's Modernist works gained momentum, the arrival of the Great Depression drastically curtailed silver sales and temporarily stunted the advance of Modern silver design in America. Compounding this situation, Modern design was manifesting itself not in costly media such as sterling silver, but in more economically viable materials such as aluminum, chromed steel, and plastic, and labor-intensive handmade processes were increasingly replaced with machined automation. Hired by Gorham in 1956, designer Donald H. Colflesh ushered in the next decades, creating futuristic forms during a transitional period that focused on space travel, nuclear power, atomic bombs, and high-tech materials. The dramatic upward thrusting lines of his *Circa '70* tea and coffee service (fig. 201) suggest a launch into the stratosphere, alluding to the space age by referencing a date a dozen years in advance in the pattern's name. Although the service's forms indicate the Modern era (fig. 219), they are countered by use of the decidedly traditional materials silver and ebony, as indicated on a design drawing (fig. 218). A modern material would enter the service in 1963, with the addition of a silver tray with a Formica center.[99]

Throughout the Gorham Manufacturing Company's existence, the dual respect for what came before and what was possible for the future was the foundation for their development and dominance of the silver industry. Their processes, ranging from administrative management and logistical organization to creative development and manufacturing methods, were recognized early on as bringing "the inheritance of an older and richer world to the quick and fertile genius of the new, and into that, comprehensive organization of all departments under one head, which gives a capital advantage to the American system of business."[100] The company was an American industrial leader, the epitome of the manufactory, a site where merchandise was produced for sale and for use through labor and machines. What the word *manufactory* often obscures, however, is that it "is not an easy thing to make a design which shall be at once delightful to the eye and convenient to the hand. . . .no talent is rarer than this, and without it, all the mechanical skill, the perfect integrity, and the courageous enterprise of the Company would not have sufficed to rear so vast . . . an establishment."[101]

202
Blueprint design for *Cubic* Sugar Bowl, 1927. Erik Magnussen, designer. Blueprint. RISD Museum

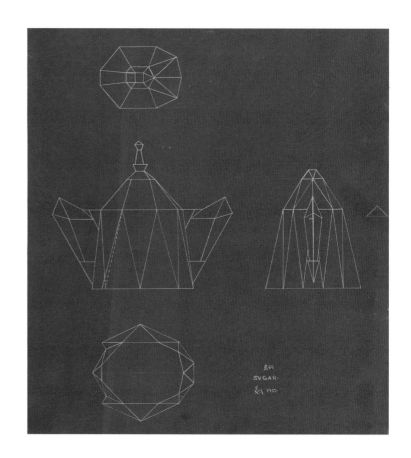

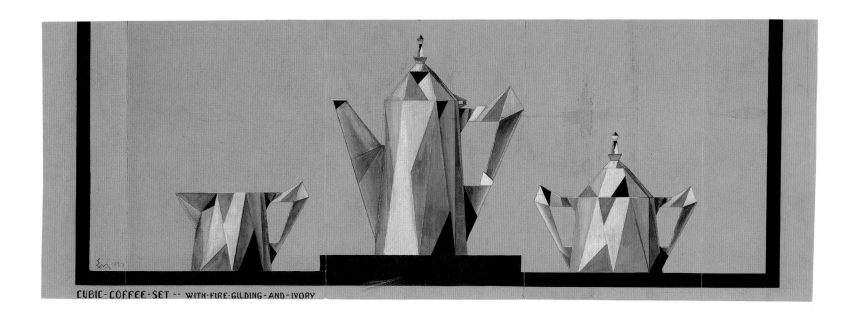

203
Design drawing for the *Cubic* Coffee
Service, 1927. Erik Magnussen, designer.
Gouache, graphite, and ink on paper.
Courtesy of Victoria Stenstream

204
Cubic Coffee Service, 1927.
Erik Magnussen, designer.
Silver with gilding and ivory.
RISD Museum

1 Welcome Arnold Greene, et al., "Important Special Manufactures," in *The Providence Plantations for 250 Years: An Historical Review of the Foundation, Rise and Progress of the City of Providence* (Providence: J. A. and R. A. Reid, 1886), 273–75.

2 "Manufacturing and Mechanical Industry of Rhode Island," *Providence Journal*, May 19, 1871.

3 Information from John Gorham, notebook with handwritten history of Gorham, 1893; and John Gorham, handwritten history of Gorham, January 13, 1894, Gorham Manufacturing Company Archive, John Hay Library, Brown University, Providence, Rhode Island (hereafter GMCA).

4 Gorham, handwritten history, January 13, 1894, GMCA.

5 Louis W. Clarke, "Ye Ancient Jewelers of Providence, Events of a Hundred Years of Jewelry Making Described and Illustrated," in *The Manufacturing Jeweler* 35 (August 30, 1894), 209–10. The author thanks Peter DiCristofaro for this information. George and Smith Owen purchased the 9 Steeple Street lot and built a four-story brick building in 1847, the lower floors of which were rented to other jewelers.

6 In 1848, $17,000 was the equivalent of about $545,000 today.

7 "Silversmithing in America Part II, Gorham Manufacturing Co.—History and Development," *Jewelers' Circular and Horological Review* 19 (June 8, 1892): 3–8.

8 John Gorham, diary of a trip to England and France, 1852, I.1 Gorham-Historical-Gorham Family, GMCA.

9 "The Modus-Operandi of Electro-Plating in Silver," in *Cincinnati Enquirer* (January 1, 1892); clipping of article in GMCA.

10 James Parton, "Silver and Silver Plate," *Harper's New Monthly Magazine* 37, no. 220 (September 1868), 433–48.

11 Gorham Manufacturing Company, ledger, 1862. The author thanks Peter DiCristofaro for access to this ledger.

12 "Manufacturing and Mechanical Industry," *Providence Journal*, May 19, 1871.

13 William C. Conant, "The Silver Age," *Scribner's Monthly* 9, no. 2 (December 1874): 202–3.

14 Ibid., 202.

15 J. D. Van Slyck, *New England Manufacturers and Manufactories: Three Hundred and Fifty of the Leading Manufacturers of New England* (Boston: Van Slyck, 1879), 295.

16 W. R. Bagnall, *Historical and Biographical Sketch of the Gorham Manufacturing Company* (Providence: Gorham Manufacturing Co., 1878), 21.

17 John Gorham, diary of a trip to Europe, 1860, information taken from entries dated June 30, August 7, and August 8, GMCA.

18 Gorham, inventory ledger, 1862, 80, 136, 145. Bagnall, *Historical and Biographical Sketch,* 10.

19 Gorham, diary, 1860, May 16 entry, "Obituary. Giovanni Franchi," in *The Art Journal London* 14 (1875): 44.

20 Gorham, handwritten history, 1893. Gorham, inventory ledger, 1862, 145. The page is identified as "Wilkinson's Room Franchi's Electrotypes."

21 Ibid.

22 "Silver and Silver Plate," *Harper's New Monthly Magazine*, 448.

23 "Manufacturing and Mechanical Industry," *Providence Journal*, May 19, 1871.

24 "Silver and Silver Plate," *Harper's New Monthly Magazine*, 440.

25 Ibid., 439.

26 The author thanks Burr Sebring (Gorham's director of design 1973–83) and Jeffrey Herman (Gorham employee 1981–83) for consulting on the production process of the teapot.

27 Gorham, inventory, 1862, 120. The handle and spout molds are listed as "chilled iron dies."

28 Gorham, inventory, 1862, 22–26, 48, 55. Lathes were costly pieces of equipment. At the time the No. 170 tea service was made Gorham had two rooms devoted to spinning, equipped with four heavy lathes and eight light lathes; the Engine Turning Room included thirteen lathes of varying sizes.

29 The item to be coated is placed into a container containing a solution of one or more metal salts and connected to an electrical circuit, forming the cathode (negative) of the circuit while an electrode typically of the same metal to be plated forms the anode (positive). When an electrical current is passed through the circuit, metal ions in the solution are attracted to the item, resulting in a layer of metal on the item.

30 Gorham, inventory, 1862, 102–3,

31 Gorham, inventory, 1871, 37, GMCA. The author thanks Charles Venable for providing copies of this now inaccessible inventory. James Napier, *A Manual of Electro-Metallurgy: The Applications of the Art to Manufacturing Processes* (London and Glasgow: Richard Griffin and Company, 1852).

32 Napier, *Manual of Electro-Metallurgy*, 131–32. For further information see "Memoirs of Mr. James Napier," in *Proceedings of the Philosophical Society of Glasgow* 16 (Glasgow: John Smith and Son, 1884–85). Napier was hired in 1842 by Elkington & Co. of Birmingham, England, to conduct and publish experiments in electro-type processes. On March 25, 1840, Elkington & Co. had secured the first patent for plating silver and gold by means of electro-plating; those patents expired in 1860.

33 Napier, *Manual of Electro-Metallurgy*, 133.

34 Parton, "Silver and Silver Plate," *Harper's New Monthly Magazine*, 436; Gorham, inventory, 1862, 149; Napier, *Manual of Electro-Metallurgy*, 43.

35 In 1801, Elgin received permission from Sultan Selim III of the Ottoman Empire, who ruled Greece until 1821, to remove most of the marble frieze to London. The Elgin Marbles were purchased by the British Museum in 1816 and put on display.

36 See Martina Droth, Jason Edwards, and Michael Hatt, *Sculpture Victorious: Art in an Age of Invention, 1837–1901* (New Haven: Yale University Press, 2014), 196–99.

37 Gorham, inventory, 1862, 144. There is a notation that the casts were "per Franchi's Bill," indicating that John Gorham purchased the casts from Giovanni Ferdinando Franchi in 1860. The Elgin Marble and Raphael casts are also listed on page 39 of the 1871 inventory.

38 Thank you to Joost During and Dianne Reilly for providing access to the Gorham casting patterns and ledgers.

39 Ibid.

40 Christopher Dresser, *Japan, Its Architecture, Art and Art Manufactures*, 1882 (repr., New York: Kegan Paul, 2001), 429–30.

41 Edwin C. Taylor, "Metal Work of All Ages," *National Repository* 6 (November 1879), 393–405.

42 Gorham, album comprising numerous formulas and processes, nineteenth and twentieth centuries, n.p. The author thanks Peter DiCristofaro for providing the album. Although previous scholarship identified a volume of formulas and processes (31236073559166) in the Gorham Archives at the John Hay Library as belonging to Tiffany and coming into Gorham's possession in 1878 (date notations in the volume begin in 1877 and end in 1882) via a Tiffany employee migrating to Gorham, further consideration in consultation with Spencer Gordon, Medill Harvey, and Ubaldo Vitali indicates that this volume was most likely composed by Tiffany designer Charles Grosjean, later acquired by his protégé Charles Osborne, and subsequently arrived at Gorham with their acquisition of the Whiting Manufacturing Company in 1905.

43 Richard Hughes and Michael Rowe, *The Colouring, Bronzing and Patination of Metals* (New York: Watson-Guptill Publications, 1991), 11–13; Carpenter, *Gorham Silver, 1831–1981*, 109.

44 A Gorham copper coffeepot (1989,0703.1) made in 1882 and currently in the collection of the British Museum, London, underwent a surface analysis by X-ray fluorescence, which detected only cuprite in the red patina.

45 Erwin S. Sperry, *The Brass World and Platers Guide* 1 (January 1905): 85–90.

46 Gorham, formula and process album; card dated 1902 calls specifically for Bowker Extract of Birch (H. L. Bowder & Co. of Boston), which was

purchased by formula author at Clafin & Co., a leading apothecary and chemist located at 62–72 South Main Street, Providence, which provided chemicals to Providence's jewelry industry.

47 Gorham, formula and process album, n.p. Sperry, 86.

48 See 1883 Gorham catalogue and photo album, GMCA. The author thanks Andrew Freedman for sharing his collection of Gorham *Banko Iron Ware*, thus allowing a survey of a large percentage of wares made.

49 Ian Ferguson, *Mokume Gane* (London: A&C Black Publishers, Ltd., 2002), 13.

50 The author thanks silversmith Jeff Herman for conducting a trial process that succeeded in closely replicating the appearance of *Curio*, thus supporting this method.

51 Gorham Manufacturing Company, *Costing Book* 34, 78, GMCA.

52 Gorham initially and consistently referred to this line as *Curio* in company ledgers, photograph labels, records and other materials. An aberration of the name, *Cairo*, appeared in later references external to the company.

53 *Silver Magazine* (September/October 2002), 27.

54 Gorham, inventory, 1862; Parton, "Silver and Silver Plate," *Harper's New Monthly Magazine*, 444.

55 "The Modus-Operandi of Electro-Plating in Silver," *Cincinnati Inquirer*, January 1, 1892.

56 Gorham, formula and process album, n.p.; typewritten memo from William N. LeCato to Mr. Aldrich, from New York, dated March 22, 1900; identified as "the formula for the Heinzelman mixture, consists of tar, wax, asphaltum and oxide of iron." Horace Townsend, *The Man and The Artist* (New York: The Gorham Manufacturing Company, for private circulation, 1918); see Charles H. Carpenter, *Gorham Silver, 1831–1981* (New York: Dodd, Mead, 1982), 132–34, for transcript.

57 Gorham Manufacturing Company costing record, 1888, GMCA.

58 Gorham Manufacturing Company, *The Sales Manual and History of the Gorham Company* (Providence: Gorham Manufacturing Co., 1932), 6, GMCA.

59 The author wishes to thank Mr. Charles Chapin, great-grandson of William Crins (Gorham president 1878–94) for providing access to these diaries. The annual diaries cover the years 1888–89 and 1894–1900. For additional diary excerpts, see Carpenter, *Gorham Silver*, 136–40.

60 Ibid, Nov. 20, 1889.

61 "Silversmithing in America. Part III. Gorham Mfg. Co.—Description of the Works," *Jewelers' Circular and Horological Review* 20 (June 15, 1892): 3–8.

62 From an album entitled *Literary Scraps, Cuttings, Extracts; Scrapbook Clippings 1891–1896,*

unsourced article entitled "The Gorham Manufacturing Co. An Interesting Visit to the company's Extensive Works Near Providence, R. I. – The Processes by which their Famous Wares are made," GMCA.

63 Gorham Manufacturing Company, *Views, Exterior and Interior of the Works of the Gorham Manufacturing Company* (Providence: 1892), n.p., GMCA.

64 Gorham Manufacturing Company, *Mythologique: Artistic Spoon and Fork Patterns in a Series of Twenty-Four Designs of Mythological Subjects* (Providence: 1895), n.p., RISD Museum 2005.118.428.

65 "American Art at the Paris Exposition—A Wonderful Exhibit," *Frank Leslie's Illustrated Newspaper* 1776 (September 28, 1889): 131.

66 Ibid.

67 "A Glimpse of the Gorham Mfg. Co. Exhibit. A View of One of the Grandest Features of the World's Fair," *Jewelers' Circular and Horological Review* 16 (May 17, 1893): 1, 34–35. "Arrangement and Condition of Exhibits in the American Jewelry Section," *Jewelers' Circular and Horological Review* 22 (May 31, 1893): 28.

68 Ibid.

69 Ibid.

70 Julia Osgood, *Silversmiths' Work in the Liberal Arts Building of the Columbian Exposition* (Providence: Gorham Manufacturing Company, 1894), 3.

71 Gorham Manufacturing Company, *Woman's Work at the Gorham Manufacturing Company* (Providence: Gorham Manufacturing Company, 1892), n.p., GMCA.

72 Ibid.

73 Janet Zapata, "American Plique-à-jour Enameling," *The Magazine Antiques* (December 1996): 812–21.

74 Research conducted by Spencer Gordon and Mark McHugh. George W. Shiebler and Co. (NY) also made plique-à-jour enamel.

75 "Fashions in Silverware and Silver Novelties," *Jewelers' Circular and Horological Review* 26 (March 1, 1893): 35.

76 "A Glimpse of the Gorham Mfg. Co. Exhibit. A View of One of the Grandest Features of the World's Fair," *Jewelers' Circular and Horological Review* 16 (May 17, 1893): 34.

77 Ibid.

78 Thank you to Spencer Gordon and Mark McHugh for identifying the pitcher as one shown at the World's Columbian Exposition.

79 "A Glimpse of the Gorham Mfg. Co. Exhibit, A View of One of the Grandest Features of the World's Fair," *Jewelers' Circular and Horological Review* 16 (May 17, 1893): 34.

80 Osgood, *Silversmiths' Work*, 13.

81 Jayne Stokes, *Sumptuous Surrounds: Silver Overlay on Ceramic and Glass* (Milwaukee: Milwaukee Art Museum, 1990), 6.

82 Gorham Manufacturing Company, *Catalogue*, Autumn 1882. GMCA.

83 "Manufacturing and Mechanical Industry of Rhode Island. Silver Ware.—Gorham Manufacturing Company," *Providence Journal*, May 19, 1871.

84 Gorham, *Catalogue*, Autumn 1882, GMCA.

85 "Jefferson Loving Cup Is Now Being Made at the Gorham Works," *Providence Journal* (January 2, 1896). "The Joseph Jefferson Loving Cup," *The Manufacturing Jeweler* (January 16, 1896): 146. Both are clippings pasted in an album.

86 Ibid.

87 Samuel Hough, *Sotheby's Important Americana* (New York, January 21, 2011, Lot 127).

88 L. J. Pristo, *Martelé: Gorham's Nouveau Art Silver* (Phoenix: Phoenix Publishing Group, 2002), 53.

89 Joseph Hall, *Biographical History of the Manufacturers and Business Men of Rhode Island at the Opening of the 20th Century* (Providence: J. D. Hall & Co., 1901), 8. See Dehan and Futter, page 252, note 125.

90 "Rare and Unique Exhibit of Hand Wrought Silver," *Jewelers' Circular*, November 17, 1897.

91 John Webster Keefe and Samuel J. Hough, *Magnificent, Marvelous Martelé* (New Orleans: New Orleans Museum of Art, 2001), 135.

92 Pristo, *Martelé: Gorham's Nouveau Art Silver*, 54.

93 Ibid., 53.

94 Charles R. Richards, Henry Creange, and Frank Graham Homes, *Report of Commission Appointed by the Secretary of Commerce to Visit and Report upon the International Exposition of Modern Decorative and Industrial Art in Paris 1925* (Washington: U.S. Government Printing Office, 1926), 18–29.

95 Charles L. Venable, *Silver in America, 1840–1940: A Century of Splendor*, 280.

96 Jewel Stern, *Modernism in American Silver: 20th-Century Design* (New Haven and London: Yale University Press / Dallas: Dallas Museum of Art, 2005), 28.

97 Elizabeth Lounsbery, "Modernistic Influence on Sterling Silver: The Lights and Shadows of a Skyscraper Are Reflected in This New Table Service," *Arts and Decoration* 28 (April 1928): 52

98 "Sculptor Revives Lost Art of Working Precious Metals," *Popular Science Monthly* 125 (October 1934): 40.

99 Stern, *Modernism in American Silver*, 257, 348–49; Amy Dehan, "Back to the Future, Gorham's *Circa '70* Service," *Gastronomica* 11, no. 4 (Winter 2011): 11–13.

100 Conant, "The Silver Age," 202.

101 Parton, "Silver and Silver Plate," *Harper's New Monthly Magazine*, 443.

GORHAM WORKS
1900s–1960s

205
Design for an *Athenic* Loving Cup, ca. 1900.
William Christmas Codman, designer.
Pencil, watercolor, ink, crayon, and gouache on paper.
RISD Museum

206
Athenic Cigar Box, 1901.
Copper, silver, and cedar.
RISD Museum

207
Martelé Chair, 1903. William Christmas Codman, designer; Joseph Edward Straker, silversmith; Franz Ziegler, carver; and Potter and Company, furniture maker. Ebony, mahogany, silver, ivory, and gilded tooled leather. RISD Museum

209
Martelé Writing Table (detail), 1903.
RISD Museum

208
Martelé Writing Table and Chair, 1903.
William Christmas Codman, designer;
Joseph Edward Straker, silversmith;
Franz Ziegler, carver; and Potter and
Company, furniture maker. Ebony, mahogany,
boxwood, redwood, thuya wood, ivory,
mother-of-pearl, silver, mirrored glass, and
gilded tooled leather. RISD Museum

210
Design for DGL *Martelé* Creamer, 1903.
Graphite and crayon on paper.
RISD Museum

211
Design for *Martelé*
Sugar Bowl, ca. 1905.
Graphite and ink on paper.
RISD Museum

212
Martelé Tea and
Coffee Service, 1901.
William Christmas Codman,
designer; Otto Colmetz,
chaser; Herbert C. Lloyd,
chaser; and William L.
MacMillan, chaser. Silver with
gilding and ivory.
RISD Museum

213
Athenic Candelabrum, 1902.
Silver. RISD Museum

214
Athenic Candelabrum (detail), 1902.
RISD Museum

215
Pair of Candlesticks, 1928.
Erik Magnussen, designer.
Silver with turquoise.
RISD Museum

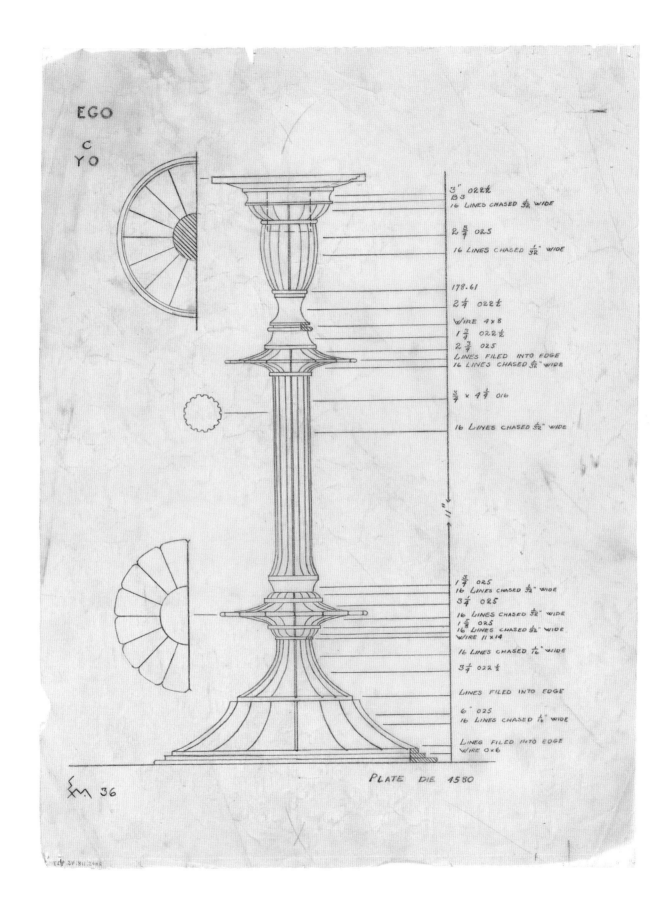

216
Design for a Candlestick, 1927.
Erik Magnussen, designer.
Graphite on tracing paper.
RISD Museum

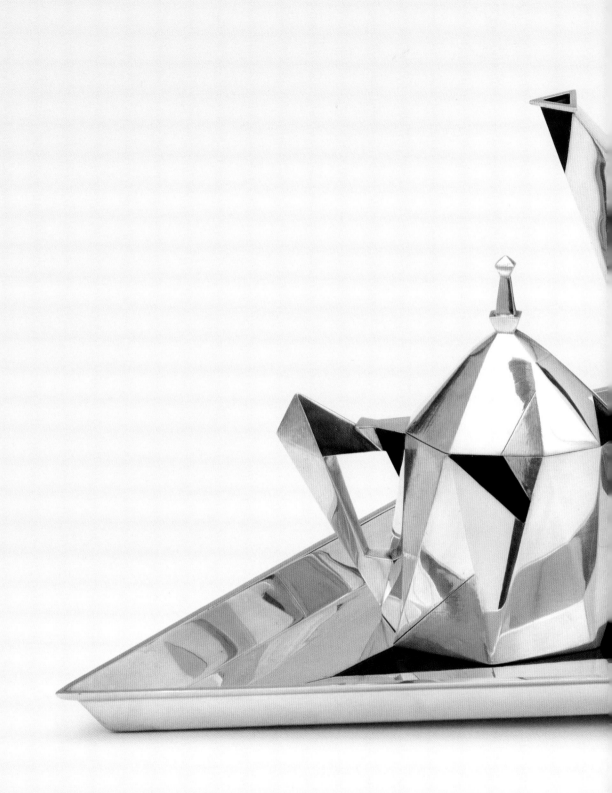

217
Cubic Coffee Service, 1927.
Erik Magnussen, designer.
Silver with gilding and ivory.
RISD Museum

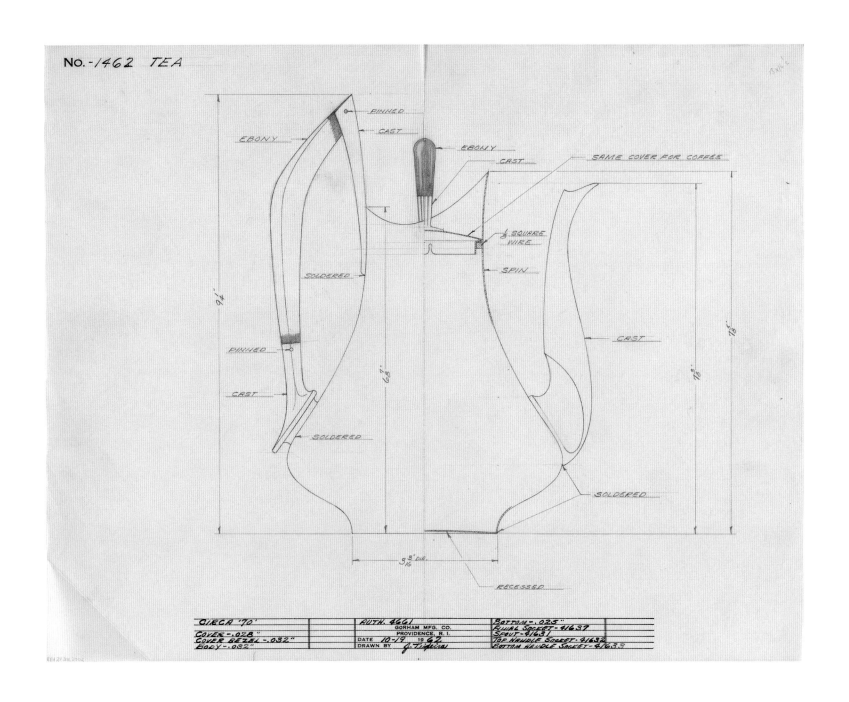

218
Design for *Circa '70* Teapot, 1962.
J. Teixeira, delineator. Graphite and ink
on waxed paper. RISD Museum

219
Circa '70 Coffee and Tea Service, 1960.
Donald H. Colflesh, designer. *Circa '70* Tray, 1963.
Silver with ebony and Formica. RISD Museum

Amy Miller Dehan and Catherine L. Futter

MARKETING GORHAM SILVER

PLACING SILVER BEFORE THE PUBLIC

220
Gorham Pavilion, Centennial
International Exhibition
of 1876, Philadelphia, in
The Century Vase, Gorham
Archive, John Hay Library

The high level of creativity and innovation manifest in Gorham's silver wares also pervaded the firm's strategies for marketing and selling their wares domestically and abroad. As an artistic firm established at the dawn of the Industrial Revolution, Gorham was among the pioneers that developed a new and evolving focus on advertising and market expansion and also established a vast sales force and network of distributors; brick-and-mortar retail and wholesale venues; the publication and circulation of printed catalogues; multimedia advertising campaigns; and participation in regional, national, and international exhibitions and world's fairs.[1]

1850–1876

Paired with John Gorham's ambition to produce all types of silver wares on a monumental scale was his desire to sell those products far and wide across the country. Gorham's business plan included the development of a national network of salesmen and retailers whose work would find support in robust advertising campaigns and public exhibitions. The success of the earliest implementations of this plan are evidenced in the firm's increased sales figures.[2] Although sales dipped briefly upon the eve of the Civil War in 1861, Gorham weathered the period with considerable ease, thanks to sound development and growth strategies.[3] Unfortunately, growth was tempered shortly thereafter by widespread economic depression (1873–79), and John Gorham's personal financial struggles, which culminated in his departure from the firm in 1878. Nevertheless, increased marketing and exposure through journal publications, advertising, participation in public exhibitions (especially the 1876 Philadelphia Centennial International Exhibition), and new leadership would eventually restore the firm's onward rise to great recognition and success.

In addition to marketing through salesmen and retailers, Gorham employed another promotional technique first introduced in the nineteenth century: the public exhibition. Gorham participated in a number of smaller local and state exhibitions and, additionally, took center stage with the first international exhibition held in the United States in 1876. Moreover, the firm was able to capitalize on another development of the mid-nineteenth century: the increase in popular and trade journals and publications. Print advertising became an effective tool in publicizing new lines and forms as well as technological developments.

Establishing a Sales Force

Working under the name of Gorham & Thurber from 1850 to 1852 (fig. 6), and then as Gorham & Co. until 1865, cousins John Gorham (fig. 2) and Gorham Thurber maintained and advertised the wholesale salesroom established in the 1820s by Jabez Gorham (fig. 4) at 12 Steeple Street (fig. 10) in Providence, Rhode Island, "nearly opposite First Baptist Church."[4] It was here, in the same building where the firm's work was manufactured, that independent peddlers would call. "Mr. Thurber took charge of the financial part, the books and the selling of the goods," while John Gorham focused on increasing production.[5]

As production increased, the firm began to develop and benefit from its own sales force. The significance of this stride is evident when considering that Jabez Gorham barely sold enough to cover his expenses in 1819 on his earliest unaccompanied sales trip, which he made to towns in Connecticut, Massachusetts, and Vermont.[6] Initially assigned to territories covering the East Coast, the Midwest, and the West Coast, Gorham's new band of salesmen traveled thousands of miles, carrying photographs and examples of representative works for the consideration of retail jewelry store owners. By the beginning of the Civil War, Gorham's distribution had expanded to include Canada.[7]

Notably, Gorham was the first American silver manufacturer to utilize industrial photography, beginning in 1855 or 1856. By the early 1860s, a full photography department had been established.[8] In 1867, John Gorham testified, "We consider [photography] a necessary part of our silverware business."[9] The workings and basis for the department were later explained:

> Each new piece of silver is immediately photographed in the factory, and the proofs, once printed, and the price set, are distributed to the traveling salesmen in order to be able, without the loss of an instant, to find out how [the design] is received by the public, receive the orders, and dedicate the amount of stock to manufacture, for the American, faithful to the old English principle, "Time is money," does not wish to lose in groping, a moment of precious time.[10]

In addition to use by the sales force, photographs were also utilized internally, mounted in large albums (fig. 13), and referenced for a variety of purposes.

A salesman's pocket notebook dating from the early 1860s provides a partial understanding of the reach and activity of a Gorham representative assigned to a territory that stretched from the East Coast to the Midwest. The book lists seventy-two targeted silverware retailers. There were twenty-eight in Boston and fifteen in New York City, while others were in Albany, New York; Baltimore, Maryland; Manchester, New Hampshire; and Chicago, Illinois. They ranged from small establishments to much larger firms including Tiffany & Co. and Ball, Black and Co. in New York City and Canfield Brothers & Co. in Baltimore.[11]

Aware of the increase in consumer wealth and cultural sophistication in California that followed statehood in 1850 and the Gold Rush (1848–55), Gorham seized an early opportunity to increase awareness of its products by assigning salesmen to the West Coast. A letter, dated July 3, 1860, written to John Gorham in Providence from New York City–based sales manager Caleb Cushman Adams, reports on a recent trip to California:

> The goods arrived there in first order and when I got them open made a fine display. . . . I sold all the stock I carried with me and got 5% advance on prices, which is 1% more than the cost of getting the goods there. I also took orders for about $15,000 which makes the present trip rising $25,000, so that I think it is a paying trip. I am confident that we shall do splendid business in the future, as the population becomes more permanent. The demand for our rich goods will increase. . . . I got well acquainted with all the trade and made some new customers up the country.[12]

Adams specifically mentions dealings with John William Tucker and George C. Shreve, both prominent importing jewelers in San Francisco, who quickly became the largest jewelry and silver retailers and manufacturers there; Gorham provided a large proportion of the silver wares they offered to western customers (figs. 29, 30).[13] In the Midwest, Chicago was an important and developing Gorham market, as was Cincinnati. In 1861, just a few months before launching their own silver manufactory, Cincinnati's Duhme & Co. advertised "Gorham Table Plate [and] Sterling Silver Table Ware, a great variety of new and elegant designs."[14] Other fancy goods retailers and jewelers of the city, including Harry R. Smith and Clemens Oskamp, also advertised as regional agents for Gorham.[15]

Perhaps the Cincinnati man with the closest ties to Gorham was William Wilson McGrew, who advertised Gorham wares as part of his line as early as 1868.[16] In an attempt to bolster business when the national economy was down, Gorham sent the center-piece known as *Hiawatha's Boat* (fig. 224) for exhibition in McGrew's booth at the 1872 Cincinnati Industrial Exposition. Works surrounding the centerpiece in the display included "a gondola berry dish in the shape of an iceberg . . . a magnificent tea set, chased in full relief, two beautiful vases in oxidized silver . . . berry and preserve spoons in gold and silver [and] a Japanese combination ladle."[17] All was likely Gorham product. The following year, McGrew anchored his exposition display with the Gorham epergne from the Furber service (figs. 73, 74).[18] Both *Hiawatha's Boat* and the epergne would later be included in Gorham's own display at the 1876 Philadelphia Centennial International Exhibition (fig. 220).

Elsewhere in the Midwest and in the South, a cursory survey of mid-1870s newspaper advertisements finds that Gorham wares were marketed by retailers and agents including Giles, Brother & Co. (Chicago),[19] George Sharp Jr. (Atlanta),[20] William Brady (Harrisburg, Pennsylvania),[21] Davidsburg & Co. (Wilkes-Barre, Pennsylvania),[22] and M. S. Smith & Co., who advertised as Gorham's sole agents in Detroit.[23] Considering the spread of aforementioned houses, large and small, William C. Conant's 1875 statement that "there has been hardly a dealer of importance in America who has not depended chiefly on the Gorham Company for first-class silver ware" was not complete hyperbole.[24]

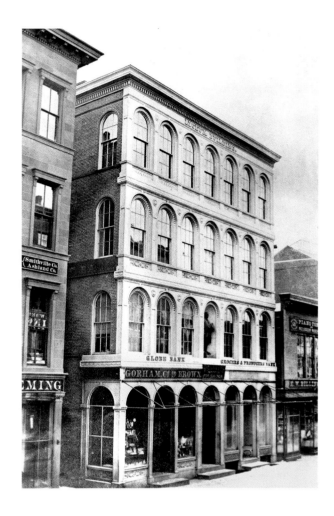

221
Gorham, Co. & Brown in the Lyceum Building, Providence, ca. 1865. Rhode Island Collection, Providence Public Library

Retail and Wholesale Activities

In 1856, Gorham ventured into its own retail business when Gorham & Company partnered with Henry T. Brown (1830–1893) to establish Gorham, Co. & Brown, a concern, managed by Brown, that sold Gorham silver and other fancy goods directly to the public.[25] By the 1860s, the shop was sited in the Lyceum Building (fig. 221) on Westminster Street in Providence.[26] While visiting Paris in 1860, John Gorham noted purchasing porcelain, bronzes, prints, ivories, opera glasses, and microscopes to supplement the store's stock.[27]

Acknowledging that a small showroom in Providence was not enough, Gorham took another leap forward in 1859 when it established a wholesale office in New York City at 4 Maiden Lane.[28] Their so-described "modest chambers" were aptly located in the silver and jewelry district of Lower Manhattan, a must-stop for silver retailers visiting from across the country to replenish stock.[29] In 1860, Gorham & Co. moved across the street and opened an expanded wholesale showroom at 3 Maiden Lane with G. & S. Owen,

manufacturing jewelers, also from Providence.[30] The firm's success in this location is suggested in the recollection that "on Christmas morning, 1864, there was left in the store in Maiden Lane . . . but seven dollars' worth of ware, out of an average stock of one hundred thousand dollars' worth."[31] An invoice dated January 27, 1865, for the purchase of more than $1,700 worth of silver suggests the variety of wares sold at the store. In addition to flatware, it lists a wine stand, cake basket, bell, casters, goblets, and a six-piece tea set.[32]

By the 1870s, many of the city's luxury goods dealers had relocated farther uptown to Bond Street. Gorham followed suit in 1871, relocating its wholesale showrooms to the new Waltham Building (fig. 222), an impressive six-story structure that occupied an entire block of Bond Street.[33] Gorham occupied the first floor of 1 Bond Street with Taylor, Olmstead & Taylor, importers of fancy goods.[34]

Gorham announced the opening of their first New York retail showroom at their Bond Street address in May 1873.[35] Previously, the firm had relied solely on others such as Howard & Co., Starr & Marcus,[36] and especially

D. APPLETON & CO.'S NEW STORE.

(*The Waltham Building, Nos. 1 to 5 Bond Street, N. Y.*)

Tiffany & Co. to sell their wares to the New York public. A combination of increased production and sales, as well as Tiffany & Co.'s decision to sell only its own silver designs, encouraged Gorham's move into the New York City retail market.[37] Not to be out-shown by competitors, they advertised "Solid Silver-Ware, Our own Manufacture Exclusively. The largest and richest stock ever shown in New York now offered at retail."[38] The showroom's December 1874 display boasted a multiplicity of silver objects at various price points. A description of the display notes the most elaborate and costly object offered as a "salver, designed in the style of Benvenuto Cellini, valued at $2,500" (fig. 14) (or about $55,500 in today's currency).[39] The point was quickly made that there were also "a variety of knick-knack, elegant trifles, and minor articles of use and ornament, at prices to suit the most economical purchaser. . . . small articles priced as low as $5, or even $3."[40]

On May 8, 1876, Gorham opened a new, expanded retail store at 37 Union Square, an important Manhattan crossroads and commercial center, and the Bond Street location returned exclusively to wholesale activities.[41] This increased the proximity of Gorham's retail business both to its wealthy private clientele and to its rival, Tiffany & Co., who had maintained a presence in the area since 1870. Wares prepared but not completed in time

for the 1876 Philadelphia Centennial were advertised and shown here alongside more typical stock wares.[42] Unfortunately, retail activities at this locale were abruptly halted by a devastating fire sparked in a basement engine room at 1, 3, and 5 Bond Street the evening of March 6, 1877. The fire raged for hours. An estimated $75,000 worth of plate was removed by members of the insurance patrol, but the whole building and most of its contents were destroyed.[43] The company's loss in sales stock was estimated at $175,000 (or approximately $4,230,000 in today's currency).[44]

Exhibitions, Fairs, and Communicating with the Public

National and international expositions became a major marketing tool for manufacturers in all industries during the nineteenth century, and Gorham used them to their full advantage. In 1852, John Gorham was drawn to London to visit the remnants of the first international fair, the Great Exhibition of the Works of Industry of All Nations, after its closing on October 15, 1851. As with other visitors, Gorham would have seen innovations in technology and artistic excellence—or the lack thereof—and been able to assess his competition. In 1860, he revisited the so-called Crystal Palace after it moved to Sydenham, outside of central London, writing in his diary of the experience: "Wonderful! Wonderful! Wonderful!"[45]

Even before Gorham's trips to London in 1852 and 1860, the company had participated in regional fairs. In 1850, Gorham & Thurber participated in the Fair of the Society for the Encouragement of Domestic Industry held in Providence. In a report from the Clocks and Watches, Silver Ware, Jewelry, and Fancy Articles Committee, the display by Gorham & Thurber was called out as "most conspicuous; the raised pieces in particular (comprising a full set of tea service) were very rich in style, and highly finished. The other portion included nearly every article of rich silver household furniture; the whole exhibited in a neat and tasteful manner, and deservedly attracted much attention."[46]

The following year, Gorham & Thurber participated in the Rhode Island State Fair, exhibiting a Chinese tea service similar to one now in the collection of the Art Institute of Chicago (fig. 111).[47] This repoussé service, produced in 1851 and seen in an advertisement for Gorham that illustrated both the service and the *Rebekah at the Well Pitcher* now in the Cincinnati Art Museum (figs. 110, 112), clearly demonstrated

Dehan and Futter

that the firm had achieved the highest quality craftsmanship in the latest Rococo chinoiserie designs in their newest endeavor, hollowware.[48] Not only did Gorham & Thurber garner the highest prize in "the graceful arts," the water kettle of the service was also described as "a new and elegant model . . . fully chased, the body being surrounded by a succession of scenes peculiar to China, which are exquisitely rendered. The feet, spout, etc., are formed of the tea plant, bearing leaves, buds and blossoms. The parts are supposed to harmonize, and the effect of the whole is in the highest degree ornate and graceful."[49]

Although there had been regional fairs, and an international fair in New York in 1853, it was the 1876 Philadelphia Centennial that established the hundred-year-old republic as a participant in the arena of international display and competition. The fair featured American manufacturers and a limited number of foreign producers. Gorham was probably the most well established of the American makers of silver and silver plate, but it was not alone in the displays. Tiffany & Co., J. E. Caldwell & Co., Meriden Britannia Co., and C. Rogers & Co. also exhibited. In the press, however, Gorham reigned supreme, with numerous illustrations in the commemorative catalogues and reports. One report stated, "[I]f the Gorham Manufacturing Company registered the number of visitors to its stall in the rotunda of the central transept, we suspect the footing up would reach several millions" (figs. 220, 223).[50] In another notice, Gorham's display was "commended for the great diversity of patterns and originality of designs; for repoussé, chased, and decorative work, with superior mechanical execution and marked excellence of material, both in solid silver and in plated ware."[51] The 1876 fair was a grand undertaking at the time of a very deep economic depression, and many of the firms, including Gorham, did not fabricate a large number of new items for display. As the circulation of images was more limited than today, and therefore audiences had not seen many of Gorham's larger productions, it was not unreasonable that the company exhibited works that had already been fabricated.[52]

Gorham's one major exception was the *Century Vase* (fig. 118). This extremely large-scale centerpiece—over 4 feet tall and 5 feet wide—reflected the ambitions of the new nation and proclaimed Gorham as the consummate producer of the most elaborate decorative and functional silver in the country. George Wilkinson and Thomas J. Pairpoint designed the program for the centerpiece. The monumental work proclaimed the triumph of America, as well as the unity of the country after the recent Civil War:

standing in a battlefield, the Genius of War holds the Dogs of War in check on one side, while the scene of children leading a lion amid a flower-strewn ground balances the other side. The motifs and figures recognized the past and present of the United States with representations of the original thirteen and then-current thirty-eight states, as well as the arts, philosophy, and diplomacy. The figures immediately beneath America signify the contributions to the exhibition from Europe, Asia, and Africa. According to one report: "aside from the mere mechanical execution, which is perfect in its way, the story of the republic has been told by fitting emblems brought together in one harmonious whole, which in itself—more, perhaps than any other feature of the design—typifies the cause of our great prosperity."[53] Very well documented in period photographs by Gorham in 1876, the centerpiece was also the subject of a stand-alone brochure. In 1878, an additional brochure with many images of the centerpiece and Gorham's stand at the Philadelphia Centennial, accompanied by a lengthy, detailed description by Providence businessman and bibliophile Alexander Farnum circulated to promote the centerpiece and Gorham's abilities.[54] Weighing two thousand troy ounces, or nearly 140 pounds, the centerpiece was priced at $25,000.[55] The centerpiece, which would also enhance Gorham's display at the 1889 Paris Exposition Universelle and the 1893 World's Columbian Exposition in Chicago, was melted down in the 1930s.[56]

In 1876, Gorham also displayed several items from the extensive service of 816 pieces made between 1866 and 1880 for Henry Jewett Furber and Elvira Irwin Furber of Chicago. The Furber works included the *Cellini Salver* (fig. 14), the *Cellini Vase* (figs. 75, 116), and a flat-sided pitcher decorated with a scene of a classically dressed woman with putti in a garden (figs. 89, 90).[57] One of the highlights of the Furber silver was a large, partially gilded centerpiece made in 1872 (figs. 73, 74). According to George Titus Ferris in *Gems of the Centennial Exhibition*, "It is pleasant to note in the leading silversmiths of America and England to-day the disposition to work out designs with freedom and boldness, with no further dependence on the past than what is essentially good and true."[58] One of the most notable of the works displayed at the 1876 fair was the large silver centerpiece produced in 1871 depicting a scene from Henry Wadsworth Longfellow's *Song of Hiawatha* (fig. 224). Fabricated of cast, hammered, and chased silver, the Iroquois chief Hiawatha sits in his masted canoe atop a mirror glass plateau gliding serenely forward. Mrs. Ulysses S. Grant purchased *Hiawatha's Boat* from the 1876 fair, and the centerpiece remains in the collection of the White House.

223
View from the southwest tower,
Main Building, Philadelphia Centennial
International Exhibition, 1876.
The Gorham Pavilion is at lower right.
Free Library of Philadelphia

Advertising

Print advertising was employed as a marketing tool from the earliest years of the firm. Some publicity was directed at the public, while other efforts were concentrated on members of the jewelry and hollowware and flatware trade. By 1852, Gorham was publicizing presentation pieces, such as commemorative ewers, or decorative pitchers in local newspapers with illustrated copy. One advertisement in the Boston *American Advertiser* included a pitcher with repoussé decoration with the copy: "Testimonials in silver, very richly embellished with appropriate designs, to order at short notice" (fig. 225).[59] Not only did Gorham market their wares, they also publicized the training and nationalities of their workers. A full-page advertisement in the December 1868 *Atlantic Advertiser & Miscellany* announced that the Gorham Manufacturing Company "have the largest manufactory of Solid Silver Plate in the world, and the only one in which all the operations involved in the production of silver ware are performed under the same roof."[60] The advertisement continues to detail the firm's transition from coin to sterling standard. In addition, it also touted "besides employing

the best native Silversmiths, the Gorham Manufacturing Company have procured the services of over one hundred of the best workmen and artists of Paris, Germany and England, who have come to this country at the company's invitation and have settled in Providence." Also, new machines and "new methods, new processes, new devices, enable the Gorham Company to manufacture silver plate of unequalled strength, durability and convenience." Finally, "The designs and patterns of the Company are *original*. They have now the most extensive and brilliant collection of original designs, patterns, and models in the country, and they are producing, every week, something new and attractive, adapted to the ever refining taste of the public." Notices in the popular press, in journals such as the *Aldine Press*, promoted Gorham's wares as editorial items, yet they are thinly disguised advertisements. At the same time, Gorham not only placed their own advertisements in journals, but retailers also promoted Gorham's products in paid advertisements for regional consumers.[61] After winning prizes at the international exhibitions, Gorham took out full-page advertisements proclaiming their successes with quotations from the reviews in the *Providence Journal*, *Boston Daily Advertiser*, *New York Evening Post*, and the *Daily Post* from Birmingham, England.[62]

224
Hiawatha's Boat, 1871.
Silver with gilding and mirror.
White House
Historical Association

article were supplied by Gorham, such as the relief from the *Cellini Vase*, the *Cellini Salver*, the flat-sided pitcher with images of Venus, and a communion service. Many, in fact were items exhibited at the 1876 Philadelphia Centennial.[65]

1877–1899

Under new leadership and increasingly favorable economic conditions, Gorham regained momentum after 1878. Edward Holbrook (1849–1919) (fig. 18) joined the sales force as a minor employee in 1870. Demonstrating an intense aptitude for sales and promotion, he quickly climbed the ranks and was "elected" agent, or manager, of all New York sales in 1876, treasurer in 1888, and president of the company in 1894. Holbrook seized upon the improvements in sales and marketing that John Gorham had set in motion. It became his mission to increase the volume

225
Gorham
advertisement, 1853

226
Illustration of the Ice Bowl
from the Furber service,
Harper's New Monthly Magazine,
September 1868

Gorham was successful in marketing through general-interest magazines. A fifteen-page article in the September 1868 *Harper's New Monthly Magazine* (fig. 226) focused on silver and silver plate, with Gorham supplying all the illustrations. The writer singled out the company as "the lead in improving this branch of manufacture in the United States," which had "improved public taste" and driven foreign competition from the American market.[63] Furthermore, the reader was encouraged to "avail himself of those free museums and galleries, the shop windows" to see Gorham's wares. "Blessed be he who first invented shop-windows, in which we can all enjoy the triumphs of ingenuity and taste without taking upon ourselves the charge of possessing them!" In 1875, the same type of article in *Scribner's Monthly* communicated the same message: Gorham reigned supreme in the manufacture of American silver, and American silver could now compete successfully and even surpass foreign-made products.[64] Once again, all the illustrations included in the

THE GORHAM MANUFACTURING COMPANY, SILVERSMITHS.
BROADWAY, NORTHWEST CORNER OF 19TH STREET.

531

227
Gorham Building,
Nineteenth Street and
Broadway, New York,
ca. 1886

fairs, encouraged the luxury, import, and desirability of Gorham's wares.

Gorham's increased focus on retail, marketing, and sales during this period is evidenced in Holbrook's 1898 incorporation of the Gorham Manufacturing Company of New York (referred to as the Gorham Company after 1906). A selling agent of the Gorham Manufacturing Company, it was established to focus solely on the retail of wares made by Gorham and its subsidiaries.[68]

Sales Force and Retail and Wholesale Venues

Following the Bond Street fire and other economic strains, Gorham announced in October 1877 that "in order to give our future attention exclusively to the manufacturing and wholesale business, we have arranged for the transfer of the sole conduct of our retail business to Mr. Theodore B. Starr . . . to his new warerooms, no. 206 Fifth Avenue."[69] Previously, the firm of Starr & Marcus had served as principal agents for Gorham in New York.[70] Extending from Fifth Ave to Broadway, Starr's warerooms opened on November 7, 1877, and the first floor was devoted exclusively to Gorham wares.[71] In turn, Gorham's location at 37 Union Square, near Seventeenth Street, converted to wholesale trade, boasting "a larger stock than any house in the trade."[72] Hailed as "one of the sights of the city," the Union Square rooms were advertised regularly in trade journals such as the *Jewelers' Circular and Horological Review* and exhibitions of "Art Silver" were held there in the "Art Room."[73]

Gorham's 1883 trade catalogue announced the company's plans to establish a New York headquarters for wholesale and retail sales at Nineteenth Street and Broadway, opening in spring 1884.[74] The new eight-story brick building (fig. 227) with terra-cotta trimmings, designed by architect Edward H. Kendall in the dominating "old Dutch style," was well placed in the fashionable Ladies' Mile shopping district. Gorham initially occupied its three lower floors. The firm's 1884 catalogue and the *Jewelers' Circular* published lengthy descriptions, providing virtual tours that began with the principal entrance on Broadway, flanked by large display windows.[75] The *Art Amateur* of December 1884 noted Gorham's shop windows: "In the field of Japanesque decoration, in which this firm is already distinguished, some marvelously good specimens of bronze and oxidized silver (fig. 228) are to be seen. The decorative purposes to which ivory (figs. 106, 107) may be applied in connection with the art of the silversmith also are notably appreciated."[76]

of sales and prestige of the firm across the globe, and that he did. At the time of his death in 1919, his business associates posited that "had it not been for him, Gorham Manufacturing Co. would not have advanced from the position of being one of many concerns to one of the most important leaders in the silverware manufacturing trade, not only of this country but of the entire world."[66]

During the 1880s and 1890s, more silver was produced in the United States than ever before.[67] This increase in production meant a rise in competition and product to sell. Gorham and its competitors enlarged their sales forces and expanded their marketing efforts. Railways made it easier and cheaper to cover more territory. Improved and more affordable printing techniques allowed for increased marketing through trade catalogues as well as advertisements placed in popular and trade magazines. A resulting surge in sales and financial flexibility allowed for the establishment of large, ostentatious showrooms, which, along with over-the-top displays and coveted awards received at international

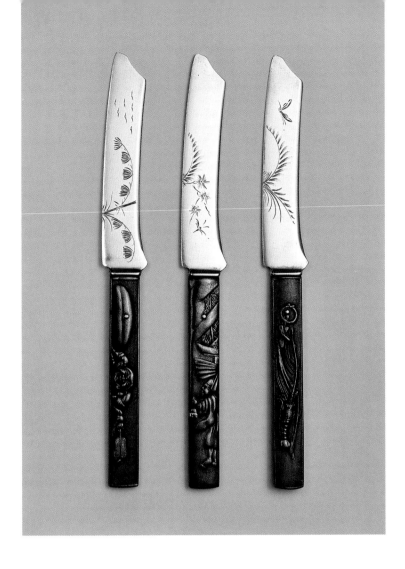

228
Knives, ca. 1880.
Silver and bronze.
RISD Museum

with a capacity of 288 lamps, "found to work admirably," both to illuminate merchandise *and* attract customers.[79] A *New York Times* article warns, "[T]he glitter of silver on each floor is ruinous to weak eyes."[80] In 1888, Gorham took over the third floor of the building for an engraving room for silver plate and the fourth floor for an additional showroom.[81] By 1894, art rooms for the display of the firm's most impressive silver "arranged as they would appear in the home" opened on the third floor.[82] By the early 1890s, 177 clerks were employed at the Broadway location, overshadowing the estimated 120 salesmen employed in Tiffany's New York store.[83]

Realizing the importance of a presence in the Lower Manhattan jewelry district (fig. 231). Gorham established a second wholesale showroom at 9 Maiden Lane in 1885.[84] Initially, Gorham shared the showroom with Boutillier & Co., purveyors of clocks and bronzes, but by 1887 they had taken over the entire store.[85] The salesroom moved to 21 and 23 Maiden Lane, the Hays Building, in 1892, and maintained a presence in this location for years, proving an essential part of their business into the mid-twentieth century.

The *Decorator and Furnisher* recognized Gorham's showrooms in 1891: "The Gorham Manufacturing Company always have new attractions. Their way of displaying their wares in large cases, flooded with electric light is perfect. From the beautifully arranged windows to the remotest corners of the store, the tasteful groupings of their goods gives one the impression of unquestionable satisfaction. . . . Every modern convenience for assisting the artistic work of their operators is employed, whose physical well-being is as much cared for as the goods they manufacture."[86]

While maintaining a New York wholesale and retail presence, Gorham also sought and secured opportunities to broaden its reach. By October 1878, it had opened a wholesale office in San Francisco at 120 Sutter Street, run by import jewelers Phelps & Miller.[87] Other independent San Francisco shops selling Gorham wares at this time included Braverman & Levy (ca. 1856–81), Schulz & Fischer (1867–90), and George C. Shreve & Co. (1858–83).[88]

In 1882, a wholesale office opened in Chicago under the management of Edward Prentiss at 170 State Street.[89] The branch was established with three employees: a cashier, a shipping clerk, and an errand boy. In 1885 George P. Gorham joined the office as a traveling salesman, and by 1888 the business had grown and moved to larger quarters at 137 and 139 State Street.[90] Walter V. Ghislin, the branch's original errand boy, was ultimately promoted and took "charge of the travelers and inside office work, acting as city salesman, cashier, etc." By the early 1890s, twelve clerks

The entrance of highly polished mahogany doors with beveled French plate glass led to the first floor, which was devoted to retail sales (fig. 229). Upon entering, "three long lines of showcases meet the eye. On the right, there extend the whole length of the building the wall cases. These sparkle with their valuable contents of crystal and silverware. Only Gorham plate is here exposed. Two rows of cases run the entire length of the room down its center; at each end a rounded case abuts these . . . and the effect is that of two immense crystal horse-shoes, placed foot to foot. On the left, six alcove cases, standing eight feet high, are arranged for the display of sterling silver."[77]

The second floor, accessible by elevator and staircase at the rear of the store, was devoted to wholesale business, and the basement held a stockroom, where "duplicates of every piece of silver and plate shown in the two immense warerooms overhead are constantly kept on hand," and where polishing, charging, packing, and shipping also took place.[78] The building boasted the Edison system of electricity

Gorham Store
Broadway & 19th St
New York

Gorham showroom,
Nineteenth Street and
Broadway, New York, ca. 1884

were employed, and continued success initiated a move to 131–137 Wabash Avenue in 1897.[91]

Recognizing that a considerable percentage of Gorham's sales came from the Midwest, Edward Holbrook seized the opportunity for increased retail sales in the region and established Spaulding & Co. in 1888 with Chicagoans Henry A. Spaulding and Levi Leiter.[92] For nearly two decades, Spaulding had maintained an office in Paris as Tiffany & Co.'s general representative in Europe, forging relationships with the principals of Europe's jewelry trade and the Continent's royal families and social elite. Not only did Gorham's collaboration with Spaulding position their wares in what would become Chicago's principal jewelry store, but it also opened channels to Europe, providing access to Spaulding's foreign network and Paris store, established in 1889 at 36, avenue de l'Opera. In 1894, Gorham's first English agency was opened at 32 Essex Street, London.[93] A Boston wholesale office was established at 45 West Street, room 56, in 1898.[94]

Territorial expansion bred a larger sales force, and an effective sales force required solid communication and coordination. To this end, Gorham held its first annual trade exhibition at the Providence factory in the summer of 1882.[95] Its purpose was to familiarize retailers and dealers with products, manufacturing techniques, and new lines. Events like this continued into the twentieth century.

Trade Catalogues

Gorham added trade catalogues to its marketing repertoire in autumn 1880 (fig. 230). By this time, catalogues were becoming commonplace tools of the trade, published by nearly all silver manufacturers of note.[96] Featuring richly detailed engravings and lithographs, they evolved into hefty publications, boasting hundreds of pages and depicting thousands of items, many illustrated to scale.[97] Intended for wholesalers and retailers, not individual customers, sales catalogues allowed retail outlets to peruse Gorham's wares without having to stock every item in a product line. As some services had hundreds of different utensils within any one given pattern, the catalogue could accomplish a great deal in terms of presenting the range of products. The issuance of a catalogue was big news, and announcements, descriptions, and reviews of catalogues often appeared in the trade journals.[98] Nearly every Gorham catalogue included an update on the superiority, achievements, and positive state of the company. The introduction published in their 1902 autumn catalogue read:

> The demands upon our resources during the past two years have been increasingly large, and have called for continual vigilance both in our artistic and mechanical departments. It is our wish, which we believe has been fully accomplished, to offer the Trade a line so complete that there need never be any occasion for looking beyond *our* stock. Certainly we have the equipment, including our own school of design and our unequaled manufactory, supported by an experience of over seventy years to meet the most exacting requirements. New designs are being constantly added to our already very full lines. We make it a point to LEAD the way in the direction of original ideas, and the Gorham name is always a well approved endorsement of newest fashions, beauty of designs, and perfection of worksmanship.[99]

Preceding the introduction, a richly illustrated frontispiece in the classical style celebrated the firm's receipt of the grand prix at the 1900 Exposition Universelle in Paris.

231
Maiden Lane,
Lower Manhattan,
New York, 1885

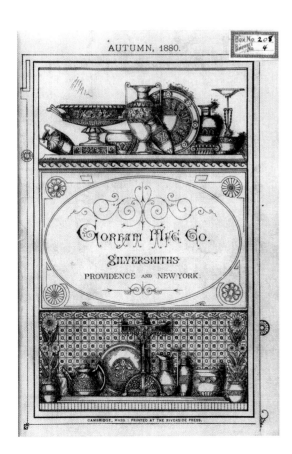

230
Gorham *Catalogue*,
Autumn 1880

The 1904 catalogue included photographs of the firm's pavilion at the Louisiana Purchase Exposition in Saint Louis (fig. 246), as well as a list of the awards and honors received there and at previous world's fairs in which they had participated.[100]

New patterns, designs, and novelties were frequently accompanied by lengthy texts meant to provide dealers with historical background and facts useful for wooing customers, as well as strategies for selling. In 1882 Gorham reported that the introduction of its copper hollowware line (figs. 91, 177), a considerable departure for the firm, "was greeted by the Trade with the most hearty sense of appreciation" and so "the variety originally confined to a few specific articles has been increased . . . until we are now enabled to offer a list of sufficient moment to constitute a distinct department of our business."[101] Despite the line's success, the company, concerned that copper might not be the most becoming metal choice for a silver company, admonished that "the dealer unaided by actual inspection and misled by the term Copper would doubtless fail to comprehend the real beauty and true merits of these goods" and assured

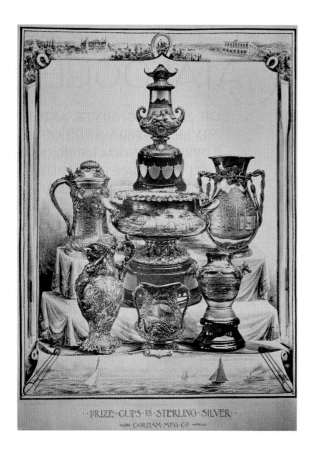

Gorham typically included one or two illustrations of its most impressive creations and filled the rest of the catalogue with less expensive stock pieces. Routinely, it reminded dealers that it was impossible to illustrate every example of its work, but hastened to add, "the facilities which our photographic department affords enable us to supply the Trade promptly with photographs of any article of our manufacture."[105] Illustrations of special commissions were featured, as well as notices such as "Designs and Estimates Furnished for Prizes and other Presentation Pieces" (figs. 135, 232).[106] Circulars dedicated to specific lines, such as spoon and fork work, are referenced as early as 1880, suggesting that Gorham utilized these smaller publications, presumably printed in larger quantities and dispersed more frequently, as another means of wholesale advertising.[107] Catalogues of all sizes, general and specialized, were produced as late as the 1980s. Featuring slick images of Gorham products accompanied by customer-enticing narratives, they remained an important element of the company's marketing efforts.

that the "skill displayed by the designer in producing the varied tones of color has given to them an indescribable charm."[102]

Gorham's catalogues were typically released in the autumn, just prior to the holiday buying season. About 1886, the firm's large general catalogues appear to have been published every other year. In the intervening years, smaller catalogues that focused on flatware were produced. The large biennial catalogues proved essential to business, although the cost to produce and disseminate them was considerable. Gorham's 1892 catalogue contained 300 pages with 1,700 illustrations depicting approximately 2,200 articles. Printed in an edition of 7,000, the books each weighed four and a half pounds and were sent by express to dealers at a total shipping expense of $2,000.[103]

Prices were not printed in the catalogues but were available separately in price lists. This eliminated the need to reprint a catalogue when prices changed. It also offered discretion to shop owners who might allow customers to browse the catalogue. Keeping the price list separate kept an item's wholesale price, and hence the seller's profit margin, confidential.[104]

American Silver Takes Center Stage

Although Gorham did not participate in the 1878 Paris Exposition Universelle,[108] most likely owing to the continuing economic depression, they would not to be left behind in international markets and participated in the Sydney International Exhibition of 1879–80.[109] The *Argus* of Sydney reported that "a good deal of instruction may be derived" from Gorham's display, especially designs in oxidized silver, overlaid on the sterling silver, cut through and then partially gilded (fig. 233). The critic observed that the oxidized silver had a "greenish tint that contrasted with the satin-like sheen of the silver, and the brilliance of the gold".[110]

The 1889 Paris Exposition Universelle set a high standard for the type and quality of American silver exhibited at world's fairs, and it brought great international attention to American silversmiths (fig. 234). Of the five American firms (Tiffany, Gorham, Meriden Britannia Co., Leroy W. Fairchild & Co., and J. F. Fradley & Co.), four of them received awards of excellence, including a *médaille d'or* for silverware for Gorham.[111] Gorham was included among winners who were hailed by the American *Jeweler's Weekly* as having "been crowned victors by belle France."[112] In the *New York Herald*, writer, journalist, and editor Margaret Frances Sullivan wrote of Gorham: "In force and individuality, as well as in exquisite manufacturers, the Gorham Company

stands in front." One visitor reflected on Gorham's 1889 display: "it is impossible to see a greater variety of silver articles in the Paris Exhibition. . . . I could go on almost indefinitely describing tea sets, punch bowls, tureens, . . . etc., all different in style and decoration."[113]

Although Gorham's displays included Saracenic, Japanese, Louis XVI, Greek, and Indian design inspirations, the predominant style was the relatively new pattern *Oriental East Indian*, described as "Strongly Oriental in feeling. Indian in style. Each piece carefully studied and each differs from the other in decoration. All motives are kept in harmony" (figs. 99, 100).[114] Derived from East Indian textiles and metalwork, these silver pieces incorporated densely chased designs of swirls, flowers, palmettes, and Greek key motifs. A six-piece tea service made 1886–89 was shown at the Paris Exposition Universelle, and is most likely the example given a prominent location to the left of the pavilion entryway, underscoring the pattern's importance.[115] Another example of this style displayed at the exposition was an exuberant pair of nine-branch candelabra with representations of elephants standing on pedestals, similar to the 1881 elephant fruit stand (fig. 131).[116]

234
Gorham Pavilion,
Exposition Universelle,
Paris, in *Frank Leslie's
Illustrated Newspaper*,
September 28, 1889

Even international critics, such as those in the British *Reports of Artisans*, admitted that American manufacturers had triumphed over European exhibitors: "[I]n making comparisons of the [silver] work, it must be conceded that America is by far the finest." The U.S. Commissioners' report further substantiated the encomium: "The United States made in their class [silver] an exhibit which attracted deserved attention and admiration from the public as well as the jury, and showed how much can be accomplished where the restless search for new forms and effects is modified and directed by good taste."[117] French jeweler Lucien Falize concludes his voluminous and repeated praise of Gorham and its display at the fair: "[O]ne of the principal causes of the Gorham Co.'s unparalleled success at the Exposition is that their goods never seem too expensive for what they are. The workmanship always looks fully up to the price."[118]

Four years later, the American silverware pavilion of the 1893 World's Columbian Exposition in Chicago was funded jointly by Gorham, Tiffany & Co., and Tiffany Glass and Decorating Company, as the American government would not financially support the enterprise (fig. 235). Designed by the New York architect John DuFais, this pavilion set the standard in opulence and refinement for future

235
Gorham and Tiffany Pavilion,
Gorham displays,
World's Columbian Exposition,
Chicago, 1893. Gorham Archive,
John Hay Library

and the gesture of the great navigator is altogether that of the man of genius pointing the way which will open to the world a new path for human activity."[120] Fairgoers were impressed by the world's largest silver sculpture, comprising more than a ton of silver at a cost of $25,000, excluding the artist's fee.[121]

On display in the pavilion were Gorham's myriad innovative silversmithing techniques, including enameling (figs. 161, 193), glass blown into silver mounts (fig. 151), and glass and ceramics with silver mounts and overlays (figs. 60, 149, 194, 238). Although Gorham showed works previously produced, such as the *Century Vase* from 1876, it was new productions, such as the *Nautilus Centerpiece* (fig. 137), that took center stage.[122] This remarkable yachting trophy was designed by William Christmas Codman specifically for the World's Columbian Exposition. In its interpretation of German Renaissance mounted nautilus shells and metalwork, the goddess Venus stands on a pedestal surrounded by four shells with the masks of Neptune; she supports a nautilus shell lavishly embellished with gilded mounts adorned with gemstones. The goddess of Victory, Nike, with her wings and arms outstretched in a gesture of triumph, perches on the mouth of the nautilus shell.

Other more modest works from the 1893 exposition demonstrated Gorham's collaboration with glass firms such as J. Hoare and Company and T. G. Hawkes & Company, both of Corning, New York.[123] Examples of these partnerships were shown at the fair, including a claret jug that combines a baluster-shaped vase with gilded cut-glass garlands supported and encased with silver-gilt mounts embellished with amethysts, garnets, and moonstones (fig. 150). In another work, partially gilded and chased scenes of nudes and putti among grapevines encircle the neck of a cut-glass decanter, which is enhanced with a large mask of Pan supporting the spout (fig. 153). Not only did Gorham win forty-five awards at the 1893 exposition, the favorable comments from international audiences, including the press and foreign government officials, helped the reputation and recognition of the firm's superlative products grow in stature. In fact, an exhibition of the 1893 World's Columbian Exposition prizewinners was held in New York at the Grand Central Palace in December 1893, furthering the standing of Gorham.[124]

In November 1897, under the direction of William Christmas Codman (fig. 134), Gorham premiered a new line of Art Nouveau silver, not yet titled *Martelé*, at the Waldorf-Astoria in New York.[125] The exhibition included "all articles for table use, excepting flat ware" and opened with a private press preview, followed by a showing for a "select group of artists,

silverware displays at world's fairs through 1915. The facade of the pavilion was crowned with a fan of American flags, surmounted by a monumental column 100 feet tall, capped with a golden American eagle atop a terrestrial globe—easily visible to the crowds of visitors to the Building of Manufacturers and Liberal Arts. Gorham and Tiffany had separate entrances, with Gorham's space measuring 3,770 square feet, decorated with a paneled ceiling and lunettes painted by Charles Frederick Naegele and medallions with portraits of the great silversmiths and designers: John Flaxman, Michelangelo, Albrecht Dürer, Peter Vischer, and Paul Revere.[119] New works created specifically for the exposition filled the cases. One of the French organizers of the 1878 Paris Exposition Universelle and the commissioner of the French section of the 1893 World's Columbian Exposition, Camille Krantz, praised Gorham, commenting that it was "the most important silver manufacturing firm in the United States" and likening it to the noted Parisian firm of Christofle. It is likely that Krantz equated Gorham to Christofle because both companies were dedicated to innovation and experimentation in metallurgical techniques.

Highlighted at the entrance of the Gorham 1893 display was an extraordinary 6-foot-tall silver figure of Christopher Columbus (fig. 236) reflecting the theme of the world's fair: the commemoration of the 400th anniversary of Columbus's landing in North America. Sculpted by the French artist Frédéric Auguste Bartholdi (1834–1904), already noted for his monumental Statue of Liberty, the figure was cast in a single pour (fig. 237). Krantz described Columbus's pose as "noble,

236
Gorham Pavilion interior,
World's Columbian Exposition,
Chicago, 1893. Gorham Archive,
John Hay Library

237
First view of the
casting for the statue of
Christopher Columbus,
1893. Gorham Archive,
John Hay Library

Dehan and Futter

architects and collectors" before opening to the public for one week. [126] According to the *Jewelers' Circular*, the exhibition featured "hand wrought silver by the Gorham Mfg. Co. different in kind from anything yet presented to the American public. . . . The exhibition is intended to awaken general interest in a renaissance of the work of the silversmith of years ago, as distinguished from the machine made wares of today."[127] The article continued: "In the hundreds of pieces shown there is not one of the company's regular productions, all being made entirely for this exhibition . . . and unduplicated."[128]

Gorham was testing the waters for what would be one of its greatest contributions to American turn-of-the-twentieth-century silver: the *Martelé* line (fig. 245), which combined the sinuous forms and lines of the Art Nouveau with the ideology of the Arts and Crafts movement. In the December 1899 issue of *House Beautiful*, author Charlotte Moffitt commented that Codman "never for a moment loses sight of the fact that he is designing for metal, and though he takes his motives from many natural forms, he expresses them only in metallic terms."[129]

Advertising

Owing to the decrease in costs of printing and the introduction of wood-pulp paper, the late nineteenth century saw tremendous growth in the number of publications. Publications were produced as a means to communicate directly with wholesalers, as in the printing of trade catalogues. In addition, the growth of weekly and monthly journals and daily papers reached consumers. Gorham also created special publications; two such volumes were produced in 1895 and 1898, entitled *Suggestions*. The 1895 version, called *Gorham Suggestions*, showed a list of "Articles priced at Ten Dollars and under, suitable for gifts, favors, etc." The booklet was produced "in response to many requests for a 'price list of novelties' suitable for gifts, favors, and prizes."[130] The eighty-two-page 1898 booklet is lavishly illustrated and arranged alphabetically, listing items for dining, writing, reading, sewing, as well as candelabra, mounted glassware, children's items, and souvenir spoons.[131] Another category of goods, which was a major income producer, was loving cups (fig. 163) and prizes for "athletic competitions and out-of-door sports." In the pages adjacent to this description are drawings of *Martelé* ewers and basins (fig. 140), three-handled loving cups (fig. 196), tankards (fig. 139), and punch bowls.[132]

Gorham also appealed directly to the consumer through newspaper and journal advertisements that presented compelling reasons to purchase silver, including weddings, trophies for competitions, and holiday gifts. Gorham's marketing efforts were under the direction of William N. Lecato, who detailed the approach the company took to promote its goods in two articles in *Printers' Ink* in 1901 and 1902.[133] According to Lecato, the "modern" marketing campaign began about 1891, with the company spending about $60,000 a year on promotion: "[T]his goes into newspapers, magazines and high-end literature. Ours are expensive goods, and their nature gives our advertising a distinctive tone. . . . Our ware is a luxury, appealing to people of means, and we trust wholly to refined, dignified methods to build up the name 'Gorham.'"[134]

1900–1940

Gorham weathered the 1893 financial panic better than most American silver manufacturers. In the spirit of John D. Rockefeller and other captains of industry, Edward Holbrook began to acquire Gorham's struggling competitors and formed his own silver manufacturing empire, which included Gorham.[135] Consolidated resources and efficiencies led to higher profits, and by 1917, Gorham sales reached more than $7 million (more than $134 million in today's currency).[136] The *Martelé* line, introduced to the world at the 1900 Paris Exposition Universelle, was an undeniable success, and the firm continued to do well with its historical revival designs as well as its modern lines. However, hardships resulting from the country's entry into World War I and the firm's expansions into munitions work, the loss of Holbrook's leadership upon his death in 1919, the recession in 1920 and 1921, and falling silver prices soon ushered in one of Gorham's darkest eras. By 1921, Gorham was effectively bankrupt.[137]

Recovery involved a much-needed reorganization and consolidation of the company and its subsidiaries. In January 1923, Gorham commissioned an extensive report on its standing and future prospects from the New York financial firm of Aldred & Co.[138] Many of the suggested actions outlined in the report were implemented by Edmund C. Mayo, who assumed Gorham's presidency in 1925. The development of marketing as a professional discipline in and of itself also took hold in this era, and Gorham made smart use of the research and expertise that prevailed. The development of a multipronged, effective marketing strategy was among Mayo's major achievements. As the years during and following the Great Depression brought yet another period of economic hardship and formed preferences for simpler, highly edited housewares and lifestyles, effective marketing became more important than ever.

least three traveling salesmen by 1906 but ceased operation in 1907.[143] The Birmingham factory closed in 1914.[144] By 1922, sales abroad were low, accounting for only $3,000 of total sales. The 1923 Aldred & Co. report advocated for a study of prospects in Mexico and Central and South America.[145]

Cultivating the Sales Force

Gorham continued to rely heavily on its vast network of retail jewelry stores for the sale and distribution of its products. The importance of retail buy-in and cooperation became especially apparent after the 1921 introduction of an ill-conceived marketing policy that allowed any retailer, including department stores, to sell Gorham ware. The short-lived policy not only failed, but it alienated many of the high-end jewelry retailers Gorham relied on.[146] Noting this, the Aldred report reiterated the importance of "constructive work with the sales force."[147]

A retail-sales study program, held in Providence, was initiated by 1925. There, Gorham assembled "the best merchandising minds of the country with the view of analyzing the situation and evolving new merchandise methods [to] increase sterling silverware sales." Applications from retail jewelers from across the country were encouraged, and fifty were accepted.[148] It was later observed that the "goodwill generated by this series of seminars was inestimable."[149] By the close of the program, it was promised that attendees would "have a complete mental picture of the world's largest sterling silver manufacturing plant—and a comprehensive knowledge of our administration from end to end."[150] Regular sales conventions and wholesale sales conferences (fig. 239) augmented these efforts by providing briefings on the state of business, new merchandise, and advertising campaigns; sessions on stock control, store management, and promotion; and the opportunity to network with other retailers and Gorham corporate leaders.[151] A report from the 1925 Sale and Factory Conference stated that it was "demonstrated that everyone . . . was determined to do his share toward the production of the merchandise . . . and that determination was going to be matched by the sales force in using every effort on their part to dispose of the merchandise. Thus was brought about a closer sympathy of feeling between our manufacturing and sales departments than we have known before."[152]

Gorham also authored written material to keep its sales force and related constituents abreast of preferred

Expanding International Sales

During the first decades of the twentieth century, Gorham developed a more strategic approach to selling its wares outside the United States. Access to Paris and other European cities came through retailer Spaulding & Co., but there were other potential markets to explore. In 1901 and 1902, a representative, likely salesman Abraham Cotton, was sent to South Africa.[139] Initial sales there were so promising that in 1904, Gorham opened a wholesale office and showroom in London at Audrey House on Ely Place, under Cotton's management, to sell to the United Kingdom, South Africa, and other territories.[140] From there, Gorham salesmen also conducted business with dealers in the Netherlands, Italy, Belgium, Switzerland, Australia, India, the Straits Settlements, Sumatra, Malta, Egypt, Java, China, and Ceylon.[141] A factory in Birmingham, England, was established in 1908 to produce wares for these markets that bore British hallmarks rather than import stamps.[142] A manufacturing center had been established in Montreal in 1901 to cater to Canadian markets. Managed by George Chillas, it had employed at practices and industry news. *To Our Salesmen*, a pocket-size book published in 1908, instructed salesmen on the proper handling of silver as to avoid fingerprints and other mishaps and impressed that treating merchandise with respect conveyed its value.[153] The booklet *Some Business Commandments*, written in the style of the biblical Ten Commandments, ministered the importance of maintaining a respectable appearance and character, solid work ethic, and professional demeanor.[154] "Thou shall not wait for something to turn up," it instructed, "but thou shalt pull off thy coat and go to work that thou mayest prosper in thy affairs and make the word 'failure' spell 'success.'"[155]

On December 1, 1924, Gorham published its first issue of the *Silver Tongue,* a quarterly booklet "for and in the interest of all employees," belonging "to the whole family . . . whether we push a pen or a truck, whether we pack a grip or a shipping case."[156] In addition to featuring company news, it also fostered camaraderie among Gorham's ranks. A weekly newsletter *Contact,* later retitled *Harmony,* was established in April 1930 to instill "a spirit of understanding and coordination between factory and salesmen."[157] In addition to social announcements for company bowling leagues, dances, picnics, and personal news, such as "Gorhamite" marriages, promotions, retirements, and babies, it included business-focused items such as price list updates and selling strategies to aid recovery following the Great

Depression. *The Gorham Mark*, a booklet containing descriptions and illustrations of advertising material available to Gorham dealers, published in about 1918, was billed as "the first piece in a campaign to cooperate more extensively with dealers in making their local advertising more productive."[158] Items available for order included literature that could be mailed to customers, show cards for window displays, electrotypes for newspaper advertising, and even movie slides. "Every family which owns a car can afford more silverware, *if they are made to want more.* Advertising made them want cars . . . Advertising can make them want more silverware."[159]

A lack of strategic merchandising, resulting in low sales and profits, was a significant problem addressed in the 1923 Aldred & Co. report. To combat this, Gorham partnered in 1927 with Wharton School faculty at the University of Pennsylvania to publish a manual for administrators of the jewelry stores that sold Gorham wares.[160] The manual was "designed to aid . . . in the solution of the many problems with which [administrators] are confronted in the conduct of their business."[161] It stressed the importance of annual marketing plans developed cooperatively among advertising, buying, and sales departments and advocated for well-rounded advertising campaigns that combined the use of direct mail, newspapers, store windows, special exhibitions, and periodic sales.[162] An extremely comprehensive 1932 sales manual equipped retailers with all of the facts and strategy one might need to impress a client and secure a sale.[163] It covered historical overviews of the Gorham firm, silver

as a material, silver design and manufacture, furniture design, and the company's flatware and hollowware patterns. It also presented a merchandising study outlining where and how different hollowware forms could be utilized in the home, and entire chapters were devoted to advertising and window display.

Windows, when smartly utilized, were deemed to be worth at least one-half the rental of an entire store. Culled from "nearly one hundred display experts" employed by the country's leading stores, the twelve cardinal points of window display were presented. These ranged from the power of attraction to timeliness. "The best lighting effects, the most beautiful colorings and the most careful selection of goods will not produce the desired results unless the window first attracts attention."[164] "Timeliness and news value of the display . . . adds materially to the power of attraction and . . . helps to impress the 'liveness' of the store."[165] When collectively applied, these twelve points

promised to "arouse the feeling of want in the customer"; appeal to "buying instincts" such as comfort, beauty, and pleasure; and transform desire into action.[166] Additionally, traveling window display kits, created by Gorham's advertising department, circulated out of the New York, Chicago, and San Francisco offices, offering retailers "hundreds of dollars of merchandise, time and thought" and promising local publicity.[167]

As time moved forward, there was a systematic modernizing or streamlining of store decor and window displays in keeping with the latest aesthetic trends. This is especially well illustrated in the 1940 renovation of the firm's Providence showrooms, located at company headquarters, adjacent to its executive offices. An invitation targeting Gorham retailers announced, "Completely new interiors, modern ideas in lighting, superb settings for silver. . . . You'll find ideas directly usable in your own business. New slants for display. Suggestions for promotion. Plan to stop off while you are East this summer."[168]

Dehan and Futter

242
First-floor interior, Thirty-Sixth Street and Fifth Avenue building, New York, 1903. Gorham Archive, John Hay Library

Designed by local architect Albert Harkness, the Providence showrooms boasted a light, elegant, modern air in the combination of clean lines, walnut and butternut woodwork, and a taupe, blue-green, and peach palette.[169] Bronze sculpture and dazzling sterling displayed in recessed cases greeted visitors upon entering the first-floor lobby. Similar displays continued down a passage that led to a round stair hall. Both the plate room and the larger sterling room on the second floor displayed wares in recessed cases, as well as in custom cupboards and on a long dining-room table (fig. 240).

Retail and Wholesale Venues

In 1903, Edward Holbrook commissioned the revered firm of McKim, Mead & White to erect an eight-story fireproof building for Gorham's New York headquarters at Thirty-Sixth Street and Fifth Avenue (fig. 241).[170] Stanford White's building gave every consideration to the company's image and goals as

well as to its operational and business requirements. Designed in the Renaissance style, the Midtown Manhattan structure assumed a more modern appearance than the old Broadway location and was intended to align the company simultaneously with both America's fashionable elite and the artistic achievements of fifteenth-century Italy. Bas reliefs of *Art* and *Industry* by American sculptor Andrew O'Connor were placed in the spandrels between the arches of the lower story, and elaborate bronze work produced in Gorham's foundry was incorporated into the facade. Large, deep display windows allowed for elaborate presentations to passersby, and clerestory windows welcomed an abundance of natural daylight into the first-floor gallery (fig. 242), which boasted more than 10,000 square feet for retail under a high, impressively decorative groin-vaulted ceiling. The second floor, reserved for display of the finest goods, included three showrooms to serve customers "individually and free from all fear of interruption."[171] A photograph of one of the showrooms (fig. 243) reveals the candelabra shown at the 1904 Louisiana Purchase Exposition in Saint Louis (figs. 213, 214, 244). The third floor of the building housed the ecclesiastical department, where a room was "fitted up as a chapel," and the company's bronze and hotel departments.

Wholesale rooms were located on the fourth floor. The stationery, engraving, and stained-glass-window departments, offices, and stockrooms occupied the floors above. When the building opened on September 4, 1905, it displayed $2.5 million worth of stock.[172] Of particular note were "massive pieces of tableware in solid silver and in gold, all in new designs and exquisitely finished . . . loving cups, tea and dinner sets, articles for the toilet, jewelry, and thousands of pieces of hammered silver."[173] In 1906, Tiffany & Co. opened a new building, also designed by McKim, Mead & White, on Fifth Avenue, only a block away from Gorham.

243
Second-floor interior,
Thirty-Sixth Street and
Fifth Avenue building, with
Athenic candelabra displayed,
1903–6. Museum of the
City of New York

Almost two decades later, in harsher times, Aldred & Co. turned a critical eye toward Gorham's retail establishments. "We doubt that it was wise to establish the stores," it asserted.[174] Gorham's principal business was the manufacture of silverwares for retailers, it stated, and its own retail stores were competing with those retailers. Acknowledging that abolishment of Gorham's already well-established retail outlets was unlikely, Aldred encouraged the firm to combine its company stores with "high-grade jewelers" or to make other arrangements that would "maintain sales without the conduct of the stores by you."[175] The Fifth Avenue store was cited as slow in the months outside the "rush season," with visitors numbering "hardly a baker's dozen" each day."[176] Clerical forces (excluding salesmen) outnumbered salespeople, and the store did not require such a large part of the building.[177] In reaction, Gorham relinquished its Thirty-Sixth Street and Fifth Avenue building and relocated its retail and wholesale showroom to Fifth Avenue and Forty-Seventh Street in 1924.[178] It was here where, in 1926, in an effort to appeal to conservative tastes for revival styles, Gorham created a period room to showcase its historically inspired silverware and to provide special instruction for salesmen in its period lines.[179]

In January 1929, the subsidiary Gorham, Inc., was formed to oversee the company-held retail stores. The store at Fifth Avenue and Forty-Seventh Street was merged with neighbors Black, Starr & Frost to form Black, Starr & Frost-Gorham, Inc., which opened showrooms at Fifth Avenue and Forty-Eighth Street and operated branch stores in the upscale communities of Southampton, Manhasset, and White Plains, New York; Millburn, New Jersey; and Palm Beach, Florida.[180] In Chicago, Gorham, Inc., took over Spaulding & Co., creating Spaulding-Gorham, Inc., which gave them control of retail stores in Chicago and Evanston, Illinois, and in Paris.[181] A year later, in Atlanta, Gorham acquired long-standing jewelers Maier & Berkele, Inc., which became Maier & Berkele-Gorham, Inc.[182]

With regard to wholesale, rooms were maintained at Gorham headquarters, which had opened in 1905 on Thirty-Sixth Street, and in the jewelry district on Maiden Lane. In 1908, the latter rooms moved from the Hays Building to "more commodious quarters" in the new Silversmith's Building at 15-17-19 Maiden Lane.[183] Areas in the twenty-story building, owned by Holbrook's Maiden Lane Realty Co., that were not occupied by Gorham were leased to other jewelry concerns, including the National Jewelers Board of Trade and the Jeweler's 24-Karat Club. This ensured that nearly everyone in the business had reason to visit and drop

244
Athenic Candelabra,
1902. Silver.
RISD Museum

by Gorham's sales rooms.[184] In 1922,
Maiden Lane annual sales measured
strong, at more than a quarter of a
million dollars. This location remained
active through the mid-twentieth
century.[185] Uptown, when Gorham left its Thirty-Sixth Street
and Fifth Avenue building in 1924, its wholesale business
moved with it to Forty-Seventh Street and Fifth Avenue.[186]
The subsidiary Gorham Co. was formed in 1929, as a counter-
part to Gorham, Inc., to manage the wholesale distribution
of Gorham wares.[187]

In order to assess the geographical distribution
of Gorham's sales and the value of its regional wholesale
offices, Aldred & Co. analyzed sales for 1922.[188] Although
New York and Philadelphia came in highest, with sales
of just over one million dollars each, their close proximity
prompted a merger in 1926.[189] Not far behind in sales, the
Chicago office merged with Spaulding & Co. in 1929 to
cut costs, and the Atlanta office was closed in 1930.[190] With
only a third of New York's sales, the Boston office was
moved to Providence in 1927, and although San Francisco
was the lowest in sales, as the firm's only West Coast
branch, it remained in operation.[191]

Firmly on an
International Stage

Although the organic, hand-wrought *Martelé* line was first
introduced in 1897, Holbrook and Codman chose the Paris
1900 Exposition Universelle to premiere this new work,
which formed half of Gorham's products shown at the fair
(figs. 139, 143, 159, 196).[192] With *Martelé*, Gorham firmly established that the company was "of the moment" and could
compete with European manufacturers in the latest fashionable style: Art Nouveau.

By far the most impressive work in the *Martelé* line
was the meticulously handcrafted dressing table and stool
(fig. 138), displayed at the Paris Exposition Universelle.
Gorham's chief designer, William Christmas Codman, was
responsible for the extravagant design, which was executed
by a team of silversmiths using more than seventy-eight
pounds of silver and laboring more than 2,300 hours.[193] The
table reflects a combination of stylistic influences: traditional eighteenth-century Rococo elements include cabriole
legs terminating in claw-and-ball feet, while the nude woman
flanked by peacocks at the top of the mirror and the rich
chasing of floral designs reveals the fluid ornamentation
of Art Nouveau. Looking both forward and backward, the

245
Vase, 1899. Silver.
Collection of
Suzanne and Joel Sugg

One writer, Herbert Sherman Houston, chose to focus on the sense of the individual in the work of Gorham—not only of the pieces but the role of the craftsman: "The Gorham Company . . . [has] shown in its exhibit that work of individual merit, giving evidence in every detail of the hand of the artist-craftsman, may reach us from the workshops of the modern factory."[196] *Martelé* was commended for marrying function with artistry: "[I]t is nothing less than an artistic awakening to stand before the sets and individual pieces of *Martelé* shown in this exhibit. Its chaste forms, classic in their simplicity, its soft grayish color and the exquisitely simple designs, which decorate rather than conceal the beautiful surface, are a rest and delight to the eye."[197] Gorham also exhibited at La Prima Esposizione Internazionale d'Arte Decorativa Moderna (First International Exposition of Modern Decorative Arts), held in Turin in 1902, winning a gold medal for their silverwork. Although Tiffany—especially Louis Comfort Tiffany—was the darling of the reports on the fair, Gorham was included in publications such as *L'Arte Decorative all'Esposizione di Torino.* The detail report includes images of pieces of *Martelé,* a copper coffer with silver strapwork (fig. 206), and a toilette set of carved ivory and gold.[198]

At the 1904 Louisiana Purchase Exposition in Saint Louis, Gorham once again took the highest honors, winning the grand prize for silverware and goldware, jewelry, bronze works, leatherwork, and for applied arts (Fine Arts Gallery) (fig. 246). As with the 1900 Paris Exposition Universelle, the centerpiece of Gorham's display was a table and chair designed by William Christmas Codman—in this instance a writing table constructed of ebony and ivory with silver mounts and marquetry panels of ebony, ivory, pearl, and silver (figs. 197, 208) with an accompanying chair (fig. 207) made of ebony, ivory, and silver. Included was a desk set of hammered silver with repoussé decoration (fig. 247). Herbert S. Houston wrote in the *World's Work Advertiser,* "The Gorham silversmiths . . . have again shown by their exhibit that their work is the standard for measuring what America is doing in combining art with craftsmanship. And this union of the two is deeply interesting in showing what can be done under the stimulating conditions of freedom. For the Gorham Company has always encouraged full expression of the artistic spirit, and the designs shown in its exhibits in St. Louis, as were those at Chicago, Buffalo and Paris, are creations, not copies."[199] The majority of the products shown by Gorham in Saint Louis were specially fabricated for the fair. Again, Houston comments: "[I]n the designs there is so much artistic distinction, of quickening individuality—all bear witness to the wisdom which has made the Gorham factories schools of freedom."[200]

design can be seen as a metaphor for the contrast between the old and the new at the 1900 Exposition Universelle.

In Paris, Codman won the gold medal and Holbrook was made a chevalier of the French Légion d'honneur. The coup de grace was the grand prix for metalwork awarded to the Gorham Manufacturing Company.[194] Even the British press noted that Gorham had "no superiors on either side of the Atlantic . . . Indeed, it is to our Transatlantic cousins that we have to look for many of the most important and instructive lessons."[195] To honor its display at the 1900 exposition, the company published *The Gorham Mfg. Co., Silversmiths* in both French and English for distribution at the fair.

In displays and advertising, Gorham ensured prospective buyers that these were unique works of art. Gorham followed up the success at the 1900 Paris Exposition Universelle with displays of *Martelé* silver at several major and some minor exhibitions, winning prizes at all of them, including the 1901 Pan-American Exhibition in Buffalo, which celebrated the economic collaboration of the two continents. Here, Gorham chose to display a number of different product lines, although *Martelé* and its companion line, *Athenic,* were favored (fig. 199).

Dehan and Futter

In addition to the magnificent writing table, Gorham also displayed a complete dinner service in the *Florentine* line as well as a Louis XVI dessert service. According to Houston, "this beautiful set is in no sense a copy, but a true creation, embodying the decorative spirit of the American craftsman, working with hammer and chasing-tool."[201] Gorham also exhibited works in gold, including a twenty-piece toilette set as well as a rose-water ewer and plateau, punch bowls, and loving cups from the *Martelé* line, some "with gray finish" and others with a "bright finish, and works from the *Athenic* line."[202] A centerpiece with a tall, swirling vase supported by a lobed four-part base all decorated with repoussé sprays of flowers was one impressive example of *Martelé* in the 1904 display (fig. 248).

At the Panama-Pacific International Exposition held in San Francisco in 1915, Gorham participated with its own large pavilion (fig. 249), which was architecturally very similar to the one it shared with Tiffany in 1893 except in this instance Gorham occupied the entire structure. The displays included a variety of products in sterling silver, gold, and silver plate as well as bronze and marble sculptures and ecclesiastical wares in a silver, gold, brass, and bronze. The remarkable ebony and silver writing table and desk, first shown in Saint Louis in 1904, was displayed in San Francisco (fig. 250), where it was awarded a gold medal (fig. 251). Here, as in earlier fairs, Gorham received numerous awards, including two grand prizes, one special gold medal for "the most artistic installation and exhibit over every other in the Varied Industries and Manufacturers Department," three gold medals of honor, and eleven additional gold medals.

The period following World War I was characterized by fewer international exhibitions owing to economic hardship, especially after the Crash of 1929. It was not until the New York World's Fair of 1939–40 that the American economy had

246
Gorham Pavilion,
Louisiana Purchase Exposition,
Saint Louis, 1904.
Missouri Historical Society

recovered enough to support an international exposition of any magnitude, but World War II would begin four months after the fair's opening.

Gorham joined Tiffany & Co. in a pavilion appealingly named the House of Jewels. In this Modernist pavilion, designed by architect J. Gordon Carr and industrial designer Raymond Loewy, the most elegant wares in the Art Deco style were displayed in simple glass cases that seemed to float. Gorham's wares, however, were clearly more historicist than Tiffany's bold rectilinear forms, many of which were designed by Arthur Leroy Barney. Gorham took a more conservative stance at the fair than Tiffany. The only Modernist silver in Gorham's display was a rather passé coffee set and cocktail shaker set that reflected an earlier form of the movement.[203]

Other Public Displays

Participation in smaller special exhibitions also increased awareness and appreciation for Gorham's products. Examples of such opportunities include the 1918 Exhibition of Manufacturers' Work, held at the Metropolitan Museum of Art, New York. Gorham supplied not only a stained-glass window but also silverwork.[204] At the 1921 Home Beautiful Exposition in Boston, Gorham joined with its local retailers to present a dining room lavishly set with examples of its *Plymouth* pattern (fig. 144).[205] There, the hundreds of thousands of people who visited the show's nearly seven hundred exhibits were meant to gain an understanding of the enduring

247
Martelé Desk Set for the Louisiana Purchase Exposition, 1904. Gorham Archive, John Hay Library

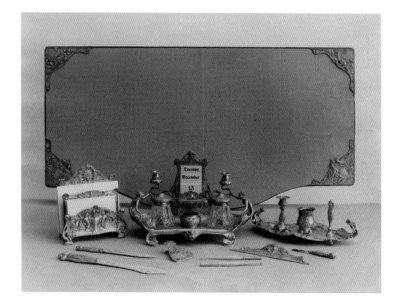

importance of silver in the home. A highlight of the show was a lecture on the history of table manners and development of dining wares, delivered by Marguerite Walker Jordan, assistant to Gorham's president.[206] Later that same year, Jordan continued her promotion of silver with a class for 325 teachers in a domestic science course at Teachers College, Columbia University, in New York. These teachers came from 183 cities across the United States and five foreign countries.

In 1928, Erik Magnussen's *Modern American* line (figs. 66, 147) and *Cubic* service (figs. 202–4, 217) were shown within room interiors designed by McBurney and Underwood at the First Annual Exhibition of Modern American Decorative Arts at the Grand Central Arts Center in New York for the Women Decorators' Club exhibition.[207] Yet Gorham really did not embrace the Modernist style popular at the time, and the company declined to participate in many of the contemporary design exhibitions held at museums in New York during this period.[208] Exceptions to Gorham's absence at exhibitions were the firm's involvement in *Decorative Metalwork and Cotton Textiles: Third International Exhibition of Contemporary Industrial Art*, organized by the American Federation of Arts in 1930, and *Contemporary Silver Made in New England*, held at Phillips Academy at Andover, Massachusetts, in 1934.[209] In 1930, Gorham's *Hunt Club* pattern, designed by Barton P. Jenks in a restrained historicist style, was featured in the third *International Exhibition of Contemporary Industrial Art* shown at the Museum of Fine Arts, Boston; the Art Institute of Chicago; the Metropolitan Museum of Art; and the Cleveland Museum of Art.[210] The new pattern was extravagantly marketed, with its own brochure claiming that the design was "inspired by the traditional elegance of the Hunt Breakfast. The keynote of *Hunt Club* is simple beauty and restrained modernity— a design created for those who maintain the standards of taste and set the new styles." The pattern's tentative modernity was marketed as "modern in spirit" that "will fit with easy grace into any period or style dining room. The simplicity of line combined with the rich detail of design makes it equally appropriate in the Elizabethan or ultra-modern dining room." Advertisements included images of the flatware superimposed over photographs of horsemen and packs of hounds.[211] The Museum of Modern Art's 1934 exhibition *Machine Art* displayed a reductivist aesthetic of the new Modernism. Although already somewhat dated, Gorham's *Covington Plain* (1914) and *Dolly Madison* (1929) lines were selected for the exhibition for their lack of decoration.[212] Gorham products were also subsequently included in the Metropolitan Museum's 1937 exhibition *Silver: An Exhibition of Contemporary American Design by Manufacturers, Designers and Craftsmen*.[213]

Marketing during
Economic Difficulty

Early in the twentieth century, Gorham
promoted *Martelé* in advertisements in
publications for the public, such as *Harper's New Monthly
Magazine.* An April 1900 notice called out the line as "the
most Exclusive Silverware for Wedding gifts . . . and for dis-
criminating art lovers."[214] Design journals were also a means
to promote Gorham's wares, as in the February and March
1902 issues of *Brush and Pencil,* which included illustrations
of two cigarette cases with repoussé decoration and four
mixed-metal vases.[215]

During this period, Gorham employed a number of
techniques to widen its audience and bring attention to
the specific holidays or markets. A survey of print advertisements in 1911 indicates the range of approach. An October
advertisement celebrated Forefather's Day by promoting
the *Plymouth* line (fig. 144) as having "historical accuracy."[216]
Shoppers for Christmas gifts were guided by the knowledge
that silver was "most appropriate; it has sentiment and
it has permanence. It will be in daily use, an ever-present
reminder of the giver; it will be steadily increasing in value
when most Christmas gifts are lost and forgotten."[217] The
readers of *Arts & Decoration* read in an advertisement that
they could purchase "Tokens of Esteem in Bronze and Silver"
to honor officers and directors with their "small and large
bronzes, statuettes, tablets, symbolic and ornamental pieces,

representative of the best art of our American Sculptors."
Gorham's silver was also suggested as "gifts that will serve
as examples of giving—not merely so much as silver metal,
but beauty and originality of design, and a variety of choice
that is rife with artistic and prac-
tical silverware suggestions."[218]

In 1922, under the direc-
tion of Marguerite Walker Jordan,
Gorham embarked on a project

to record "the South's heirloom silver." The cities of Atlanta, Memphis, and Nashville were visited with the goal of making as complete a record as possible of all silver with family histories—and, according to *Hardware and House Furnishing Goods*, "a national program to popularize sterling." The program also included displays of local heirloom silver with "window arrangements

featuring ancestral plate as 'Today's Heirlooms' and modern ware under the caption of 'Tomorrow's Heirlooms.'"[219] Jordan embarked on a tour of various cities in New England, Middle Atlantic, Southern, and Midwestern states to spread the word on "Sterling Silver as an Art Product"—and to promote Gorham in particular.[220]

Gorham also continued to exhibit their products in a number of venues: a twenty-piece silver service (fig. 252) commissioned in 1907 by the people of Rhode Island for the battleship U.S.S. *Rhode Island*, launched in 1904, was shown at the State House in Providence in 1922 after the decommissioning of the ship in 1920.[221] A note in *The Jewelers' Circular* commented on not only how beautiful the service was when it was produced, but also on its sad state of preservation after fifteen years at sea.

Print advertising addressed various audiences from the trade and its needs to a range of consumers. A 1929 magazine promotion featured Mrs. John Hering of Portland, Oregon, who "chose her wedding silver in the smart *King Albert* pattern." By focusing on her lifestyle, Gorham positioned silver as a necessity for "an altogether modern, somewhat amazing, completely adorable young American woman." For Mrs. Hering, the *King Albert* pattern "is the true aristocrat of all modern silverware patterns—distinctive in its simplicity and charming in design." The advertisement

continued: "Gorham designs are the work of rarely gifted artists who share the creed of Michael Angelo that 'trifles make perfection and perfection is no trifle.' Each lovely Gorham piece bears the mark of their genius and infinite care."[222]

Leading up to the stock market crash of 1929, sales of luxury goods had been in decline. Gorham, along with other silver manufacturers, had gone through a difficult period in the 1920s, when silver and other luxury commodities seemed out of the reach of most American consumers. Even in 1921, Gorham and others were strategizing about how to encourage the buying of silver. According to an article in the *New York Times* of June 26, 1921, Gorham was the leader of the silver companies, promoting among their wholesalers sterling over plated silver. Franklin A. Taylor, Gorham's president at the time, sought to remove "the ignorance and indifference which have hampered the sale of sterling ware and even placed it at a disadvantage with plated goods."[223] The campaign sought to promote the lasting qualities of the material over cheaper, less robust goods such as china or plate. Taylor hoped to "inaugurate educational publicity that will arouse desire and quicken the will to possess in millions of persons now indifferent to the charms and advantages, the economy, usefulness, durability, beauty and lasting satisfaction which silver brings."[224] Marguerite Walker Jordan's exhibitions and talks must have been part of the campaign to raise awareness of the beauty, utility, and enduring qualities of sterling silver.[225]

Erik Magnussen's iconic *Cubic* service (figs. 202–4, 217), an early example of Modern design, debuted at Gorham's Fifth Avenue showroom in late 1927, where the theatrical display featured the service dramatically illuminated by a spotlight and placed on a black stepped cube, positioned in front of a sign illustrated with soaring skyscrapers and radiating beams of light, proclaiming: "Silver Like This Has Never Been Seen Before" (fig. 253). The service created an immediate sensation and was hailed in an article by Elizabeth Lounsbery of *Arts & Decoration* as a "strong response to the spirit of America."[226]

Once again, Gorham innovated in order to preserve sales. In June 1929, Gorham entered into a contract with Commercial Credit Companies, the International Silver Company, and eleven other silver manufacturers to sell silver and silver plate on an installment basis. With this arrangement, over 2,800 jewelers throughout the United States were involved in the installment scheme.[227] The following year, the silver industry was lowering its prices by 10 percent on "standard sterling silver flatware." The stated reason was the lower cost of the material; silver bullion had dropped.[228]

252
U.S.S. *Rhode Island*
Silver Service, 1907.
Rhode Island Collection,
Providence Public Library

254
*Gorham Sterling, New York,
1930 (Juxtapositions).*
Edward Steichen, artist.
Gelatin silver print, negative 1930,
printed 1984–86.
Museum of Fine Arts, Boston

1941–70

Marketing and sales of silver came to a near halt with the advent of World War II and manufacturing limits set by the War Production Board.[229] Gorham's hollowware production was reduced by 70 percent, and only the top thirteen flatware patterns were available, and only in larger six-piece place settings. The company was forced to ration its silver among its network of retailers.[230] Following the war, most Americans sought simpler, more casual lifestyles that generally did not include silver. Domestic servants, who had cared for a household's silver in earlier days, were now a rarity. Although some brides still registered for silver patterns, five-piece place settings replaced the countless specialized utensils required at nineteenth-century meals. The sale of stainless-steel flatware usurped sterling, and new materials such as plastic, aluminum, and chrome began to replace silver in the fabrication of dishes, trays, utensils, and other household items. Retailers like Black, Starr & Gorham remained hopeful: "Young couples may start their married life with stainless because it is less expensive. . . . However, after four or five years of living with only stainless, they buy sterling" (fig. 255).[231] But, despite this sentiment, the recruitment of up-and-coming designers such as Donald H. Colflesh who were charged with infusing contemporary design into Gorham products, and extensive advertising campaigns, Gorham silver never regained its former stature.[232]

In the late 1950s and early 1960s, Gorham president Wilbur H. Norton began to acquire other silver firms, including Quaker Silver Co. and Graff, Washbourne & Dunn, as well as businesses including Eaton Paper Co. and Pickard & Burns Inc., an electronic research and development firm, to diversify company interests.[233] Norton confided that the 1960–61 recession had "its effect on our industry and our company."[234] Nevertheless, thanks to careful planning and a rise in silver prices that bolstered the value of their inventory, Gorham was a cash-rich entity by the mid-1960s.[235] This led to its acquisition in 1967 by the Providence-based industrial conglomerate Textron.[236] New ownership and increased diversification ultimately changed Gorham's production focus from silver to stainless-steel and pewter flatware and more diverse lines such as ceramics, glass, and collectibles.

Communication and Distribution in Sales

In the spring of 1960, as Gorham acquired other entities and pursued a diversity of interests, the firm introduced the

253
Erik Magnussen's *Cubic* Service
in Gorham's New York
showroom window, ca. 1927.
Gorham Archive,
John Hay Library

In 1930, to promote its streamlined *Fairfax* pattern, the company made a bold statement by hiring American photographer Edward Steichen, known at the time for his highly styled fashion photography for Condé Nast's *Vogue* and *Vanity Fair* as well as his work for New York advertising agencies. Steichen created a series of avant-garde images of the pattern (fig. 254), promoting its moderately priced "elegance and simplicity" that "harmonizes with the decoration of most dining rooms." His straightforward yet stylish layout of the flatware suggested efficiency for a fast-paced world unwilling to sacrifice taste, especially in economically challenging times. The inclusion of Steichen's photograph in the advertisement would stand as an important connection between Gorham's wares and their efforts to retain the relevancy of their creations in the constantly changing interests and status of their consumers.

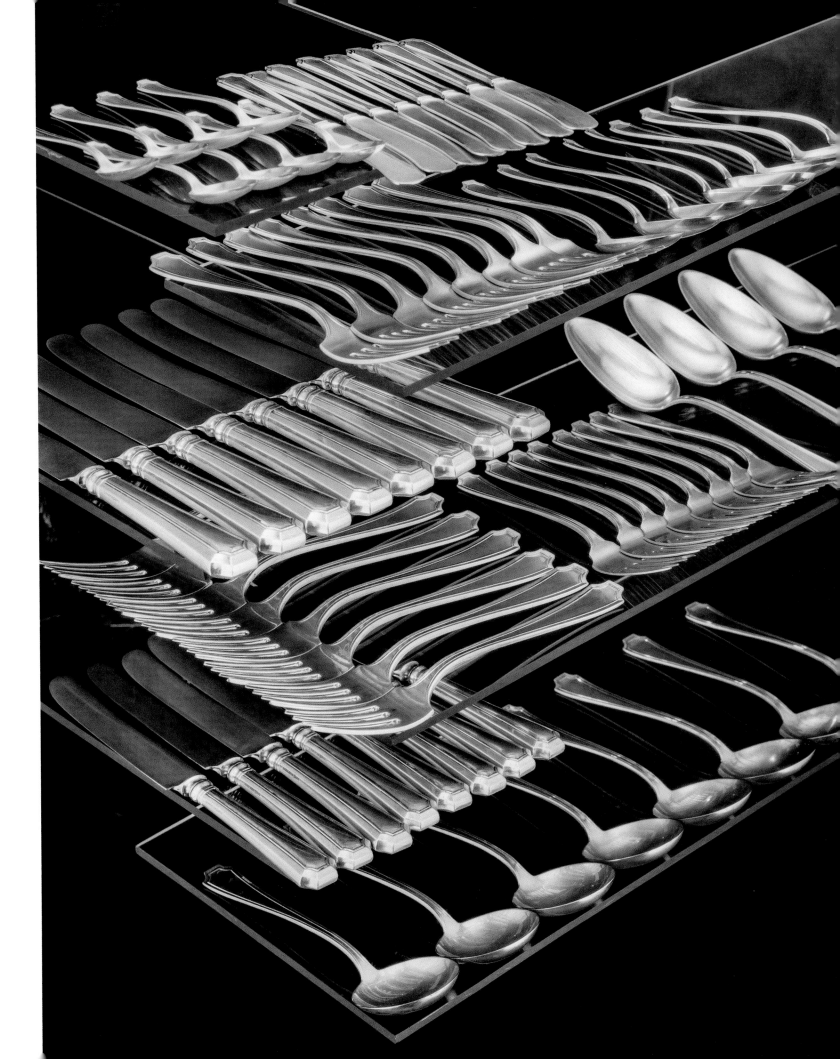

publication *Gorham Perspectives* for its Elmwood plant employees.[237] This bimonthly newspaper, following in the footsteps of the previously published *Harmony,* promised "newsworthy items about your activities and reporting on matters of interest to every Gorham employee," including company policies and programs.[238] In the inaugural issue, Wilbur H. Norton wrote, "I am relatively new to Gorham and so are many others in our growing organization; some are new to the Company, as I am, others may have new jobs or responsibilities. A newspaper can help us all to become better acquainted, not only personally, but business-wise."[239]

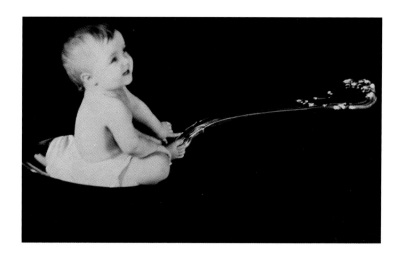

Specifically published for salesmen, the *Gorham Salesmaker* was introduced by 1951.[240] Running

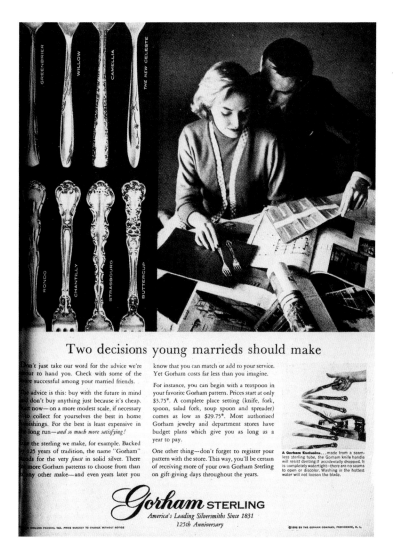

Two decisions young married should make

Don't just take our word for the advice we're about to hand you. Check with some of the more successful among your married friends.

The advice is this: buy with the future in mind and don't buy anything just because it's cheap. Start now—on a more modest scale, if necessary —to collect for yourselves the best in home furnishings. For the best is least expensive in the long run—*and so much more satisfying!*

Take the sterling we make, for example. Backed by 125 years of tradition, the name "Gorham" stands for the very *finest* in solid silver. There are more Gorham patterns to choose from than in any other make—and even years later you

know that you can match or add to your service. Yet Gorham costs far less than you imagine.

For instance, you can begin with a teaspoon in your favorite Gorham pattern. Prices start at only $3.75*. A complete place setting (knife, fork, spoon, salad fork, soup spoon and spreader) comes as low as $29.75*. Most authorized Gorham jewelry and department stores have budget plans which give you as long as a year to pay.

One other thing—don't forget to register your pattern with the store. This way, you'll be certain of receiving more of your own Gorham Sterling on gift-giving days throughout the years.

A Gorham Exclusive . . . made from a seamless sterling tube, the Gorham knife handle will resist denting if accidentally dropped. It is completely watertight—there are no seams to open or discolor. Washing in the hottest water will not loosen the blade.

Gorham STERLING
America's Leading Silversmiths Since 1831
125th Anniversary

about four pages an issue, these periodicals focused on particular sterling lines, providing tips on introducing the line to customers, stories behind the design, and special selling points. Featured in the June 1951 issue, the *Melrose* pattern was touted as a "traditional and fashionable line completely at home on modern table," and a 4-foot-long spoon in the pattern was produced for traveling promotional displays (fig. 256).[241] Methods for selling were presented, such as "Build the sale up, not down. If your customer is willing to spend $10.00, show interesting items in a slightly higher bracket."[242] Encouragement was given to engage customers in careful observation and discussion of Gorham quality and manufacturing practices: "Show your customers trays or other pieces with rolled or turned borders. Point out the fine detail in border, the smooth finish of the silver as it meets the border, the absence of tiny hairline wrinkles."[243] Occasionally, sales contests meant to generate competition and enthusiasm among salesmen were announced.

Gorham's continued plans for expanded markets and sales are outlined in a 1946 report submitted in support of continued TWA air service to and from Providence.[244] It projects the number of territorial salesmen will increase to fifty (compared with a pre–World War II force of forty) and states that international interest had been secured from at least fourteen countries in Europe, northern Africa, and southern Asia. However, it is unclear—and unlikely—that any progress of great consequence was made in these areas.

Retail and Wholesale Venues

Of Gorham's wholesale offices, the New York branch was the only one to remain open during World War II.[245] The Atlanta branch closed in 1940, and the San Francisco branch closed in 1941.[246] In Chicago, Spaulding-Gorham, Inc., was acquired in 1943 by Gordon Lang, and Gorham left the New York retail business completely when it voted in March 1962 to sell its shares in Black, Starr & Gorham, Inc.[247] Proceeds from the sale were used to support Gorham's diversified corporate objectives.

Department stores increasingly served as the best spots for Gorham's promotional displays. In 1955, Gorham was one of fifty companies that displayed sterling-silver teapots at B. Altman, promoting "tea time" and showing the integration of hollowware and flatware.[248]

Continued Promotion at Exhibitions

In 1959, the Albright Art Gallery of the Buffalo Fine Arts Academy organized a traveling exhibition entitled *20th Century Design: USA* that featured industrially produced—rather than handcrafted—works. The products were promoted for sale in an accompanying catalogue, which included model numbers for easy ordering. The exhibition, which included more than eleven hundred objects, traveled to seven museums between 1959 and 1960, including the Cleveland Museum of Art, Dallas Museum of Art, Dayton Art Institute, Minneapolis Institute of Arts, Portland Art Museum, Saint Louis Art Museum, and San Francisco Museum of Art. Gorham was one of the largest exhibitors, with nine objects shown in the Metal Ware and Cutlery section.[249]

In a more modest display, staff designer Burr Sebring was awarded a fifty-dollar prize for his entry of a silver and ivory bonbon dish in the Rhode Island Arts Festival, held in May 1960. A silver necklace by Sebring's colleague Alexandra Solowij was also chosen for display. In 1961, the firm took out twelve pages of advertising in the *New Yorker* to celebrate the company's 130th anniversary.[250] Except for the *Circa '70* four-piece coffee service, all the silver designs included in the advertisements were historicist. In 1963, sterling and silver-plate Gorham flatware was included in *New York's Ten Best Dressed Tables*, an exhibition at the Georg Jensen store on Fifth Avenue. Gorham was the sponsor for a ten-city tour of the winning design.[251] At the New York 1964 World's Fair, Gorham followed more current styles, incorporating, like many of its competitors, silver plate and wood in designs that were more organic and ergonomic. One of the works displayed for sophisticated audiences with more modest financial means was a silver-plate butter dish nestled in an oiled walnut tray.[252]

257
Gorham advertisement, ca. 1960. Gorham Archive, John Hay Library

In the mid-twentieth century, Gorham was employing the same marketing techniques it had used to great effect over the previous century. Brochures and print advertisements promoted flatware and serving pieces in new patterns (fig. 257). Department stores and jewelers carried these new lines, hoping to reach more consumers. Exhibitions continued to feature Gorham's most innovative patterns in room settings. In the 1950s and 1960s, however, silver came to suggest not elegance and refined dining, but a formality indulged in only at family gatherings such as Thanksgiving. Fewer wedding registries included requests for sterling flatware, with more young people opting for casual wares and modern conveniences. Aluminum and the dishwasher became ubiquitous. Major shifts in American lifestyles, rather than a lack of creativity in marketing and promotion, spelled the end of one of America's greatest manufacturers.

1   The authors acknowledge with great apprecia-
    tion Charles H. Carpenter Jr. and Charles L.
    Venable, who laid significant groundwork on the
    subject of Gorham's marketing and distribution
    methods in their research and publications.

2   Sales recorded for 1841–50: $236,000;
    1851–60: $1,549,400; 1850 sales: $29,000;
    1859 sales: $397,000; Gorham Manufacturing
    Company Archive, I.4 Histories Written
    About Gorham, Box 1, John Hay Library,
    Brown University, Providence, Rhode Island
    (hereafter GMCA).

3   In 1865, sales hit $759,000, peaking in 1872
    at $1,024,000. Charles H. Carpenter Jr.,
    Gorham Silver, 1831–1981 (New York: Dodd,
    Mead, 1982), 62, 90.

4   John Gorham, John Gorham's history, 1893,
    GMCA; Gorham & Thurber advertisement,
    The Rhode Island Almanac for the Year 1852
    (Providence: H. H. Brown, 1852).

5   John Gorham, John Gorham's history, 1893,
    GMCA; *The Biographical Cyclopedia of
    Representative Men of Rhode Island,* vol. 2
    (Providence: National Biographical Publishing
    Co., 1881), 434.

6   Correspondence between Jabez and
    Amey Gorham, 1819, GMCA; for tran-
    scription, see Carpenter, *Gorham Silver,
    1831–1981,* 25–27.

7   W. R. Bagnall, "Historical and Biographical
    Sketch of Gorham Manufacturing Co.,"
    unpublished, October 25, 1878, 10, GMCA.

8   Augustus E. Alden vs. The Gorham
    Manufacturing Company, 1867, 66. John
    Gorham, John Gorham's history, 1893, 18,
    Sidney S. Rider Collection, John Hay Library.

9   Ibid., 74.

10 For more on Gorham's use of photography
    see Charles L. Venable, *Silver in America,
    1840–1940: A Century of Splendor* (Dallas and
    New York: Dallas Museum of Art / Harry N.
    Abrams, 1994), 26 and endnotes 57, 58, and 59.

11 This notebook is cited as belonging to C. B. Y.
    Gorham, who has yet to be identified as a
    Gorham employee. Purportedly passed down
    through the Gorham family, C. B. Y. Gorham
    may note the donor of the notebook, possibly
    Catherine B. Yerrington Gorham, wife of
    Charles Field Gorham and sister-in-law of John
    Gorham. See Georgiana Guild, *The Gorham
    Family in Rhode Island, Notes on the Providence
    Line,* (Boston: David Clapp & Son, 1900), 6.
    The dating of the notebook is based on address
    listings of the retailers included. See Venable,
    Silver in America, 1840–1940, 47, endnote 26.
    Although this notebook is included in the
    GMCA, it could not be located at the time of
    publication. Photocopies of the original
    notebook were provided by Charles Venable.

12 For a transcription, see Carpenter, *Gorham
    Silver, 1831–1981,* 63. This letter could not be
    located at the time of this publication.

13 See Edgar W. Morse, "Silver in the Golden
    State" in *Silver in the Golden State* (Oakland, CA:
    Oakland Museum History Department, 1986),
    3 and 16–20; "John W. Tucker," in *Sketches
    of Leading and Representative Men of San
    Francisco,* ed. Oscar T. Shuck (London: London
    and New York Publishing Co., 1875).

14 Duhme & Co. was founded in 1843. Duhme &
    Co. advertisement, *Cincinnati Commercial
    Tribune,* August 13, 1861, 5.

15 Harry R. Smith advertised as an agent for
    Gorham in 1867 and 1868. Harry R. Smith & Co.
    advertisements, *Cincinnati Daily Gazette,*
    December 23, 1867, 2; May 19, 1861, 2;
    December 21, 1861, 1. Clemens Oskamp
    advertised Gorham stock "guaranteed to be
    of sterling quality." "The Holidays," *Cincinnati
    Daily Gazette,* December 2, 1870, 1. For other
    Cincinnati agents for Gorham, see Amy Miller
    Dehan, *Cincinnati Silver 1788–1940* (London:
    D. Giles Ltd., 2014).

16 William Wilson McGrew advertisement,
    Cincinnati Daily Gazette, December 17,
    1868, 2. This advertisement refers to Gorham
    plated wares.

17 "Exposition Items, Description of the Great
    Industrial Exposition of 1872," *Cincinnati Daily
    Gazette,* September 9, 1872, 2. The Japanese
    combination ladle refers to a ladle in Gorham's
    Japanese pattern introduced June 17, 1871.
    Cost Book Silver Flatware No. 1 1867–1880,
    61–66, GMCA.

18 "The Useful and the Beautiful at the Cincinnati
    Exposition. Silver and Jewelry," *Cincinnati
    Daily Gazette,* September 26, 1873. For more
    on William Wilson McGrew and his ties with
    Gorham, see Amy Miller Dehan, *Cincinnati
    Silver: 1788–1940,* 236–37.

19 Advertisement, *Chicago Tribune,*
    December 17, 1876.

20 Advertisement, *Atlanta Constitution,*
    December 23, 1876.

21 Advertisement, *Carlisle Weekly Herald,*
    July 6, 1876.

22 Advertisement, *Record of the Times*
    (Wilkes-Barre, PA), October 18, 1876.

23 Advertisement, *Detroit Free Press,*
    December 22, 1876.

24 William C. Conant, "The Silver Age,"
    Scribner's Monthly 9, no. 2 (December
    1874): 201.

25 While some sources indicate the Gorham, Co.
    & Brown was established in 1859, the correct
    date is most likely 1856. "Death of Henry T.
    Brown," *Jewelers' Circular* 27, no. 14 (November
    1, 1893), 16; Russell J. De Simone, *A Survey of
    Nineteenth Century Rhode Island Billheads,*
    Technical Services Department Faculty Publica-
    tions, paper 9, Tilden Thurber Company
    billhead, figure 68, http://digitalcommons.uri.edu/
    lib_ts_pubs/9, accessed April 6, 2018;
    "Providence: Rapid Growth of the New England
    Jewelry Industry in the past Fifty Years,"
    Jewelers' Circular-Weekly 78, no. 1 (February 5,
    1919), 283; Carpenter, *Gorham Silver,
    1831–1981,* 59.

26 Rental receipt for Lyceum Building, dated July 1,
    1864, includes rendering of Gorham, Co. &
    Brown storefront, Rhode Island Currency,
    Globe Bank, http://www.ricurrency.com/
    bank-name/globe-bank-providence/, accessed
    April 6, 2018.

27 John Gorham, diary of a trip to Europe, 1860,
    entries for August 3–8, 19–21, 25, GMCA;
    Henry Brown to John Gorham, July 3, 1860,
    I.1 Gorham-Historical – Gorham Family, Box 2,
    GMCA; Gorham, Co. & Brown later became
    Henry T. Brown & Co. and eventually the
    Tilden Thurber Company. "Death of Henry
    T. Brown," *Jewelers' Circular* 27, no. 14
    (November 1, 1893), 16, GMCA.

28 Date of establishment is given as 1859 in
    "Historical Data," June 17, 1921, GMCA. City
    directory searches indicate the date of
    establishment between May 1858 and May
    1859; 1858/59 New York City Directory;
    1859/1860 New York City Directory.

29 "The Gorham Manufacturing Co.," *Biographical
    History of the Manufacturers and Business Men
    of Rhode Island at the Opening of the Twentieth
    Century* (Providence: J. D. Hall & Co., 1901), 8.

30 "Historical Data," June 17, 1921, GMCA;
    "Providence: Rapid Growth of the New England
    Jewelry Industry in the past Fifty Years,"
    Jewelers' Circular-Weekly 78, no. 1 (February 5,
    1919), 287.

31 "Among the Silver Workers," *Atlantic Monthly,*
    December 1867, 732.

32 Invoice, January 27, 1865, I.2 Gorham –
    Historical – 19th Century Documents, GMCA.

33 "Bond St. Improvements—The Waltham
    Building," *New York Tribune,* October 5, 1871.

34 Ibid.

35 Gorham advertisement, *New York Tribune,*
    May 13, 1873, 8; Gorham advertisement,
    New York Times, May 24, 1873.

36 Starr & Marcus advertisement, *New York
    Times,* May 17, 1871.

37 Conant, "The Silver Age," 201; Edmund C.
    Mayo, "Three Men in an Industrial Century:
    Jabez Gorham, John Gorham, Edward
    Holbrook," *Rhode Island History* 1, no. 11
    (January 1952).

38 Gorham advertisement, *New York Times,*
    November 17, 1873.

39 "The Gorham Manufacturing Company," *New York Times,* December 4, 1874.

40 Ibid.

41 Notice, *Sun* (New York), May 7, 1876, 4; I.10.A; I.10.B Gorham Historical Product, GMCA.

42 "An Elegant Display of Silver-Ware," *New York Times,* May 17, 1876.

43 "A Great Bond Street Fire," *New York Times,* March 7, 1877.

44 "The Gorham Company," *Jewelers' Circular and Horological Review,* September 1877, 129.

45 John Gorham diary, May 24, 1860, GMCA.

46 *Transactions of the Rhode-Island Society for the Encouragement of Domestic Industry in the Year 1850* (Providence: Joseph Knowles, 1851), 65.

47 See Elizabeth A. Williams in *American Silver in the Art Institute of Chicago* (Chicago: Art Institute of Chicago, 2017), 128–30. The Art Institute of Chicago example (2015.606.1–.5) was produced a year before the example shown at the 1851 fair. An 1868 *Harper's New Monthly Magazine* article tells the story of the Chinese tea service in detail. James Parton, "Silver and Silver Plate," *Harper's New Monthly Magazine* 37, no. 220 (September 1868): 438.

48 See Amy Miller Dehan, "An Apt and Noble Gift: Gorham's Rebekah Pitcher," *Gastronomica: The Journal of Food and Culture* 9, no. 4: 14–18, and Venable, *Silver in America, 1840–1940,* 25.

49 *Providence Journal,* September 13, 1851, 2, cited in full in Carpenter, *Gorham Silver, 1831–1981,* 43–45, and Williams, *American Silver in the Art Institute of Chicago,* 128–30.

50 Sandhurst, Phillip T., et al. *The Great Centennial Exhibition* (Philadelphia & Chicago: P. W. Ziegler & Co., 1876), 152–53.

51 United States Commission, *International Exhibition, 1876, Reports and Awards,* V, Group XI, no. 91, 413.

52 According to Samuel J. Burr, *Memorial of the International Exhibition* (Hartford, CT: L. Stebbins, 1877), 291, the *Century Vase* was the only work produced for the exhibition.

53 Sandhurst, *The Great Centennial Exhibition,* 156.

54 The 1878 brochure even entered the collection of the South Kensington Museum the same year.

55 James D. McCabe, *The Illustrated History of the Centennial Exhibition* (Philadelphia: National Publishing Company, 1877), 359–60. The current equivalent of $25,000 then would be approximately $634,000.

56 Venable, *Silver in America, 1840–1940,* 118.

57 Gorham Manufacturing Co., *The Century Vase* (Cambridge, MA: Riverside Press, 1878), n.p.; Also included is an engraving of the central panel of the vase. The same engraving of the central panel is illustrated in George Titus Ferris, *Gems of the Centennial Exhibition* (New York: D. Appleton & Company, 1877), 13–14. The vase is visible in one of the photographs of the 1876 Gorham stand.

58 Ferris, *Gems of the Centennial Exhibition,* 13–14.

59 *American Advertiser* (Boston), 1853.

60 *Atlantic Advertiser & Miscellany* 134, December 1868, n.p.

61 See *Aldine Press* 2, no. 12 (December 1869), 121.

62 Venable, *Silver in America, 1840–1940,* 111, cites *Jewelers' Circular-Keystone* 8, no. 6 (July 1877): n.p.

63 Parton, "Silver and Silver Plate," *Harper's New Monthly Magazine,* 433–48.

64 Conant, "The Silver Age," 193–209.

65 Ibid. 197, 198, 200, 203.

66 "Last Honors Paid to Edward Holbrook," *Jewelers' Circular,* May 23, 1919, 73; Edmund C. Mayo, "Three Men in an Industrial Century: Jabez Gorham, John Gorham, Edward Holbrook," *Rhode Island History* 11 (January 1952).

67 By 1899, it was estimated that the value of solid silver and plated wares produced in the United States had risen to $26,114,000, an amount that doubled estimates from 1869. United States Tariff Commission, *Silverware, Solid and Plated,* report no. 139, 2d s (Washington, DC: Government Printing Office, 1940), Government Document no. C 18.9:23/a.

68 "New York Notes," *Jewelers' Circular* 37, no. 4 (November 2, 1898), 20; Gorham Company, *The Sales Manual and History of the Gorham Company* (Providence: Gorham Company, 1932) 6; Venable, *Silver in America, 1840–1940,* 245.

69 "Announcement," *New York Times,* October 3, 1877. Starr had recently purchased the interest of his partner, Herman Marcus, in Starr & Marcus. "New York Jewelers of a Half Century Ago," *Jewelers' Circular Weekly* 78, no. 1 (February 5, 1919), 188.

70 Starr & Marcus advertisement, *Appletons' Journal of Literature, Science and Art* 5, no. 113 (May 27, 1871): 628; Starr & Marcus advertisement, *New York Times,* May 17, 1871. See also Venable, *Silver in America, 1840–1940,* note 31, 47. "Minutes of the Board of Directors, 1868–1892" at the GMCA were not accessible at the time of this publication.

71 "Mr. Starr's New Wareroom," *New York Times,* November 8, 1877, 8; *Jeweler, Silversmith and Watchmaker* 4, no. 3 (November 1877), 41.

72 "Gorham Manufacturing Co.," *New York Times,* December 13, 1877, 5.

73 "Art Silverware," *Sun,* New York, October 22, 1881, 4; advertisement, *Jewelers' Circular* 9 (October 1878), xiii; advertisement, *Jewelers' Circular* 10, November 1878; advertisement, *Jewelers' Circular* 10, no. 3 (April 1878), xi.

74 Gorham Manufacturing Company, *Catalogue of Sterling Silver and Silver Plated Wares of the Gorham M'f'g Company: Including Examples of Their Production in Other Metals* (New York: Gorham Manufacturing Company, Autumn 1883); 1884/85 New York City Directory, 653.

75 Gorham Manufacturing Company, *Catalogue of Sterling Silver and Silver Plated Wares of the Gorham M'f'g Company: Including Examples of Their Production in Other Metals* (New York: Gorham Manufacturing Company, Autumn 1884), 6; "The Gorham Manufacturing Co.'s New Building," *Jewelers' Circular* 15, no. 5 (June 1884), 155–56; "Gorham Mfg. Co.'s New Building," *Jewelers' Circular* 15, no. 6 (July 1884), 176.

76 "Decorative Arts Notes," *Art Amateur* 12, no.1 (December 1884), 23.

77 Gorham Manufacturing Company, *Catalogue of Sterling Silver and Silver Plated Wares of the Gorham M'f'g Company: Including Examples of Their Production in Other Metals* (New York: Gorham Manufacturing Company, Autumn 1884), 6.

78 "Gorham Mfg. Co.'s New Building," *Jewelers' Circular* 15, no. 6 (July 1884), 176.

79 "Gorham Mfg. Co.'s New Building," *Jewelers' Circular* 15, no. 5 (June 1884), 156.

80 "The Art of the Silversmith," *New York Times,* April 4, 1885.

81 New York City Landmarks Preservation Commission, "Gorham Building, 889–891 Broadway," Designation Report, LP-1227, June 19, 1894, 4. http://s-media.nyc.gov/agencies/lpc/lp/1227.pdf.

82 "An Art Exhibit of Silverware," *New York Times,* January 23, 1894.

83 "Employees of the Gorham Mfg. Co," I.8/9.a.2 Gorham – Historical – Silversmiths Co., GMCA; M. Camille Krantz, *International Exposition of Chicago, 1893* (Paris: Imprimerie nationale, 1894), 3; Gorham moved out of this location in 1907. New York City Landmarks Preservation Commission, "Gorham Building, 889-891 Broadway," Designation Report, LP-1227, June 19, 1894, 2. http://s-media.nyc.gov/agencies/lpc/lp/1227.pdf.

84 "Maiden Lane Store," historical plant, GMCA.

85 Gorham Manufacturing Company, *Catalogue of Sterling Silver and Silver Plated Wares of the Gorham M'f'g Company: Including Examples of Their Productions in Other Metals* (New York: Gorham Manufacturing Company, Autumn 1892); historical data, June 17, 1921, GMCA; histories written about Gorham, GMCA; "History of Gorham Mfg. Company," *Silver Tongue* 1, no. 3 (September 1, 1925), 2; "New York News," *Silver Tongue* 3, no. 25 (June 1, 1927), 26.

86 "The Art Trades Supplement," *Decorator and Furnisher* 17, no. 6 (March 1891), 229.

87 Advertisement, *Jewelers' Circular* 9, no. 9 (October 1878), xiii.

88 Morse, *Silver in the Golden State*, 4, 13, 16.

89 Gorham Manufacturing Company, *Catalogue of Sterling Silver and Silver Plated Wares of the Gorham M'f'g Company: Including Examples of Their Productions in Other Metals* (New York: Gorham Manufacturing Company, Autumn 1884), 10; *Silver Tongue* 1, no. 3 (September 1, 1925), 1; employees of the Gorham Mfg. Co., GMCA.

90 Gorham Manufacturing Company, *Catalogue of Sterling Silver and Silver Plated Wares of the Gorham M'f'g Company: Including Examples of Their Productions in Other Metals* (New York: Gorham Manufacturing Company, Autumn 1888).

91 After 1911, Chicago streets were renumbered and 137–139 Wabash became 10–16 South Wabash; "Historical Data," June 17, 1921, I.4 Histories Written About Gorham, Box 1, GMCA. "Old Papers from Mr. Holbrook's files," I.8/9.a.2 Gorham – Historical – Silversmiths Co., GMCA.

92 Venable, *Silver in America, 1840–1940,* 95; "Spaulding & Co.," *A History of the City of Chicago, Its Men and Institutions* (Chicago: Inter Ocean, 1900), 268–69; "Prominent Wholesale Merchants," *Industrial Chicago: The Commercial Interests,* vol. 4 (Chicago: Goodspeed Publishing Co. 1894), 426–34.

93 John Culme, *The Directory of Gold and Silversmiths, Jewellers and Allied Traders 1838–1914* (Woodbridge, UK: Antique Collector's Club, 1987), 187.

94 Little is known about the Boston office, although it was, for some time, noted on Gorham's corporate letterhead. *The Boston Directory* (Boston: Sampson, Murdock & Co, 1898), 654; 13 West Factory Prices, undated, GMCA.

95 Gorham Manufacturing Company, *Catalogue of Sterling Silver and Silver Plated Wares of the Gorham M'f'g Company: Including Examples of Their Productions in Other Metals* (New York: Gorham Manufacturing Company, Autumn 1882), 34.

96 The first silver trade catalogues appeared in the late 1850s and 1860s; Venable, *Silver in America, 1840–1940,* 101. Sales manager Hiram Bliss recalled that prior to publishing the first catalogue in 1880, small booklets were issued for flatware patterns. I.8 Gorham – Historical – Personnel Box 1 A-L, GMCA.

97 By 1888, Gorham catalogues contained to-scale illustrations.

98 "Art Employed as the Servant of Art," *The Manufacturing Jeweler* (no date). "The Gorham Mfg. Co.'s Marvelous Catalogue," *Jewelers' Circular* 25, no. 11 (October 12, 1892), 38; "A Notable Catalogue," *American Architect and Building News,* November 5, 1892. "Another Artistic Catalogue from the Gorham Mfg. Co.,"

Jeweler's Journal, 1892. All above found in I.5 Gorham Historical Articles – Clippings, 1891–1896 Scrapbook, GMCA.

99 Gorham Manufacturing Company, *Catalogue of Sterling Silver and Silver Plated Wares of the Gorham M'f'g Company: Including Examples of Their Productions in Other Metals* (New York: Gorham Manufacturing Company, Autumn 1902), n.p.

100 Gorham Manufacturing Company, *Catalogue of Sterling Silver and Silver Plated Wares of the Gorham M'f'g Company: Including Examples of Their Productions in Other Metals* (New York: Gorham Manufacturing Company, Autumn 1904), n.p.

101 Gorham Manufacturing Company, *Catalogue of Sterling Silver and Silver Plated Wares of the Gorham M'f'g Company: Including Examples of Their Productions in Other Metals* (New York: Gorham Manufacturing Company, Autumn 1882), 27.

102 Ibid.

103 "The Gorham Mfg. Co.'s Marvelous Catalogue," *Jewelers' Circular* 25, no. 11 (October 12, 1892): 38. The current equivalent of that sum is approximately $55,600.

104 For further discussion of price coding, see Venable, *Silver in America, 1840–1940,* 101.

105 Gorham Manufacturing Company, *Catalogue of Sterling Silver and Silver Plated Wares of the Gorham M'f'g Company: Including Examples of Their Productions in Other Metals* (New York: Gorham Manufacturing Company, Autumn 1883), 8.

106 Gorham Manufacturing Company, *Catalogue of Sterling Silver and Silver Plated Wares of the Gorham M'f'g Company: Including Examples of Their Productions in Other Metals* (New York: Gorham Manufacturing Company, Autumn 1890), 76. Similar instances appear in Gorham catalogues published in 1886 and 1888.

107 Gorham Manufacturing Company, *Catalogue of Sterling Silver and Silver Plated Wares of the Gorham M'f'g Company: Including Examples of Their Productions in Other Metals* (New York: Gorham Manufacturing Company, Autumn 1880), 5. Later in the decade, references are made to small separate catalogues published for toiletware, and catalogues devoted solely to sterling silver vases and lunch sets were published in 1908.

108 See Venable, *Silver in America, 1840–1940,* for a rationale for the limited number of American silver firms displaying at the 1878 Paris exposition: 112.

109 *United States Court Official Catalogue* (Sydney: Gibbs, Shallard & Co., 1879).

110 *Argus*, September 30, 1879, 5.

111 In addition to the work by Venable (see *Silver in America, 1840–1940,* 115), Elizabeth A.

Williams undertook research on Gorham and the 1889 Paris Exposition Universelle in 2006, when the Nelson-Atkins Museum of Art acquired the tea service. Her research is invaluable to this discussion. See also Lucien Falize, "Last Glimpses of the Exposition," *Jewelers' Circular and Horological Review* 20, no. 10 (November 1889), 46.

112 "The Exposition Awards," *Jewelers Weekly* 8, no. 24 (October 10, 1889), cover story; cited in Venable, *Silver in America, 1840–1940,* 115.

113 "The Gorham Exhibit," *Jewelers' Weekly* 8, no. 8 (June 20, 1889): 35–39; cited in Venable, *Silver in America, 1840–1940,* 115.

114 Gorham Manufacturing Company, *Choice Examples of Sterling Silver Ware: The Productions of the Gorham M'f'g Co., Silversmiths* (New York: Gorham Manufacturing Company, 1889), n.p.

115 This service is owned by the Nelson-Atkins Museum of Art, 2006.20.1–.5

116 Katharine Morrison McClinton, *Collecting American 19th-Century Silver* (New York: Scribner's and Sons, 1968), 77, note 136.

117 *Reports* cited in Venable, *Silver in America, 1840–1940,* 115.

118 Lucien Falize, "A Retrospect of the Paris Exposition," *Jewelers' Circular and Horological Review* 20, no. 11 (December 1889): 49.

119 Venable, *Silver in America, 1840–1940,* 116. Not all of the critics liked the Gorham and Tiffany pavilion. According to a writer for *American Architect and Building News*: "The outsides of the Gorham and Tiffany exhibits, which stood side by side, were decidedly disappointing. The Tiffany section was less aggressively bad, but anything more meaningless than the Gorham design it would be hard to find in the whole building." XLII.933 (November 11, 1893), 74. See also clipping preserved in 1891–1896 Scrapbook, "Beautiful Silverware," *Providence Sunday Journal*, March 26, 1893.

120 M. Camille Krantz, *International Exposition of Chicago, 1893* (Paris: National Press, 1894), 85; translated, typescript copy in I.5.B + I.5.C Gorham Historical Articles – Awards and Exhibits, GMCA.

121 The current equivalent of this sum is more than $700,000.

122 Krantz, *International Exposition of Chicago, 1893*, 242; see also Venable, *Silver in America, 1840–1940*, 116–88, and the Dallas Museum of Art website (https://collections.dma.org/artwork/5020783).

123 Hawkes had displayed cut glass at the 1889 Paris Exposition Universelle and garnered wide acclaim and a grand prix.

124 *The Jewelers' Circular* 17, no. 20 (December 13, 1893), 7.

125 For the history of the introduction of *Martelé*, see Carpenter, *Gorham Silver, 1831–1981*, 237;

Venable, *Silver in America, 1840–1940*, 95, 253–54; John Webster Keefe and Samuel J. Hough, *Magnificent, Marvelous Martelé* (New Orleans: New Orleans Museum of Art, 2001), 9–10, 17–18; and L. J. Pristo, *Martelé: Gorham's Nouveau Art Silver* (Phoenix: Phoenix Publishing Group, 2002), 14–19, 48. The first piece of *Martelé* was a loving cup (8454) made on November 21, 1896. Gorham established a school to train silversmiths in traditional handcrafted methods in 1896. Gorham's display at the Boston Arts and Crafts Society exhibition at Copley Hall on April 5–16, 1897 may have included early examples of *Martelé*, although this cannot be confirmed via contemporary literature or company records. Gorham held an invitational event at the Waldorf-Astoria in New York beginning November 15, 1897, for a viewing of their new line of "Wrought Sterling Silverware, representing examples of the handwork of the most skilled artisans"; although the name *Martelé* was not used, the description of the wares in the November 17, 1897 issue of *Jewelers' Circular* indicates that they were *Martelé*. Gorham applied for a trademark protection for the name *Martelé* on November 22, 1899. Trade advertisements as early as August 1898 and magazine articles dating from 1899 (see Charlotte Moffitt, "New Designs in Silver," *House Beautiful* 7, no. 1 [December 1899], 56) indicate that *Martelé* was available for purchase or special order at Gorham salesrooms, including Spaulding in Chicago.

126 "Exhibit of Artistic Silver Ware at the Waldorf-Astoria Hotel," *Jewelers' Circular* 10 (November 1897), 20; *Illustrated American* 22, no. 406 (November 20, 1897), n.p.

127 "Rare and Unique Exhibit of Works in Hand Wrought Silver," *Jewelers' Circular* 17 (November 1897), 16.

128 Ibid.

129 Charlotte Moffitt, "New Designs in Silver," *House Beautiful* 7, no. 1 (December 1899), 57–58. The article was illustrated with photographs said to have been supplied by Spaulding & Company of Chicago.

130 Gorham Manufacturing Company, *Gorham Suggestions*, 1895.

131 Gorham Manufacturing Company, *Gorham Suggestions*, 1898. The introductory text states, "[T]his book is not a price list. It outlines simply a stock ever changing and growing in variety. The Gorham Company will be glad to supplement it by furnishing detailed information regarding any particular article, accompanied by illustrations and prices of all the style in which the goods are made."

132 Ibid., 36–43.

133 James H. Collins, "Dignified Publicity," *Printers' Ink: A Journal for Advertisers* 37, no. 5 (October 30, 1901): 3–4, and "An Extensive Silverware Campaign," *Printers' Ink: A Journal for Advertisers* 41, no. 6 (November 5, 1902): 12–13. See also Venable, *Silver in America, 1840–1940*, 102, for a discussion of the marketing in trade publications for Gorham and other silver manufactories during the late nineteenth century.

134 Collins, "Dignified Publicity," 3. The current equivalent of that sum is approximately $1.67 million.

135 For more on Holbrook's acquisitions, see Venable, *Silver in America, 1840–1940*, 224–26.

136 Aldred & Co., *The Silversmith Company of New York*, 7, GMCA. The current equivalent of that sum is approximately $134 million.

137 Ibid., condensed consolidated balance sheet, statement A-1. See also Venable, *Silver in America, 1840–1940*, 228.

138 Aldred & Co. assumed control of Gorham Company in 1924; Aldred & Co., *The Silversmith Company of New York*; "Spaulding of Chicago Joins Gorham Merger," *New York Times*, April 30, 1929.

139 Samuel Hough, *Gorham Roster of Craftsmen*.

140 For a more in-depth look at Gorham's activities in England, see John Culme, *The Directory of Gold & Silversmiths, Jewellers & Allied Traders 1838–1914*, vol. 1 (Woodbridge, UK: Antique Collectors' Club, 1987), 187–88.

141 I.7 Gorham – Historical – Plant, GMCA.

142 Manufacturing at the plant began in 1909. "Historical Data," June 17, 1921, GMCA; John Culme, *The Directory of Gold & Silversmiths, Jewellers & Allied Traders 1838–1914*, 187.

143 Manufacturing in Canada allowed Gorham to avoid import duties. On January 3, 1907, this Gorham plant, located in the Stephens business block, was destroyed by fire. Photographs of the burnt building include a sign that indicates Gorham had relocated its offices and showroom temporarily to the Inglis Building (St. Catherine Street). Later that year, Gorham's Canadian silver factory was taken over by the Canadian jewelers Henry Birks & Sons, Ltd.; "Historical Data," June 17, 1921, GMCA; "Canada and the Provinces," *Jewelers' Circular*, March 3, 1897, 20; "Canada Notes," *Jewelers' Circular Weekly*, December 5, 1906, 66; "Building Occupied by Well-Known Jewelers Wiped Out by Fire in Montreal, Can.," *Jewelers' Circular Weekly*, January 9, 1907, 45, I.7 Gorham – Historical – Plant, GMCA. Allan C. Fox, *Presentation Pieces and Trophies from the Henry Birks Collection of Canadian Silver* (Ottawa: National Gallery of Canada, 1985), 82.

144 John Culme, *The Directory of Gold & Silversmiths, Jewellers & Allied Traders 1838–1914*, 188.

145 Aldred & Co., *The Silversmith Company of New York*, 16.

146 Venable, *Silver in America, 1840–1940*, 239.

147 Aldred & Co., *The Silversmith Company of New York*, 16.

148 Gorham Manufacturing Company, *Leadership* (Providence: Gorham Company, 1926), 12, GMCA.

149 "History of the Gorham Manufacturing Company," 7, I.4 Histories Written about Gorham, Box 2, GMCA.

150 "Retail Salespeople to Attend Special Conference," *Harmony* 1, no. 48 (March 7, 1931), 1.

151 These meetings were held in Providence, New York, Chicago, and San Francisco. *Silver Tongue* 1, no. 20 (April 1, 1925) 11; *Silver Tongue* 2, no. 2 (October 1926), 6, 9; *Harmony* 1, no. 1 (January 24, 1931), 2; *Harmony* 1, no. 48 (March 7, 1931), 1. Reports on these events are found throughout Gorham publications such as the *Silver Tongue, Contact,* and *Harmony*. GMCA.

152 "Convention News," *Silver Tongue* 2, no. 1 (April 1, 1925), 11.

153 "To Our Salesmen," published by Gorham on May 27, 1908, pages 1–2. See Venable, *Silver in America, 1840–1940*, 93.

154 Per Venable, *Silver in America, 1840–1940*, 94, note 8, this publication and "Our Creed," which emulates a catechism, were part of Gorham's design library at the plant in Providence and were published between 1905 and 1915.

155 Ibid.

156 *Silver Tongue* 1, no. 1 (December 1, 1924), 8.

157 Gorham Company, *A Merchandising Manual* (Providence: The Gorham Company, 1927), GMCA.

158 Gorham Manufacturing Company, *The Gorham Mark*, n.d. [ca. 1918], notice inside cover, GMCA.

159 Ibid., 625.

160 Gorham Company, *A Merchandising Manual* (Providence: The Gorham Company, 1927), GMCA.

161 Ibid., preface.

162 Ibid., 10.

163 Gorham Manufacturing Company, *The Sales Manual and History of the Gorham Company*, 1932, I.4 Histories Written about Gorham, Box 2, GMCA.

164 Ibid., 68.

165 Ibid., 72.

166 Ibid., 67–69.

167 *Harmony* 1, no. 50 (March 21, 1931), 1.

168 Invitation, 1940, Albert Harkness Collection, File B11 F30, Rhode Island Historical Society, Providence.

169 "Gorham Showrooms, Providence, RI," *Pencil Points,* January 1942, 11–14.

170 "Three Men in an Industrial Century: Jabez Gorham, John Gorham, Edward Holbrook," *Rhode Island History*, January 9, 1952, 1–9, I.5.A Gorham – Historical – Articles Arranged Chronologically, GMCA; New York City Landmarks Preservation Commission, "Gorham

Building, 390 Fifth Avenue," Designation Report, LP-2027, December 15, 1998; available at http://s-media.nyc.gov/agencies/lpc/lp/2027.pdf.

171 John S. Holbrook, "The Gorham Building," *New York Architect* 1, no. 11 (November 1908), 5.

172 The current equivalent of this sum is approximately $71.8 million.

173 "Gorham Building Ready," *New York Times*, September 5, 1905; "Gorham Store Opened," *New York Tribune*, September 5, 1905.

174 Aldred & Co., *The Silversmith Company of New York*, 23, GMCA.

175 Ibid., 23.

176 Ibid., 25.

177 Ibid., 25.

178 Alfred A. Smith, "Gorham 1873 Store Set Elegant Pace," *Christian Science Monitor*, May 21, 1960; "Gorham Leaving Retailing Field," *New York Times*, March 23, 1962; "Gorham Building Sold," *New York Times*, November 2, 1923. Before moving, Gorham sold the lease to its building at Fifth Avenue and Thirty-Sixth Street in 1920. "Fifth Av. Lease Sold By Gorham," *New York Times*, May 30, 1920.

179 *Silver Tongue* 2, no. 2 (October 1926), 17–18, GMCA.

180 Black, Starr & Frost was one of Manhattan's oldest jewelry firms, established in 1904. In September 1940, the name Black, Starr & Frost-Gorham, Inc. was shortened to Black, Starr & Gorham, Inc. Alfred A. Smith, "Gorham 1873 Store Set Elegant Pace," *Christian Science Monitor*, May 21, 1960; Advertisement, *Brooklyn Daily Eagle*, May 9, 1929; "Two 5th Av Jewelers in Remodeled Home," *New York Times*, October 30, 1929; "Black, Starr & Frost, Gorham Co. to Merge," *Brooklyn Daily Eagle*, January 5, 1929; "Gorham Co. and Black, Starr & Frost to Merge," *New York Times*, January 5, 1929; "Jewelry House Expands," *New York Times*, September 19, 1949; "Official Describes Gorham Companies," *New York Times*, September 4, 1929; Announcement, *Ithaca Journal*, Ithaca, New York, April 30, 1929; "Aldred Gets Option on Gorham's 5th Av. Retail Store," *Brooklyn Daily Eagle*, April 1, 1929; "Gorham Plant to Expand. Plans Holding Company to Take Over Retail Stores," *New York Times*, March 23, 1929.

181 "Spaulding of Chicago Joins Gorham Merger," *New York Times*, April 30, 1929.

182 "Gorham Adds Store," *New York Times*, June 5, 1930.

183 Announcement, undated [1908], I.7 Gorham – Historical – Plant, GMCA.

184 "Last Honors Paid to Edward Holbrook," *Jewelers' Circular*, May 23, 1919, 73; "New Office Buildings," *Architect and Builders' Magazine* 9, no. 9, 412.

185 Aldred & Co. recommended "tighter management, paring expenses and pushing sales" to build on and increase these results. Aldred & Co., *The Silversmith Company of New York*, 26, GMCA.

186 "Official Describes Gorham Companies," *New York Times*, September 4, 1929; "Gorham to Quit Fifth Avenue Home," *New York Times*, February 14, 1932.

187 "Black, Starr & Frost, Gorham Co. to Merge," *Brooklyn Daily Eagle*, January 5, 1929; "Gorham Co. to Quit Fifth Avenue Home," *New York Times*, February 14, 1932.

188 Based on data collected in 1922, sales in New York ($1,110,126) and Philadelphia ($1,077,461) were the highest, with Chicago ($869,843), Atlanta ($570,989), Boston ($395,244), and San Francisco ($238,754) following. Aldred & Co., *The Silversmith Company of New York*, 15, GMCA.

189 "District Offices," I.4 Histories Written about Gorham, Box 2, GMCA, as cited by Venable, *Silver in America, 1840–1940*, 239, note 34.

190 Samuel J. Hough, "Service de Toilette, Martelé," *Silver* 23, no. 6 (November/December 1990), 24–26.

191 The San Francisco branch at 140 Geary Street was listed through 1941. Polk's Crocker-Langley San Francisco City Directory (San Francisco: R. L. Polk & Co., 1941), 562; "District Offices," Histories Written about Gorham, GMCA, as cited by Venable, *Silver in America, 1840–1940*, 239, note 34.

192 L. J. Pristo, *Martelé: Gorham's Nouveau Art Silver* (Phoenix, AZ: Heritage Antiques, 2002), 53, cited by Williams, "Designing a New Mold," 182.

193 Samuel J. Hough, "Service de Toilette, Martelé," *Silver* 23, no. 6 (November/December 1990), 24–26.

194 Pristo, *Martelé: Gorham's Nouveau Art Silver*, 53, cited by Williams, "Designing a New Mold," 183.

195 "The Paris Exhibition 1900," *Art Journal* (London: Art Journal Office, 1901), 248–49.

196 Herbert S. Houston, "The Arts and Crafts," *World's Work Advertiser* 2, no. 4 (August 1901), n.p.

197 Ibid.

198 Vittorio Pica, *L'Arte Decorativa all'Esposizione di Torino del 1902* (Bergamo: Istituto Italiano d'Arti Grafiche, 1903), 66–69.

199 Herbert S. Houston, "The Arts and Crafts," *World's Work Advertiser* 8, no. 4 (August 1904), n.p.

200 Ibid.

201 Ibid. See also R. Rücklin, "Die grösste Silberwarenfabrik der Welt," *Deutsche Goldschmiede-Zeitung* 7 (1904), 161–66.

202 Houston, "The Arts and Crafts," n.p.; see also *Gorham Exhibit 1904* booklet, NK7101.S2 G6 1904.

203 Jewel Stern, *Modernism in American Silver: 20th Century Design* (New Haven and London: Yale University Press / Dallas Museum of Art, 2005) 174–76; see also Braznell, "Modern Expression in American Silver," 292.

204 Christine Wallace Laidlaw, "The Metropolitan Museum of Art and Modern Design: 1917–1929," *Journal of Decorative and Propaganda Arts* 8 (Spring 1988), 92.

205 "The Home Beautiful Exposition in Boston," *Jewelers' Circular* 84, no. 14 (May 4, 1921), 103–4.

206 Ibid. See also "Several Centuries of Table Manners," *Jewelers' Circular* 84, no. 16 (May 18, 1921), 69. A similar display mounted by Marguerite Walker Jordan and Gertrude Mayo of Gorham at the Evanston, Illinois, County Fair was reportedly attended by upwards of twenty thousand visitors. "Unusual Exhibit of Silver at Evanston's 'County Fair' for Charities," *Jewelers' Circular*, June 29, 1921, 97. Jordan traveled around the country giving a series of talks in the 1920s and presenting Gorham silver as essential to the modern home.

207 See Patricia E. Kane, "Master of Modern Silver: Erik Magnussen," *Antiques & Fine Arts Magazine* (Summer 2014); online version available at https://www.incollect.com/articles/master-of-modern-silver-erik-magnussen; "Twentieth-Century Decoration: The Modern Theme Finds a Distinctive Medium in American Silver," *Vogue* 72 (July 1, 1928): 94, 98; "Interior Decoration at its Best: Four Rooms Assembled and Exhibited by the Decorators' Club of New York," *Country Life* (July 1928): 68; and Helen Appleton Read, "Twentieth-Century Decoration: The Modern Theme Finds a Distinctive Medium in American Silver," *Vogue* 72 (July 1, 1928): 94, 98. See also "Gallery Notes: American Decorative Arts Show," *Art Center Bulletin* (New York: Art Center, October 1928), 1–3; "American Decorative Art at the Art Center," *Good Furniture Magazine* 32 (Jan. 1929), 46–48.

208 W. Scott Braznell, "Modern Expression in American Silver: The Designs of the Weimar Emigré Albert Feinauer (1886–1955)," *Winterthur Portfolio* 44, no. 4 (December 2010), 291.

209 Ibid.

210 *Harmony* 1, no. 17 (August 2, 1930), GMCA.

211 Gorham Manufacturing Company, *The Hunt Club, Gorham's New 1931 Design*, 1931, GMCA.

212 Stern, *Modernism in American Silver*, 134–35. A mayonnaise bowl from 1934, now in the collection of the Dallas Museum of Art (2002.29.5), was also included.

213 *Silver: An Exhibition of Contemporary American Design by Manufacturers, Designers and Craftsmen* (New York: The Metropolitan Museum of Art,

1937), 193; see also Braznell, "Modern Expression in American Silver," 291.

214 Gorham advertisement, *Harper's Magazine*, April 1899, 100; *Bulletin* (Saint Louis Art Museum) 17, no. 1 (Winter 1984), 52–53.

215 "Examples of Decoration and Design," *Brush and Pencil* 9, no. 5 (February 1902), 300 and plate 11; *Brush and Pencil* 9, no. 6 (March 1902), 372 and plate 13.

216 *Fine Arts Journal* 25, no. 4 (October 1911), n.p.

217 *Fine Arts Journal* 25, no. 6 (December 1911), n.p.

218 *Arts & Decoration* 7, no. 3 (January 1917), 160.

219 McDonald, "Listing the South's Ancestral Silver," *Hardware and House Furnishing Goods* (January 1922), 25–26.

220 *Allen Monthly* (October 1923), 9. Marguerite Walker Jordan spoke to about three hundred guests at the American National Retail Jewelers' Association Breakfast at the Biltmore Hotel in Providence in 1923.

221 "Silver Service of Battleship 'Rhode Island' to be Exhibited at the State House in Providence," *Jewelers' Circular*, June 14, 1922, 76.

222 *International Studio*, September 1929, 83.

223 "To Create Demand for Silverware," *New York Times*, June 26, 1921.

224 Ibid.

225 "The 'Home Beautiful' Exposition in Boston," 103–4; "Several Centuries of Table Manners," 69. "Unusual Exhibit of Silver at Evanston's 'County Fair' for Charities," 97.

226 Elizabeth Lounsbery, "Modernistic Influence on Sterling Silver: The Lights and Shadows of a Skyscraper Are Reflected in This New Table Service," *Arts & Decoration* 28 (April 1928), 52.

227 *New York Times*, June 18, 1929.

228 *New York Times*, July 8, 1930.

229 In April 1932, Gorham president Edward Mayo reported, "Sales for the year showed an improvement of 3.8 percent from the preceding year. There is no doubt that our Christmas business was adversely affected by our entrance in the war." "Gorham, Inc. Reports," *New York Times,* April 13, 1942.

230 "History of the Gorham Manufacturing Company," 8–9, I.4 Histories Written about Gorham, Box 2, GMCA.

231 Rita Reif, "Stores Look to a Harvest in Flatware," *New York Times*, April 15, 1958, 39.

232 Donald H. Colflesh was recruited by Gorham while studying at Pratt Institute. He went to work for Gorham in 1956, just a year after he received a bachelor of arts degree in industrial design. While at Gorham, his most significant design was the *Circa '70* line. Colflesh left Gorham in 1962. Stern, *Modernism in American Silver*, 334.

233 See Carpenter, *Gorham Silver, 1831–1981*, 266.

234 "[A]t this point the so-called 'recession' has very definitely had its effect on our industry and our company. This same condition is expected to continue into the early part of 1961 and we are making our plans accordingly," said Wilbur H. Norton. *Gorham Perspective* 2, no. 1 (January–February 1961), 1, GMCA.

235 By September 1962, silver had risen to its highest since 1920. "Silver Industry Feels Price Rise," *New York Times,* September 6, 1962.

236 "Textron Set to Acquire Gorham," *New York Times,* July 7, 1967.

237 Gorham Manufacturing Company, *Gorham Perspectives* 1, no. 1 (April–May 1960), GMCA.

238 Ibid., 1.

239 Ibid., 2.

240 Gorham Manufacturing Company, *Gorham Salesmaker,* introduced 1951. Select issues are held in the Fleet Library, Rhode Island School of Design.

241 Gorham produced oversized promotional spoons in at least six patterns, as well as 2-½-foot-tall coffeepots.

242 Gorham Manufacturing Company, *Gorham Salesmaker,* June 1953, n.p.

243 Ibid.

244 Gorham Manufacturing Company, *Statement of Facts Concerning Gorham Manufacturing Company in Support of the Application of Transcontinental & Western Air, Inc. to Provide Scheduled Air Transportation to and from Providence, R.I.,* January 8, 1946, I.5.A Gorham – Historical – Articles Arranged Chronologically, GMCA.

245 Ibid.

246 *Polk's Crocker-Langley San Francisco City Directory* (San Francisco: R. L. Polk & Co., 1941), 562; "District Offices," I.4 Histories Written about Gorham, Box 2, GMCA.

247 Dorothy T. Rainwater and Martin and Colette Fuller, "Spaulding & Co.," *Encyclopedia of American Silver Manufacturers* (Atglen, PA: Schiffer Publishing, 2004), 234; "Gorham Leaving Retailing Field," *New York Times,* March 23, 1962.

248 "Sterling Tea Pots Match Flatware," *New York Times*, April 19, 1955.

249 Stern, *Modernism in American Silver*, 278.

250 *New Yorker*, April 8, 1961: 19–30

251 "Table Décor Display Goes on View Today," *New York Times*, August 20, 1963.

252 Stern, *Modernism in American Silver*, 234–35.

Ingrid A. Neuman

GORHAM SILVER CONSERVATION PROJECT

Three years before the 2019 opening of the exhibition *Gorham Silver: Designing Brilliance, 1850–1970*, the RISD Museum embarked on a monumental conservation project to prepare the majority of its 2,220-piece Gorham silver collection for display (fig. 258). What was initially conceived primarily as a cleaning project quickly transformed into a major conservation initiative that resulted in a range of treatments, tailored to each object's conservation needs. Not only can each piece of silver possess a unique chemical makeup, but each could also have been created using different techniques, treatments, and secondary materials. As functional works of art, many of these objects were handled and used by their original owners, sometimes on a daily basis, which significantly affected their surfaces and overall condition. Previous conservation treatments, such as lacquer coatings, also presented issues that required careful assessment.

Silver is a precious metal and very sensitive from both a physical and chemical standpoint. Its atoms form a lattice of molecules, giving silver its characteristic malleability, allowing it to be formed in many ways, including hammering, rolling, chasing, and casting. Silver's easily pliable properties, however, equally render it susceptible to scratches, surface deformations, and sensitivity to outside agents, polishes, and pollutants. Exposure to elements in the air such as sulfur, nitrogen, and oxygen result in a discoloration or darkening commonly known as tarnish.

For silver to gain durability and ultimately serve in a functional capacity, its pure form must be chemically combined, or alloyed, with other metals, most commonly copper. The sterling standard we use today was first established in Britain during the Middle Ages, in the year 1238, defining sterling silver as no less than 92.5 percent silver by weight. The standard was adopted in the United States in the 1870s, became internationally recognized, and continues today. Gorham began using sterling silver in 1868, typically alloying the silver with copper. For some wares, Gorham used a higher percentage of silver, such as 95 percent and 95.84 percent, known as the Britannia standard. Copper gives silver strength, but it is also a less stable element and therefore makes the sterling alloy more susceptible to tarnish and corrosion. When the copper within the sterling alloy begins to corrode, green by-products are often visible. Identifying the metal composition of each object was essential to understanding its condition and to formulating a conservation treatment plan.

Prior to cleaning, a thorough conservation analysis was undertaken for each object, and, in consultation with the curators of the RISD Museum's Decorative Arts and Design Department, Elizabeth A. Williams and Emily Banas, treatment plans were formulated based upon a mutual agreement of how each object should look at the end of the process. Each determination considered the original intent of the object's

appearance, which sometimes led to the research of archival images of Gorham wares. Some objects, such as a set of egg spoons and knife rests featuring unicorn heads, had suffered deformation during their prior use as functional tableware. The delicate horns of the unicorns had been bent, a condition that extended beyond the work of a conservator (fig. 259).[1]

The scale of the conservation initiative necessitated additional participants in order to finish the project on time. Fortunately, a vetting process yielded experienced RISD and Brown University students, faculty, and staff, as well as members of the community, willing to dedicate their skills and time to the initiative. In particular, archaeology students from Brown University who possessed prior experience handling fragile collections objects, and students and faculty from RISD's Jewelry and Metalsmithing Department,

provided invaluable insight. An exciting synergy occurred between students from different departments and various institutions of higher learning. Emerging artists were inspired by the historical Gorham works they were cleaning, resulting in new manifestations of Gorham imagery in contemporary art making.

The variety of methods Gorham used to create its silver objects meant that each piece potentially had a unique surface treatment or application of ornament that required a special cleaning strategy. Before conservation work began, cleaning tools, solvents, and methods of polishing were demonstrated, emphasizing a slow, controlled approach. Each participant wore nitrile or cotton gloves while handling or polishing an object. This was a crucial part of the process, as chlorides and acids naturally present on human hands can etch the surface of the metal and can eventually lead to corrosion, leaving a darkened imprint of the handlers' fingerprints.[2]

The degree to which the objects, or elements thereof, were to be polished was an important consideration. The goal of conserving historical works in silver is not to make them look brand-new. Even after a thorough cleaning, their appearance should remain consistent with their age and wear. Additionally, silver wares are often designed so that raised areas have a high sheen, which contrasts with lower or recessed areas that are intentionally allowed to remain darker to highlight the three-dimensional aspect of the decorative work, adding sculptural emphasis. Many intricately hammered surface details were enhanced with niello, a black compound of sulfur, silver, copper, and lead that often mimics tarnish and is used in the crevices of a design to highlight the raised shinier silver parts. For these objects, polishing had to be especially controlled so as to avoid overcleaning, which might have misrepresented the original intent of the ornamentation.

Cleaning commenced with the removal of particles from the surface using a dry soft brush. The next step often involved the careful use of a solvent such as denatured alcohol to remove accumulated grease and old polish residue on the surface and in corners. A mildly abrasive polishing compound—a slurry of precipitated calcium carbonate in distilled water—was custom-formulated for use in this project. Volunteers moistened hand-rolled cotton swabs with this solution and then moved a swab in circles to slowly and gently polish the

259
Knife rest from the Furber service, with repaired unicorn horn

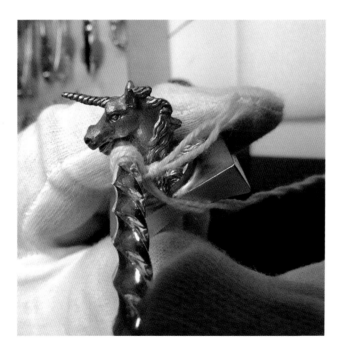

surface of the object (fig. 260). This method allowed localized areas to be cleaned to a higher or lower sheen and assured that objects were not overpolished.

260
A conservation team member cleans a Furber service fruit stand (shown on page 170)

After the cleaning slurry was removed with ethanol applied by cotton swabs, the work was polished, sometimes through use of a dry cloth infused with clay particles, known as a jeweler's rouge cloth. Clay particles are mildly abrasive and commonly used for polishing in the metalworking industry. After polishing, rouge was removed by buffing with a dry cloth and in many cases also through the use of solvents.

Many of the objects conserved for the exhibition feature accents in other metals, such as copper, brass, or, most commonly, gold. The application of gold onto silver, also known as gilding, can be achieved through a variety of processes, yielding different results. Gold was applied to many of Gorham's objects through electroplating. This technique uses an electric current to deposit gold onto the silver, producing a very smooth surface. Other objects, such as the *Cubic* coffee service and salad set (figs. 148, 217), were amalgam gilded, or mercury gilded. In this process, mercury is mixed with gold and applied to the surface of the object. The gold adheres to the surface after the object is heated, which causes the mercury to evaporate. Unlike electroplating, this technique leaves the gold surface much more uneven. The quantity of gold deposited also depends on several factors, including the electrical current, the solution composition, and the amount of time allotted for the process. In both electroplating and mercury gilding, the layer of gold is very thin and quite susceptible to removal through abrasion, which can result from general use or a cleaning method that is too aggressive. Throughout the conservation project, objects that featured gold were handled and cleaned with great care. No solvents or wet-cleaning methods were employed; only rouge cloths were used to gently clean the surfaces.

Analysis of the objects was undertaken in January 2017 at the Museum of Fine Arts, Boston, by Richard Newman, conservation scientist and head of that museum's Scientific Research Laboratory. During evaluation, it was determined that a significant number of objects had at some point been coated in specific areas with cellulose nitrate. While cellulose nitrate is highly revered for its leveling characteristics on metal surfaces, it yellows as it ages, imparting a warmer coloration to the overall silver tone. This protective, plastic-like coating was most likely applied by Gorham to inhibit tarnishing while the objects traveled from store to store as commercial examples, prior to their acquisition by the RISD Museum. The coating, applied in some instances to tarnished or dirty surfaces, sometimes with fingerprints present, was removed using organic solvents such as acetone prior to other cleaning and polishing processes (fig. 261). It was decided that the reapplication of a coating material after cleaning would not be

261
A conservation team member removes lacquer from a Furber service tureen (shown on page 88)

desirable, owing to the poor aging characteristics of many silver coatings.

In order to protect the objects after conservation, they were wrapped in acid-free, neutral-pH tissue paper and enclosed in inert polyethylene bags infused with copper particles to absorb pollutants. This procedure reduced the amount of air that could physically and chemically interact with newly polished surfaces while the objects awaited placement in their display vitrines.

To date, the conservation of objects for the Gorham silver exhibition is the largest cleaning project the RISD Museum has ever undertaken. The number of volunteers varied on a weekly basis, but by the end, more than eighty-five people had participated. Gorham's reputation and its importance in the community of Providence, Rhode Island, no doubt played a significant role in generating interest on the part of project volunteers, some of whom participated for more than two years, coming back regularly for more direct interaction with these remarkable creations.

Conservation Volunteers

It is with gratitude on an exponential level that I extend my sincerest thanks to all the volunteers who participated in this conservation project between 2016 and 2019, and made it so rewarding on an educational level for all. In chronological order of participation: Elizabeth A. Williams, Emily Banas, Heather McLeod, Denise Bastien, Brianna Turner, Danielle Kachapis, Marny Kindness, Sionan Guenther, Lillian Webster, Charlotte Tisch, David Elitzer, Ruby Huh, Alexandra Poterack, Rachel Hauser, Cammie Curtin, Isabel Newton, Sophie Swartz, Ellen Nigro, Thom Morin, Anna Owens, Megan Donnelly, Ashley Chen, Rhea Stark, Luiza Silva, Xiao Rui, Haley Moen, Melissa Tyson, Johan van Aswegen, Ellie Choi, Jess Pedigo, Juri Rhyu, Laura Spellman, Luke Towne, Kaining Wang, Tess Kline, Julia D'Amico, Laurana Hogan, Janie Merrick, Menghan Zhou, Etta Zasloff, Freeman T. Freeman, Chris Cruz, Pamela Provan, Sean O'Keefe, Barbara Seidenath, Peter Prip, Lilly Prip, Maryann Manoli, Christina Alderman, Julia Gualtieri, Penny Stein, Winny Qiu, Chubai Liu, Sang Kon Kwon, You Dam Son, Bailey Franzoi, Kennan Liu, Bridget Provan, Lauren Inoue, Alex Dunwoodie, Moira Anderson, Macy Nobles, Rachel Maynard, Erik Maldonado, Hampton Smith, Anna Rose Keefe, Irene Wei, Rachele Romano, Matthew Bird, Lucy Green, Victor Badami II, Sophia Mongeon, Nicole Amaral, Murphy Chang, Holly Ewald, Catherine Cooper, Cathryn Jasterzbski, Selin Ozulkulu, Jon Gewirtzman, Alex Goldstein, Alessandra Pozzuoli, Hannah Hines, Anabeth Bostrup, Cheri Sivik, Sarah Ellis, Gemma Lurie, Tammie Worthington-Witczak, Kiku Langford McDonald.

1   Peter Prip, a local Rhode Island silversmith and faculty member in the Industrial Design Department at RISD, repaired the gilded unicorn horns adorning the knife rests and egg spoons.
2   See Vanessa Cheel, Peter Northover, Chris Salter, Donna Stevens, Geoff Grime, and Brian Jones, "The Effects of Fingerprints on Silver" (report, Metal 2010: International Conference on Metal Conservation, Charleston, SC, October 11–15, 2010), 173–77.

GORHAM DOCUMENTATION PROJECT

262
Gorham Manufacturing
Company, Office of
the President, 1997

A number of inexorable factors converged in the 1980s, causing the Gorham Manufacturing Company to downsize and move out of the facility in the Elmwood neighborhood of Providence, Rhode Island, where they had been in continual operation since 1890. The complex of brick buildings, including offices, design studios, warehouses, and manufacturing plant, remained empty for more than ten years, and although many efforts were made to find alternative uses for the complex, no workable offers arose. In 1997, the City of Providence planned for demolition but first consulted with the Rhode Island Historical Preservation and Heritage Commission in accordance with the Rhode Island Historical Preservation Act, as the complex had been deemed eligible for listing on the state and national registers of historic places. In response, the Gorham Documentation Project was initiated to compile photographic and written documentation recording the historic and architectural significance of the complex and the individual buildings therein.

The photographic documentation of the site was undertaken by Erik Gould in 1997 and 1998. His photographs simultaneously document and record the evidence of its existence while palpably capturing the essence of the place, which was still vital, still vividly present, even after a decade of disuse. Through Gould's images, powerful machinery operating within arched steel frameworks can be heard and the intense heat of molten metal can be felt. Although the enterprising manufactory no longer exists, Gorham's legacy continues with every spoon laid on a table, every work exhibited in a museum, and every familiar memory of and future encounter with this extraordinary company and the work it produced.

263
Gorham Manufacturing
Company, Foundry, 1997

264
Gorham Manufacturing
Company, Preparatory Room, 1997

Emily Banas

OBJECTS AND ILLUSTRATIONS

Coffeepot: STERLING / D / [lion] [anchor] G A / 850 / 6 ½ PINTS / [star/x-symbol] 6; Teapot: STERLING / D / [lion] [anchor] G A / 850 / 5 ½ PINTS / [star/x-shape] O; Hot-Milk Pitcher: [lion] [anchor] G / 850 / STERLING / [M/H?] .T BROWN / E; Creamer: STERLING / D / [lion] [anchor] G A / 850 / [star/x-shape]; Sugar Bowl: STERLING / D / [lion] [anchor] G / 850 / [star/x-shape] / 11; Slop Bowl: STERLING / D / [lion] [anchor] G A / 850 / [star / × shape]. All objects inscribed: MAL / December 16th / 1870. RISD Museum, Gift of Miss Mary Ann Lippitt, 2001.74

Page 44: Creamer and Sugar Bowl, ca. 1865. George Wilkinson (1819–1894), designer, and Shreve, Stanwood & Company (1860–69), retailer. Silver. Creamer: 18.8 × 14.3 × 8.3 cm (7 ⅜ × 5 ⅝ × 3 ¼ in); Sugar Bowl: 17.6 × 12 × 11 cm (6 ¹⁵⁄₁₆ × 4 ¾ × 4 ⁵⁄₁₆ in.). Both marked: SHREVE STANWOOD&CO. / [lion] [anchor] G / COIN / 0390. Inscribed: ABT. RISD Museum, Gift of the Wunsch Americana Foundation, Inc., 1986.170, 1986.076.2

Page 45: Detail of Creamer. RISD Museum, Gift of the Wunsch Americana Foundation, Inc., 1986.170

Page 46: Ice Bowl, 1866. Silver with gilding. 24.2 × 31.6 × 25 cm (9 ½ × 12 ⁷⁄₁₆ × 9 ¹³⁄₁₆ in.). Marked: [lion] [anchor] G / 110. Inscribed: EIF. RISD Museum, The Gorham Collection. Gift of Textron Inc., 1991.126.54; Ice Tongs, 1869. Silver. 29.3 × 8.7 × 5.8 cm (11 ⁹⁄₁₆ × 3 ⁷⁄₁₆ × 2 ⁵⁄₁₆ in.). Marked: [lion] [anchor] G / STERLING / 68. Inscribed: EIF. RISD Museum, The Gorham Collection. Gift of Textron Inc., 1991.126.45.25

Page 47: Detail of Ice Bowl. RISD Museum, The Gorham Collection. Gift of Textron Inc., 1991.126.54

Page 48: Isis Ice Serving Spoon, ca. 1871. George Wilkinson (1819–1894), designer. Silver with gilding. 26 × 7.6 × 5.3 cm (10 ¼ × 3 × 2 ¹⁄₁₆ in.). Marked: [lion] [anchor] G STERLING. RISD Museum, Museum Purchase: Gift of the Friends of the Decorative Arts Department, 1992.009

Page 49: Detail of Isis Ice Serving Spoon. RISD Museum, Museum Purchase: Gift of the Friends of the Decorative Arts Department, 1992.009

Page 50: Pattern 500 Tea and Coffee Service, 1871. Silver with ivory. Urn with Stand: 37 × 25.7 × 24.2 cm (14 ⁹⁄₁₆ × 10 ⅛ × 9 ½ in.) (overall); Coffeepot: 22.9 × 22.6 × 14.4 cm (9 × 8 ⅞ × 5 ¹¹⁄₁₆ in.); Teapot: 18.7 × 21.4 × 14.6 cm (7 ⅜ × 8 ⁷⁄₁₆ × 5 ¾ in.); Creamer: 14.2 × 11.5 × 8.9 cm (5 ⁹⁄₁₆ × 4 ½ × 3 ½ in.); Sugar Bowl: 10.7 × 15 × 13

cm (4 ³⁄₁₆ × 5 ⅞ × 5 ⅛ in.); Waste Bowl: 13.7 × 15.7 × 12.8 cm (5 ⅜ × 6 ³⁄₁₆ × 5 ¹⁄₁₆ in.); Tray: 13.5 × 78.5 × 51 cm (5 ⁵⁄₁₆ × 30 ⅞ × 20 ¹⁄₁₆ in.). Urn with Stand marked: D / STERLING / [lion] [anchor] G D / 500 / 13 ½ PINTS; Coffeepot: D / 500 / [lion] [anchor] G D / STERLING / 7 ½ PINTS / 2; Teapot: D / 500 / [lion] [anchor] G D / STERLING / 6 ½ PINTS / 1; Creamer: D / STERLING / [lion] [anchor] G D / 500; Sugar Bowl: 500 / [lion] [anchor] G D / STERLING / D; Waste Bowl: 500 / [lion] [anchor] G D / STERLING / D / 6; Tray: [anchor] / GORHAM MFG.CO / 090 / D IN. / 26. All objects inscribed: CBN. RISD Museum, Gift of Elizabeth Mayer Buchanek, 2001.86

Page 51: Detail of Pattern 500 Urn with Stand. RISD Museum, Gift of Elizabeth Mayer Buchanek, 2001.86.1ad

Page 52: Hot-Water Kettle and Stand, 1874. Silver with gilding and ivory. 37.3 × 29.6 × 21.9 cm (14 ¹¹⁄₁₆ × 11 ⅝ × 8 ⅝ in.). Marked: GORHAM MFG CO. / H. Inscribed: EIF. RISD Museum, The Gorham Collection. Gift of Textron Inc., 1991.126.23abc

Page 53: Detail of Fruit Stand. RISD Museum, The Gorham Collection. Gift of Textron Inc., 1991.126.26. For complete information, see listing for page 79.

Gorham Silver and Social Aspirations

Page 54: Water pitcher, 1851. George Babcock (1814–1883), engraver, and Gorham & Thurber, 1850–52. Coin silver. 31.6 × 23.4 × 17.7 cm (12 ⁷⁄₁₆ × 9 ³⁄₁₆ × 6 ¹⁵⁄₁₆ in.). Marked: GORHAM & THURBER / PROVIDENCE RI / PURE COIN. Inscribed: Presented / by Ladies of / the First Universalist / Society / to / Rev. Henry & Mrs. Eliza Ann Bacon / Providence R.I. Sept. 4th 1851 / "Your memory will be to us a joy for ever." RISD Museum, Museum Purchase: Bequest of Eliza Taft, by exchange, 2003.26

Page 56 (above): William Henry Lippincott, Infantry in Arms, 1887. Oil on canvas. Pennsylvania Academy of the Fine Arts, Gift of Homer F. Emens and Francis C. Jones, 1922.10

Page 56 (below): Gems of Deportment and Hints of Etiquette by Martha Louise Rayne, 1881.

Page 57: Tea and Coffee Service, 1873–75. Silver with gilding and ivory. Waiter (for reference): 12.4 × 85.3 × 52.6 cm (4 ⅞ × 33 ⁹⁄₁₆ × 20 ¹¹⁄₁₆ in.).

All objects marked: STERLING / [lion] [anchor] G, and inscribed: EIF. All RISD Museum, The Gorham Collection. Gift of Textron Inc. 1991.126.14–24, 43

Page 58 (left): Cake Basket, 1874. Silver with gilding. 20.4 × 26.4 × 17.8 cm (8 ¹⁄₁₆ × 10 ⅜ × 7 in.). Marked: 770 / [lion] [anchor] G / STERLING / G. Inscribed: EIF. RISD Museum, The Gorham Collection. Gift of Textron Inc., 1991.126.28

Page 58 (right): Oyster Forks (set of 24), 1879. Silver with gilding. 15.8 × 2 × 1.5 cm. (6 ¼ × ¹³⁄₁₆ × ⁹⁄₁₆ in.). Marked: [lion] [anchor] G / STERLING. Inscribed: EIF. RISD Museum, The Gorham Collection. Gift of Textron Inc., 1991.126.764

Page 59 (left): Celery Vase, 1875. Silver. 19.4 × 20 × 12.8 cm (7 ⅝ × 7 ⅞ × 5 ¹⁄₁₆ in.). Marked: [lion] [anchor] G / STERLING / H. Inscribed: EIF. RISD Museum, The Gorham Collection. Gift of Textron Inc., 1991.126.35

Page 59 (right): Terrapin Tureen, 1890. Silver with gilding. Tray: 3.2 × 41.9 × 38.1 cm (1 ¼ × 16 ½ × 15 in.). Tureen: 16.5 × 36.4 × 24.1 cm (6 ½ × 14 ½ × 9 ½ in.). Tray marked: [lion] [anchor] G / 455 / STERLING / [rooster date mark, 1890]. Tureen marked: [lion] [anchor] G / 455 / STERLING. Private collection, courtesy of the Indianapolis Museum of Art at Newfields

Page 60 (left): Ice Cream Hatchet, ca. 1880. Silver. 28.5 × 8.6 × 1.3 cm (11 ¼ × 3 ⅜ × ½ in.). Marked: [lion] [anchor] G STERLING. Inscribed: Elise. RISD Museum, Gift of Kathy Field Malavasic in memory of her mother Doris Coles Field, 2016.68

Page 60 (right): Salad Set, ca. 1875. Ivory and silver. Fork: 29.7 × 3.5 × 3 cm (11 ¹¹⁄₁₆ × 1 ⅜ × 1 ³⁄₁₆ in.); Spoon: 29.5 × 5.4 × 3 cm (11 ⅝ × 2 ⅛ × 1 ³⁄₁₆ in.). Marked: GORHAM CO. RISD Museum, Helen M. Danforth Acquisition Fund, 1988.066

Page 61: Ice Cream Spoon (one of a set of 24), 1879. Silver with gilding. 15.3 × 3.2 × 2.6 cm (6 × 1 ¼ × 1 in.). Marked: STERLING / [lion] [anchor] G. Inscribed: EIF. RISD Museum, The Gorham Collection. Gift of Textron Inc., 1991.126.71.1

Page 62 (above left): Table setting for dinner à la française, ca. 1870, in Wendell Schollander and Wes Schollander, Forgotten Elegance: The Art, Artifacts, and Peculiar History of Victorian and Edwardian Entertaining in America, 2002. Page 62 (below left): Dining room, Leland Stanford residence, ca. 1878. Eadweard Muybridge Photograph Collection (PC0006), Department of Special

Collections and University Archives, Stanford Libraries, Stanford, California

Page 62 (below right): Diagram of a table set for a multi-course dinner, Demorest's Family Magazine 28, 1891.

Page 63 (left): Potter Palmer house, dining room with table set, ca. 1895–1902. Art Institute of Chicago

Page 63 (right): Match Safes, clockwise from top left (all objects RISD Museum, Gift of the estate of Richard Harrington): ca. 1889. Silver. 7.3 × 4.3 × 1.5 cm (2 ⅞ × 1 ¹¹⁄₁₆ × ⁹⁄₁₆ in.). Marked: [lion] [anchor] G STERLING. 1990.061.11; 1895. Silver with gold and copper. 6 × 4.5 × 1.6 cm (2 ⅜ × 1 ¾ × ⅝ in.). Marked: [lion] [anchor] G STERLING & OTHER METALS. 1178. 1990.061.35; 1881. Silver with copper. 6.7 × 3.8 × 1.5 cm (2 ⅝ × 1 ½ × ⁹⁄₁₆ in.). Marked: [lion] [anchor] G STERLING. 141 N & OTHER METALS. 1990.061.19; ca. 1900. Silver. 6 × 5 × 1.6 cm (2 ⅜ × 1 ¹⁵⁄₁₆ × ⅝ in.). Marked: [lion] [anchor] G STERLING. Inscribed: HGL. 1990.061.12; ca. 1889. Silver. 6 × 4.1 × 1.4 cm (2 ⅜ × 1 ⅝ × ⁹⁄₁₆ in.). Marked: [lion] [anchor] G STERLING 670. COPYRIGHTED 1888. 1990.061.23; ca. 1889. Silver. 6.5 × 3.5 × 1.3 cm (2 ⁹⁄₁₆ × 1 ⅜ × ½ in.). Marked: [anchor] GORHAM CO. 035. 1990.061.46

Page 64: "Gossip—at every sip a reputation dies," 1899. Stereographic photograph by Strohmeyer & Wyman, New York.

Page 65: Black Coffeepot, 1881. Silver with rattan. 21.3 × 15.8 × 9.1 cm (8 ⅜ × 6 ¼ × 3 ⁹⁄₁₆ in.). Marked: [lion] [anchor] G STERLING / F17 /N. RISD Museum, Gift of Kathy Field Malavasic in memory of her mother Doris Coles Field, 2016.68.1ab

Page 66: Decanters, 1913. Silver and glass. Each 23 × 12.6 cm (9 ¹⁄₁₆ × 4 ¹⁵⁄₁₆ in.). Marked on stopper: [lion] [anchor] G STERLING. Marked on body: P. Dawson / Dufftown Glenlivet. Monogramed: JSH. RISD Museum, The Gorham Collection. Gift of Textron Inc., 1991.126.491.1ab

Page 67: "For Tiny Hands," Gorham advertisement in House and Garden, April 1924. GMCA

Page 68: Dressing Set, ca. 1890. Silver. All objects are RISD Museum, The Gorham Collection. Gift of Textron Inc. All objects marked: [lion] [anchor] G / STERLING. Clockwise from left: Comb: 20.2 × 4.7 × 1 cm (7 ⅞ × 1 ⁵⁄₁₆ × ¼ in.). 1991.126.599.1. Marked C181;

Hair Brush: 24.3 × 8.8 × 4.6 cm
(9 9/16 × 3 7/16 × 1 13/16 in.). 1991.126.239.
Marked C1451; Hand Mirror: 21 ×
13.8 × 2 cm (8 1/4 × 5 7/16 × 13/16 in.).
1991.126.244. Marked C17; Whisk
Brush: 16.2 × 9 × 2 1880 cm (6 3/8 ×
3 9/16 × 13/16 in.). 1991.126.243. Marked
C9 [1901 date mark]; Buttonhook:
20.6 × 2 × 1.5 cm (8 1/8 × 13/16 × 9/16 in.).
1991.126.599.2. Marked B675;
Nail File: 20 × 2 × 1.5 cm (7 7/8 × 13/16 ×
9/16 in.). 1991.126.599.3. Marked B675;
Clothes Brush: 5 × 18.1 × 6 cm
(1 15/16 × 7 7/8 × 2 3/8 in.). 1991.126.240.
Marked C1456

Page 69 (left): *Wedding Presents*, ca.
1880. James Wells Champney, 1843–
1903, artist. Oil on canvas. Museum of
the City of New York, Gift of Mr. and
Mrs. Luke Vincent Lockwood, 42.254

Page 69 (right): "Wedding Silver"
Gorham advertisement in *Vogue*,
October 10, 1910. GMCA

Page 70 (left and right): "A Dining
Room—Louis XV Period" and "The
Chantilly Pattern—Cold Meat Fork,
Soup, Ladle, Tomato Server and Salad
Fork," from S*ilver for the Dining Room:
Selected Periods*, by John S. Holbrook,
1912. Special Collections, Fleet Library
at Rhode Island School of Design

Page 72: *Modern American* Coffee
Service, 1928. Erik Magnussen
(1884–1961). Silver with ebony and
ivory. Tray: 2.2 × 38.1 × 30.5 cm
(7/8 × 15 × 12 in.); Coffeepot: 20.7 ×
20.6 × 9.8 cm (8 1/8 × 8 1/8 × 3 7/8 in.);
Milk Pot: 7.3 × 15.6 × 8.9 cm (2 7/8 ×
6 1/8 × 3 1/2 in.); Sugar Bowl: 7.3 ×
16.8 × 8.9 cm (2 7/8 × 6 5/8 × 3 1/2 in.).
All objects marked: EM / [pattern
number] / STERLING / [lion] [anchor]
G / GORHAM / JUNE 29 / 1904–1929.
Individual pattern numbers: Tray:
14054; Coffeepot: 14051; Sugar Bowl:
14052; Milk Pot: 14053. Philadelphia
Museum of Art, 2001-8-1-4

Page 73: Ring Basket, 1965. Sheila
M. Chandler, designer. Silver plate
and plastic. 8.6 × 24. 5 × 24.5 cm
(3 3/8 × 9 5/8 × 9 5/8 in.). Marked: Gorham
/ E [anchor] P / YC 744. Dallas Museum
of Art, The Jewel Stern American Silver
Collection, Decorative Arts Fund
2002.29.252

Page 75: *Modern* Beverage Server
and Stirrer, 1959. Donald H. Colflesh
(b. 1932), designer. Silver and plastic.
28.4 × 15.7 × 7.7 cm (11 3/16 × 6 3/16 ×
3 1/16 in.). Marked: Gorham E [anchor]
P / YC 845 / CAP. 40 OZS. RISD Museum,
Gift of Sam Hough, 2006.113.1

The Gorham Furber Service

Page 78 (left): Elvira Irwin Furber, ca. 1869.
Neville Public Museum of Brown County,
Green Bay, Wisconsin

Page 78 (right): Henry Jewett Furber,
1869. Neville Public Museum of Brown
County, Green Bay, Wisconsin

Page 79: Pair of Fruit Stands, 1871. Silver
with gilding. .25 × 32.4 × 46.4 × 23.5 cm
(12 3/4 × 18 1/4 × 9 1/4 in.). .26 × 26 × 52.2 ×
23.8 cm (10 1/4 × 20 9/16 × 9 3/8 in.). Marked:
[lion] [anchor] G / STERLING / 775 / D.
Inscribed: EIF. RISD Museum, The Gorham
Collection. Gift of Textron Inc.,
1991.126.25–.26

Page 81: Fruit Knife (one of a set of 24),
1879. Silver with gilding. 17.1 × 2 × .2 cm
(6 3/4 × 13/16 × 1/16 in.). Marked: [lion]
[anchor] G / STERLING. Monogramed:
FURBER. RISD Museum, The Gorham
Collection. Gift of Textron Inc., 1991.
126.767.1

Page 82: Epergne, 1872. Thomas Pairpoint
(1838–1902), designer. Silver with gilding.
65 × 90 × 54.5 cm (25 9/16 × 35 7/16 ×
21 7/16 in.). Marked: [lion] [anchor] G /
STERLING / 965 / E. Inscribed: EIF. RISD
Museum, The Gorham Collection. Gift
of Textron Inc., 1991.126.80. Plateau, 1876.
Thomas Pairpoint (1838–1902), designer.
Silver with gilding and mirror. 15 × 73.5 ×
43 cm (5 7/8 × 28 15/16 × 16 15/16 in.). Marked
under base: STERLING / [lion] [anchor]
G / I. Marked on top: GORHAM & CO. /
UNION SQUARE N.Y. RISD Museum, The
Gorham Collection. Gift of Textron Inc.,
1991.126.79.1

Page 83: Detail of Epergne 1872. RISD
Museum, The Gorham Collection. Gift
of Textron Inc., 1991.126.80

Page 84: *Cellini Vase*, 1875. Thomas
Pairpoint (1838–1902), designer. Silver
with gilding. 42 × 23.2 × 12.7 cm (16 9/16 ×
9 1/8 × 5 in.). Marked: GORHAM / [lion]
[anchor] G / STERLING / H. Monogramed:
EIF. RISD Museum, The Gorham Collection.
Gift of Textron Inc., 1991.126.52

Page 86: Case for Dessert Set, *Gorham
Photo Catalogue*, 1873–79. GMCA

Page 88: Soup Tureen, 1873. Silver. 29.2 ×
47 × 26.7 cm (11 1/2 × 18 1/2 × 10 1/2 in.).
Marked: [lion] [anchor] G / STERLING /
F / 190. Inscribed: EIF. RISD Museum, The
Gorham Collection. Gift of Textron Inc.,
1991.126.30ab

Page 89 (above): Tureens, Sauceboats,
Salts, Compotes, Fruit Stand, Pickle Dish,
and Butter Dish, 1873. Silver with gilding.

Largest dimension: 19 × 50 × 27.5 cm
(7 1/2 × 19 11/16 × 10 13/16 in.); smallest
dimension: 6.7 × 15 × 7 cm (2 5/8 × 5 7/8 ×
2 3/4 in.). All objects marked: [lion]
[anchor] G / STERLING / F. RISD Museum

Page 89 (below): Oil and Vinegar Cruet,
1875. Silver with gilding and glass. 36 ×
21.8 × 12.3 cm (14 3/16 × 8 9/16 × 4 13/16 in.).
Marked: [lion] [anchor] G / [heart] H /
STERLING / GORHAM. Inscribed: EIF. RISD
Museum, The Gorham Collection. Gift
of Textron Inc., 1991.126.39

Pages 90–91: *Angelo* Flatware Set, ca.
1870. Silver with gilding. RISD Museum

Page 92 (above): Candelabra, 1879.
Silver with gilding. Each 87.6 × 53.3 ×
53.3 cm (34 1/2 × 21 × 21 in.). Both
marked: Gorham & CO / [lion] [anchor]
G / STERLING / L / B92. Both inscribed:
EIF. RISD Museum, The Gorham Collection.
Gift of Textron Inc., 1991.126.81.1–.2

Page 92 (below): Detail of Candelabrum.
RISD Museum, The Gorham Collection.
Gift of Textron Inc., 1991.126.81.1

Page 93 (above): Ice Cream Plate (one
of a set of 24), 1879. Silver with gilding.
1.2 × 15.2 cm (1/2 × 6 in.). Marked: [lion]
[anchor] G / STERLING / L. Inscribed:
EIF. RISD Museum, The Gorham Collection.
Gift of Textron Inc., 1991.126.64.19

Page 93 (below): Melon Forks (set of 24),
1879. Silver with gilding. 19.6 × 2 × 2 cm
(7 11/16 × 13/16 × 13/16 in.). Marked: [lion]
[anchor] G / STERLING. Inscribed: EIF.
RISD Museum, The Gorham Collection.
Gift of Textron Inc., 1991.126.73

Page 94 (above): Waiter, 1873.
Thomas Pairpoint (1838–1902), designer.
Silver with gilding. 12.4 × 85.3 × 52.6 cm
(4 7/8 × 33 9/16 × 20 11/16 in.). Marked:
GORHAM MFG. CO. / 1 BOND ST. NY. G
[lion] [anchor] G [trefoil] / STERLING /
1000 / 28. Inscribed: EIF RISD Museum,
The Gorham Collection. Gift of Textron
Inc., 1991.126.43

Page 94 (below): Nutcrackers, 1879.
Silver with gilding. Each 16.8 × 4.2 × 1.6
cm (6 5/8 × 1 5/8 × 5/8 in.). Marked: STERLING
[lion] [anchor] G. Monogramed: FURBER.
RISD Museum, The Gorham Collection.
Gift of Textron Inc., 1991.126.78.8

Page 95 (above): Bread Plate, 1871.
Silver with gilding. 2.3 × 26.7 ×
26.7 cm (7/8 × 10 1/2 × 10 1/2 in.).
Marked: D / [lion] [anchor] /
G / [trefoil] / 20 / STERLING.
Inscribed: EIF. RISD Museum, The
Gorham Collection. Gift of Textron
Inc., 1991.126.51

Page 95 (below): Grape Shears, 1879.
Silver with gilding. 17.1 × 5.9 × 1.3 cm
(6 3/4 × 2 5/16 × 1/2 in.). Marked: STERLING /
[lion] [anchor] G. RISD Museum, The
Gorham Collection. Gift of Textron Inc.,
1991.126.78.1–.2

Page 96: Pitcher, 1874. Silver with
gilding. 28.4 × 28 × 16.2 cm (11 3/16 ×
11 × 6 3/8 in.). Marked: 885 / [lion]
[anchor] G / STERLING / G. Inscribed: EIF.
RISD Museum, The Gorham Collection.
Gift of Textron Inc., 1991.126.55

Page 97: Detail of Pitcher. RISD Museum,
The Gorham Collection. Gift of Textron
Inc., 1991.126.55

Gorham Works 1870s–1890s

Page 99: Coffeepot, ca. 1890. Copper
and silver with ivory. 32.8 × 17.8 ×
13 cm (12 15/16 × 7 × 5 1/8 in.). Marked:
[anchor] / GORHAM CO. RISD Museum,
Mary B. Jackson Fund, 84.161

Page 100: Katsushika Hokusai, *Manga*,
1878, volume 15. Special Collections,
Fleet Library at Rhode Island School
of Design

Page 101: Vase, 1880. Silver with copper
and brass. 22.2 × 13 × 10.5 cm (8 3/4 ×
5 1/8 × 4 1/8 in.). Marked: [lion] [anchor]
G / STERLING & OTHER METALS / B86 /
M / GORHAM & CO. RISD Museum,
Elizabeth T. and Dorothy N. Casey
Fund, 2015.43

Page 102: Salad Servers, ca. 1880. Silver
with gilding. Salad Fork: 24.8 × 8.8 ×
2.4 cm (9 3/4 × 3 7/16 × 15/16 in.); Salad
Spoon: 25.2 × 6.3 × 2.5 cm (9 15/16 ×
2 1/2 × 1 in.). Both objects marked: [lion]
[anchor] G / STERLING / 330. RISD
Museum, The Gorham Collection. Gift
of Textron Inc., 1991.126.534

Page 103: Tureen on Stand, 1881.
Silver with copper. Tureen: 20.3 × 33 ×
22.9 cm (8 × 13 × 9 in.); Stand: 26 × 26 ×
1.8 cm (10 1/4 × 10 1/4 × 11/16 in.).
Collection of Kathy Field Malavasic

Page 104: Tureen, 1884. Silver. 17 ×
27.7 × 20.7 cm (6 11/16 × 10 7/8 × 8 1/8 in.).
Marked: [lion] [anchor] G STERLING
255 / Q. RISD Museum, Gift of
Mrs. Pierre Brunschwig, 81.072ab

Page 105 (left): Detail of Teapot and
Stand. RISD Museum, Mary B. Jackson
Fund, 80.155ad

Page 105 (right): Teapot and Stand, 1871.
Silver. 28.5 × 18 × 13.7 cm (11 1/4 × 7 1/16 ×
5 3/8 in.). Marked: T. KIRKPATRICK / 10 /

[lion] [anchor] G / STERLING / D 5 ½ pints. RISD Museum, Mary B. Jackson Fund, 80.155ad

Page 106: Coffee and Tea Service, 1886. Silver with gilding and wood. Kettle on Stand: 31.4 × 23 × 20.6 cm (12 ⅜ × 9 ¹/₁₆ × 8 ⅛ in.); Coffeepot: 19.8 × 24.1 × 16.3 cm (7 ¹³/₁₆ × 9 ½ × 6 ⁷/₁₆ in.); Teapot: 14.1 × 24 × 15.1 cm (5 ⁹/₁₆ × 9 ⁷/₁₆ × 5 ¹⁵/₁₆ in.); Sugar Bowl: 12.8 × 18 × 13.6 cm (5 ¹/₁₆ × 7 ¹/₁₆ × 5 ⅜ in.); Cream Jug: 9.5 × 15.4 × 12.2 cm (3 ¾ × 6 ¹/₁₆ × 4 ¹³/₁₆ in.); Waste Bowl: 8.2 × 13.5 × 13.5 cm (3 ¼ × 5 ⁵/₁₆ × 5 ⁵/₁₆ in.). All marked: [lion] [anchor] G / 1940 THEODORE B. STARR. / STERLING / [Latin cross]. RISD Museum, Elizabeth T. and Dorothy N. Casey Fund, 2014.25

Page 107: Detail of Cream Jug. RISD Museum, Elizabeth T. and Dorothy N. Casey Fund, 2014.25.5

Page 108: Fish Forks (set of 24), 1879. Silver with gilding. 17.6 × 3 × 2 cm (6 ¹⁵/₁₆ × 1 ³/₁₆ × ¹³/₁₆ in.). Marked: [lion] [anchor] G STERLING. Inscribed: EIF. RISD Museum, The Gorham Collection. Gift of Textron Inc., 1991.126.765

Page 109 (above): Water Set, 1878. Silver with gilding. Tray: 2 × 27.3 × 20.6 cm (¹³/₁₆ × 10 ¾ × 8 ⅛ in.); Pitcher: 16 × 18 × 10.7 cm (6 ⁵/₁₆ × 7 ¹/₁₆ × 4 ³/₁₆ in.); Cups: Each 9.8 × 6.2 × 6.2 cm (3 ⅞ × 2 ⁷/₁₆ × 2 ⁷/₁₆ in.). All objects marked: [lion] [anchor] G / STERLING / [pattern number] / K. Individual pattern numbers: water pitcher: 936, tray: A23, cups, 41. RISD Museum, The Gorham Collection. Gift of Textron Inc., 1991.126.48–.50

Page 109 (below): Detail of Sardine Tongs, ca. 1879. Silver with gilding. 15.3 × 5.9 × 6.7 cm (6 × 2 ⁵/₁₆ × 2 ⅝ in.). Marked: [lion] [anchor] G STERLING. Monogramed: F. RISD Museum, The Gorham Collection. Gift of Textron Inc., 1991.126.77

Page 110: Vase, 1879. Silver with copper and brass. 27.94 × 9.53 cm (11 × 3 ¾ in.). Marked: [lion] [anchor] G / B66 / L. Inscribed: BAILEY BANKS & BIDDLE. The Nelson-Atkins Museum of Art, Kansas City, Missouri. Purchase: William Rockhill Nelson Trust through exchange of the gifts of Mr. and Mrs. Frank P. Burnap, Mrs. E. A. Grosvenor Blair, Hilliard Hughes, Nettie Yanoff Brudner, Miss M. H. Bogie, and Mrs. John B. Stover; the bequests of Mary B. B. Crouch and Christine Hall Hough; and other Trust properties, 92–17. Photo courtesy The Nelson-Atkins Media Services / Robert Newcombe

Page 111: Gorham casting patterns from the 1800s in original drawer, 2018.

Page 112 (above): Trophy Cup, 1883. Ivory, silver, and glass. 13.8 × 25.5 × 11.3 cm (5 ⁷/₁₆ × 10 ¹/₁₆ × 4 ⁷/₁₆ in.) Marked: [lion] [anchor] G STERLING P A7. Inscribed: FIRST PRIZE GENTLEMENS SINGLE'S. N.Y.T.C. SEPT. 29, '86. RISD Museum, Gift of Kathy Field Malavasic, 2017.69.4

Page 112 (below): Detail of Trophy Cup. RISD Museum, Gift of Kathy Field Malavasic, 2017.69.4

Page 113: Tea Caddy, 1880. Silver with gilding. 9.3 × 10.3 × 10.3 cm (3 ¹¹/₁₆ × 4 ¹/₁₆ × 4 ¹/₁₆ in.). Marked: [lion] [anchor] G / STERLING / 150 / M. RISD Museum, Museum Collection, S44.26

Designing Gorham Silver

Page 114: Urn with Stand, 1871. Silver. 37 × 25.7 × 24.2 cm (14 ⁹/₁₆ × 10 ⅛ × 9 ½ in.). Marked: Marked: D / STERLING / [lion] [anchor] G D / 500 / 13 ½ PINTS. Inscribed: CBN. RISD Museum, Gift of Elizabeth Mayer Buchanek, 2001.86.1ad

Page 116 (above): Gorham & Company advertisement, 1852. GMCA

Page 116 (below): Tea Service, 1850. Gorham & Thurber, 1850–52. Silver. Teapot: 21.9 × 23.8 × 14.6 cm (8 ⅝ × 9 ⅜ × 5 ¾ in.); Coffeepot: 21 × 15.9 × 12.1 cm (8 ¼ × 6 ¼ × 4 ¾ in.); Sugar Bowl: 18.4 × 16.2 × 16.2 cm (7 ¼ × 6 ⅜ × 6 ⅜ in.); Creamer: 17.1 × 14.9 × 11.4 cm (6 ¾ × 5 ⅞ × 4 ½ in.); Waste Bowl: 11.4 × 16.2 × 16.2 cm (4 ½ × 6 ⅜ × 6 ⅜ in.). All objects marked: GORHAM & THURBER / PROVIDENCE RI / PURE COIN. All objects inscribed: EMA. Teapot inscribed: Almy. Mary Swissler Oldberg Fund, 2015.606.1–.5. Art Institute of Chicago. Photo Credit: The Art Institute of Chicago / Art Resource, NY. Hot-Water Pot (far left in group image): Gorham & Thurber, 1850–52. Silver. 21.3 × 24.1 × 14.6 cm (8 ⅜ × 9 ½ × 5 ¾ in.). Art Institute of Chicago, Bequest of Mrs. Frederick H. Wickett, 1952.1107

Page 117 (above): *Rebekah at the Well Pitcher*, 1852. Gorham & Company, 1852–65. Silver. 34.29 × 18 × 15.24 cm (13 ½ × 7 ⅛ × 6 in.). Marked: GORHAM & COMPANY / STERLING [upside down] / PROVIDENCE, R.I. Inscribed: Louise J. F. Whiteman / from her Father / Oct. 12, 1854. Cincinnati Art Museum, Gift of Angeline Russell Faran, 1978.267

Page 117 (below): *Union Vase*, 1864. George Wilkinson (1819–1894), designer, in Gorham, *Photo Catalogue*, 1872. GMCA

Page 118: Fruit Dish, 1866. Starr & Marcus (1862–77), retailer. Silver with gilding. 42.5 × 35.2 × 29.8 cm (16 ¾ × 13 ⅞ × 11 ¾ in.). Marked: 164 [lion] [anchor] G. Inscribed: George Peabody / to / Cyrus W. Field / in testimony and commemoration / of an act of very high / commercial integrity and honor. / New York 24 Nov. 1866. SANS DIEU RIEN. Gorham Manufacturing Company for Starr & Marcus / Museum of the City of New York. 34.346.2

Page 119: Designing and Modeling Room in *Views, Exterior and Interior, of the Works of the Gorham Manufacturing Company, Silversmiths*, 1892. GMCA

Page 120 (left): *Cellini Vase*, 1875. Thomas Pairpoint (1838–1902), designer. Silver with gilding. 42 × 23.2 × 12.7 cm (16 ⁹/₁₆ × 9 ⅛ × 5 in.). Marked: GORHAM / [lion] [anchor] G / STERLING / H. Inscribed: EIF. RISD Museum, The Gorham Collection. Gift of Textron Inc., 1991.126.52. *Cellini Stand*, 1874. Thomas Pairpoint (1838–1902), designer. Silver with gilding. 4.5 × 50.2 × 32.5 cm (1 ¾ × 19 ¾ × 12 ¹³/₁₆ in.). Marked: [lion] [anchor] G / STERLING / G. Inscribed: EIF. RISD Museum, The Gorham Collection. Gift of Textron Inc., 1991.126.57

Page 120 (right): Plate 12 in Martin Riester, *Ornements du 19me siecle: inventès et dessinès par divers artistes industriels et gravès* (Paris: Turgis, ca. 1851). Special Collections, Fleet Library at Rhode Island School of Design

Page 121: *Century Vase,* 1876. Thomas Pairpoint and George Wilkinson, designers. As illustrated in *Gorham Photobook Silver No. 1*, 1872–79. GMCA

Page 122 (left): Florentin Antoine Heller in his studio, 1892, as illustrated in Charles H. Carpenter Jr., *Gorham Silver, 1831–1981* (New York: Dodd, Mead, 1982)

Page 122 (right): *American Shield* and the Furber Candelabrum, in *Choice Examples of Sterling Silver Ware: The Products of the Gorham Mfg Co: Silversmiths*, an exhibition book show at the 1893 World's Columbian Exposition, Chicago. GMCA

Page 123 (above): Ice Bowl, 1871. M. W. Galt Bro. & Co., retailer. Silver. 17.8 × 27.3 × 17.1 cm (7 × 10 ¾ × 6 ¾ in.). Marked: [lion] [anchor] G / 125 / STERLING / D. Inscribed: M.W. Galt Bros.

& Co. Washington, D.C. Dallas Museum of Art, The Eugene and Margaret McDermott Art Fund, Inc., 1989.5.1.McD. Ice Spoon, 1874. M. W. Galt Bro. & Co., retailer. Silver. 28.6 × 5.7 cm (11 ¼ × 2 ¼ in.). Marked: 63 / STERLING / [lion] [anchor] G. Dallas Museum of Art, The Eugene and Margaret McDermott Art Fund, Inc., 1989.5.1.McD

Page 123 (below): Salt (one of a set of 24), 1879. Silver with gilding. 3.5 × 5.4 × 4.4 cm (1 ⅜ × 2 ⅛ × 1 ¾ in.). Marked: [lion] [anchor] G / STERLING / 1620 / L. RISD Museum, The Gorham Collection. Gift of Textron Inc., 1991.126.66.13

Pages 124–25: Butter Plates (set of 24), 1879. Silver with gilding. .8 × 7.5 × 7.5 cm (⁵/₁₆ × 2 ¹⁵/₁₆ × 2 ¹⁵/₁₆ in.). Marked: [lion] [anchor] G / STERLING / L. Inscribed: EIF. RISD Museum, The Gorham Collection. Gift of Textron Inc., 1991.126.68

Page 126 (left): Tray, 1881. Silver. 2.5 × 27.8 × 30.6 cm (1 × 10 ¹⁵/₁₆ × 12 ¹/₁₆ in.). Marked: [lion] [anchor] G / STERLING E42 / N GORHAM & CO / H. Dallas Museum of Art, 1993.10

Page 126 (right): Pitcher, 1882. Silver. 22.9 × 21 × 17.5 cm (9 × 8 ¼ × 6 ⅞ in.). Marked: [lion] [anchor] G STERLING 1095 / O. The Metropolitan Museum of Art 2013.26

Page 127 (left): Fruit Plate, 1881. Silver with gilding and copper. 7.6 × 31.4 × 31.1 cm (3 × 12 ⅜ × 12 ¼ in.). Marked: [lion] [anchor] G / STERLING / &OTHER METALS / C24 / N. Dallas Museum of Art, The Eugene and Margaret McDermott Art Fund, Inc. 1989.6.McD

Page 127 (right): Oyster Tureen, 1885; Stand, 1884. Silver. Tureen: 22.8 × 26.3 × 22.2 cm (9 × 10 ⅜ × 8 ¾ in.); Stand: 1.9 × 19 × 24.1 cm (¾ × 7 ½ × 9 ½ in.). Tureen marked: [lion] [anchor] G / STERLING / 291 / [boar's head, date mark for 1885]; Stand marked: [lion] [anchor] G STERLING / Q [date mark for 1884]. Dallas Museum of Art, Discretionary Decorative Arts Fund and gift of David T. Owsley via the Alvin and Lucy Owsley Foundation 2005.9.A-C

Page 128: Wine Decanter Stand, 1873. George Wilkinson (1819–1894), designer. Silver with gilding and glass. 44 × 25.4 × 24.8 cm (17 ⁵/₁₆ × 10 × 9 ¾ in.). Marked: 105 / [lion] [anchor] G / STERLING / F. Inscribed: EIF. RISD Museum, The Gorham Collection. Gift of Textron Inc., 1991.126.38

Page 129 (left): Detail of Wine Decanter Stand. RISD Museum, The Gorham Collection. Gift of Textron Inc., 1991.126.38

Page 129 (right): Bud Vase with Enameled Decoration, 1877. Silver and gilding with enamel. 13.97 × 5.71 × 5.71 cm (5 ½ × 2 ¼ × 2 ¼ in.). Marked: [lion] [anchor] G / STERLING / J. Newark Museum, Purchase 1984 Sophronia Anderson Bequest Fund, 84.334

Page 130: Elephant Fruit Stand, 1881. Silver with gilding. 26.7 × 50.8 × 40.6 cm (10 ½ × 20 × 16 in.). Marked: [lion] [anchor] G STERLING N 1800. Inscribed: RA. Manoogian Foundation, courtesy the Detroit Institute of Arts

Page 131: Gorham silver in Gorham Mfg. Co., Catalogue, Autumn 1880.

Page 132 (left): Atalanta Prize Cup, 1887. Silver. 65.8 × 38.9 × 31.1 cm (25 ⅞ × 15 ⁵⁄₁₆ × 12 ¼ in.). Marked: [lion] [anchor] G / 23. GORHAM & CO. / STERLING. Philadelphia Museum of Art, Gift of Dr. and Mrs. Joseph Sataloff, 1982-128-1

Page 132 (right): William Christmas Codman (1839–1921), ca. 1895, as illustrated in Charles H. Carpenter Jr., Gorham Silver, 1831–1981.

Page 133 (above): Advertisement for Gorham prize cups, Gorham, Catalogue, Autumn 1888. GMCA

Page 133 (below): Der Moderne Stil, published 1895, owned by William Christmas Codman. Special Collections, Fleet Library at Rhode Island School of Design

Page 134: Nautilus Centerpiece, 1893. William Christmas Codman (1839–1921), designer. Silver with gilding, pearls, turquoise, jade, garnet, tourmaline, amethyst, and shell. 50.8 × 39.4 × 31.8 cm (20 × 15 ½ × 12 ½ in.). Marked: [lion] [anchor] G / STERLING / 4700 [in oval] / [intersecting globes, 1893 World's Fair mark]. Inscribed: LUDWIG VOGELSTEIN / UPON THE OCCASION OF HIS / FIFTIETH BIRTHDAY / WITH AFFECTION AND ESTEEM FROM / HIS FRIENDS AND ASSOCIATES OF / THE AMERICAN METAL COMPANY, LIMITED / FEBRUARY 3, 1921. Dallas Museum of Art 1990.176

Page 135: Martelé Dressing Table and Stool, 1899. William Christmas Codman (1839–1921), designer. Silver, glass, fabric, and ivory. 152.4 × 137.2 × 83.8 cm (60 × 54 × 33 in.). Table marked: Martelé / [eagle] / [lion] [anchor] G / 950-1000 fine / 2117 [in oval]; Stool marked: Martelé / [eagle] / [lion] [anchor] G / 950-1000 fine / 3709

[in oval] / sickle, date mark for 1899]. Dallas Museum of Art, The Eugene and Margaret McDermott Art Fund, Inc., in honor of Dr. Charles L. Venable 2000.356.A-B.MCD

Page 136 (left): Martelé Tankard, 1900. Silver. William E. Jordan (1861–1945), chaser. 40 × 20.3 × 18.2 cm (15 ¾ × 8 × 7 ⅛ in.). Collection of Suzanne and Joel Sugg

Page 136 (right): Ewer and Dish, 1900. Robert Bain (1866–1946), chaser. Silver. Ewer: 49.2 × 20.3 × 14.6 cm (19 ⅜ × 8 × 5 ¾ in.); Dish: 5.7 × 45.1 × 45.1 cm (2 ¼ × 17 ¾ × 17 ¾ in.). Collection of Suzanne and Joel Sugg

Page 137: Centerpiece, 1903. Edwin Everett Codman (1876–1955), attributed modeler, and Robert Bain (1866–1946), chaser. Silver. 45.1 × 62.2 × 35.6 cm (17 ¾ × 24 ½ × 14 in.). Marked: Martelé / [lion] [anchor] G / SL [mark for 1904 St. Louis Exposition]. Inscribed: THE GORHAM CO. A3362 / 275 ozs. Cincinnati Art Museum, 1999.1

Page 138: Tankard, 1898. Silver and ivory. 36.8 × 22.9 × 16.2 cm (14 ½ in. × 9 in. × 6 ⅜ in.). Marked: [lion] [anchor] G / STERLING / 7857 [in rectangle] / PINT / 2 ¼. Inscribed: GP. Purchase, The Metropolitan Museum of Art. Ambassador and Mrs. W. L. Lyons Brown Gift, 2014

Page 139 (left): Martelé Claret, 1900. George W. Sauthof (1852–1927), chaser, and J. Hoare & Company (1853–1920), glassmaker. Silver and glass. 41.9 × 17.8 × 14 cm (16 ½ × 7 × 5 ½ in.). Collection of Suzanne and Joel Sugg

Page 139 (right): Plymouth Coffee and Tea Service, as illustrated in The Gorham Mark, 1916, Tea and Coffee Services. GMCA

Page 140: Erik Magnussen at work in studio, ca. 1927. GMCA

Page 141: Candy Dish, 1926. Erik Magnussen (1884–1961), designer, and Spaulding & Co., retailer. Silver and ivory. 22.23 × 16.51 × 16.51 cm (8 ¾ × 6 ½ × 6 ½ in.). Marked: GORHAM / [lion] [anchor] G / STERLING / EHH and MADE FOR SPAULDING & COMPANY / EM. Dallas Museum of Art, 1990.230.a–b

Page 142: Design for Modern American Coffeepot, 1928. Erik Magnussen (1884–1961), designer. Pencil on paper. 34.6 × 37.5 cm (13 ⅝ × 14 ¹³⁄₁₆ in.). Marked: EM. 427. / 1928 / JUNE 22. TURN. 12 LINES FILED / IVORY / OR / BACHALITE. (BLACK) / TURN. COVER. RISD Museum, Gift of Lenox, Incorporated 2005.118.45.891

Page 143: Cubic Salad Set, 1927. Erik Magnussen (1884–1961), designer. Silver with patinated and gilt decoration and ivory. Fork: 26 × 5.1 × 1.3 cm (10 ¼ × 2 × ½ in.); Spoon: 24.7 × 5.9 × 4.2 cm (9 ¾ × 2 ⁵⁄₁₆ × 1 ⅝ in.). Marked: EM / 30 / STERLING / GORHAM / [lion] [anchor] G. RISD Museum, The Gorham Collection. Gift of Textron Inc., 1991.126.489

Gorham Works 1890s–1900s

Page 149: Whiskey Decanter, 1892. Silver and glass. 19.1 × 14.5 × 9.8 cm (7 ½ × 5 ¹¹⁄₁₆ × 3 ⅞ in.). Marked on bottom: GORHAM MFG. CO. / S 1099 / GORHAM MFG. CO. Marked on neck: [lion] [anchor] G STERLING [helmet, date mark for 1892]. Inscribed: MB. RISD Museum, Helen M. Danforth Acquisition Fund, 1988.065

Page 150: Claret Jug, 1893. Silver with gilding, glass, amethysts, garnets, and moonstones. 37.5 × 11.4 × 11.4 cm (14 ¾ × 4 ½ × 4 ½ in.). Marked: [lion] [anchor] G / [1893 date mark, two globes] / S1434 / STERLING. Inscribed: 1892 [underside of base]. MB [on foot]. Marion E. Davis Fund 2006.1246a–b. Museum of Fine Arts, Boston. Photograph © Museum of Fine Arts, Boston

Page 151: Design drawing for a pitcher, ca. 1893. GMCA

Page 152 (above and below): 1893 World's Fair Ring, 1892. Silver. .6 × 1.9 × 1.9 cm (¼ × ¾ × ¾ in.). Marked on exterior: RECUERDO / 1492 / ESPOSICION DE CHICAGO / DE LA 1893 / ELANILLO / YSABEL. Marked on interior: GORHAM MFG CO / REGISTERED [lion] [anchor] G STERLING / 1892 / 6 ½. RISD Museum, Gift of Kathryn S. Smyth, 2016.34

Page 153: Wine Pitcher, 1893. Silver with gilding and glass. 30.48 × 22.86 × 17.78 cm (12 × 9 × 7 in.). Marked: [lion] [anchor] G STERLING S1067 1/22 [1893 date mark, two globes]. The Nelson-Atkins Museum of Art, 2006.19. Photo courtesy Nelson-Atkins Media Services / John Lamberton

Page 154: Sugar Tongs depicting Minerva, Mythologique Pattern, 1894. Florentin Antoine Heller (1839–1904), designer. Silver. 11.3 × 2.8 × .6 cm (4 ⁷⁄₁₆ × 1 ⅛ × ¼ in.). RISD Museum, Gift of Lenox, Incorporated, 2005.118.42.11

Page 155: Apostle Spoons, 1894. Silver. Largest Spoon (Jesus): 19.2 × 4.5 × 2 cm (7 ⁹⁄₁₆ × 1 ¾ × ¹³⁄₁₆ in.), all other Spoons: 16.5 × 3.5 × 1.8 cm (6 ½ × 1 ⅜ × ¹¹⁄₁₆ in.).

Marked: STERLING / [lion] [anchor] G. Each spoon marked with the name of its apostle. RISD Museum, The Gorham Collection. Gift of Textron Inc., 1991.126.565

Page 156: Joseph Jefferson Cup, 1895–96. William Clark Noble (1858–1938), modeler. Silver. 56.5 × 55.9 × 55.9 cm (22 ¼ × 22 × 22 in.). Marked: GORHAM CO. SILVERSMITHS. / [lion] [anchor] G / STERLING / 5715 [in rectangle]. W. CLARK NOBLE SCULPTOR. GORHAM CO. SILVERSMITHS. Inscribed: "Here's your good health / And your Family's, / And may They all live long and prosper." / To / THE DEAN OF THE DRAMATIC PROFESSION / With the loving Greeting and Affection / of his Brother and Sister Players / Nov. 8 1895. / "He Touched Nothing he did not Adorn." / JOSEPH JEFFERSON. New Orleans Museum of Art, Gift of Jolie and Robert Shelton in honor of John Webster Keefe and E. John Bullard, 2011.3

Page 157 (left): Admiral Dewey Cup, 1899. William Christmas Codman (1839–1921), designer. Silver with porcelain and oak. 254 × 85.7 × 85.7 cm (100 × 33 ¾ × 33 ¾ in.). Marked: [lion] [anchor] G / STERLING. Inscribed: THE DEWEY LOVING CUP / PRESENTED TO / THE CONQUERING ADMIRAL / BY SEVENTY THOUSAND / AMERICAN CITIZENS / AS A TRIBUTE / OF THEIR GRATITUDE. Chicago History Museum

Page 157 (right): Design for the Admiral Dewey Cup, 1899. William Christmas Codman (1839–1921), designer. Graphite, watercolor, and gouache on paper. 185.4 × 66 cm (73 × 26 in.). Inscribed: MANILA BAY / MAY 1ST 1898. Plan of cup / 3 handles. RISD Museum, Gift of Lenox, Incorporated, 2005.118.95

Page 158: Martelé Wine Pitcher, 1900. William Christmas Codman (1839–1921), designer; Edward Zior (1868–1927), chaser; J. Hoare & Company, glass manufacturer; and Shreve, Crump & Low, retailer. Silver and glass. 35.2 × 17.7 × 14.9 cm (13 ⅞ × 7 × 5 ⅞ in.). Marked: 950.1000 FINE. SHREVE, CRUMP, & LOW CO. High Museum of Art, Atlanta, Virginia Carroll Crawford Collection, 1982.306

Page 159: Design for a Martelé Ewer, ca. 1900. Graphite, watercolor, and gouache on paper. 82.9 × 54 cm (32 ⅝ × 21 ⁵⁄₁₆ in.). RISD Museum, Gift of Lenox, Incorporated, 2005.118.59.

Pages 160 and 161 (above): Bonbon Spoon, ca. 1893. Silver with gilding and plique-à-jour enamel. 13.3 × 5 × 1.5 cm (5 ¼ × 1 ¹⁵⁄₁₆ × ⁹⁄₁₆ in.). Marked:

[lion] [anchor] G / STERLING / 5650 [in oval]. RISD Museum, Anonymous gift, 54.184

Page 161 (below): Pendant, 1900. Gold, pearls, frosted green glass, diamonds, enamel, and rubies. Pendant: 8.3 × 3.2 cm (3 1/4 × 1 1/4 in.). Marked: [lion] / [anchor] / 18K / XEX. RISD Museum, Helen M. Danforth Acquisition Fund, 1997.80

Page 162: *Martelé* Billings Cup, 1899. William Christmas Codman (1839–1921), designer; Herbert C. Lloyd (1865–1951), chaser; and Spaulding & Co. (1888–1973), retailer. Silver. 19.8 × 24.7 × 23.5 cm (7 13/16 × 9 3/4 × 9 1/4 in.). Marked: SPAULDING & CO. / CHICAGO / [eagle] / [lion] [anchor] G / 950-1000 FINE / 9164. Inscribed: THE BILLINGS CUP / GIVEN BY / C.K.G. BILLINGS / FOR / MORGANS UNDER SADDLE / VERMONT STATE FAIR / 1913. RISD Museum, Helen M. Danforth Acquisition Fund, 1990.004

Page 163 (above and below): Match Safe, ca. 1889. Silver. 6 × 4.1 × 1.4 cm (2 3/8 × 1 5/8 × 9/16 in.). Marked: [lion] [anchor] G STERLING 670. COPYRIGHTED 1888. RISD Museum, Gift of the estate of Richard Harrington, 1990.061.23

Creating Gorham Silver

Page 165: Gorham casting patterns from the 1800s in original drawer, 2018

Page 167: Design Drawing, *Pattern 170* Coffeepot, ca. 1869. GMCA

Page 168: Tea Service, 1860. Silver with gilding. Tea Urn: 27 × 28 × 27.4 cm (10 5/8 × 11 × 10 13/16 in.); Teapot: 21.5 × 23.2 × 14.8 cm (8 7/16 × 9 1/8 × 5 13/16 in.); Creamer: 15 × 13.8 × 10.1 cm (5 7/8 × 5 7/16 × 4 in.); Sugar Bowl: 16 × 19.4 × 13.5 cm (6 5/16 × 7 5/8 × 5 5/16 in.); Slop Bowl: 6.7 × 17.1 × 13.5 cm (2 5/8 × 6 3/4 × 5 5/16 in.). All objects marked: [lion] [anchor] G / COIN / 170. RISD Museum, Museum Acquisition Fund, 2001.37

Page 170 (above): Pair of Fruit Stands, 1871. Silver with gilding .25: 32.4 × 46.4 × 23.5 cm (12 3/4 × 18 1/4 × 9 1/4 in.), .26: 26 × 52.2 × 23.8 cm (10 1/4 × 20 9/16 × 9 3/8 in.). Marked: [lion] [anchor] G / STERLING / 775 / D. Inscribed: EIF. RISD Museum, The Gorham Collection. Gift of Textron Inc., 1991.126.25–.26

Page 170 (below): Presentation Drawing, Furber Fruit Stand, ca. 1871. GMCA

Page 171: Stamped Borders in *Gorham Old S Book*, 1885. GMCA

Page 172 (above): Miniature Cast of the Parthenon Frieze, 1820. John Henning I (1771–1851). Plaster. 5.4 × 18.9 × .6 cm (2 1/8 × 7 7/16 × 1/4 in.). RISD Museum, Gift of Edward Carrington, 05.153.1C

Page 172 (below): Detail of Candelabrum. Silver with gilding. RISD Museum, The Gorham Collection. Gift of Textron Inc., 1991.126.81.2

Page 173: Detail of Sauceboat. Silver. 10.8 × 20.3 × 9.5 cm (4 1/4 × 8 × 3 3/4 in.). Marked: [lion] [anchor] G / STERLING / 190 / F. Inscribed: EIF. RISD Museum, The Gorham Collection. Gift of Textron Inc., 1991.126.10

Page 174: Pepper Shaker (one of a set of 24), 1879. Silver with gilding. 8.3 × 3.4 × 3.4 cm (3 1/4 × 1 5/16 × 1 5/16 in.). Marked: [lion] [anchor] G / STERLING / 1620 / L. Inscribed: EIF. RISD Museum, The Gorham Collection. Gift of Textron Inc., 1991.126.67.23

Page 175 (left and right): Butter Plate (from a set of 24, top and bottom views), 1879. Silver with gilding. .8 × 7.5 × 7.5 cm (5/16 × 2 15/16 × 2 15/16 in.). Marked: [lion] [anchor] G / STERLING / L. Inscribed: EIF. RISD Museum, The Gorham Collection. Gift of Textron Inc., 1991.126.68.3

Page 176: Pitcher, 1879. Silver with copper and gilding. 19.68 × 11.11 × 19.36 cm (7. 3/4 × 4 1/8 × 7 5/8 in.). Marked: [lion] [anchor] G / STERLING / L / B95. Museum of Fine Arts, Houston, Gift of Eleanor Freed in memory of her parents, Esther and David W. Kempner, 82.529

Page 177: Cigar Lighter, ca. 1900. Copper with mixed metals. 6.5 × 12.8 × 7.6 cm (2 9/16 × 5 1/16 × 3 in.). Marked: [anchor] / GORHAM CO / BY147 / Muschenheim. RISD Museum. Gift of Deborah L. Maxwell, in memory of her father, Norman W. Baker, RISD Class of '57, 2009.107

Page 178 (left): Toddy Kettle, 1883. Iron with copper, brass, silver, and ebony. 16.8 × 21.5 × 12.5 cm (6 5/8 × 8 7/16 × 4 15/16 in.). Marked: [anchor] / GORHAM CO / W 22 / P / STERLING / IRON. RISD Museum, The Gorham Collection. Gift of Textron Inc., 1991.126.203abc

Page 178 (right): Katsushika Hokusai, *Manga*, 1878, volume 15. Special Collections, Fleet Library at Rhode Island School of Design

Page 179: Vase, 1879. Silver with copper and brass. 27.9 × 9.5 cm (11 × 3 3/4 in.). Marked: [lion] [anchor] G / B66 / L. Inscribed: BAILEY BANKS & BIDDLE. Nelson-Atkins Museum of Art, Kansas City, Missouri. Purchase: William Rockhill Nelson Trust through exchange of the gifts of Mr. and Mrs. Frank P. Burnap, Mrs. E. A. Grosvenor Blair, Hilliard Hughes, Nettie Yanoff Brudner, Miss M. H. Bogie, and Mrs. John B. Stover; the bequests of Mary B. B. Crouch and Christine Hall Hough; and other Trust properties, 92-17. Photo courtesy Nelson-Atkins Media Services / Robert Newcombe

Page 180 (above): *Curio* Fork, 1879–80. Silver with copper and brass. 15.8 × 2.3 × 1.5 cm. (6 1/4 × 7/8 × 9/16 in.). Marked: [lion] [anchor] G STERLING & OTHER METALS. Inscribed: H. RISD Museum, Gift of Kathy Field Malavasic in memory of her mother Doris Coles Field, 2016.68.2

Page 180 (below): Chasing Room, in *Views, Exterior and Interior, of the Works of the Gorham Manufacturing Company, Silversmiths*, 1892. GMCA

Page 181 (left): Gorham employee pouring pitch into a vessel. GMCA

Page 181 (right): Punch Bowl and Ladle, 1885. Silver with gilding. Punch Bowl: 25.7 × 38.7 × 23.5 cm (10 1/8 × 15 1/4 × 9 1/4 in.); Ladle: 9.5 × 35.6 cm (3 3/4 × 14 in.). Punch Bowl marked: [lion] [anchor] G / STERLING / 1980 [boar head date mark for 1885]; Ladle marked: STERLING. Edwin E. Jack Fund 1980.383. Museum of Fine Arts, Boston. Photograph © Museum of Fine Arts, Boston

Page 182: Snake Pitcher, 1885. Silver. 25.4 × 19.4 × 13.2 cm (10 × 7 5/8 × 5 3/16 in.). Marked: [lion] [anchor] G / STERLING / 1295 / [boar's head date mark for 1885]. Edwin E. Jack Fund 1983.331. Museum of Fine Arts, Boston. Photograph © Museum of Fine Arts, Boston

Page 183: *Narragansett* Salad Set, ca. 1885. Silver with gilding. Fork: 28 × 5.8 × 2.2 cm (11 × 2 5/16 × 7/8 in.). Spoon: 29 × 7.2 × 3 cm (11 7/16 × 2 13/16 × 1 3/16 in.). Both marked: STERLING. RISD Museum, Museum purchase: Bequest of Ida Littlefield, 84.060.

Page 184: Front View (facing east), in *Views, Exterior and Interior, of the Works of the Gorham Manufacturing Company, Silversmiths*, 1892. GMCA

Page 185: South Section of Preparatory Room, in *Views, Exterior and Interior, of the Works of the Gorham Manufacturing Company, Silversmiths*, 1892. GMCA

Page 186 (above): *Mythologique* Flatware Pattern Booklet, 1894. Paper, bound with string. RISD Museum, Gift of Lenox Incorporated, 2005.118.42.30

Page 186 (below): Employee engraving a steel die, no date. GMCA

Page 187: *Mythologique* Flatware Design Samples, 1894. Florentin Antoine Heller (1839–1904), designer. Silver. RISD Museum, Gift of Lenox, Incorporated, 2005.118.42

Page 188 (left): Woman painting silver overlay on ceramic, in *Woman's Work at the Gorham Manufacturing Company*, 1892. GMCA

Page 188 (right): Jewelry Box, ca. 1890. Count Gyula de Festetics (1846–1922), enameler. Silver and enamel. 9.9 × 21.7 × 16 cm. (3 7/8 × 8 9/16 × 6 5/16 in.). Marked: [lion] [anchor] G / STERLING / 1430 M. RISD Museum, Gift from the M. F. Collection, 2013.120.2

Page 189: Pitcher, 1893. Constance Amelia Baker (active 1892–1904), decorator, and Rookwood Pottery (1880–present). 16.8 × 21 × 15.2 cm (6 5/8 × 8 1/4 × 6 in.). Earthenware with glaze and silver. Marked: R1056 GORHAM MFG CO. Signed: CAB. Museum of Fine Arts, Boston, 1989.200

Page 190 (left): Presentation Drawing for *Martelé* Loving Cup, 1904. GMCA

Page 190 (right): *Martelé* Loving Cup, 1900. George W. Sauthof (1852–1927), chaser. Silver with enamel. H: 26.7 cm (10 1/2 in.). Collection of Suzanne and Joel Sugg

Page 191: *Martelé* Writing Table, 1903. William Christmas Codman (1839–1921), designer; Joseph Edward Straker (1843–1912), silversmith; Franz Ziegler (1869–1934), modeler; and Potter and Company (active 1878–1910), cabinetmaker. Ebony, mahogany, boxwood, redwood, thuya wood, ivory, mother-of-pearl, silver, mirrored glass, and gilded tooled leather. Table: 124 × 136.5 × 76 cm (48 13/16 × 53 3/4 × 29 15/16 in.); Chair: 76 × 46 × 63.5 cm (29 15/16 × 18 1/8 × 25 in.). Table marked: [lion] [anchor] G STERLING CCX. Signed inside center drawer: W C Codman 1903; chair marked [lion] [anchor] G / CCY / STERLING. RISD Museum, Gift of Mr. and Mrs. Frederick B. Thurber, 58.095ab

Page 192 (left): Costing Slips for *Martelé* Table and Chair, 1903. GMCA

Page 192 (right): *Athenic* Vase, 1901. Silver with copper and enamel. 39.4 × 15.9 cm (15 ½ × 6 ¼ in.). Marked: Athenic / [lion] [anchor] G / STERLING / &OTHER METALS AV212. Chrysler Museum of Art, Gift of Walter P. Chrysler, Jr., 71.969

Page 193: Drawing of *Athenic* Vases, 1901. GMCA

Page 194 (left): Gorham advertisement, *Circa '70* Coffee and Tea Service, 1961. GMCA

Page 194 (right): Blueprint for *Cubic* Sugar Bowl, 1927. Erik Magnussen (1884–1961), designer. Blueprint. 43.5 × 39.4 cm (17 ⅛ × 15 ½ in.). Marked: 259 / SUGAR. / EM. 1927. RISD Museum, Gift of Lenox, Incorporated, 2005.118.45.832

Page 195 (above): Design Drawing for *Cubic* Coffee Service, 1927. Erik Magnussen (1884–1961), designer. Gouache, graphite, and ink on paper. 30.5 × 90.2 cm (12 × 35 ½ in.). Courtesy of Victoria Stenstream

Page 195 (below): *Cubic* Coffee Service, 1927. Erik Magnussen (1884–1961), designer. Silver with gilding and ivory. Tray: 2.2 × 56 × 34.5 cm (⅞ × 22 1/16 × 13 9/16 in.); Coffeepot: 23.7 × 22.9 × 10 cm (9 5/16 × 9 × 3 15/16 in.); Sugar Bowl: 15.2 × 19.6 × 10 cm (6 × 7 11/16 × 3 15/16 in.); Creamer: 9.9 × 14.9 × 8.4 cm. (3 ⅞ × 5 ⅞ × 3 5/16 in.). All objects marked: GORHAM EM [lion] [anchor] G / 28 / STERLING / DESIGNED AND EXECUTED / BY / ERIK MAGNUSSEN / 1927. RISD Museum, The Gorham Collection. Gift of Textron Inc., 1991.126.488

Gorham Works 1900s–1960s

Page 199: Design for an *Athenic* Loving Cup, ca. 1900. William Christmas Codman (1839–1921), designer. Graphite, watercolor, ink, crayon, and gouache on paper. 48.3 × 35.2 cm (19 × 13 ⅞ in.). RISD Museum, Collection of Gorham Division of Textron, Inc. EL006.84.15

Page 200 (above and below): *Athenic* Cigar Box, 1901. Copper, silver, and cedar. 14.6 × 22.5 × 17.5 cm (5 ¾ × 8 ⅞ × 6 ⅞ in.). Marked: Athenic / [anchor] / GORHAM CO. / BY238 / 7 / [hourglass date stamp for 1901]. RISD Museum, Abby Rockefeller Mauze Fund, 80.099

Pages 201–3: *Martelé* Writing Table and Chair, 1903. William Christmas Codman (1839–1921), designer; Joseph Edward Straker (1843–1912), silversmith; Franz Ziegler (1869–1934),

modeler; and Potter and Company (active 1878–1910), cabinetmaker. Ebony, mahogany, boxwood, redwood, thuya wood, ivory, mother-of-pearl, silver, mirrored glass, and gilded tooled leather. Table: 124 × 136.5 × 76 cm (48 13/16 × 53 ¾ × 29 15/16 in.); Chair: 76 × 46 × 63.5 cm (29 15/16 × 18 ⅛ × 25 in.). Table marked: [lion] [anchor] G STERLING CCX. Signed inside center drawer: W C Codman 1903; chair marked [lion] [anchor] G / CCY / STERLING. RISD Museum, Gift of Mr. and Mrs. Frederick B. Thurber, 58.095ab

Page 204: Design for DGL *Martelé* Creamer, 1903. Graphite and crayon on paper. 16.5 × 12.7 cm (6 ½ × 5 in.). RISD Museum, Gift of Lenox, Incorporated, 2005.118.45.2208

Page 205 (above): Design for *Martelé* Sugar Bowl, ca. 1905. Graphite and ink on paper. 26 × 30.5 cm (10 5/16 × 12 in.). RISD Museum, Gift of Lenox, Incorporated, 2005.118.45.2065

Page 205 (below): *Martelé* Tea and Coffee Service, 1901. William Christmas Codman (1839–1921), designer; Otto Colmetz (1863–1950), chaser; Herbert C. Lloyd (1865–1951), chaser; and William L. MacMillan (1867–1928), chaser. Silver with ivory and gilding. Kettle on Stand: 35 × 25.4 × 19.5 cm (13 ¾ × 10 × 7 11/16 in.); Coffeepot: 27.3 × 24.1 × 14.6 cm (10 ¾ × 9 ½ × 5 ¾ in.); Teapot: 19 × 25.9 × 15.3 cm (7 ½ × 10 3/16 × 6 in.); Creamer: 16.2 × 14.3 × 10.6 cm (6 ⅜ × 5 ⅝ × 4 3/16 in.); Sugar Bowl: 16.4 × 19.5 × 12.9 cm (6 7/16 × 7 11/16 × 5 1/16 in.); Waste Bowl: 8.8 × 14.4 × 13.1 cm (3 7/16 × 5 11/16 × 5 3/16 in.). All objects marked: Martelé / [eagle] / [lion] [anchor] G / 950-1000 FINE. 4606 [in oval]. RISD Museum, Gift of Mrs. Kirkland H. Gibson, 1992.075

Page 206: *Athenic* Candelabrum, 1902. Silver. 49.3 × 42.3 × 42.3 cm (19 7/16 × 16 ⅝ × 16 ⅝ in.). Marked: [lion] [anchor] G / STERLING / A3357 / [two globes for St. Louis World's Fair mark]. RISD Museum, Elizabeth T. and Dorothy N. Casey Fund 2017.28.1

Page 207: Detail of *Athenic* Candelabrum, 1902. RISD Museum

Page 208: Pair of Candlesticks, 1928. Erik Magnussen (1884–1961), designer. Silver with turquoise. 34.9 × 16.8 × 16.8 cm (13 ¾ × 6 ⅝ × 6 ⅝ in.). Marked: GORHAM EM [lion] [anchor] G / STERLING / 45. RISD Museum, The Gorham Collection. Gift of Textron Inc., 1991.126.182

Page 209: Design for a Candlestick, 1927. Erik Magnussen (1884–1961), designer. Graphite on tracing paper. 38.1 × 28.6 cm (15 × 11 3/16 in.). RISD Museum, Gift of Lenox, Incorporated, 2005.118.45.927.

Pages 210–211: *Cubic* Coffee Service, 1927. Erik Magnussen (1884–1961), designer. Silver with gilding and ivory. Tray: 2.2 × 56 × 34.5 cm (⅞ × 22 1/16 × 13 9/16 in.); Coffeepot: 23.7 × 22.9 × 10 cm (9 5/16 × 9 × 3 15/16 in.); Sugar Bowl. 15.2 × 19.6 × 10 cm (6 × 7 11/16 × 3 15/16 in.); Creamer: 9.9 × 14.9 × 8.4 cm (3 ⅞ × 5 ⅞ × 3 5/16 in.). All objects marked: GORHAM EM [lion] [anchor] G / 28 / STERLING / DESIGNED AND EXECUTED / BY / ERIK MAGNUSSEN / 1927. RISD Museum, The Gorham Collection. Gift of Textron Inc., 1991.126.488

Page 212: Design for *Circa '70* Teapot, 1962. J. Teixeira, delineator. Graphite and ink on waxed paper. 33 × 42.2 cm (13 × 16 ⅝ in.). RISD Museum, Gift of Lenox, Incorporated, 2005.118.45.633

Page 213: *Circa '70* Coffee and Tea Service, 1960. Donald H. Colflesh (b. 1932), designer; Tray, 1963. Silver with ebony and Formica. Tray: 31 × 172.7 × 147.3 cm (12 3/16 × 68 × 58 in.); Coffeepot: 29.6 × 18.6 × 14.7 cm (11 ⅝ × 7 5/16 × 5 13/16 in.); Teapot: 23.5 × 18.1 × 15.4 cm (9 ¼ × 7 ⅛ × 6 1/16 in.); Sugar Bowl: 11.6 × 16.7 × 12.3 cm (4 9/16 × 6 9/16 × 4 13/16 in.); Creamer: 16.1 × 10 × 9.1 cm (6 5/16 × 3 15/16 × 3 9/16 in.). All objects marked: Gorham / STERLING / [lion] [anchor] G / [pattern number] / [hexagon]. Individual marks: Tray: 1468; Coffeepot: 1461 / 3 PINT; Lid: 45; Teapot: 1462 / 2 ¾ PINT / 9; Lid: 9; Sugar Bowl: 1463 / 18; Lid: 18; Creamer: 1464 / ¾ PINT. RISD Museum, Gift from the M. F. Collection, 2017.47.1–.5

Marketing Gorham Silver

Page 214: Gorham Pavilion, Centennial International Exhibition of 1876, Philadelphia, in *The Century Vase*, Gorham Manufacturing Company. GMCA

Page 217: Lyceum Building, Providence, ca. 1865. Rhode Island Collection, Providence Public Library

Page 218: Waltham Building, New York, in *Publisher's Weekly*, June 1880

Pages 220–21: View from the southwest tower, Main Building, Philadelphia Centennial International Exposition, 1876. Free Library of Philadelphia

Page 222: *Hiawatha's Boat*, 1871. Silver with gilding and mirror. 83.4 × 113 × 48.3 cm (34 × 44 ½ × 19 in.). Marked: [lion] [anchor] G / STERLING / D. White House Collection / White House Historical Association. © 2019 White House Historical Association

Page 223 (left): Gorham advertisement, 1853, in the *American Advertiser* (Boston)

Page 223 (right): Illustration of the Ice Bowl from the Furber service, *Harper's New Monthly Magazine*, September 1868

Page 224: Gorham Building, Nineteenth Street and Broadway, New York, 1886. The Library of Congress

Page 225: Knives, ca. 1880. Silver and bronze. 19.6 × 2.1 × .5 cm (7 11/16 × 13/16 × 3/16 in.). Marked: [lion] [anchor] G / STERLING / 5. RISD Museum, Georgianna Sayles Aldrich Fund and Walter H. Kimball Fund, 1989.007.1–.3

Page 226: Gorham Showroom, Nineteenth Street and Broadway, New York, ca. 1884

Page 227 (left): Gorham Mfg. Co., *Catalogue*, Autumn 1880

Page 227 (right): Maiden Lane, New York, 1885. New York Public Library

Page 228: Prize Cups in Gorham, *Catalogue*, Autumn 1888. GMCA

Page 229: Flask, 1879. Silver with gilding. 15.6 × 9.7 × 4.1 cm (6 ⅛ × 3 13/16 × 1 ⅝ in.). Marked: AA / [lion] [anchor] G / STERLING / J. Inscribed: H.J.F. RISD Museum, The Gorham Collection. Gift of Textron Inc., 1991.126.213ab

Page 230: Gorham Pavilion, Exposition Universelle, Paris. *Frank Leslie's Illustrated Newspaper*, September 28, 1889

Page 231: Gorham and Tiffany Pavilion, Gorham displays, World's Columbian Exposition, Chicago, 1893. GMCA

Page 232 (above): Gorham Pavilion interior, World's Columbian Exposition, Chicago. 1893. GMCA

Page 232 (below): First view of the casting for the statue of Christopher Columbus, 1893. GMCA

Page 234: Ewer, 1890. Kitaro Shirayamadani (1865–1948), decorator; Pitts Harrison Burt (1837–1907), designer; and Rookwood Pottery Company (1880–present), manufacturer. Earthenware with glaze and silver. 24.1 × 22.9 ×

21.9 cm (9 ½ × 9 × 8 ⅝ in.). Marked: GORHAM MFG CO. S. 1225 C. [mark of Kitaro Shirayamadani]. William W. Taylor Endowment. Cincinnati Art Museum

Page 235: Gorham's Semiannual Sales Conference, June 23–24, 1925. GMCA

Page 236 (left): Gorham Showroom, Providence, ca. 1941. GMCA

Page 236 (right): Gorham Building, Thirty-Sixth Street and Fifth Avenue, New York, 1903. GMCA

Page 237: First-floor interior, Thirty-Sixth Street and Fifth Avenue building, New York, 1903. GMCA

Page 238: Second-floor interior, Thirty-Sixth Street and Fifth Avenue building, with *Athenic* Candelabra displayed, 1903–6. McKim, Mead & White / Museum of the City of New York. 90.44.1.1039

Page 239: *Athenic* Candelabra, 1902. Silver. Each: 49.3 × 42.3 × 42.3 cm (19 ⁷⁄₁₆ × 16 ⅝ × 16 ⅝ in.). Marked: [lion] [anchor] G / STERLING / A3357 / SL [St. Louis World's Fair mark]. RISD Museum, Elizabeth T. and Dorothy N. Casey Fund, 2017.28.1

Page 240: Vase, 1899. Silver. Collection of Suzanne and Joel Sugg

Page 241: Gorham Pavilion, Louisiana Purchase Exposition, Saint Louis, 1904. Courtesy of the Missouri Historical Society, Saint Louis

Page 242: *Martelé* Desk Set for the Louisiana Purchase Exhibition, 1904. GMCA

Page 243 (above): *Martelé* Centerpiece and Base, 1904. Silver. 46 × 60 × 38.3 cm (18 ⅛ × 23 ⅝ × 15 ¹⁄₁₆ in.). Centerpiece marked: [lion] [anchor] G / STERLING / FFM / SL [St. Louis World's Fair mark]. Base marked: [lion] [anchor] G / STERLING / FCT / SL [St. Louis World's Fair mark]. RISD Museum, The Gorham Collection. Gift of Textron Inc., 1991.126.180ad

Page 243 (below): Gorham Pavilion, Panama-Pacific International Exposition, San Francisco, 1915. GMCA

Page 244 (above): Gorham Pavilion interior, Panama-Pacific International Exposition, San Francisco, 1915. GMCA

Page 244 (below): Gold-medal certificate awarded to Gorham at the Panama-Pacific International

Exposition for the Writing Desk and Chair, 1915. GMCA

Page 245: U.S.S. *Rhode Island* Silver Service, 1907. Rhode Island Collection, Providence Public Library

Page 246: Erik Magnussen's *Cubic* Service in Gorham's New York Showroom window, ca. 1927. GMCA

Page 247: *Gorham Sterling, New York, 1930 (Juxtapositions)*, Photograph by Edward Steichen (1879–1973), artist; George Tice (b. 1938), printer. Negative 1930, printed 1984–86. Gelatin silver print. 33.6 × 26.4 cm (13 ¼ × 10 ⅜ in.). Gift of Janet Singer 2000.1103. Museum of Fine Arts, Boston. Photograph © Museum of Fine Arts, Boston

Page 248 (left): Gorham advertisement in *Glamour Magazine*, May 1956. GMCA

Page 248 (right): Baby in Monumental Spoon, ca. 1950. GMCA

Page 249: Gorham advertisement, ca. 1960. GMCA

Gorham Silver Conservation Project

Page 257: RISD Museum conservator Ingrid A. Neuman (second from right) oversees the Gorham conservation project.

Page 258 (left): Knife Rest from the Furber service, with repaired unicorn horn.

Page 258 (right): Conservation team member cleaning a Furber service fruit stand.

Page 259: Conservation team member removing lacquer from a Furber service tureen.

Gorham Documentation Project

Page 260: Gorham Manufacturing Company, Office of the President, 1997.

Page 261: Gorham Manufacturing Company, Foundry, 1997.

Pages 262–63: Gorham Manufacturing Company, Preparatory Room, 1997.

Glossary

Page 275: Gorham tools.

Page 279: Servingware, ca. 1870. Silver with gilding. RISD Museum, Providence, Rhode Island

Opposite page 288: Date stamp on Volume 10, Katsushika Hokusai, *Manga*, from the Gorham design library. Fleet Library at Rhode Island School of Design

Back endpaper: Gorham Factory at Elmwood, in *Views, Exterior and Interior, of the Works of the Gorham Manufacturing Company, Silversmiths*, 1892. GMCA

Back cover: Gorham marks, Covered Butter Dish, 1873. Silver with gilding. Overall: 17.2 × 26.8 × 13.4 cm (6 ¾ × 10 ⁹⁄₁₆ × 5 ¼ in.). The Gorham Collection. Gift of Textron Inc., 1991.126.13abc

SELECTED REFERENCES

American Cut Glass Association. *The Glass of Gorham.* Corning, NY: American Cut Glass Association in collaboration with the John Hay Library, Brown University, Providence, RI; and the Rakow Research Library, Corning Museum of Glass, Corning, NY, 2012.

Art Institute of Chicago and Elizabeth McGoey. *American Silver in the Art Institute of Chicago.* Chicago: Art Institute of Chicago; Distributed by Yale University Press, New Haven, CT, 2017.

Augustus E. Alden v. The Gorham Manufacturing Company, 1867. Sidney S. Rider Collection [Manuscripts, 1666–1883] [31236096867208], John Hay Library, Brown University, Providence, RI.

Buhler, Kathryn C. *American Silver, 1655–1825, in the Museum of Fine Arts, Boston.* Greenwich, CT: New York Graphic Society, 1972.

Burke, Doreen Bolger, et al. *In Pursuit of Beauty: Americans and the Aesthetic Movement.* New York: The Metropolitan Museum of Art and Rizzoli, 1986.

Carpenter, Charles H. Jr. *Gorham Silver, 1831–1981.* New York: Dodd, Mead, 1982.

Coffin, Sarah, et al. *Feeding Desire: Design and the Tools of the Table, 1500–2005.* New York: Smithsonian, Cooper-Hewitt, National Design Museum, 2006.

Conant, William C. "The Silver Age." *Scribner's Monthly* 9, no. 2 (Dec. 1874): 193–209.

Culme, John. *Nineteenth-Century Silver.* London: Country Life Books, 1977.

Ensko, Stephen Guernsey Cook, and Dorothea Ensko Wyle. *American Silversmiths and Their Marks IV.* Boston: Godine, 1989.

Farnum, Alexander. *The Century Vase.* Providence, RI: Livermore & Knight, 1876.

Ferris, George Titus. *Gems of the Centennial Exhibition.* New York: D. Appleton & Company, 1877.

Gordon, Spencer, and Mark McHugh. "Global Exchange: How the Craftsmanship of Two Cultures Met in Gorham's 'Japanese Work' Silver." *Antiques* 185 (January/February 2018): 102–9.

Gorham, Henry S. *The Gorham Family in Rhode Island.* Boston: David Clapp & Son, 1900.

———. *The Gorham Manufacturing Company, Silversmiths.* New York: Cheltenham Press, 1900.

Gorham Manufacturing Company. *Gorham Suggestions.* New York: Gorham, 1895.

———. *Gorham Suggestions.* New York: Gorham, 1898.

Gould, Erik, Erik Carlson, and Joshua Safdie. Gorham Documentation Project for The City of Providence Department of Planning and Development and The Rhode Island Historical Preservation and Heritage Commission. June 8, 1998.

Greene, Welcome Arnold. *The Providence Plantations for 250 Years.* Providence, RI: J. A. and R. Reid, 1886.

Grover, Kathryn. *Dining in America 1850–1900.* Amherst, MA, and Rochester, NY: University of Massachusetts Press, 1972.

Hood, Graham. *American Silver: A History of Style, 1650–1900.* New York: Praeger Publishers, 1971.

Hughes, Richard, and Michael Rowe. *The Colouring, Bronzing and Patination of Metals.* New York: Watson-Guptill Publications, 1991.

Keefe, John Webster, and Samuel J. Hough. *Magnificent, Marvelous Martelé: American Art Nouveau Silver: The Jolie and Robert Shelton Collection.* New Orleans: New Orleans Museum of Art, 2001.

Kovel, Ralph M., and Terry H. Kovel. *Kovels' American Silver Marks.* New York: Crown Publishers, 1989.

McCabe, James D. *The Illustrated History of the Centennial Exhibition.* Philadelphia, Chicago, and Saint Louis: National Publishing Company, 1876.

Michie, Thomas S., and Museum of Art, Rhode Island School of Design. *Selected Works.* Providence, RI: RISD Museum, 2008.

Newman, Harold. *An Illustrated Dictionary of Silverware.* London: Thames & Hudson, 2000.

Parton, James. "Silver and Silver Plate." *Harper's New Monthly Magazine* 37 (September 1868): 432–38.

Pristo, L. J. *Martelé: 950–1000 Fine. Gorham's Nouveau Art Silver.* Phoenix, AZ: Heritage Antiques, 2002.

Rainwater, Dorothy T., and Judy Redfield. *Encyclopedia of American Silver Manufacturers,* 4th ed. Atglen, PA: Schiffer, 1998.

Rainwater, Dorothy T., ed. *Sterling Silver Holloware.* Princeton, NJ: Pyne Press; Distributed by Scribner, New York, 1973.

Rhode Island School of Design, Carla Mathes Woodward, and Franklin Westcott Robinson. *A Handbook of the Museum of Art, Rhode Island School of Design.* Providence, RI: RISD Museum, 1985.

Sandhurst, Phillip T. *Great Centennial Exhibition.* Philadelphia: P. W. Ziegler, 1876.

Shapiro, Neil, and George Sparacio. *Gorham Match Safes.* Riverdale, NJ: International Match Safe Association, 2009.

Smith, Andrew F. *The Oxford Encyclopedia of Food and Drink in America,* 2 volumes. New York: Oxford University Press, 2004.

Stern, Jewel. *Modernism in American Silver: 20th-Century Design.* Edited by Kevin W. Tucker and Charles L. Venable. New Haven, CT, and London: Yale University Press, 2005.

Stokes, Jayne. *Sumptuous Surround: Silver Overlay on Ceramic and Glass.* Milwaukee: Milwaukee Art Museum, 1990.

Tompkins, George, and Carolyn Tompkins. *The Handbook of Gorham Salt Dishes.* Rockport, ME: Archimedes Press, 1987.

Venable, Charles L. *Silver in America, 1840–1940: A Century of Splendor.* Dallas and New York: Dallas Museum of Art / Harry N. Abrams, 1994.

Ward, Barbara McLean, and Gerald W. R. Ward. *Silver in American Life: Selections from the Mabel Brady Garvan and Other Collections at Yale University.* Boston: David R. Godine, 1979.

Waters, Deborah Dependahl, Kristen H. McKinsey, and Gerald W. R. Ward. *Elegant Plate: Three Centuries of Precious Metals in New York City.* New York: Museum of the City of New York, 2000.

Williams, Susan. *Savory Suppers and Fashionable Feasts.* New York: Pantheon Books, 1985.

**Gorham Manufacturing Company
Archival Materials**

**GORHAM MANUFACTURING COMPANY ARCHIVE
(GMCA), JOHN HAY LIBRARY, BROWN UNIVERSITY,
PROVIDENCE, RHODE ISLAND**
Approximately 6,200 linear feet of company records, dating from the founding of the company by Jabez Gorham in 1831 to its final disposition in 2005, constitute the Gorham Manufacturing Company Archive at the John Hay Library.

SELECTED COLLECTIONS AND SERIES
Trade catalogues of silver and electroplated silver,
    ca. 1880–1960
Costing ledgers and slips, ca. 1869–1920
Large books of photographs of silver and electroplated
    silver hollowware, flatware, and smallwares
    (approx. 45 albums), ca. 1869–1905
Gorham Manufacturing Company Employee Periodicals
    and Newsletters: *The Silver Tongue* (ca. 1924–27),
    Mettle (ca. 1926–30), *Harmony* (ca. 1930–32),
    Contact (ca. 1930–32), *Gorham Perspective*
    (ca. 1960–85).

SELECTED ARCHIVAL REFERENCES
There is an inventory of the materials in the Gorham Manufacturing Company Archive compiled by the John Hay Library. The inventory is organized by section titles and often identified with a barcode.

SELECTED SECTION TITLE CROSS-REFERENCED
WITH BARCODE:

I.1 Gorham-Historical–Gorham Family, Files 1–10,
    Box 1 [31236073558978]
I.1 Gorham-Historical–Gorham Family, Files 11–20,
    Box 2 [31236073558960]
I.2 Gorham-Historical–19th Century Documents
    [31236073559059]
I.4 Histories Written about Gorham, Box 1
    [31236073558796]
I.4 Histories Written about Gorham, Box 2
    [31236073558887]
I.5 Gorham Historical Articles–Scrapbook Clippings
    1891–96 [31236073558861]
I.5.A Gorham-Historical–Articles Arranged
    Chronologically [31236073558879]
I.5.B + I.5.C Gorham Historical Articles–Awards and
    Exhibits [31236073559208]
I.7 Gorham-Historical–Plant [31236073559174]
I.8 Gorham-Historical–Personnel
    Box 1 A–L [31236073559158]
I.8 Gorham-Historical–Personnel
    Box 2 M–Z [31236073559141]
I.8/9.a.2 Gorham-Historical–Silversmiths Co.
    [31236073559133]
I.10.A; I.10.B Gorham Historical Product
    [31236073559075]

I.13 Gorham-Historical–Technical Process
    [31236073559166]
II.3.F Gorham-Financial–Inventory 1871 [n/a]
Archival Box 22 [31236071170974]
Archival Box BBB [31236072052809]

Gorham, 1806
    Jabez Gorham's indenture of apprenticeship with
    Nehemiah Dodge, April 2, 1806 [GMCA I.1 Box 1].
Gorham, 1819
    Gorham, Jabez. Correspondence with Amy
    Thurber Gorham, October–November 1819
    [GMCA I.1 Box 1].
Gorham, 1852
    Gorham, John. Diary of a trip to England and
    France, 1852 [GMCA I.1 Box 2].
Gorham, 1860
    Gorham, John. Diary of a trip to Europe, 1860
    [GMCA I.1 Box 2].
Gorham, 1869
    Will of Jabez Gorham, 1869 [GMCA I.1 Box 1].
Gorham, 1871
    Gorham Manufacturing Company. Gorham List
    of Assets, 1871 [GMCA II.3.F].
Gorham, 1878
    Bagnall, W. R. *Historical and Biographical
    Sketch of the Gorham Manufacturing Company.*
    Providence, RI: The Gorham Manufacturing
    Company, 1878 [GMCA I.4 Box 1].
Gorham, 1891–96
    *Literary Scraps, Cuttings, Extracts; Scrapbook
    Clippings 1891–1896* [GMCA I.5].
Gorham, 1892
    Gorham Manufacturing Company. *Views,
    Exterior and Interior of the Works of the Gorham
    Manufacturing Company.* Providence, RI:
    Gorham Manufacturing Company, 1892.
Gorham, 1892
    Gorham Manufacturing Company.
    *Woman's Work at Gorham Manufacturing
    Company, Silversmiths, Providence,
    and New York.* Providence, RI: Gorham
    Manufacturing Company, 1892.
Gorham, 1893
    Gorham, John. "John Gorham's History," 1893
    [GMCA I.1 Box 1–2].
Gorham, 1893
    "Photographs Exhibited at Chicago Columbian
    Exposition 1893" [GMCA Archival Box 22].
Gorham, 1894
    Gorham, John. Draft notes on the history of the
    Gorham Company [GMCA I.1 Box 1].
Gorham, 1900
    Townsend, Horace. *An Artistic Experiment.* New
    York: Gorham Manufacturing Company, 1900.
Gorham, 1912
    Holbrook, John S. *Silver for the Dining Room:
    Selected Periods.* Cambridge, MA: The Gorham
    Company, 1912.

Gorham, 1918
    Holbrook, John S. *The Art of the Silversmith
    and Its Development.* New York: Greenwich
    Press, 1918.
Gorham, 1921
    "Historical Data" [GMCA I.4 Box 1].
Gorham, 1923
    Aldred & Co. *The Silversmith Company of
    New York, Gorham Manufacturing Company
    and Affiliates Report,* 1923 [I.8/9.a.2].
Gorham, 1930
    Codman, William. *An Illustrated History of
    Silverware Design.* Providence, RI: The Gorham
    Company, 1930.
Gorham, 1931
    "The Gorham Company present the
    Hunt Club, the new design in Sterling," 1931
    [GMCA Archival Box BBB].
Gorham, 1932
    Gorham Manufacturing Company. *The Sales
    Manual and the History of the Gorham Company.*
    Providence, RI: Gorham Manufacturing
    Company, 1932 [GMCA I.4 Box 2].

**RHODE ISLAND SCHOOL OF DESIGN,
FLEET LIBRARY, SPECIAL COLLECTIONS, PROVIDENCE**
The Gorham Manufacturing Company's Design Library, located at the Rhode Island School of Design (RISD) Fleet Library, comprises more than 950 catalogued design volumes and a collection of uncatalogued portfolios, scrapbooks, drawings, photographs, and ephemera and is organized by a finding aid.

GLOSSARY

This listing was adapted from the "Manufacturing Vocabulary" in Gorham's company publication, *The Sales Manual and History of the Gorham Company* (Providence, 1932). This manual helped familiarize salespeople with the vocabulary and processes of silver making to better sell Gorham's products.

Alloy
Metal produced by combining two or more compatible metals to achieve greater strength and/or resistance to corrosion.

Annealing
Process by which a metal is made more malleable by the application of heat.

Applied Decoration
A decorative element soldered to an object.

Assaying
Process of testing the purity of metal in an alloy.

Blank
Piece of flat sheet metal that can be rolled, worked with hammers, or die stamped.

Blanking
Process by which the spoon and fork blanks are cut from the sheet metal.

Bobbing
Process of removing file marks and scratches with pumice and oil and a walrus hide buff.

Britannia Silver
Silver alloy of 95.84 percent silver, 4.16 percent copper; more malleable than sterling silver.

Brushing
Finishing process of removing file marks and scratches with pumice and oil on a hair brush.

Burnishing
Process of creating a highly reflective polish by rubbing a metallic surface with a metal tool.

Butler Finish
Medium-bright silver finish produced using siliceous rottenstone (Tripoli polish).

Casting
Process of creating an object or part thereof by pouring molten metal into a prepared mold to reproduce the model from which the mold was made.

Chasing
Process of decorating an object by hammering a blunt tool against the surface of the metal.

Coin Silver
Silver alloy of 90 percent silver, 10 percent copper.

Coloring
Process of polishing with rouge to give a bright finish and remove the blueish cast that is created by bobbing.

Die
Tool used to cut or shape material using a press.

Die Sinking
Process of cutting a design or pattern out of steel to form a die.

Die Stamping
Process of creating a design on a blank sheet of metal by pressing it into a die.

Drawing
Process of elongating silver into a tubular shape so that it may be spun on a lathe (also referred to as drafting). Also the process of creating wire by pulling it through a die, successively making it thinner.

Dripping
Process of immersing an object in an acid solution to remove oxidation and other impurities caused by heating.

Embossing
Process of ornamenting metal by stamping with a die.

Engraving
Process of decorating by cutting into the surface with faceted tools to remove metal.

Etching
Process of ornamenting metal by eating away its surface with acid.

Facing
Process of smoothing a metal edge, especially the edges of a bow of a spoon, on a belt or wheel.

Finishing
Process of polishing silver or refining a metal surface by use of abrasive compounds applied by hand or a polishing wheel.

Firestain / Firescale
An oxide causing a dark stain on or under the surface of silver when the metal is overheated, often during the processes of annealing or soldering.

Flatware
Eating and serving utensils such as knives, forks, and spoons. Knives are also referred to as cutlery.

French Finish
A gray finish produced by buffing silver with a mixture of pumice and oil.

Gilding
Process of coating a metal with gold:
1) Electroplating
Process utilizing a cyanide solution and electricity to deposit gold onto a metal.
2) Mercury Gilding
Process in which mercury is mixed with gold and applied to the surface of the object, which is then heated, causing the mercury to evaporate and the gold to adhere to the surface.

Grading
Process of gauging to mathematical scale the varying thicknesses of a piece of flatware.

Hallmark
Official mark stamped on an object to indicate the quality of silver (or gold) of the object.

Hollowware
Vessels such as bowls, platters, tureens, coffeepots, vases, etc.

Knurling
Process of making borders or moldings on a metal object by rolling the design onto the piece between two circular dies.

Lacquer
A coating, usually cellulose nitrate, applied to the surface of a metal to act as a protective barrier.

Litharge
A type of cement made from lead and glycerin, used to fill the hollow handles of cutlery items.

Maker's Mark
Mark, or series of marks, stamped on an object to identify the maker.

Milling
Process of cutting away metal using a milling machine with revolving cutters.

Niello
Decorative technique of embedding engraved areas with a dark silver-sulphide mixture and heating it until the alloy melts, creating a high contrast with polished areas.

Oxidizing
Process of darkening the surface of the metal by dipping it into a solution of boiling water and sodium sulphide.

Patination
Process of coloring metal to highlight a surface texture or design. Patinas can occur naturally (through the object's exposure to air, wear through handling, etc.) or be applied intentionally through chemical processes.

Piercing
Process of cutting away metal using cutting dies or a saw.

Planishing
Process of smoothing the surface of metal through light hammering to refine the surface after raising; may also be used as a decorative element.

Profiling
Process of removing the projecting rim from the stamped halves of hollowware pieces.

Raising
Process of hammering a flat sheet of metal over an anvil or metal stake to raise it into a vessel.

Repoussé
Process of creating relief decoration by hammering the metal from the back, using chasing tools or a snarling iron, to raise the design on the front. From the French verb *pousser* (to push up).

Rolled Edge
Edge of a hollowware piece formed by rolling the metal back.

Rolled Wire
Wire or strip rolled between circular dies and used as an applied design, border, or molding.

Rolling
Process by which a blank is flattened between rollers in one direction to reduce it to a uniform thickness, while rendering it thinner and easier to work with.

1) Cross Rolling
Process by which the bowl section of a spoon blank is flattened and widened.

2) Pinch Rolling
Process by which the bowl section of a spoon blank is flattened and lengthened.

Satin Finish
Matte finish created by brushing the surface of the metal with a long-haired steel-wire brush.

Snarling
Process of raising the metal from underneath or inside a hollowware object by using a long-armed steel tool known as a snarling iron.

Soldering
Process of joining pieces of metal using a metal with a lower melting temperature.

Spinning
Process of forming a vessel by mounting a flat metal disc on a lathe and pressing it against a wooden form as it spins.

Sterling Silver
Silver alloy of 92.5 percent silver, 7.5 percent copper.

Stoning
Process of removing scratch marks and other imperfections from flat surfaces using pumice stones.

Tining
Process of stamping out the tines of a fork with a cutting die.

Turning
Process of cutting away metal as a piece fitted over a form turns on a lathe.

265
Gorham tools

SELECTED GORHAM MARKS

Early Marks

Below is a selection of marks used by Gorham during the period covered by this publication (1850–1970). The company name, which went through several iterations between its founding in 1831 and its incorporation in 1865, was sometimes preceded by a mark for Providence, Rhode Island, and later by other maker's and date marks. Although Gorham did not use date marks prior to 1868, objects can often be dated based on the type of marks. Prior to 1868, Gorham used coin silver, an alloy of 90 percent silver and 10 percent copper.

Gorham & Thurber, 1850–52

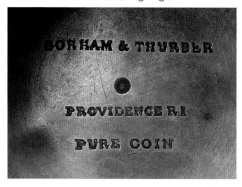

Maker's Mark: Lion / Anchor / G

First used in the 1850s, the traditional mark of a lion, anchor, and letter *G* have long been associated with Gorham. The lion represents silver, the anchor is the symbol for Rhode Island, and the *G* is for Gorham. The marks were registered at the United States Patent and Trademark Office on December 19, 1899 (No. 33902).

Gorham & Co., 1852–65

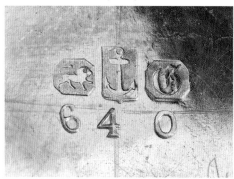

Date and Silver Marks

In 1868, Gorham adopted the British standard alloy for sterling silver (92.5 percent silver and 7.5 percent copper) and began stamping their objects *STERLING* to signify the change. In the same year, Gorham also began using a system of letters and symbols that indicated the year the piece was made, beginning with the letter A to represent 1868, B for 1869, on through Q for 1884. Beginning 1885, they used a different symbol for each year.

Letter/Symbol	Year		Symbol	Year
A.	1868			1903
B.	1869			1904
C.	1870			1905
D.	1871			1906
E.	1872			1907
F.	1873			1908
G.	1874			1909
H.	1875			1910
I.	1876			1911
J.	1877			1912
K.	1878			1913
L.	1879			1914
M.	1880			1915
N.	1881			1916
O.	1882			1917
P.	1883			1918
Q.	1884			1919
	1885			1920
	1886			1921
	1887			1922
	1888			1923
	1889			1924
	1890			1925
	1891			1926
	1892			1927
	1893			1928
	1894			1929
	1895			1930
	1896			1931
	1897			1932
	1898			1933
	1899			
	1900			
	1901			
	1902			

During 1933 year marks were discontinued.

January 1941 year marking was resumed on Sterling Holloware except lower priced items.

1941
The square frame indicates the decade of the '40s. The numeral indicates the year of the decade.

1950

1951
The pentagon indicates the decade of the '50s. The numeral indicates the year of the decade.

1960

1961
The hexagon indicates the decade of the '60s. The numeral indicates the year of the decade.

The heptagon was used for the 1970s, and the octagon for the 1980s.

Cruet Set (detail), 1875.
Silver, gilding, and glass.
RISD Museum 1991.126.40

Record of the Sachem Tray
(detail), 1889.
Silver and bronze.
RISD Museum 2016.123.1

Retailer Marks

Before 1873, most Gorham wares were sold wholesale through retailers whose marks were stamped on the silver. Gorham continued this wholesale practice after it began retailing its own works.

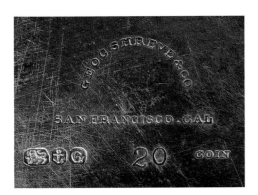

Shreve & Co. (retailer),
Wine Decanter Set,
ca. 1865. Silver and
glass. RISD Museum
2017.69.3

Spaulding & Co. (retailer),
Billings Cup, 1899. Silver.
RISD Museum 1990.004

Martelé

Gorham's handmade line *Martelé*, first produced in 1896, was stamped with a special mark and was initially made in sterling silver. By 1898, the *Martelé* mark incorporated an eagle, signifying the upgrade from sterling to an alloy containing 95 percent silver, which was further increased in 1905 to the Britannia standard of 95.84 percent silver. Code numbers or letters were often included with the marks.

Martelé Coffeepot
(detail), 1901.
Silver with ivory.
RISD Museum
1992.071.2

Martelé Bowl
(detail), 1901.
Silver with ivory.
RISD Museum
1991.126.183

Athenic

In 1901, Gorham introduced their *Athenic* line, which featured not only objects in silver but also copper, glass, and ivory.

Athenic Cigar Box
(detail), 1901.
Copper, silver, and cedar.
RISD Museum 80.099

World's Fair Marks

Objects created for world's fairs were often marked with specific stamps to commemorate the occasion, such as the interlocking SL for the 1904 St. Louis World's Fair, the Louisiana Purchase Exposition.

Athenic Candelabrum (detail), 1902. Silver. RISD Museum 2017.28.1

Erik Magnussen, 1925–29

Erik Magnussen was the only Gorham designer allowed to put his own mark on Gorham objects. His designs carried his signature *EM* stamp, which he continued to use after he departed Gorham.

Cubic Creamer (detail), 1927. Silver with gilding and ivory. RISD Museum 1991.126.488.4

Other Metals

Silver objects with applications of other metals such as copper and brass, or objects made of iron, were noted accordingly.

Tureen on Stand (detail), 1881. Silver with copper. Collection of Kathy Field Malavasic

For additional information and illustrations of marks on hollowware and flatware, see Charles H. Carpenter, *Gorham Silver, 1831–1981* (New York: Dodd, Mead, 1982), and L. J. Pristo, *Martelé: Gorham's Nouveau Art Silver* (Phoenix, AZ: Heritage Antiques, 2002).

Selected Gorham Marks

CONTRIBUTORS

266
Servingware, ca. 1870.
Silver with gilding. RISD Museum

Elizabeth A. Williams is the David and Peggy Rockefeller Curator of Decorative Arts and Design at the RISD Museum.

Emily Banas is Assistant Curator of Decorative Arts and Design at the RISD Museum.

David L. Barquist is the H. Richard Dietrich, Jr., Curator of American Decorative Arts at the Philadelphia Museum of Art.

Gerald M. Carbone is an independent writer, historian, and journalist.

Amy Miller Dehan is Curator of Decorative Arts and Design at the Cincinnati Art Museum.

Jeannine Falino is an independent art historian and curator.

Catherine L. Futter is Director of Curatorial Affairs at the Nelson-Atkins Museum of Art.

Erik Gould is the photographer at the RISD Museum.

Ingrid A. Neuman is a conservator at the RISD Museum.

John W. Smith is the Director of the RISD Museum.

Holly Snyder is Curator of American Historical Collections and the History of Science at the John Hay Library, Brown University.

INDEX

This publication complements the exhibition *Gorham Silver: Designing Brilliance 1850–1970*, on view at the RISD Museum (May 3–September 15, 2019), the Cincinnati Art Museum (March 13–June 7, 2020), and the Mint Museum (July 25–November 1, 2020). Lenders to the exhibition are Museum of Fine Arts, Boston; Art Institute of Chicago; Chicago History Museum; Chrysler Museum of Art; Cincinnati Art Museum; Dallas Museum of Art; High Museum of Art; Museum of Fine Arts, Houston; private collection, courtesy of the Indianapolis Museum of Art at Newfields; Manoogian Foundation, courtesy the Detroit Institute of Arts; Metropolitan Museum of Art; Nelson-Atkins Museum of Art; New Orleans Museum of Art; Philadelphia Museum of Art; RISD Fleet Library Special Collections; John Hay Library at Brown University; Kathy Field Malavasic; Suzanne and Joel Sugg; and Victoria Stenstream. A full checklist of objects included in the exhibition is available at www.risdmuseum.org.

Gorham Silver: Designing Brilliance 1850–1970 is made possible by an exhibition sponsoring grant from the Henry Luce Foundation, with additional support from the National Endowment for the Arts, the RISD Museum Associates, Textron Inc., the Rhode Island Council for the Humanities, Virginia and Alan Nathan, Cindy and Scott Burns, and a generous in-kind gift from Spencer Marks, Ltd. Educational programming associated with the exhibition is made possible by a lead sponsorship from the Zennovation Fund and additional support for Critical Encounters from Victoria Veh. A gift from Joseph A. Chazan, MD, made this publication possible. The RISD Museum is supported by a grant from the Rhode Island State Council on the Arts, through an appropriation by the Rhode Island General Assembly and a grant from the National Endowment for the Arts, and with the generous partnership of the Rhode Island School of Design, its Board of Trustees, and the RISD Museum Board of Governors.

Library of Congress Control Number: 2018966356

ISBN: 978-0-8478-6252-8 (hardcover)
ISBN: 978-0-9856189-2-6 (paperback)

First published in the United States of America in 2019 by

Rizzoli Electa
A Division of Rizzoli International Publications, Inc
300 Park Avenue South
New York, NY 10010
www.rizzoliusa.com

and

RISD Museum
20 North Main Street
Providence, RI 02903
www.risdmuseum.org

For RISD Museum:
John W. Smith, Director
Amy Pickworth, Editor of Publications

For Rizzoli Electa:
Charles Miers, Publisher
Margaret Rennolds Chace, Associate Publisher
Andrea Danese, Editor

Design: James Goggin & Shan James at Practise
This volume was set in Sackers Gothic (Gary Sackers, 1974–75), Scotch Modern, and Figgins Sans (both Nick Shinn, 2008)

2019 2020 2021 2022 / 10 9 8 7 6 5 4 3 2 1

Printed in China

Image Credits:

Cover and page 8
Fruit Stand, 1872. Silver with gilding. RISD Museum

Front endpaper
View of the Gorham Manufacturing Company's works, ca. 1885. Gorham Manufacturing Company Archive, John Hay Library

Opposite page 1
Gorham Manufacturing Company bookplate, designed by Florentin Antoine Heller. Special Collections, Fleet Library at Rhode Island School of Design

Pages 2–3
Plan of land belonging to the Gorham Manufacturing Company, ca. 1890. GMCA

Pages 4–5
Experimental room, in *Views, Exterior and Interior, of the Works of the Gorham Manufacturing Company, Silversmiths*, 1892. GMCA

Pages 6–7
Martelé Writing Table (detail), 1903. RISD Museum

Opposite
Date stamp on Volume 10, Katsushika Hokusai, *Manga*, from the Gorham design library. Fleet Library at Rhode Island School of Design

Back endpaper
Gorham Factory at Elmwood, in *Views, Exterior and Interior, of the Works of the Gorham Manufacturing Company, Silversmiths*, 1892. GMCA

Back cover
Gorham marks, Covered Butter Dish, 1873. Silver with gilding. RISD Museum

GORHAM M'F'G CO.
WORKS AT
(ELMWOOD)
PROVIDENCE, R.I.